Teaching in the Elementary School

Sixth Edition

Teaching in the Elementary School

A REFLECTIVE ACTION APPROACH

ADRIENNE L. HERRELL
California State University, Emeritus

MICHAEL JORDAN
California State University, Emeritus

JUDY W. EBY
Reflective Action Research Center, San Diego

PEARSON

Boston • Columbus • Indianapolis • New York • San Francisco • Upper Saddle River
Amsterdam • Cape Town • Dubai • London • Madrid • Milan • Munich • Paris • Montreal • Toronto
Delhi • Mexico City • São Paulo • Sydney • Hong Kong • Seoul • Singapore • Taipei • Tokyo

Vice President, Editiorial Director: Jeffery W. Johnston
Senior Acquisitions Editor: Kelly Villella Canton
Development Editor: Anne Whittaker
Editorial Assistant: Annalea Manalili
Executive Marketing Manager: Darcy Betts
Production Editor: Paula Carroll
Editorial Production Service: Electronic Publishing Services Inc.
Manufacturing Buyer: Megan Cochran
Electronic Composition: Jouve
Interior Design: Electronic Publishing Services Inc.
Photo Researcher: Annie Fuller
Cover Designer: Diane Lorenzo

Library of Congress Cataloging-in-Publication Data

Herrell, Adrienne L.
    Teaching in the elementary school : a reflective action approach / Adrienne L. Herrell, Michael Jordan,
        Judy W. Eby. — 6th ed.
            p. cm.
    Prev. ed. cataloged under Eby, Judy W.
    Includes bibliographical references and index.
    ISBN-13: 978-0-13-269618-0 (pbk.)
    ISBN-10: 0-13-269618-5 (pbk.)
    1. Elementary school teaching.   2. Reflective teaching.   3. Curriculum planning.   4. Educational
tests and measurements.   I. Jordan, Michael   II. Eby, Judy W.   III. Title.
    LB1555.E29 2012
    372.1102—dc23

                                                                                    2011045112

4   17

ISBN-10: 0-13-269618-5
ISBN-13: 978-0-13-269618-0

Dedication

Adrienne and Michael dedicate this book to the loving memory of Stephanie Collom, outstanding teacher and friend.

Judy dedicates her portion of this book to her family and friends who have generously supported her efforts.

About the Authors

Adrienne Herrell received her Ph.D. from Florida State University in early childhood education/early literacy. She retired from California State University, Fresno, where she was a professor in the department of literacy and early education; she taught classes in early literacy and teaching second-language learners before she retired and moved back to Florida in 2004. Adrienne recently retired from Florida State University.

Adrienne is the author or coauthor of 15 other books published by Pearson, including *Fifty Strategies for Teaching English Language Learners* (4th ed.), with Michael Jordan; *Reflective Planning, Teaching, and Evaluation K–12*, with Judy Eby and Michael Jordan; and *Thirty-Five Classroom Management Strategies: Promoting Learning and Building Community*, with Michael Jordan. Adrienne taught for 23 years in public schools in Florida but considers raising five sons to be her most challenging and valuable life experience.

Michael Jordan also recently retired from California State University, Fresno, where he was an associate professor in the Department of Curriculum and Instruction, teaching classes in curriculum, classroom management, and social foundations. He has taught primary grades through high school in Georgia, Alabama, Florida, and California. Dr. Jordan is also an actor, musician, and former B-52 pilot. His work in live theater is dedicated to providing access to the arts for children and youth. He and Dr. Herrell incorporate many dramatic reenactment strategies into their joint research working with English learners. This is Dr. Jordan's ninth book for Pearson.

Judy Eby began her teaching career at a Head Start program in Coronado, California. She has been a classroom teacher, a gifted program coordinator, a teacher educator (DePaul University, University of San Diego, and San Diego State University), and a mentor teacher in the Beginning Teacher Support Academy with the San Diego Unified School District. In 1983, she wrote a master's thesis on gifted behavior and published two articles on that subject in *Educational Leadership* in 1983 and 1984. One of those articles caught the attention of Benjamin S. Bloom, and this led to the opportunity to attain her Ph.D. at Northwestern University with Bloom as her dissertation chairman and advisor.

Turning her attention to teacher education as a professor of education at DePaul University in Chicago, Judy reinterpreted her construct of gifted behavior in terms of teacher education, calling this related construct "reflective action in teaching."

Judy has actively used her own research to make decisions about her life choices. She feels that using reflective action has benefited her in her marriage, child rearing, friendships, and leisure and volunteer activities. She participates in children's literacy programs on both sides of the San Diego–Tijuana border. Her most treasured project is the Tecolote Centro de Comunidad, a children's center in Tijuana, where she has created a children's library for the community. She also participates in before- and after-school programs on both sides of the border.

Brief Contents

Contents

CHAPTER 3   Lesson Planning and Sequencing   51

CHAPTER 4   Planning Curriculum Units   85

CHAPTER 5 Differentiating Instruction 113

CHAPTER 6 Using Teaching Strategies That Engage Students in Active, Authentic Learning 139

CHAPTER 8 Engaging Students in Classroom Discussions 183

CHAPTER 9 Balancing Standards and Creative Activities 202

Preface

Beginning with the first edition of this book, we have aspired to make it much more than an academic textbook. Our goal has always been to inspire and encourage teachers to become as reflective, creative, and independent as possible throughout their teaching careers. We have tried to achieve this goal by searching out the most creative and adventurous teachers we could find and weaving their real-life stories into the text.

At this time in history, we recognize that requiring accountability and meeting state standards are on the forefront of everyone's minds in education. In this text, we seek to balance the reality of today's rather uniform educational expectations with our message that true satisfaction in teaching comes from being a caring and creative artist in the classroom, always striving for improvement.

As we wrote this edition, we became excited as we began to collect the stories of teachers who are not only succeeding in a standards-based environment but also excelling in it. So we are happy to offer this edition with what we believe is a balanced description of the realities of a standards-based curriculum and the truly exhilarating stories of teachers who see these standards not as a goal but as a baseline.

Our new aspiration is to inspire teachers to view federal, state, and local standards as meaningful and important but not the end goal of teaching. We provide the stories of real teachers who begin with standards and then exceed them by creating highly original and creative curricula that take into account and meet the diverse needs of their students. This edition provides you with the knowledge base you need to become highly professional and creative teachers who meet and exceed standards with confidence.

New Features of This Edition

To accomplish our new aspiration, we have revised this edition to emphasize these added features:

- **A View into the Classroom.** This section begins each chapter, and each view tells the story of one teacher and the ways in which the topic of the chapter is implemented in an exemplary classroom.

- **Group Focus Activity.** Since we strongly advocate active involvement throughout this text, we have added new activities to the feature titled "Group Focus Activity" in each chapter. These activities are hands-on engagements for readers, allowing them to further explore the concepts featured in each chapter and giving them examples of a variety of hands-on activities they can use with their future students in the elementary classroom.

- **Portfolio of Professional Practices Activity.** A new chapter ending feature called "Portfolio of Professional Practices Activity" provides simulated experiences and reflective essays that invite reflection and focus readers on ways they can meet standards while still providing a rich, meaningful curriculum for their students. These activities serve as the basis for an interview portfolio that readers can use when applying for their first teaching positions.

- **Preparing for Your Licensure Exam.** A new feature titled "Preparing for Your Licensure Exam" serves two purposes. It helps you to review and reflect on the chapter content by using the "View into the Classroom" as a case study, and it prepares you to succeed on your licensure examination.

- **Technology Applications.** Sections that are marked with a technology icon throughout the text highlight ways that the use of technology can be infused into the curriculum.

- **Reflective Action Case Study.** In each section titled "Reflective Action Case Study," a classroom example models how teachers create school curricula and programs, select teaching strategies, and plan appropriate assessments for their students that achieve the standards of their school districts. These real-life examples of teachers' reflections can serve as models for beginning teachers to think and act with creativity and originality.

- **Two New Chapters.** We have added two new chapters, titled "Involving the Larger Community: Collaboration to Support Continuous Improvement" and "Improving the Effectiveness of Your Teaching," to this sixth edition.

- **Involving the Larger Community.** Preservice teachers can make use of the "Involving the Larger Community" sections that illustrate how to elicit the involvement of parents, volunteers, and community members to improve learning in their classrooms. The Continuous Improvement Model (CIM) is one example of a highly successful district-wide collaboration project.

- **Improving the Effectiveness of Your Teaching.** The last chapter, titled "Improving the Effectiveness of Your Teaching," provides support to beginning teachers in reflecting on and improving their teaching effectiveness. This final chapter also includes self-reflection rubrics in several areas of teaching. Preservice and beginning teachers can use these rubrics to help assess their continuing growth in such areas as use of voice, body language, and enthusiasm; clarity and pacing of instruction; and classroom management.

Acknowledgments

We gratefully acknowledge the contributions made by professors and students who have provided us with meaningful feedback on our previous edition. You are our eyes and ears. With your feedback, we are confident that we can continue to provide a realistic and hopeful view of the teaching profession today. We wish to especially thank Elaine Chakonas, Northeastern Illinois University; Angela Cresswell, Holy Family University; Lisa Hyde, Athens State University; Karen Robinson, Otterbein University; Dana Simel, American University; and Pamela R. Stockinger, Shenandoah University.

Teaching in the Elementary School

Reflective Action in Teaching

Annie Fuller/Pearson

"Reflection commences when one inquires into his or her experiences and relevant knowledge to find meaning in his or her beliefs. It has the potential to enable teachers to direct their activities with foresight and to plan according to ends-in-view."

John Dewey, 1933

I t is vitally important that teachers reflect on their teaching processes and procedures on an ongoing basis. Monitoring successes and challenges before, during, and after teaching provides timely input for adapting instruction that results in robust learning experiences for students.

Questions for Reflection as You Read the Chapter

1. What does it mean to be a reflective teacher?
2. What is the difference between reflection and reflective action?
3. Why is it important to reflect on our teaching as it relates to the students' learning?

A View into the Classroom

Susan McCloskey is a first-grade teacher in an inner-city school where most of her students are learning English as a second language. Susan has been teaching for 8 years, and during that time her school district has adopted a number of different programs in reading and language arts. For the past 2 years, the primary-grade teachers in her district have been trained in a phonics program that relates each of the sounds of the alphabet to an animal. The students are taught the sounds by singing a song and making motions to help them remember the sound represented by the letter and the animal whose name begins with the sound. Susan is concerned about this new phonics program and its appropriateness for her students who have limited knowledge of the English language and the animal names.

One morning during writing workshop, one of her students, Thao, asks her how to spell the word house. *As she always does, Susan asks, "What do you hear at the beginning?"*

Thao immediately begins to make the sound he hears. "Huh-huh-huh," he says.

Susan then asks, "Which letter do you use to spell that sound?" Thao just shakes his head.

Maria, who is standing next to Thao, starts to make the motion for the horse, which is the animal used to connect the sound and letter H in the phonics program. Thao still shakes his head.

Susan takes both Thao and Maria over to the alphabet strip that she has displayed at the students' eye level in the classroom. Next to the letter H is a picture of a horse, the animal that represents the sound in the phonics program. Susan asks, "What is the letter we use to spell the sound "Huh"? Although the letter is clearly displayed next to the picture of the horse, neither child is able to identify the letter. Susan has each child trace the letter H on the alphabet strip and say "H" as they trace the letter, and Thao returns to his seat to continue work on his story.

Susan reflects on this interaction at the end of the day. She is concerned that this new phonics program seems to assume that her students are familiar with the English labels for the animals. The program requires about 45 minutes a day in which the students are singing the song that connects the animals, the animal motions, and the letters. Susan knows that the first-grade language arts standards require that her students be able to represent sounds with letters in writing but do not require that those sounds be taught in any specific way, so she makes an appointment with her principal to discuss this problem.

Susan describes the scene that occurred in her classroom and explains to Mrs. Calmes, her principal, that these incidents seem to occur frequently. Mrs. Calmes asks Susan what she believes would work better than this prescribed phonics strategy.

"I think my students need a much more direct connection between the letters and the sounds," responds Susan. *"I want to try an approach one of my professors explained in my master's class the other evening."*

"What does this other approach entail?" asks Mrs. Calmes.

"My professor demonstrated the use of drawing the letters in the air while singing a song that connects the name of the letter and the sound it makes," explains Susan. *"I think that will make a more direct connection for my students since they are not familiar with the names of the animals. The animals seem to be introducing another layer of information that confuses them,"* she adds.

"I think you have a good solution," replies Mrs. Calmes. *"Give it a try and let me know how it works. Maybe we need to take another look at the new phonics program and see if it is serving our students well."*

"Thank you for listening," replies Susan with a smile. *"I'll document how this works and keep you informed."*

"If it works well, I'll want you to share your results with the rest of the primary teachers," Mrs. Calmes reminds Susan.

REFLECTING ON THE CLASSROOM EXPERIENCE

As Susan's story demonstrates, teachers are called upon to make many difficult decisions every day. In fact, it is quite possible that teachers make literally thousands of decisions every day. While it is not possible to reflect thoroughly on every decision, there are many occasions in which reflective teachers search their hearts and minds to find good solutions to problems that confront them and their students on a daily basis.

The Reflective Action Model

Our first chapter describes a method teachers can use to reflect on the many thorny issues that arise in their classrooms each day. We call our concept reflective action in teaching.

Our opening reflective action classroom example shows Susan McCloskey pondering over a phonics program that doesn't seem to meet her students' needs. After considering the problem, Susan talks to her principal and discusses another program that she feels might be more appropriate. Her principal, Mrs. Calmes, encourages Susan to try the new program and document the results, leaving the door open for further adaptations, if needed. This example shows Susan's willingness and ability to reflect on changes that can be made to better meet the needs of her students.

In a recent study funded by the National Institutes of Health, researchers found that children have only a 1 in 14 chance of having a rich, supportive elementary school experience. The findings suggest that not enough time is focused on teachers being engaging and supportive. The overwhelming majority of classroom time, based on the observations of this study, is spent in passive teacher-directed activity. They also noted that classrooms can be dull, bleak places where students don't get much teacher feedback or personal attention. These teachers consistently scored low on measures such as having "richness of instructional methods" and providing "evaluative feedback." Such studies point out the importance of teachers' constantly recognizing the need to evaluate their own teaching, especially as it relates to student needs and interests. The "whole child" is such an important part of our educational pursuits.

This model is a way of clarifying just how teachers think systematically about their practices and learn from their experiences. We wholeheartedly agree: Accomplished teachers are inventive in their teaching. They recognize the need to explore new findings and continue learning while incorporating ideas and methods developed by others. It is important for teachers to seek the advice of others and draw on education research and scholarship to improve their practices. We illustrate this concept by showing a teacher investigating new methods that may help students learn better and by discussing the problem with trusted colleagues. Our teacher uses reflective action to take new actions that will better fit students' needs. We cannot overemphasize the importance of teachers thinking systematically about their practices and learning from experience.

Definitions of Reflective Thinking and Action

In *How We Think: A Restatement of the Relation of Reflective Thinking to the Educative Process*, Dewey (1993) defined reflective thinking as the "active, persistent and careful consideration of any belief or supposed form of knowledge in light of the grounds that support it" (p. 9). An analysis of this carefully worded statement creates a powerful verbal image of the reflective thinker and correlates with the concept presented here of a person consciously choosing to use reflective action in teaching:

- **Active**—Voluntarily and willingly taking responsibility for personal actions.
- **Reflective**—Searching for information and solutions to problems that arise in the classroom; identifying the strengths and needs of individual students.
- **Persistent**—Being committed to thinking through difficult issues in depth; consistently and continually fine-tuning teaching approaches.
- **Relational**—Striving for quality interactions in the classroom to set the tone for learning.
- **Evidence seeking**—Trying new approaches while documenting their effectiveness and making adaptations based on evidence in the form of student learning.

Although persistent and careful thinking is important to the reflective teacher, such thinking does not automatically lead to change and improvement. Dewey (1937) also acknowledged the importance of translating thought into action and specified that attributes of open-mindedness, responsibility, and wholeheartedness are needed for teachers to translate their thoughts into reflective actions.

The Reflective Practitioner

Schon (1990) concurs with Dewey and others' (1937) emphasis on action as an essential aspect of the reflective process. He defines the reflective practitioner as one who engages in "reflection-in-action." This kind of thinking includes observing and critiquing our own actions and then changing our behaviors based on what we see. Reflection in action gives rise to an on-the-spot experiment. We define a problem, consider how we have addressed it in the past, and then think up and try out new actions to test our tentative understandings of them. This process helps us determine whether our moves change things for the better. An on-the-spot experiment may work, or it may produce surprises that call for further reflection and experiment.

Schon (1990) also notes that reflectivity in teaching leads to "professional artistry," a special type of competence displayed by some teachers when they find themselves in situations full of surprise, ambiguity, or conflict. Just as physicians respond to each patient's unique array of symptoms by questioning, inventing, testing, and creating a new diagnosis, Schon believes that reflective teachers also respond to the unexpected by asking questions such as, "What are my students experiencing?" "What can I do to improve this situation?" "How does my students' performance relate to the way I am teaching this material?"

Reflective thinking involves personal consideration of your own learning. It considers achievements and failures—what worked and what didn't—and strives to find ways to improve (Given, 2002). It involves active metacognition: thinking about your own thinking.

Often, during the process of reflection, teachers find that a new, surprising event contradicts something they thought they already "knew." When this happens, reflective individuals are able to cope with paradoxes and dilemmas by reexamining what they already know, by restructuring their strategies, or by reframing the problem. They often invent on-the-spot experiments to put their new understandings to the test or to answer the puzzling questions that have arisen from the event.

Reflective action is made up of many elements and is related to an individual's willingness to be curious and assertive in order to increase self-awareness, self-knowledge, and new understandings of the world in which we live and work. It is not something that occurs easily for most of us, and it takes time to develop. Writing of this idea, Brubacher, Case, and Reagan (1994) cite the children's story *The Velveteen Rabbit* to suggest that becoming a reflective practitioner has much in common with the process of becoming "real." As the Skin Horse explained to the Rabbit, becoming "real" takes time and happens after a toy has been loved so much that it loses its hair and becomes shabby. In the same way, becoming a truly reflective teacher involves time, experience, and inevitably a bit of wear around the edges!

Developing reflective practitioners has become a goal of many institutions educating future teachers. In a recent survey of websites of colleges and universities engaged in teacher education, we found one of the most common visions stated to be "to develop reflective practitioners." Research in the role of reflection in developing effective teachers (Bracken & Bryan, 2010) shows reflection as an important part of self-evaluation and growth in new teachers and teachers-in-training.

Developing as a Reflective Practitioner

Reflective thinking is a learned behavior that requires time and practice to develop and improve. Starting this process during the teacher education process is vital if it is to become a part of your daily routine. Some ways to ensure that you, as a teacher-in-training, develop the habits and skills needed to become a reflective practitioner include:

1. Take the time to reflect on all lessons that you plan and teach. Keeping a reflective journal where you write your thoughts after each lesson is one way to monitor your own development and the effectiveness of your teaching. Reflect on your organization, presentation, and interaction with students while also focusing on the reactions, successes, and any obvious confusions that the students exhibit. Make a practice of identifying areas in which you want to improve and documenting your progress in your journal.

2. Video- or audiotape yourself teaching. Review the recordings, focusing on your instruction and the responses of the students. Reflect on the clarity of your explanations and interactions with the students. Do you have to repeat directions? How can you clarify your instruction in order to avoid unnecessary repetitions? Do your interactions with the students sound like you are interested in them? Are you actively listening to their input? How often do you give encouragement? Reflecting on the lesson requires thought and focus. Your goal is to improve your teaching in future lessons.

3. Identify students who seem to need more assistance from you. Document the times you need to work individually with particular students and the results of those interactions. Keep track of the approaches you try, and reflect on their effectiveness. Be sure you allow time for students to become comfortable with new approaches before changing them. Be sure you are alert to indications from them that they are not benefiting from any of the interactions. Don't be afraid to talk to the students and get their verbal reactions to new approaches.

Reflective Action Builds on Withitness

This book describes classroom strategies and methods that you can use to become a caring and reflective teacher so that you will thrive in the classroom, not just "get by." We believe that two major traits help teachers achieve the kind of caring relationships that encourage students to relate to ideas, to their peers, and to others in their world. The first trait is withitness, which refers to a combination of caring and perceptiveness that allows teachers to focus on the needs of their students. The second trait, reflective action, is rooted in withitness. It is the ability to monitor your own behaviors, feelings, and needs and to learn from your mistakes. One of the most important things you can do to develop both withitness and reflective action is to get to know yourself and understand your own needs and desires for approval and acceptance from your prospective students. We will return to this theme repeatedly because your need to receive respect and affection from your students is something you must come to recognize and deal with effectively before you can care for others.

We will begin by examining the concept of withitness and then describe reflective action as it relates to withitness.

Defining Withitness

When you go into classrooms and observe teachers at work, you probably are curious to discover the differences between classrooms that are well managed and those that are disorderly and chaotic. Kounin (1977) hypothesized that smoothly functioning classrooms were governed by a clear set of rules and that chaotic classrooms had vague rules and discipline strategies. When he took his video camera into classrooms, however, he found that his hypothesis was wrong. What he observed was that the most smoothly functioning classrooms were those that were led by a teacher whose management style was characterized by a high degree of alertness and the ability to pay attention to more than one thing at the same time.

Kounin (1977) labeled the teacher characteristic that distinguished good classroom managers from poor ones as *withitness*. Good classroom managers, he observed, knew what was going on in their classrooms at all times. They were aware of who was working and who was not. They were also able to carry out their instruction while at the same time monitoring student behavior. In the midst of a sentence, they were willing and able to alter their lessons at the first sign of student restlessness or boredom. If a minor disruption occurred between students, the teacher perceived it immediately and was likely to walk toward a student, using eye contact that said, "I am watching you. You can't get away with that behavior in here."

Withitness is expressed more through teacher perceptiveness and behavior than through rules or harsh words. Eye contact, facial expressions, proximity, gestures, and actions such as stopping an activity demonstrate teacher withitness to students. These teachers are able to continue teaching a lesson while gesturing to a group or standing next to an overactive student who needs to refocus on the lesson. More importantly, the withit teacher can acknowledge students who are working well with a thumbs up, a smile, or a pat on the back, all while not interrupting the flow of the lesson. These are examples of the concept of *overlapping*, in which the teacher is able to deal with both student behavior and the lesson at the same time.

Kounin (1977) also studied what he called the *ripple effect*, a preventive discipline strategy that he found to be particularly useful in elementary classrooms. Kounin observed a student in his own college class reading a newspaper during the lecture. When Kounin reprimanded the student, he observed that his remarks caused changes in behavior among the other members of the class as well. Side glances to others ceased, whispers stopped, eyes went from windows or the instructor to notebooks on the desk. In subsequent observations in kindergarten classrooms, Kounin found that when teachers spoke firmly but kindly to a student, asking that student to desist from misbehavior, the other students in the class were also likely to desist from that behavior as well. When teachers spoke with roughness, however, the ripple effect was not as strong. Children who witnessed a teacher reprimand another child with anger or punitiveness did not conform more or misbehave less than those witnessing a teacher correcting another without anger or punitive actions.

Herrell and Jordan (2011) add another dimension to withitness, that of cultural sensitivity. They found that a culturally sensitive teacher not only evoked positive responses from students of other cultures but also started a ripple effect of cultural sensitivity among the students who spoke only English. This cultural sensitivity involved the recognition of word meanings and nuances in the students' first languages and the recognition of special aspects of the second culture. It also involved expressing general admiration of a student's ability to function in more than one language.

Recent research in teaching effectiveness adds to our understanding of the importance of withitness. It also indicates ways that teachers can work toward making themselves more aware of their own responses to interactions with students.

Malcolm Gladwell (2008) identifies "the gift of noticing," or withitness, as a vital attribute of a great teacher. Snoeyink's research (2008), using videos of student teachers, examined ways to improve withitness and reflectiveness to increase both teacher and student success.

Reflective Action as It Relates to Withitness

We all hear that it is good to be reflective and that teachers who are reflective are likely to grow and mature into excellent teachers. But what does it mean to be reflective, and how do you get that way? As educators, we want to create a word picture in our readers' minds that describes positive, caring, reflective teachers in action. We believe that reflectiveness starts with withitness, because it is first and foremost a type of perceptiveness. Perceptive, withit teachers constantly observe conditions and gather information to make good judgments about what is happening in a classroom and what can or should be done to address it. Withitness continually raises the quality and level of reflective thinking because it helps teachers observe more accurately and collect more complete information about classroom conditions. Reflective teachers plan for variations in student responses, constantly monitor students' reactions to classroom events, and are ready to respond when students show confusion or boredom. Reflective teachers actively monitor students during group activities and independent seat work, looking for signs that students need clarification of either the task or the teacher's expectations. They also consider the quality of developing student relationships, not how students interact with ideas, peers, and others in various settings.

Can withitness and reflective action be learned? We believe so. If you are willing to examine the cause-and-effect relationships in your classroom honestly and search for reasons for students' behaviors, then you are likely to develop withitness in the process. If you are willing to ask other adults to observe your interactions with students and give you feedback on how you respond to various situations, then you will be able to make changes and improve the quality of your withitness radar and responses. If you are willing to discuss classroom problems openly and honestly with your students in a problem-solving manner, then you are likely to learn from them what their signals mean.

When Michael Jordan (this book's co-author, not the basketball player) supervises student teachers, he always videotapes their lessons, focusing the camera on the children in the classroom. As he views the video with the student teachers, they always notice behaviors that they hadn't seen while they were teaching. They begin to reflect on their own withitness and ways that they respond to various students. Some of their comments include:

- "I never noticed that puzzled look on Jeremy's face. He obviously was not understanding."
- "My instructions must not be clear; look at how they're all asking each other what to do."
- "I can't believe that I never noticed how often I call on the same students."

Principals and supervising teachers often note that withitness and reflective thinking grow with experience. They grow in a symbiotic way. The more withitness teachers develop, the more reflective they are likely to become. Similarly, the more reflective teachers are about how their own needs may conflict with the needs of their students, the more withitness they display. Withitness is gradually developed by teachers as they actively reflect on the effects of their actions and decisions on their students' behavior.

For example, a beginning teacher may gradually become aware that her lessons are too long for students' attention spans. From that time on, she will be sensitive to whether a particular lesson is moving too slowly or lasting too long. On another day, the teacher may notice that whenever eye contact is made with a certain student, the student ceases to misbehave; the teacher reflects on this and actively begins to use eye contact as a way to connect not only with this student but also with others. Then, after further observation and discussion with a colleague, the teacher may also become aware that in some cultures children avoid eye contact with adults as a sign of respect. In response to a serious disruption, the teacher may notice that using a strong, confident voice causes the students to pay attention, whereas using a tentative, meek voice causes their attention to wander. Through reflecting on these experiences, the teacher develops two effective strategies for redirecting student behavior and begins to learn which is more effective in a given situation. Her active self-reflection is the first step toward developing greater withitness, and her increasing withitness contributes to greater self-reflection.

Improving Your Withitness

Set up a video camera to focus on your students while you teach a lesson. After the lesson, view the video and ask yourself the following questions:

1. Which student behaviors did I notice and correct or commend?
2. Did I call on a variety of students?
3. Are there students whose expressions or actions indicate that they are not understanding the lesson?
4. What did I do to make the lesson appropriate for students who did not appear to be understanding it?
5. Did I move around the room so that all students were in my close proximity at times?
6. What do I need to do differently or more consistently next time?

Do this exercise periodically to note your improvements and consistency. To see characteristics of teachers who exhibit withitness, see Figure 1.1.

Figure 1.1   Characteristics of a teacher who demonstrates withitness.

Characteristics	Examples
Teacher is alert and monitors multiple actions and behaviors at the same time.	• Teacher continues to teach and move into close proximity to students who are not listening. • Teacher points to correct part of textbook page for a student who looks confused.
Teacher provides timely correction/commendation for students as appropriate.	• Teacher monitors seat work and provides support and encouragement based on observation. • Teacher uses hand signals to let students know she is aware of student behaviors, both positive and negative, while continuing to teach.
Teacher adjusts lessons based on student restlessness, boredom, or confusion.	• Teacher plans several approaches to use in the event that the lesson is too hard or too easy for some students. • Teacher plans lessons that require all students to respond using a variety of methods such as individual whiteboards, show-me cards, or hand signals.

A Graphic Model of Reflective Action in Teaching

Consider that, as writers, it is our responsibility to connect with you in the same way teachers must connect with their students. We reflect on our memories as beginning teachers and think about what we wanted to learn and needed to know to be successful. In this sixth edition, we use feedback from readers of previous editions, as well as our own continuing research, to fine-tune the material we present.

We know that sometimes students learn better by seeing a picture or a graphic model of a complicated idea. The model of reflective action we present in this edition has changed from earlier editions because we are continually reflecting on how to make it more understandable and usable. Still, we recognize that any model is oversimplified and relies on the readers to fill in details and examples with their own imagination. With feedback from you, we will continue to refine our thinking in future editions. This is exactly how your own teaching can improve over the years if you are willing to seek critical feedback, reflect, and grow as a result of your experiences. In addition, changes in education policies and current research often influence what is expected of teachers. Standards-based teaching requires that you focus on a set of predetermined goals established by your local and state boards of education. This may present challenges for teachers who strive to design programs to meet the diverse needs of their students. When all students must meet the same standards, teachers have an enormous task to create lessons that also allow each student to experience success.

The Spiral Curriculum

Jerome Bruner (1960) describes children as active problem solvers who are ready and eager to take on difficult learning tasks in a supportive learning environment. His now-classic text The Process of Education describes the concept of the spiral curriculum, which "revisits basic ideas repeatedly, building upon them until the student has grasped the full formal apparatus that goes with them" (p. 13).

When you think of your school years, perhaps you recall subjects that were taught year after year, each time reviewing past learning and then revisiting it with increased complexity. The concept of the spiral curriculum allows teachers to adapt lessons to ensure that all students succeed. Maybe you had a favorite teacher who made a recurring subject such as U.S. history or geometry come "alive" to you in a way that made you feel stimulated and motivated to learn very difficult material. Perhaps one of the reasons you are reading this book is because your interactions with a caring teacher helped instill the desire to awaken a love of learning in others in the same way you were influenced.

The Art of Teaching

You have probably heard the term art of teaching. One aspect of the art of teaching is that each of us enters the teaching profession with a unique set of experiences with people and with institutions. From these individual experiences, we as teachers develop a unique perspective, or set of expectations, through which we view the world and from which we determine what we think life in a classroom should be like.

In the field of education, our perspectives or expectations are a little bit like the visual artist's perspective. For example, imagine that three different artists have been asked to paint the same landscape. Figure 1.2 shows the artist on the left painting the scene as she views it. Notice how she has chosen to depict the boat in relation to the sunset and the lake.

In contrast, note how the middle artist's view differs. He focuses on a close-up of the pine tree, with the boat farther in the distance. If you compared the two paintings, you might not realize from the first that there were pine trees in the original scene. Finally, look at the third artist's canvas. How does her view compare to the first two views? There is no lake at all in her painting.

Figure 1.2 Different perspectives create a point of view.

Over time, artists develop particular perspectives that become associated with their style of art. In the same way, your unique teaching and learning perspective will lead you to notice some things and overlook others—during your teacher preparation courses, and throughout your teaching career. There is nothing wrong with having a perspective or set of expectations about teaching—in fact, you can't help having one. However, it is important to remember that your personal perspective is not the only view or interpretation of events. As a teacher, you need to look at events and planning as if you were using a three-way mirror. In fact, there are at least as many different perspectives for an event as there are participants in it!

The Planning Process

The process of planning any type of classroom event is also unique for each teacher. The particular steps you take in planning a lesson or other types of classroom activities will be unique and may vary from day to day or lesson to lesson. As a teacher, you will consider aspects such as what your students' prior knowledge is, what the standards call for the students to learn, and what your expectations are for the outcome of the lesson. In this vein, we are proposing a general set of steps or guidelines here that we call a model of reflective action in teaching.

Reflective action, as the term implies, is a series of steps or processes in which you reflect on what you want to occur in your classroom and then take some type of action. While you are taking the action, you are also likely to be evaluating how well it is working. That evaluation may cause you to adapt or modify your course of action or plan an entirely new and different action.

Teachers establish learning goals in response to state standards, district requirements, students' needs, availability of resources, time commitments, and personal limits of energy and creativity. The process that teachers use is most likely to be reflective in nature. At the beginning, teachers sketch out in their minds a teaching action in the simplest terms. For example, a teacher may have a simple vision of teaching a math lesson on fractions using pizza to motivate the students. The teacher sees students cutting pizzas into halves, quarters, sixths, and so on. Upon further reflection, however, the teacher sees the possibility of a huge clean-up to follow and modifies the plan from cutting pizzas to cutting up cardboard "pizzas." The teacher may even prepare cardboard circles and pass them out to the students. But as the lesson develops, the teacher reflects on how difficult it is for students to cut accurate fractional sections of the cardboard circles. Seeing the ragged "fourths" and sixths" cut by the students, the teacher reevaluates the lesson to improve it. Each time the teacher modifies this lesson and plans a new set of actions, more details are added to ensure success. In this way,

Figure 1.3 Graphic model of reflective action in teaching.

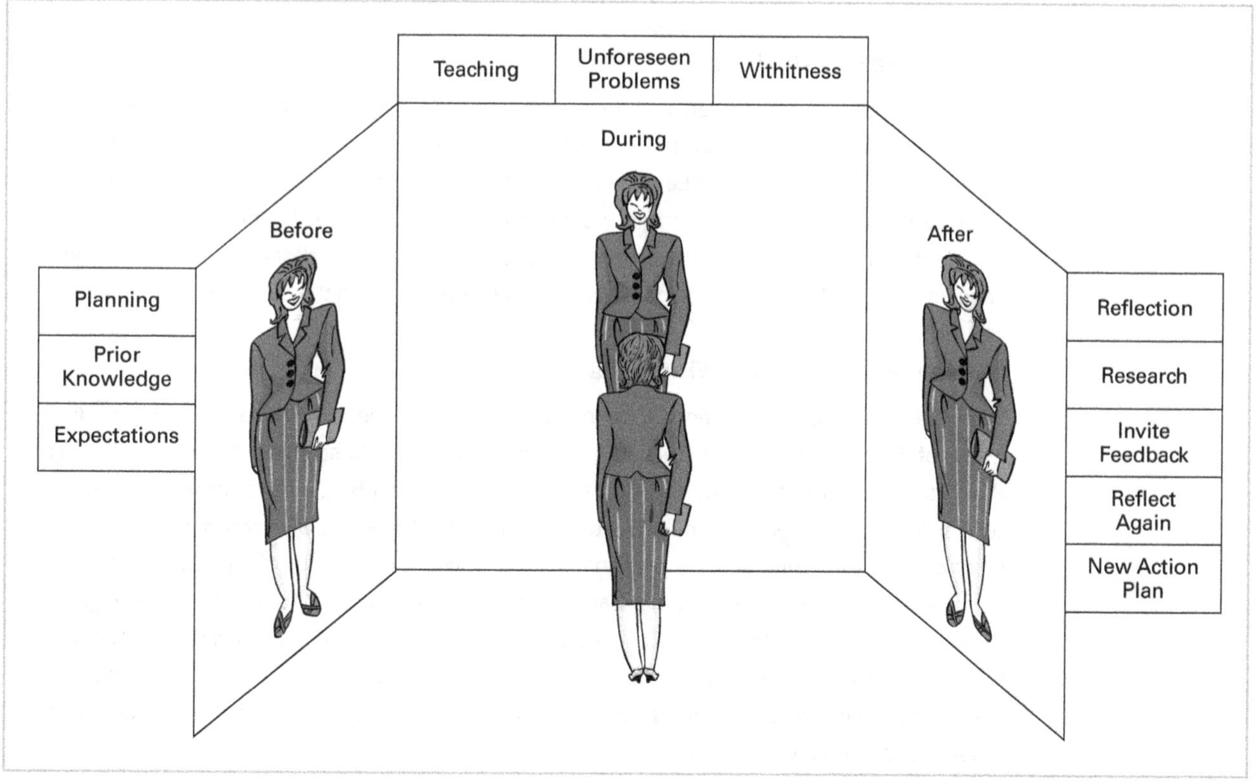

the reflective actions resemble looking in a three-way mirror in order to see a reflection from multiple perspectives.

In Figure 1.3 we represent the multiple perspectives involved in reflective action, showing some of the many adaptations teachers make from their first vision of a teaching event to the first attempt to teach the event and then subsequent modifications that are made over time.

Teacher Begins to Plan

In the left-hand mirror, the teacher begins to plan a lesson based on state content standards for the grade level and subject matter and to meet school district requirements and goals. Many teachers form a picture in their heads of what is about to occur. This mental image may even be in the form of a moving picture, with a script that the teacher intends to follow. The teacher has expectations that by following the script, the goal for this lesson will be achieved.

Next, **the teacher considers students' prior knowledge** and what they need to learn next. Reflective teachers think about the general needs or readiness of their class as a whole, and they also consider the individual needs of students. Some students will need more scaffolding in order to be successful, while others may have already mastered the material and need a more challenging assignment.

Teacher Teaches the Lesson

During the teaching of the lesson, unforeseen problems may occur, and students' responses may not match what was expected. Reflective teachers immediately begin to rethink their lesson plans. This can occur for a number of reasons. Perhaps the students' experiences with school differ greatly from those of the teacher, or perhaps a physical need (e.g., hunger, fatigue) prevents a student from paying full attention to the teacher's input. For any number of reasons, an unforeseen problem or challenge may (and often does!) arise during even the best-prepared lessons.

Reflective Teachers Use Withitness

Withit teachers monitor students' responses and adapt their lessons based on the individual needs of their students. Withit teachers immediately attend to these students while continuing their lessons. They use a variety of approaches such as eye contact, a closer proximity, a touch on a shoulder, or a predetermined nonverbal signal. Withit teachers also recognize exemplary work and behavior with positive responses. They notice the behavior of all students and respond quickly to unexpected events. Caring, reflective teachers monitor the ever-changing climate of the classroom by paying close attention to students' nonverbal and verbal responses. When events deviate from expectations, a teacher who uses reflective action responds by changing pace in a lesson, moving about the room, and interacting with students in an effort to redirect and refocus attention and learning.

Withitness is a form of *reflection in action* (Schon, 1990). This means that the teacher is perceiving cues from students, pondering what they mean, and talking out loud or continuing with a demonstration—all at the same time! This is an amazingly difficult feat to accomplish, and most beginning teachers do not achieve this easily. It takes practice and more practice. It also takes commitment and more commitment to teach and reflect at the same time. You will find that your withitness grows as you become more practiced at looking at events from multiple perspectives.

After Teacher Teaches the Lesson

After a lesson is taught, the teacher reflects again and tries to understand the reasons problems may have occurred. This is also known as reflection on action (Schon, 1990). Reflective teachers do not stop thinking about a problem when the bell rings. They try to understand what happened and why. They want to know how the problem might have been prevented. While nonreflective teachers may blame it all on the students, reflective teachers will not be satisfied with such a hasty conclusion. We cannot emphasize enough the importance of this step. Without reflection on practice, there is unlikely to be any growth of withitness. Without reflection, there is little or no opportunity to be creative, identify and solve problems, or devise and take a new approach.

Teacher Invites Feedback

A teacher's honest self-reflection leads to the next important action step on the reflective action model, inviting the feedback of respected colleagues or looking for other resources to help explain the unexpected classroom event. A concerned teacher might share a discouraging classroom experience with a colleague, who is likely to have a different perspective to offer.

Teacher Does Proactive Research

Perhaps the colleague will recommend a book or an article about the subject or suggest a workshop the teacher could attend. By taking the proactive step of seeking new information, the reflective teacher grows stronger and more capable with each such learning experience. These teachers are increasing their capacity for planning, teaching, and evaluating interesting learning events tailored to fit the needs of the students they teach. Rather than simply adopting a colleague's perspective or idea, the reflective teacher formulates a unique creative idea of how to reteach the lesson.

Teacher Creates New Action Plan

The next step is to devise a new action plan. The teacher imagines the scene in the classroom again and writes a new script—one with greater and more accurate awareness of the students' existing knowledge, skills, and interests. There are likely to be additional action steps needed, such as locating appropriate materials and getting them set up in the classroom in time for the next lesson. The entire reflective action process begins again with this newly adapted lesson. Perhaps all will go smoothly, but if a new problem occurs, the reflective teacher uses withitness to perceive the problem and begins the whole reflective action process again.

We hope that you can adapt this reflective action model to situations that arise in your classrooms. We hope that you will recognize the importance of reflecting before, during, and after a lesson. By reflecting before the lesson, you may be able to imagine or picture what is likely to occur. Then you can take preventive action by changing your lesson plan to better fit the needs of your students.

In the midst of the lesson, we hope that you will use your withitness and reflect on the actions you are taking in real time. What is happening? How are the students responding? Who is paying attention and who isn't? Why do some students seem overwhelmed or bored by this lesson? What can I do to improve the learning experience for them right now? These are questions that reflective teachers ask themselves while they are in front of their class.

After the lesson is over, it is time to reflect on what went well and what didn't. Beginning teachers may tend to get discouraged when lessons don't go as planned, but experienced teachers know that unforeseen circumstances are not only possible but likely. They reflect on what happened without assigning blame to themselves or to their students. They recognize that by reflecting and adapting this lesson, they are learning from their own experience.

The reflective action model never really ends. Instead, caring, reflective teachers begin the whole process again—planning, teaching, using withitness, getting feedback, researching, and creating. We believe that reflective action is an integral part of creativity. In addition, the self-awareness that grows from reflection on practice enhances teachers' self-confidence and makes them thrive and grow in their chosen career.

Standards That Apply to Reflective Action in Teaching

Certain guidelines assist teachers in making good decisions about their curricula and other classroom management issues. Each state has a board of education that publishes a set of standards for teachers to use when planning school programs. A standard is a goal or expectation intended to ensure high-quality educational experiences for all students. In the past, school districts made most curriculum decisions independently, but now each state has adopted standards that apply to all schools, so it is important for you to become familiar with those published by your state. Content standards describe what the state wants students to learn for each subject in the elementary curriculum: reading and language arts, mathematics, science, history and social science, physical education, and visual and performing arts. These content standards identify grade-level goals that you as teacher will be responsible to teach. It is the standards, not the textbooks, that determine what must be taught. The textbooks adopted by your state are simply classroom resources you can use to help your students gain the knowledge and skills defined in the content standards.

As a teacher, you will be planning a sequence of lessons designed to help your students learn and grow toward the grade-level expectations defined in each of the content standards. You will be responsible for monitoring their performance and progress throughout the year, and you must be ready to plan and adapt your lessons to support their achievement of the state standards. State assessments will be used to determine whether students in your school are mastering the content standards.

The curriculum consists of three elements: content, process, and product (Tomlinson, 1999).

1. *Content* defines what the student will know and understand.
2. *Process* involves giving students the opportunity to use and own the content.
3. *Product* involves providing students ways to demonstrate and expand their knowledge.

Two additional elements of curriculum, *learning environment* and *affect,* are closely related to the reflective action model and require that teachers know their students' individual needs and interests. In summary, planning curriculum includes the consideration of a number of elements:

- State and national content standards
- Students' past experiences
- Students' present levels of functioning
- Opportunities for students to process and use information and knowledge
- State-adopted textbooks
- Children's literature (trade books)
- Skills instruction (how to read, write, and conduct research)

National Teaching Standards

State boards of education also have responsibility for awarding teachers with teaching credentials or licenses. When you complete your teacher education program, you will be awarded a license or credential to teach in your state. However, if you move to another state, you must satisfy the requirements for that state's teaching credential as well. A new national organization has been formed that awards nationally recognized teaching credentials. The National Board for Professional Teaching Standards (NBPTS) has a mission to advance the quality of teaching and learning by providing rigorous standards for teachers. While state boards of education provide certificates for beginning teachers who demonstrate competence in teaching, the NBPTS provides the voluntary opportunity to experienced teachers to earn an additional certificate that demonstrates their high levels of proficiency in their chosen profession. This organization synthesized the research on teaching excellence and has produced a document describing five core propositions that define standards of excellence that teachers may attain during their careers (NBPTS, 2002–2003). The NBPTS seeks to identify and recognize teachers who effectively enhance student learning and demonstrate a high level of knowledge, skills, abilities, and commitment to the teaching profession.

Reflecting on Your Ethics, Beliefs, and Principles

Reflective action is a time-consuming practice that requires a willingness to examine why you choose to do something, how you can do something better, and how your actions affect other people. When you engage in reflective thinking about actions you have just taken or are about to take, you may become critical of your own behavior or your motives. Peters (1991) observes that reflective practice involves a personal risk because it requires that practitioners be open to an examination of beliefs, values, and feelings about which there may be great sensitivity.

When teachers are engaged in reflection about their decisions, actions, and behaviors, they are likely to begin asking themselves questions such as, "Why do I have this rule?" "Why do I care so much about what happens in my classroom?" "How did I come to believe so strongly about this element of my teaching?"

As teachers ask themselves this type of searching question, they are likely to reexamine their core beliefs and values. For example, if a teacher has grown up and gone to school in a traditional setting where children were "seen but not heard" unless they were responding to a direct question by an adult, then the teacher may expect the same type of behavior from students. But imagine that this teacher observes a classroom where students are allowed to interact, discuss their ideas with other students, and take part in spirited discussions with the teacher. Based on past assumptions, the beginning teacher may feel uncomfortable in a classroom with this noise level and consider the behavior of the students to be rude. This teacher should then ask the following questions: "Why am I uncomfortable with this noise level? Is it because I was never allowed to speak up when I was a child? How did I feel about the rules when I was a child? How do I feel about them now? What are the differences in the way these children are learning and the way I learned? What do I want my future students to learn—how to be quiet and orderly or how to be curious and assertive?"

When you confront confusing and ambiguous questions like these with honesty, your self-reflection can lead to new understandings of how your beliefs influence your present choices and actions. Continued reflective thinking can lead you to begin to clarify your philosophy of life and teaching, ethical standards, and moral code.

Do you think that it is necessary for you as a teacher to know what you stand for, what you believe and value? Is it important that you be able to state clearly the ethical and moral basis for your decisions? Strike (1993) notes two important reasons for teachers to have a well-articulated philosophy of teaching and code of ethics: (1) They work with a particularly vulnerable clientele, and (2) the teaching profession has no clear set of ethical principles or standards. Strike believes that, in the matter of discipline and grading, the most important ethical concepts are honesty, respect for diversity, fairness, and due process. He also believes that teachers must be willing to consider the ethical implications of equity in the way teachers distribute their time and attention to students, avoiding playing favorites. Are these part of your personal code of ethics?

It is likely that you believe your students ought to have the attributes of honesty, respect for diversity, and fairness. If so, it is vital that you demonstrate these behaviors for them, for it is well known that teachers are important models of moral and ethical behavior for the students they teach. When you begin teaching, we want you to accept the responsibility for beliefs and ethics. Teachers are important role models for behavior and character (see Figure 1.4). In classrooms that we observe, the teacher's character and moral code set the standards and the tone or climate for the classroom. If the teacher is fair, students are influenced to treat others fairly. If the teacher is impulsive and selfish, students are likely to behave in the same way. When teachers demonstrate a willingness to listen openly and honestly to others' points of view, students begin to respect the opinions of others as well. When teachers are closed and rigid in their approach to teaching and learning, students mold their behavior into a search for right answers and rote learning.

Figure 1.4 Implementing teacher beliefs.

Examples of beliefs	Ways the beliefs become evident
Students learn best in a supportive environment.	• Teacher consistently recognizes student achievement in classroom displays and verbal encouragement. • Teacher provides lessons that meet student needs and allow them to succeed.
Students learn best in a collaborative environment.	• Students are seated in groups so that they can work together. • Areas of the classroom are available for group projects, and materials are available nearby.
Students learn at different rates and with different methods.	• Teacher knows her students and plans lessons based on student needs, encouraging the use of different approaches and responses.
Students learn best when they are actively involved.	• Teacher plans lessons that require students to use manipulatives and ways for all students to respond. • Teacher involves students in planning units of study based on curriculum standards and the students' interests and strengths.

Professional Organizations and Ethical Standards

The National Association of Education of Young Children (NAEYC) recognizes that many daily decisions required of those who work with young children are of a moral and ethical nature. The association has produced a code of ethical conduct that offers guidelines for responsible behavior and sets forth a common basis for resolving the principal ethical dilemmas encountered in early childhood care and education. The following core values of their document offer a basis for ethical and moral decision making (NAEYC, 1997):

- Appreciating childhood as a unique and valuable stage of the human life cycle
- Basing our work with children on knowledge of child development
- Appreciating and supporting the close ties between the child and family
- Recognizing that children are best understood and supported in the context of family, culture, community, and society
- Respecting the dignity, worth, and uniqueness of each individual (child, family member, and colleague)
- Helping children and adults achieve their full potential in the context of relationships that are based on trust, respect, and positive regard

Because as an elementary school teacher you will be responsible for teaching multiple subjects, you should become familiar with the professional organizations that set the standards and ethical considerations for these different subjects. The following organizational websites will provide you with the most current information on standards and support available to their membership:

International Reading Association (IRA)

www.reading.org

National Council for Social Studies (NCSS)
www.socialstudies.org

National Council of Teachers of English (NCTE)
www.ncte.org

National Council of Teachers of Mathematics (NCTM)
www.nctm.org

National Science Teachers Association/National Research Council (NSTA/NRC)
www.nsta.org
www.nationalacademies.org/nrc

Ethical Caring

Noddings (2005) expresses the need for ethical caring in schools because schools are places where human beings learn how to interact. She proposes that caring is the basis of the Golden Rule. Caring as a moral attribute is no doubt high on the list of most aspiring teachers. Many people choose the career of teaching because they care deeply about the needs of children in our society. They are also likely to feel responsible for meeting the needs of their students. Occasionally, you may observe teachers who seem to have lost the ability to care for others because they are overwhelmed with meeting their own needs. They tend to blame others when their students fail to behave or achieve. Reflective, caring teachers, however, willingly accept that it is their responsibility to design a program that allows their students to succeed. They take responsibility for problems that occur during the school day rather than blaming others. They work every day to balance their own needs with the needs of their students. They are committed to growing as professional educators. To achieve these goals, they are willing to learn systematic ways of reflecting on their own practice so that they can enhance their students' likelihood to succeed. Other moral attributes that teachers cite as important in their personal lives and in their work with children are honesty, courage, and friendliness (Noddings, 2005).

Involving the Larger Educational Community

This reflective model extends beyond planning for individual lessons or units of teaching. It also involves considering the multiple perspectives of the broader community responsible for educating our children. Involving the larger educational community is a crucial part of this model.

Sharing your philosophy of education with parents, peers, and administrators is an important aspect of enlisting them as members of the learning team. Use back-to-school night, parent meetings, and parent conferences to help parents understand your beliefs about education and the ways in which they are implemented in your classroom. For example, if you believe that children should develop intrinsic motivation and do not believe in giving rewards and prizes in the classroom, you need to share this with the parents. You need to become familiar with research that supports your beliefs and be prepared to defend them and the related practices. You can then enlist parents in helping to develop students' intrinsic motivation by using encouraging words or special time to work together on projects as incentives rather than buying them presents or giving them material rewards.

Developing your philosophy of education will be an ongoing project. As you study educational psychology and teaching methods, your ideas and beliefs will change. For this reason, revisiting your ideas and the related philosophy should become a part of your reflection on teaching. Every time you observe in a classroom or plan a lesson, you should get into the habit of reflecting on the practices you've seen or planned. In this text, we will include regular activities that will support your reflection and help you develop a clear and concise philosophy of education.

Group Focus Activity

After the teaching event, the teacher should reflect again and try to understand the reasons for any problems that might have occurred or ways in which the lesson might be strengthened. They try to understand what happened and why. While nonreflective teachers may blame it all on the students, reflective teachers will not be satisfied with such a hasty conclusion. Without reflection on practice, there is unlikely to be any professional growth. Your professor might choose to involve you in the following small-group activity:

1. Have each group examine one of the following teaching scenarios.

2. Use blank transparencies and nonpermanent markers to record group responses to the following tasks:

   - Read the scenario your group is given.

   - Discuss what happened and why.

   - Discuss resources that might be accessed for deciding what action you could take.

   - Decide on appropriate actions.

   - Write responses (actions) on the transparency provided.

   - Share your group's suggestions on the overhead.

Teaching Scenario 1

While teaching a math lesson on multiplication, I realize that several of my students haven't mastered their addition facts. They have to count each item to figure out the arrays that I am using to demonstrate that multiplication is repeated addition. They are not able to complete the repeated additions because of their lack of basic skills.

Teaching Scenario 2

While teaching a social studies lesson about the Civil War, I realize that my students are obviously disinterested: passing notes, having to be redirected to the text, and talking to one another. We are reading a chapter in the social studies book and answering the questions at the end of the chapter.

Teaching Scenario 3

My second-grade class and I read a descriptive paragraph and discuss the words that make it "descriptive." I ask my students to write a paragraph about their favorite place using as many descriptive words as possible. About half of my students seem to have no idea how to begin.

Teaching Scenario 4

Several of my third graders have great difficulty reading the third-grade textbooks. I have them placed in appropriate books for their reading instruction, but they can't read the social studies and science textbooks. I'm at a loss as to how to help them.

Teaching Scenario 5

I have several students in my class who are just learning English. They all speak Spanish at home. I need to do something to help them understand the instruction in my class. What can I do?

Teaching Scenario 6

I have a child included in my classroom from a learning disabilities resource class. He has great difficulty keeping up with any writing tasks in my class due to his poor fine-motor skills. He tries to keep up, but it takes him twice as long as any of my other students to do any written work.

Teaching Scenario 7

I have several students who don't seem to be able to pass their spelling tests. They go through the weekly routine of looking up the words in the dictionary, writing sentences using the words, and filling in blanks in sentences using the words, yet they continue to fail their tests each week.

Teaching Scenario 8

There is a child in my class who is being left out of everything by the others. He is overweight and prefers to read a book on the playground instead of joining in the games. The other students won't pick him for teams anyway. He is becoming increasingly isolated.

This activity provides an opportunity to explore a variety of resources available for reflecting on and implementing modifications to instruction.

Preparing for Your Licensure Exam

In this chapter, you read about reflective action in teaching. Reread "A View into the Classroom" at the beginning of the chapter, and think about it as a case study you might encounter on your licensure exam. Answer the following questions to demonstrate your understanding of the role of standards in today's classroom, the steps in reflective action, and the teacher's responsibility for adapting curriculum and teaching approaches to students' needs:

1. What evidence is there that Susan is familiar with the state standards relative to the teaching of phonics in the first grade?
2. How does Susan demonstrate that she recognizes a need for continuing her education and growth as a teacher?
3. Cite some examples of Susan's withitness.
4. Are there examples of Susan's awareness of her students' abilities and background?
5. In implementing the reflective action model, how could you document the results of using a different teaching approach?

Portfolio of Professional Practices Activity

Developing an electronic portfolio as a model for working with student electronic portfolios

To help you develop your philosophy of education, a personal statement of your values and beliefs relating to the education of children, it is important for you to explore position statements and codes of ethics adopted by professional organizations in the field. This begins the process

of developing and clarifying your personal philosophy of education. Visit the following websites to select statements that reflect your personal beliefs relating to teaching at this stage in your professional development, and list those statements, paraphrasing them in a format that best suits your personal philosophy:

National Association for the Education of Young Children
www.naeyc.org/about/position/PSETH05.asp

National Education Association
www.nea.org/aboutnea/code.html

References

Bracken, M., & Bryan, A. (2010). The reflective practitioner model as a means of evaluating development education practice: Post-primary teachers' self-reflections of "doing" development education. *Monitoring and Evaluation (11)*, 17–21.

Brubacher, J., Case, C., & Reagan, T. (1994). *Becoming a reflective educator: How to build a culture of inquiry in the schools.* Thousand Oaks, CA: Corwin Press.

Bruner, J. (1960). *The process of education.* Cambridge, MA: Harvard University Press.

Dewey, J. (1933). *How we think: A restatement of the relation of reflective thinking to the education process* (Rev. ed.). Lexington, MA: D.C. Heath.

Dewey, J., Kilpatrick, W., Hartmann, G., & Melby, E. (1937). *The teacher and society.* New York: Appleton-Century.

Given, B. (2002). *Teaching to the brain's natural learning systems.* Washington, DC: Association of Supervision and Curriculum Development.

Gladwell, M. (2008, December 15). Most likely to succeed. *The New Yorker*, 16–18.

Herrell, A., & Jordan, M. (2011). *Fifty strategies for teaching English language learners* (4th ed.). Upper Saddle River, NJ: Pearson Education.

Kounin, J. (1977). *Discipline and group management in classrooms.* New York: Holt, Rinehart and Winston.

National Association for the Education of Young Children (NAEYC). (1997). *Ethical standards for teachers.* Retrieved from www.naeyc.org

National Board for Professional Teaching Standards. (2002–2003a). *Middle childhood/generalist portfolio.* Washington, DC: NCATE Webmaster. Retrieved from www.nbpts.org/candidates/portfolios.cfm

Noddings, N. (2005). *The challenge to care in schools* (2nd ed.). New York: Teachers College Press.

Peters, J. (1991). Strategies for reflective practice. *Professional and Continuing Education, 51*, 83–102.

Schon, D. (1990). *Educating the reflective practitioner.* San Francisco: Jossey-Bass.

Snoeyink, R. (2008). *Using video-analysis to improve withitness of student teachers.* Paper presented at the 2009 National Education Computing Conference (NECC) of the International Society for Computing in Education, Washington, DC.

Strike, K. (1993). The legal and moral responsibility of teachers. In J. Goodlad, R. Soder, & K. Sirotnik (Eds.), *The moral dimensions of teaching* (pp. 188–223). San Francisco: Jossey-Bass.

Tomlinson, C. (1999). *The differentiated classroom: Responding to the needs of all learners.* Upper Saddle River, NJ: Pearson Education.

chapter two

Creating a Safe, Healthy, and Happy Classroom

iStockPhoto

"In school there is no greater motivation for a student than the knowledge that at least one adult knows them well and cares about what happens to them."

J. Mathews, Washington Post Education Columnist

One thing that has not changed, despite rapid growth and dependence on technology, is that we all still need to feel that someone cares for us. All students who enter a classroom to begin a new year yearn for a teacher who will like them, inspire them to do their very best, listen to them, and respond to their needs and longings. There is no high-tech shortcut for this fundamental truth.

Nel Noddings (2005) recognizes that "the desire to be cared for is almost certainly a universal human characteristic. Not everyone wants to be cuddled or fussed over. But everyone wants to be received, to elicit a response that is congruent with an underlying need or desire" (p. 17). Caring is a way of relating to one another's needs and points of view, not a set of specific behaviors.

The best, most creative, caring, and reflective teachers realize that, like parenting, good teaching takes time and understanding. Good teaching resembles good parenting in that both require long periods of time and continuity to develop. Good parents and teachers start by creating an environment that encourages trusting relationships, and they work continually to strengthen that foundation of trust (Noddings, 1992).

Questions for Reflection as You Read the Chapter

1. What elements must be considered in order for students to learn in a secure setting?
2. How does the arrangement of the room affect the learning that takes place there?
3. How does a standards-based classroom support students' success in acquiring academic skills?

A View into the Classroom

Jennifer Bateman teaches second grade at Burnsville Elementary School in Lumpkin County, Georgia. This is Jennifer's story of how she adapted her classroom to a standards-based format.

Nearly two years ago I was given the opportunity to participate in a professional development program within my school district. My principal invited a primary and an intermediate-level teacher to join a cohort of county educators that would provide classroom laboratories for our standards-based classroom initiative.

Lumpkin County was going to be pursuing the standards-based classroom initiative that was the next step in implementation of the academic standards that were established by our state.

When the opportunity came to participate in the standards-based cohort for my district, I didn't just jump in and go. I took a few days and talked it over with my husband and a few other key people. I wanted to be sure I knew what I was getting into because it would be a yearlong program and I'd be responsible for maintaining my classroom as a standards-based exemplar that district and school personnel could visit at any time.

After weighing the positives and negatives, I decided to accept the professional development opportunity. My first meetings would be held the week prior to the beginning of the new term. That gave me 8 weeks of summer break to prepare.

The first thing I did involved research about what was considered to be an "ideal" standards-based classroom. I researched books, school websites, professional development portals like PBS online, and many Internet articles. I came to the conclusion that some of it would be the same as my normal activities in the classroom: planning, teaching, assessing, and reteaching as necessary to meet student needs.

The main differences appeared to be the following:

- *The expectations students meet are more specific, clearly stated, and clearly understood by both teachers and students and require a high level of academic standards in each of the content areas taught. For instance, in the past students had not always known why they were learning about adding and subtracting money. They were just told it was just necessary, leaving them without a clear understanding about where that learning would be used.*

- *The classroom environment should be one of inquiry, problem solving, formative and summative assessments, collaboration between students and teachers, and higher-order activities and essential questions that promote student interest. In the past, teachers knew that reaching the highest order in Bloom's taxonomy was ideal, but it wasn't always the first choice. Many teachers appeared to be satisfied with knowledge and application-level learning and assessments.*

- *The students and teachers need a common language and foundation of knowledge so that conversations, investigations, and learning opportunities can be the most productive. In the past, teachers seemed to have a language different from that of students, and it put students at a disadvantage in the learning process.*

I began researching the qualities of a true standards-based design and discovered the following criteria:

- *Standards-based classrooms are not classrooms where lessons are taught in isolation. Instead, teachers and students both have a clear understanding of the standards and expectations as well as a common knowledge of the relevance and process for learning the material as it relates to the standards.*

- *Standards-based classrooms employ a sense of community where the students and teachers understand their roles in the learning process. This is especially important in reaching at-risk students and enriching all students to enable them to reach the highest possible level of learning.*

- *Standards-based classrooms are filled with opportunities for learning that truly make sense to the students. If something doesn't make sense, it needs to be rethought and retaught until it does make sense. This may require using different texts and different learning tools (music, hands-on approaches, computer-based approaches, manipulatives, peer involvement, mentors, etc.) to differentiate the learning to accommodate the students' learning style.*

- *Unlike other classroom practices that just address topics as they appear in the list of standards to be taught or as they appear in a purchased text, standards-based classrooms are filled with daily explanations of where we were, where we are, and where we will be going with each concept. This is especially important with concepts that are not continued at the next grade level. Sometimes students are taught basic understandings in one grade, and then the topic isn't addressed again until several grades later. It is assumed that students have already mastered this concept at the grade level where it was introduced and that they are ready to tackle the next phase of the learning process.*

Standards-based classrooms provide bodies of evidence in that when you talk to students in the classroom, you should get a picture of what they are learning, where they are in the learning process, and why it's important for them to learn the concept.

Once the cohort began in July, I soon discovered that all of the research I had done and the matrices I had worked on were valuable assets for my own learning. My cohort of K–12 colleagues provided me with a wealth of knowledge about how my teaching and student learning, at even the primary level, were impacting all levels, K–12, within our district. It also gave me a yearlong look at my own teaching and the ways my children and I were able to grow and learn throughout the year.

As I began setting up my classroom that year, I found that everything I did seemed to be related to standards in some way. Deciding on the classroom arrangement is a good example.

In the past, I had used a variety of classroom arrangements to accommodate and promote the most beneficial learning opportunities for my students' academic, physical, and emotional needs. Rest assured that the arrangements changed throughout the year based on what was working and what needed improvement.

The classroom layout and setup were usually based on the grade level I was teaching at the time as well as various circumstances and specific criteria that had to be addressed (inclusion, mainstreaming, coteaching, etc.). The type of adjustment usually dictated specifics (like obtaining physical therapy devices for children needing certain accommodations or having a desk in the front of the room for a child who had partial hearing loss).

Many times my classroom also included a computer area and other media devices for use when I needed students to complete certain classroom activities and tasks. I always had believed that while the room was somewhat important for the flow and comfort of the students and me, the main focus should be on what was to be taught and how learning was to be delivered or shared.

This time I would be tackling something a little different. I had no idea that the physical layout of the standards-based classroom was such a crucial element to student success. The room layout of chairs and desks would not change a great deal as long as it allowed for flexible grouping and a sense of community. The students and I would be working collectively as a community, and the learning needed to be kid centered instead of teacher centered. In addition to the student desks, I set up a computer station, a listening station and reading center, a small-group activity table, a math transparency and manipulative station, and a science and social studies station.

Following are the necessary physical elements of a standards-based classroom:

- *Posting of essential higher-order questions that children would be pursuing each week*
- *Posting of the standards that children would be expected to know and understand*
- *Posting of curriculum maps (I chose to make time lines) to help everyone have an understanding of when things would occur throughout the year*
- *Places for displaying authentic work—examples of student work that educates rather than just decorates*
- *Displays of rubrics and expectations for success*

Additionally, I had to use a large portion of my whiteboard for a new interactive SMART Board. I was looking forward to finding ways to use the interactive board to improve my students' learning and participation.

My biggest hurdle throughout the setup process involved getting the standards and the curriculum maps displayed in a way that the students could digest, especially when teaching second grade. I solved this in two ways:

1. *Curriculum map. I created time lines that ran vertically up the walls of my classroom with pictures or brief titles representing each of the different standards we would be covering throughout the year. The only difference was for writing. I ran the writing time line horizontally across the room, with the expectations for the beginning and end of the year at the ends and the four genres to be mastered in the appropriate time location within the time line. This was great for providing work samples for each genre to show the student growth throughout the year.*

2. *Standards. I researched some other districts/states to see how they were displaying the standards. My first attempt was to print out the huge matrix I had developed over the summer. Reading/ELA and math each went floor to ceiling, were 150 pages in length and width that had to be taped together, and were typed with the smallest print, showing the articulation for K–6 standards (with "WE ARE HERE" on the second-grade sections). It was overwhelming to the kids and scary to the parents. Instead, I went with changing the standards to kid speak with a visual cue. I had seen some similar examples at other websites. It was a huge improvement.*

Instead of the formal language about students using multiple ways to represent and make connections between symbols and quantities. The Kid Speak version would say

"I can show my numbers in many ways (models, number sentences, and diagrams)."

Place value model.

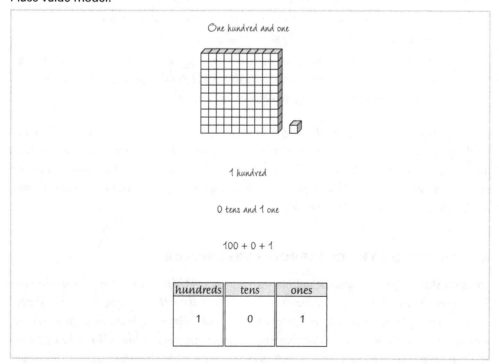

Setting up the classroom in preparation for the standards-based lab was another step in the reflective process. I didn't feel ill-prepared, but I did feel like I still had a lot to learn . . . and I am still learning today.

Another part of the reflective process is recognizing the importance of gaining information about each individual student in order to know how to approach the teaching of skills and standards. Analysis of every student's math, reading, and English/language arts (ELA) level upon arrival is critical to really understanding what that student's needs are for the coming year. My standards-based classroom analysis of each student involves several tools:

- *Screening for high-frequency word identification and accuracy for all K–2 levels*
- *Reading fluency analysis (including retelling comprehension)*
- *Text-based pretest of fluency and comprehension*
- *Math benchmark pretest*
- *Reading/ELA benchmark pretest*
- *Math skills analysis*
- *ELA pretest to determine mastery of skills from previous grade*
- *Accelerated Reader STAR Reading Diagnostic analysis to determine student performance in comparison to national percentiles*

Once I have accumulated all of the data, I meet with the parents to discuss my findings.

If the student has mastered the first-grade standards and is ready to begin working on second-grade standards, there is no need for overall catch-up strategies or enrichment strategies, but there may be individual areas in which catch-up or enrichment is needed. Two scenarios dictate specific differentiation:

1. *Catch-up. When a child does not show beginning grade-level performance in these analyses, I begin a Response to Intervention (RTI) to track classroom interventions that I will be using to bring the child up to grade-level performance.*
2. *Enrichment. When a child obviously exceeds beginning grade-level performance in these analyses, I look for ways to enrich and move the child toward higher expectations and learning levels, sometimes moving into higher-level material.*

Now, nearly two years after the original invitation, I look at the huge growth both in my teaching and in the academic growth of my students, and I know that we've come a very long way . . . and there is much more to do. This process will never be something that is a closed cycle. There isn't one set end that we seek; there is only a range of opportunities for students and teachers to grow as a productive learning unit.

REFLECTING ON THE CLASSROOM EXPERIENCE

Jennifer's story helps us to understand how experienced teachers continue to grow as they are involved in changes that occur in education. Jennifer uses the reflective action model as she researches new approaches and learns from her colleagues. Her story helps us to focus on the importance of implementation. Studying new methods and approaches will not benefit your students unless you implement them effectively in your classroom. Translating theory into practice is one of the most important roles a teacher performs.

Withitness: Observing Students to Learn from Them

In this text, we use the term *withitness* to refer to this attitude teachers have that compels them to listen, watch, and learn from their students. In their daily practice, reflective, withit teachers adjust their expectations, plans, and schedules to keep students interested and motivated to do well in their studies. For instance, if a reflective teacher becomes aware of a family circumstance that may prevent a student from paying full attention to school tasks, then the teacher will talk with the student to learn more about the situation and then modify the classroom expectations accordingly.

In this chapter, we will provide descriptions and examples of classroom management strategies and discipline techniques that respect the rights of each individual in the classroom and promote growth of self-esteem and self-responsibility. While there are many discipline methods that seem to work in the sense that they cause students to listen quietly and perform adequately, they are not included here if they rely on bribery, threats, sarcasm, or harsh punishments. We believe that you can establish classroom rules and expectations with your students, respecting their rights as well as your own. We believe that you can create a classroom community where the character of each student is encouraged to grow and expand during the school year. We hope that you want to be the type of teacher who is recalled by students later in life as the one who helped them understand the need for self-responsibility and respect for others. We also hope that you want to establish a classroom environment that is a happy and satisfying place to work and learn.

Practical Classroom Management Strategies

Connectedness

Joy! Does this word remind you of classroom environments you have participated in as a student or an observer? Glasser has been researching classroom management methods that have this goal since the early 1960s. His original work, *Schools without Failure* (1969), persuades teachers to see the necessity for creating a therapeutic environment that would allow all students to succeed. Glasser (2001) continues to create models of school environments that are characterized by joy, cooperation, and a feeling of connectedness.

In classrooms where students and teachers alike appear to be doomed to fail, there is a noticeable lack of teacher reflectiveness. Instead, Glasser (2001) observes that nonreflective teachers seem trapped in seven deadly habits: criticizing, blaming, complaining, nagging, threatening, punishing, and rewarding to control the behaviors of their students. The mistaken goal of the teacher who uses these negative habits is to control the behavior of students. He suggests that we replace these deadly habits with seven connecting habits: caring, listening, supporting, contributing, encouraging, trusting, and befriending. The teacher's goal should be connecting with students rather than attempting to control or blame them.

But teachers may say, "What am I supposed to do when a kid in my class is disruptive and obviously testing my authority?" Glasser (2001) responds, "Students who give you a hard time have already chosen to separate from you. That's why they're disrupting. If you can't connect with them, they'll give you a hard time all year, resisting your direction, which is their way of trying to control you" (p. 25). This type of student may keep disrupting the classroom until you start to threaten and punish. It's like a game of "Gotcha!" When students see you struggling for control, *they* may surmise that they are now in control. As the situation escalates, the students are very likely blaming the entire situation on the teacher.

How do you avoid this? Glasser describes a couple of familiar situations and suggests a way to use connecting behaviors rather than resorting to blaming behaviors. A third-grade boy starts to hum and keeps humming louder and louder while watching carefully to see what the teacher will do about it. Other students are also aware of the situation and are watching to see what will happen. This is a situation that demands withitness, followed by an appropriate and constructive response. Glasser suggests that the teacher stop teaching, look at the boy, and say, "Tom, I'm having trouble teaching with what you're doing. I'd like to talk with you for a few minutes."

Tell the other students to go back to their work, but do not be concerned if they watch and listen as you talk with Tom, as they can learn from this lesson on human interaction.

When you and Tom are sitting eye to eye, begin by saying, "Tom, I'm concerned about you. I don't think you are happy in this classroom. I'd like you to be happier. I think if you were happier, you wouldn't have been humming this morning. What do you think?"

Tom may be surprised and disarmed by this approach. He expects anger, threats, and punishment. His surprise will likely mean that he is paying attention to you, but he may not know how to answer your question. Instead, he may try to ignore you or pretend that he does not need you to care about him. He may answer, "I'm okay; don't worry about it." This is a weak effort to suggest that he does not need a connection with you, but he does. All children need to feel connected to the important adults in their lives, and as their teacher, you are one of the most important adults in your students' lives.

Continue to talk quietly with Tom. You might say, "I'm worried about you. If I weren't worried about you, I wouldn't take this time to talk with you about it. You are a smart kid. I'd like to help you get some good work done in this class. I think you'd feel a lot better if you did some work that you are proud of."

Tom may respond with something like, "I hate history. It's boring. Who cares about that old stuff anyway?"

To continue your connective interaction, you might respond, "That's a good question. Why should anyone care about history? We can talk about that with the whole class later this morning. But for now, I need to get back to teaching. I hope that you will get back to your report and finish it in a way that will make you proud of your work, or please sit quietly and think about all of this until the period is over."

Tom and the whole class have heard this important exchange. If Tom cooperates at this point, an important victory has been achieved for all members of the class. If Tom begins to hum again with a defiant look in his eye, it may be necessary to send Tom to the principal's office or another quiet place. You can say quite honestly, "Tom, I can't devote any more time to this problem right now. Go to the principal's office and wait for me there. I will come and talk to you during recess." After Tom leaves, you may want to talk to the class about what just happened. Ask the students to give their opinion of what just happened. Allow them to give suggestions for what you might say to Tom when you meet with him during recess. Explain to your students that you want to create a classroom where everybody can work and where everyone feels connected and supported.

Strategies to Meet Students' Needs

In *Motivation and Personality*, Maslow (1954) describes a hierarchy of human needs. He recognizes that people have basic physical and emotional needs that must be satisfied before the individual can attend to the higher need for achievement and recognition. If the lower needs are not satisfied, the individual is preoccupied by trying to meet them, and higher-level needs are pushed into the background. This explains why hungry or tired students cannot learn efficiently. All their capacities are focused on satisfying the need for food or sleep. To satisfy the real hunger needs experienced by many students, some schools provide breakfast or snacks so that students can pay attention to school tasks.

What happens when the student has plenty of food and adequate shelter and is well rested? Then "at once other (and higher) needs emerge" (Maslow, 1954, p. 375), and these become dominant. Once basic physiological needs are met, humans need safety and security. Next come the needs for love and belonging. Imagine two classrooms: One is led by either an autocratic or a permissive teacher, and students feel threatened, insecure, and isolated; the other is led by a democratic teacher, and students feel safe, secure, cared for, and connected to other members of the class community. In the latter setting, students are more likely to have their needs met and therefore be ready and able to achieve greater success in academic work.

Glasser (2001) believes that students need to feel safe, happy, and proud of themselves in a classroom if they are going to become convinced that schoolwork is worth the time and effort. To enlist their support, he recommends that you allow your students to know you as a human being, not just as an authority figure. Isn't it true that the better you know someone and the more you like them, the harder you will work for that person? Glasser asks you to use that same principle when establishing the expectations and procedures for your classroom. He suggests that during the first few months you are with your students, you look for natural occasions to tell them about the following:

Who you are

What you stand for

What you will ask them to do

What you will not ask them to do

What you will do for them

What you will not do for them

Glasser suggests that you may want to begin the school year in a way that creates a sense of connectedness among you and your students. One way to accomplish this is to involve your students in decisions about how to arrange the desks and tables in order to promote good two-way communication and make the students feel connected to you and to one another.

Building a Cooperative Climate

When your students walk into your classroom for the first time, they can sense a particular climate or environment within a few moments. A multitude of sensory images enter their consciousness—sights, sounds, and smells for the most part. The way the room is arranged, its messiness or neatness, wall decorations, open or shut windows, and the smell of chalk dust or an animal cage all combine to create a unique flavor or climate in a classroom.

What do you want your students to see, hear, smell, and feel when they enter your classroom? The appearance of your classroom makes a statement about the extent to which you care for the environment in which you and your students will spend several hours each day. It may be untidy, neat, colorful, or drab; it could be filled with objects, plants, animals, and children's art or undecorated and unkempt. No two classrooms are alike; each has its unique environment. However, some classrooms (and their occupants) bloom with health, vitality, and strength, whereas others appear sickly, listless, and debilitated.

Reflective teachers want to come to school several days before their contract calls for them to be there. They hang posters, decorate bulletin boards, and carefully consider ways to arrange the students' desks, tables, bookcases, and other furniture to fit their curriculum plans and the needs of their students. You know from the many years you have spent in classrooms as students that a bright, colorful, and stimulating classroom leads you to expect that school will be interesting and that the teacher celebrates life and learning. You also know that drab, undecorated spaces lead to expectations of dullness and boredom.

How to arrange the desks is a complex issue. Even though you may decide to involve your students in helping to rearrange the furniture as a way of connecting with them during the first week of class, you must still select an arrangement for the first day of school. Often the room contains many more desks than it was designed to hold comfortably. The number of students in a classroom may vary from 15 to 35, and the precise number of students is not known until the last minute, making preplanning difficult. Generally, though, teachers know approximately how many students they will have in their classrooms, and they set about arranging the desks in a way that uses space economically and strategically. Their plans are governed by an image of themselves and their students in teaching and learning experiences.

While arranging the classroom, reflective teachers envision its "activity flow"—what it will be like when the classroom is filled with students. This imaging process helps reflective teachers decide how to arrange the furniture in the room. As with other important decisions, each option has both advantages and disadvantages. Desks can be arranged in rows, circles, semicircles, and small groups. Each arrangement influences how students work and how they perceive their environment. Rows of desks provide an advantage in keeping order but leave little space for activities (Figure 2.1). A large circle of desks can be used if the teacher envisions that teaching and learning experiences will take place in the center of the circle, but it will be difficult for all students to see the chalkboard (Figure 2.2).

Arranging desks into small-group configurations results in students spending more time working together, initiating their own tasks, and working without teacher attention when compared with students in traditional rooms. Teachers who value cooperative group learning experiences over teacher-centered learning experiences often use clusters of four to six desks (Figure 2.3).

Activity and workspaces can be arranged by using bookcases and room dividers or simply by arranging tables and chairs in the corners of the room. Some teachers bring in comfortable furniture and rugs to design a space just for quiet reading. Computer or listening stations must also be designated. Room arrangement and use of space are highly individualized decisions. Teachers make these decisions to fit their personal image of what a classroom should be by considering what they value most highly and how the room arrangement fits their values as well as the curriculum and grade level of the class.

Reflective teachers also consider the effects of the physical arrangement of the room on developing a healthy classroom environment. Rows of desks imply order and efficiency but do little to build a sense of community. Clusters of desks promote cooperation and communication among groups of students. A large circle or concentric circle arrangement

Figure 2.1 Classroom arrangement: rows of desks.

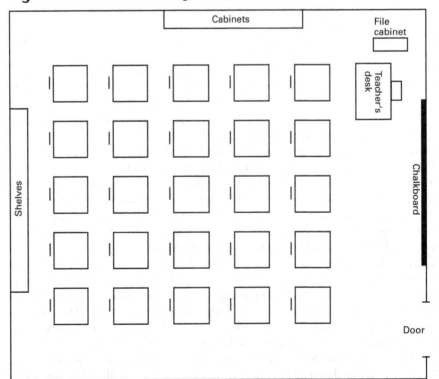

Figure 2.2 Classroom arrangement: circle of desks.

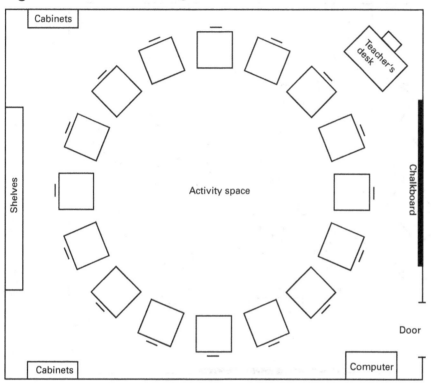

Figure 2.3 Classroom arrangement: clusters of desks.

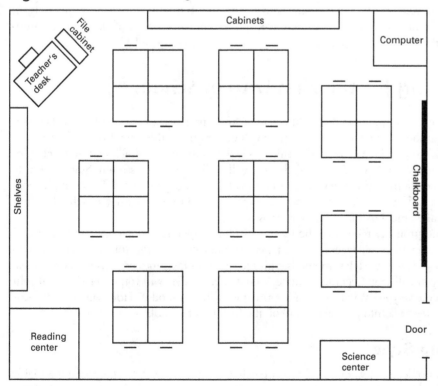

Figure 2.4   Classroom arrangement: concentric circles.

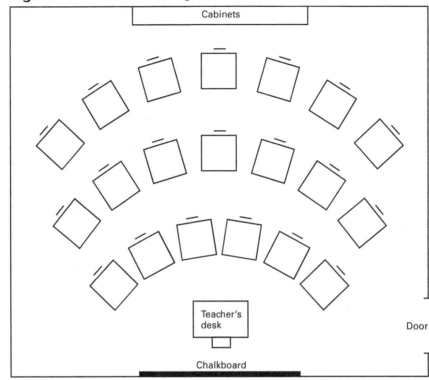

(Figure 2.4) encourages communication and sharing among all the members of the class. Many reflective teachers change their room arrangements from time to time, depending on the goals of a particular learning experience, and thus create a variety of classroom environments to fit a variety of purposes.

Planning for the First Day of School

The physical environment and schedule of the classroom may lead students to expect certain things about the way teaching and learning will occur during the school year. Thus, as you will recall from your own experiences, students look forward to meeting their new teacher for the first time so that they can discern what life will be like in this classroom. Students create lasting expectations during the first few minutes of the first day of school. For example, consider Figure 2.5, which describes students' experiences on their first day of school in four hypothetical elementary classroom scenarios.

You can probably recognize the teachers in these opening-day scenarios and can give them different names and faces from your own experiences in school. You have been exposed to a variety of teaching styles, methods, attitudes, and philosophies as consumers of education. Now you will soon become a teacher yourself. What style will you have? How will your students perceive you? What values and principles will you model? How will your students feel when they walk into your classroom on the first day of school?

Teaching Style

Each scenario depicts a variation of what we call a teaching style. A *teaching style* is a highly individualized and complex concept made up of personality, philosophy, values, physical and

***Figure* 2.5**   Scenarios of the first day of school.

The scene is an elementary school. It is the first day of the new school year. In one corridor, several classroom doors are open. We see and hear four teachers greet the students in their classes.

Room 101

Miss Adams is standing at the doorway. As children walk in, she says in a calm, even-toned voice to each of them, "You'll find your name on a desk," as she gestures toward eight clusters of desks. "Sit in that desk and wait quietly." The children obey and the room is quiet. When all the children have entered, Miss Adams goes into her classroom and quietly shuts the door behind her. The beginning bell rings at precisely that moment.

Room 102

Mr. Baron is nowhere to be seen. Children enter the classroom looking for him, but when they don't see him, they begin to talk and walk around the room. The desks are arranged in a circle. Two boys try to sit in the same desk, and a scuffle breaks out. The beginning bell rings. Suddenly Mr. Baron comes running down the hall, enters the room, and yells, "All right, you guys, sit down and be quiet. What do you think this place is? A zoo?"

Room 103

Mr. Catlin is standing at the door wearing a big smile. As each child enters, he gives the child a sticker with his or her name on it. "Put this sticker on a desk that you like and sit in it," he says. The children enter and quickly claim desks, which are arranged in four concentric arcs facing the front of the room. They talk with each other in the classroom. When the bell rings, Mr. Catlin enters, leaving the door ajar for latecomers.

Room 104

Mrs. Destry is sitting at her desk when the children enter. Without standing up, she tells the children to line up along the side of the room. They comply. When the bell rings, she tells a student to shut the door.

If we were able to enter the classrooms with the students, this is what we might see, hear, and experience.

Room 101

Miss Adams stands in front of the class. She has excellent posture and a level gaze. As she waits quietly for the children to find their seats, she looks each child in the eye. They settle down quickly. When the classroom is perfectly quiet, she begins to talk.

"I see that you have all found your desks. Good. Now we can begin. I like the way you have quieted down. That tells me that you know how to behave in school. Let's review some of the important rules of our classroom."

Pointing to a chart titled "Class Rules," she reads each aloud and tells the children its significance.

"'Rule 1: Students will pay attention when the teacher is speaking.' This is important because we are here to learn, and there can be no learning if you do not hear what the teacher is saying. 'Rule 2: Students will use quiet voices when talking in the classroom.' This rule is important because a quiet, orderly classroom is conducive to learning. 'Rule 3: No fighting, arguing, or name calling is allowed.'"

The children listen attentively to all items. They do not ask questions or comment on the rules. After the rules are read, Miss Adams assigns helpers for class jobs. The newly appointed monitors pass out the reading books, and the children begin to read the first story in their books. Miss Adams walks quietly from desk to desk to see that each child is reading.

Room 102

Mr. Baron rushes in and slams some books and papers on the desk. Some of them land on the floor nearby. Stooping to pick them up, he says, "Sit down, sit down, or I'll find cages for you instead of desks." The children sit down, but the noise level remains high.

"Enough! Do you want to begin the school year by going to the principal's office? Don't you care about school? Don't you want to learn something?" Gradually, the noise diminishes, but children's voices continue to interrupt from time to time with remarks to their teacher or to fellow classmates.

Mr. Baron calls roll from an attendance book. He does not even look up when a child says "Here" but stares intently at the book. He has several children pass out books at one time, resulting in more confusion about whether each child received all the necessary books. Finally he tells them to begin reading the first story in their reading books. Some do so; others do not. Mr. Baron begins looking through his file cabinet, ignoring the noise.

Room 103

Mr. Catlin walks through the room as he talks to the class. From time to time, he stops near a child and puts

(continued)

Figure 2.5   *Continued.*

his hand on the child's shoulder, especially a child who appears restless or insecure. This action seems to help the child settle down and pay attention.

"Welcome back to school! This year should be a good one for all of us. I've got some great new ideas for our math and social studies programs, and we'll be using paperback novels to supplement our reading series. But first, let's establish the rules for our classroom. Why are we here?"

A student raises her hand. Mr. Catlin reads the name tag sticker on her desk and calls on her by name. "To learn," she says timidly.

"Exactly!" Mr. Catlin agrees. "And what rules can help us to learn the most we've ever learned in a single year?"

Several children begin to call out responses at the same time.

"Wait a moment, class. Can we learn anything like this?"

A chorus of "No's" is heard.

"Then what rule do we need to solve this problem?"

A child raises his hand, is called on, and says, "We need to raise our hands before we talk."

"What a fine rule," Mr. Catlin says with a broad smile. "How many agree?" The hands of most children

go up. Mr. Catlin spots one child whose hand is not raised. He walks over to that child, kneels next to the child's desk, and says, "Do you agree that this rule will help you learn this year?"

"Yes," says the child, and his hand goes up.

After the class has established and agreed on several other class rules, Mr. Catlin talks about the reading program. He offers the children their choice of five paperback novels, distributes them, and tells the children to begin reading. As they read, he circulates, stopping from time to time to ask questions or make comments about the stories to individual children.

Room 104

Mrs. Destry regards the children in their line with an unfriendly gaze. When a child moves or talks, she gives that child a withering stare. From a class list, she begins to read the students' names in alphabetical order, indicating which seat they are to take. The students sit down meekly. No one says a word or makes a sound.

"Now, class, you will find your books in your desks. Take out your reading books and turn to the first page." Going down the rows, each child reads a paragraph aloud while the other children sit silently and listlessly, following along in their books.

emotional health, past experiences, and current knowledge about the effects of a teacher's behavior on the classroom environment.

Perhaps you may be considering the important question, "Is it possible to control and decide on my teaching style, or is it simply a function of my personality?" The more information you can gather about how teachers create healthy climates for learning, the more power you have to gain self-understanding and control over this and other important matters pertaining to teaching and learning.

Parents and administrators should be kept informed of your teaching style and expectations. In one case, during Adrienne Herrell's early years of teaching first grade, she had a principal who often made comments like, "I wonder why we even have desks in your classroom. I always see your students working at tables or on the floor." Adrienne simply had forgotten to communicate her desire for the students to learn to work cooperatively, so the room was equipped with individual desks that did not fit the class's needs or her teaching style.

Classroom Management Strategies

To identify the most effective classroom management strategies, Evertson and Harris (2002) review and evaluate the findings of many major studies on classroom management strategies. They found that even under the best circumstances, half or less of the school day is used for instruction. They also noted that the more effective classroom managers are able to conserve instruction time and minimize noninstruction time by appropriately sequencing, pacing, monitoring, and providing feedback for student work. The most effective managers were those who had rules and procedures planned for their classes. During the first week of school, the more effective managers spent a major part of the first day and much time during the next 3 weeks helping their students adjust to their classroom expectations and learn to understand the rules and procedures established for the class. Like Miss Adams and Mr. Catlin (in Figure 2.5), as soon as most students had arrived, the teachers began describing the rules and procedures they had selected. In some cases, but not always, students were invited to suggest rules for the class. The rules and procedures were explained clearly, with examples and reasons.

More effective managers did not rely simply on a discussion of the rules. They spent a considerable amount of time during the first week of school explaining and reminding students of the rules. One of the most effective ways to communicate your expectations to your class is to model the procedures they will be using. Effective teachers take time to rehearse procedures such as how students should line up for lunch or what students should take out of their desks for math class. Many teachers teach students to respond to specific signals, such as a bell or a hand signal used to gain their attention. Evertson and Harris (2002) observe that the effective managers began the school year by clearly establishing themselves as confident leaders. They prepared and planned classroom procedures in advance, communicated their expectations clearly, and demonstrated their withitness by signaling their awareness of student participation. After the first 3 weeks, teachers who use these methods have few discipline challenges for the rest of the year.

Leadership Style

The reflective teacher, guided by moral principles, also recognizes that it is not simply a matter of establishing leadership that is important; the style of leadership counts as well. Miss Adams and Mr. Catlin both quickly established that they were the classroom leaders, but Mr. Catlin better exhibited the underlying moral principles of caring, consideration, and honesty as he interacted with his students. The result is that students in such an environment return the caring, consideration, and honesty to the teacher and exhibit it in their interactions with one another.

Monitoring of Behavior

The way teachers monitor the behavior of their students is also a critical factor in establishing a clear set of expectations for students. The Evertson and Harris (2002) study discloses that less effective teacher-managers did not actively monitor students' behavior. Instead, they busied themselves with clerical tasks or worked with a single student on a task while ignoring the rest of the class. The consequence of vague and untaught rules and poor monitoring was that the children were frequently left without enough information or a good enough example to guide their behavior.

From this study, you can conclude that if you expect your students to obey the rules of your classroom, you must give them clear directions. Allow them to rehearse the procedures until they get them right, and actively monitor your students at work. Show them that you expect them to focus on the task and do their work. Remember the sad finding that less than half of the school day is actually used for teaching and learning. Resolve to use your withitness to ensure that you are using your time as effectively as possible.

Teacher Body Language

Jones (2000) found that effective classroom management and control of student behavior depend a great deal on the teacher's body language. Strong, effective teachers are able to communicate many important things with eye contact, physical proximity, bodily carriage, gestures, and facial expressions. A teacher's physical stature need not be a determining factor in successful classroom management. Indeed, it is fascinating to observe teachers who are smaller in stature managing disruptive students by simply moving into closer proximity or tossing a furtive glance in their direction.

Consider the eye contact of the teachers in the first-day scenario. Miss Adams had a level gaze and met the students' eyes as she looked at each of them at their first meeting. In a positive and nonthreatening manner, she communicated that she was aware and confident. In contrast, Mrs. Destry gave the students "withering stares" that probably caused them to feel anxious and fearful about the year ahead. Mr. Baron never met the eyes of his students at all, communicating his lack of preparedness and confidence to manage the classroom. Mr. Catlin used physical proximity as well as eye contact to put his students at ease while communicating his leadership role.

A teacher's personal bearing also sends messages to students. The strong, straight posture of Miss Adams reinforced the students' perception that she was an authority worthy of their respect. Good posture and confident bodily carriage convey strong leadership, whereas a drooping posture and lethargic movements convey weakness, resignation, or fearfulness (Jones, 2000).

Gestures are also a form of body language that can communicate positive expectations and prevent problems. Teachers can use gestures to mean "stop," "continue," or "quiet, please" without interrupting their verbal instruction. When used with positive eye contact, physical proximity, bodily carriage, or facial expression, gestures can prevent small disruptions from growing into major behavior problems.

Facial expressions also vary greatly among teachers. They can show enthusiasm, seriousness, enjoyment, and appreciation, all of which encourage good behavior; or they can reveal boredom, annoyance, and resignation, which may tend to encourage misbehavior (Jones, 2000). Facial expressions that display warmth, joy, and a sense of humor are those that students themselves report to be the most meaningful. You may even want to look in the mirror to see how students will see you when you are happy, are angry, are feeling good about yourself, or are upset.

Proximity Control

Jones (2000) recommends the concentric circle desk arrangement that Mr. Catlin used because it causes students to focus their attention on the teacher and enables the teacher to provide help efficiently by moving quickly to the side of any student who is having difficulty. A teacher can help students allay their fears and turn the focus to the classroom activity by moving close to a restless student and placing a hand on the student's shoulder. However, to use physical proximity effectively, the teacher must be able to step quickly to the side of the misbehaving student, as Mr. Catlin did. Thus, room arrangement can help or hinder a teacher's ability to manage classroom movement.

Establishment of Rules and Consequences

In a healthy democratic community, the citizens understand and accept the laws that govern their behavior; they also understand and accept that if they break the laws, certain consequences will follow. Healthy democratic classrooms also have laws that govern behavior, although they are usually called *rules*. In the most smoothly managed classrooms, students also learn to understand and accept the consequences for breaking a rule from the very first day.

In the first-day scenarios, each teacher established rules and consequences for the classroom differently. Miss Adams established a set of rules before school began. She read them to the class and explained why each was important. Neither Mr. Baron nor Mrs. Destry presented a clear set of rules. Their actions indicated that they expected the students to discover the rules of the classroom. These are likely to be quite consistent in Mrs. Destry's classroom, but in the case of Mr. Baron, we suspect that the rules might change from day to day. Mr. Catlin had planned an entire process for establishing rules. His process involved the students in helping to establish the class rules based on shared expectations and consequences.

Two different types of consequences are used to guide or shape student behavior. Natural consequences are those that follow directly from a student's behavior or action. For example, if a student gets so frustrated while working on an assignment that he rips the paper in half, the natural consequence is that the work will have to be redone from the beginning. If another student wakes up late, the natural consequence is that she misses the bus, has to walk to school, arrives late, and suffers the embarrassment of coming to class tardy. In these cases, there was no adult intervention; the consequence grew directly from the student's behavior.

Logical consequences are those the teacher selects to fit students' actions; they are intended to cause students to change their behavior. For example, a teacher may decide that the logical consequence for not turning in a paper on time is that the student must stay in for recess or come in for a detention after school to finish the paper. When the paper is turned in, the logical consequence is that the student may go out to recess or leave the detention hall.

The difference between a punishment and a consequence is that a consequence is not arbitrary, and it is not dispensed with anger or any other strong emotion. In his book *What Works in Schools*, Marzano (2003) recommends seven action steps in establishing rules and procedures that will have the effect of managing your classroom with a sense of success for you and a sense of belonging and acceptance for your students (pp. 95–102):

Action Step 1. Articulate and enforce a set of classroom rules and procedures.

Action Step 2. Use strategies that reinforce appropriate behavior, and recognize and provide consequences for inappropriate behavior.

Action Step 3. Institute a schoolwide approach to discipline.

Action Step 4. Develop a balance of dominance of and cooperation with students.

Action Step 5. Develop your awareness of the needs of different types of students, and learn ways to alleviate those needs.

Action Step 6. Use withitness to heighten your awareness of the actions of your students in your classes.

Action Step 7. Maintain healthy emotional objectivity with your students.

By establishing a clear set of rules with objective consequences and clearly communicating these rules and their consequences to your students, you can fulfill many of these seven action steps. In many classrooms, teachers write a set of rules on a large piece of poster board that is prominently displayed. Many teachers try to word the rules in positive ways, describing what they expect rather than what they forbid. They write specific consequences for each rule on the same poster for all students to see. For example:

Our class rules	Consequences if you do not follow the rule
We wait in line courteously.	You will go to the end of the line.
We listen to the teacher.	You will lose 5 minutes of free time.
We turn in work on time.	You will do your work at free time.
We work and talk quietly.	You will take a time-out.
We treat others with respect.	You will write a letter of apology.

CONDUCTING A RULES-SETTING ACTIVITY WITH YOUR CLASS. The most effective rules are those that the students help set. The discussion that takes place in setting rules for the classroom community is as important as the rules themselves. Students need to understand the rules and their purposes. Guidelines for conducting a rules-setting activity include:

1. Gather your class together and initiate a discussion of the purpose of rules.
2. Ask the students to suggest some rules that would make their classroom a better place to work. As students make suggestions, ask them to state the rule in a positive manner, telling what you should do instead of what you shouldn't. As a rule of thumb, five to seven rules should be sufficient.
3. Discuss each suggestion and ask the students to identify what consequences students should face if they break the rule.

4. Create a chart of rules and consequences as the class makes suggestions.

5. Tell the group that you will be trying the new rules for a week and that they will be asked to evaluate the rules' helpfulness at the end of that time.

6. Provide a place on the chalkboard or bulletin board for the students to make suggestions for any additional rules that are needed during the trial week.

7. Conduct a second rules-setting activity at the end of the week. Use this time to discuss how the rules worked, their benefits and negatives. Give the students a chance to suggest any additional rules they think necessary at that time.

USING POSITIVE CONSEQUENCES AND REWARDS.   Many beginning teachers believe that they can reward students with tokens or awards to earn their cooperation and respect. Jones (2000) examines the familiar incentive systems of using grades, awarding gold stars, and being dismissed first. He discovered that these systems appear to benefit only the top achievers; they are not genuine incentives for students who cannot realistically meet the established criteria.

Jones (2000) also notes that if teachers offer incentives that are not particularly attractive to many students, then the incentives will not positively affect student behavior or achievement. He uses the term *genuine incentives* to distinguish those that students perceive as both valuable and realistic for them to earn from those that students perceive to be of little benefit or impossible to achieve. His system of "responsibility training" focuses on preventing discipline problems by helping students to develop self-control and insight into what is meaningful and important in life.

One important way to develop self-responsibility is a form of time management training that provides genuine incentives for students to waste less time during the day. If they work efficiently and cooperatively, they can earn their own time to do what they want. Jones (2000) has observed enough classrooms to conclude that without genuine incentives to save time, many students will simply fritter it away: They move slowly getting to their seats in the morning; they waste time coming to attention, getting out their materials, or lining up.

Jones suggests that teachers think about time in the same way they think about money.

To train a child to become more responsible with money, it is essential that they earn some money in the first place. Once they have money of their own, it is the adult's responsibility to help them learn how to manage their money effectively. They have to learn that they cannot use credit or borrow more money. They need to learn that if they want more money, they have to earn it. Responsibility training with time is analogous to learning to manage money. Teachers can establish a classroom system that allows students to earn *preferred activity time* (PAT) to make their own choices. If they fritter away their class work time, then they earn less PAT. If they work effectively and cooperatively during work periods, they become rich (!) in time for their own preferred activities. In this type of system, you can maintain an objective demeanor that is nicely balanced between dominance and cooperation, because you are not rewarding or punishing student behavior as much as you are simply keeping an accurate record of the students' decisions and giving them their payoff in time.

If students are to continue to perceive these favored activities as genuine incentives, they must be delivered as promised. Teachers must plan well so that time is available for PAT. Failure to deliver on promises can upset the balance of trust between students and teacher, so that when the teacher establishes incentives, the students are skeptical that they will be delivered.

Counterproductive practices include continually threatening to reduce or eliminate the incentive or delivering the reward when work is not appropriately completed. Students then learn that they can have dessert even if they do not eat their dinner—that is, they can get the reward without doing their work.

Genuine incentives can promote increased achievement among individuals and groups and can encourage good behavior. Caring reflective teachers attempt to understand the real needs and desires of their students and to provide incentives that meet these needs.

Classroom Meetings

One method democratic teachers often use to build mutual caring, consideration, and honest expression of opinions and perceptions is to hold classroom meetings to discuss problems confronting the class. Some teachers hold regularly scheduled classroom meetings each week; others schedule them only when necessary. When Judy Eby taught fifth grade, she scheduled her meetings just before lunch on Wednesdays so that they were in the middle of the week. She found that one of the most important effects of a classroom meeting is the sense of community created when the students and teacher sit down to solve problems together.

CONDUCTING A CLASSROOM MEETING.   The seating arrangement for a classroom meeting is a single circle of chairs so that each member of the class can see both the teacher and all other members of the class. The teacher has the responsibility of establishing rules and consequences for the meeting. These usually consist of a rule about one person speaking at a time and accepting the ideas and opinions of others without criticism or laughter. It is important that, as the leader of the meeting, the teacher be nonjudgmental. When expressing anger or other feelings, class members are encouraged to use *I* statements.

The meeting should begin with positives. The teacher starts with a statement such as "I am proud of the way you all came to the class meeting and sat down quietly." Each student in the circle then responds with something they are proud of. Encourage them to compliment each other during this section of the meeting. Make it clear that students may simply say "Pass" if they can't think of anything to say. Additional opening statements could include "I wonder about . . ." or "I am concerned about. . . ." Give everyone a chance to share. It's best to use only one opening statement per meeting, however.

The second part of the meeting can be devoted to students' concerns. The teacher opens this discussion by asking who has a concern. When a problem is expressed, the teacher moderates discussion on that issue alone until it is resolved. Issues are seldom resolved easily in one meeting, but class members can raise a problem, express different ideas and opinions, and then offer possible solutions. When a reasonable solution is worked out, the teacher's role is to restate the solution and suggest that the class try it for a time and discuss how it worked at the next classroom meeting. Other student concerns can then be expressed.

The third part of the classroom meeting can address the teacher's concerns. The teacher can bring up a problem by expressing personal feelings or stating expectations for future work. Students' responses can be brought out and discussed and solutions proposed. The sense of community that develops from expressing needs and opinions, hearing other perspectives, and solving problems together is translated into all aspects of life in the classroom. When an argument occurs during recess or when students perceive something as unfair, they know they can discuss it openly and freely in a classroom meeting. When the teacher needs more cooperation or wants higher-quality work, this issue can be brought up in a classroom meeting. Mutual understanding, tolerance for opposing views, and development of ways to resolve conflicts result in a strong sense of ownership and commitment to the academic, social, and emotional goals of the class as a whole.

The teacher concludes by proposing an action plan to address the concerns that have been discussed and setting a time for the next classroom meeting when the action plan will be reviewed and evaluated.

Issues in Classroom Management

Dealing with Economic and Social Differences

Laughter and fun may seem to be scarce commodities in many school districts today. School violence, bullying, and suicide make the headlines these days, even in elementary schools.

Many people think that inner-city schools serving less affluent students are deadly and sterile, whereas suburban schools serving middle-class students are vital and stimulating. In reality, though, within each school a great variety of classroom environments exists. Talented, caring, and reflective teachers in inner-city schools can and do make learning a joyful experience, and their classrooms shine with goodwill, understanding, wit, and creativity.

Unfortunately, great social and economic disparities exist in the world. Children who have not created these differences are their victims. Historically, school has been the great equalizer — the means to rise out of poverty, the chance to make the most of one's potential. Reflective, caring, and creative teachers know they can make a significant difference in students' lives, and they work especially hard at creating a positive, healthy classroom environment to counteract the effects of poverty, discrimination, and neglect.

Whether you teach in a small town, a wealthy suburb, or the inner city, there are some social issues that are universal and seem to be growing at an alarming pace. One of these problems is a trend toward ethical and moral bankruptcy. As national corporations demonstrate, there is a growing sense that winning is everything and that rules are for the other guys. As a classroom teacher, you will have the opportunity to convince your students that honesty and integrity matter. You will have to model it for them if you expect them to understand or accept that moral discipline is worth achieving.

Lickona (1992) warns that some students come to school with distorted and disrespectful attitudes toward adults or schools; "many are astonishingly bold in their disrespect for teachers and other authority figures" (p. 109). He has observed student teachers and first-year teachers confront the harsh realities of working with students who bring their anger and resentment to school each day. Lickona believes that the teacher is the central moral authority in the classroom and that for many children the teacher functions as the primary moral "mentor" in their lives. "Exercising authority, however, doesn't mean being authoritarian. Authority works best when it's infused with respect and love" (p. 111).

To create a moral discipline system for your classroom, Lickona (1992) suggests involving your students in establishing the rules in a cooperative, mutually respectful manner. He describes how Kim McConnell, a sixth-grade teacher at Walt Disney Elementary School in San Ramon, California, develops rules with her students on the second day of school.

She arranges her classroom into groups of four students each, because she believes it is important for students to have a support group. She asks each group to work as a team to brainstorm rules that will help everyone in the class feel safe, get their work done, and be glad they are in school.

When they have written their rules on large pieces of paper, Kim transcribes them into a list of all ideas generated by the teams. As a group, the class synthesizes the best elements into one list that serves as the class rules for that year.

A SYSTEM OF MORAL DISCIPLINE.   Lickona (1992) proposes a system of moral discipline that focuses on the specific needs of each class and uses logical consequences that help students understand what they have done and what they must do to improve their moral conduct.

For example, with a rule such as "Use respectful language in this classroom," the consequences (designed by the students in cooperation with their teacher) might be as follows:

First occasion. Take a time-out of 5 minutes, and state or write the language you used that was disrespectful. Tell why it was disrespectful and to whom.

Second occasion. Write a letter of apology to the person or class to whom you were disrespectful.

Third occasion. Bring up your own behavior at a class meeting; ask for feedback on how you can stop using this type of language. Write a plan for improving your language, and present it to the class.

CHEATING BY STUDENTS AND TEACHERS.   One important element of character development is demonstrating an awareness of right and wrong concerning cheating on schoolwork. Cheating is easier than ever before because of material available to students on the Internet. In earlier eras, children might copy word for word from an encyclopedia. Today, they can go online and buy a term paper or essay to turn in as their own. Confounding this trend is the fact that teachers and school administrators have shown an increasing tendency to cheat. Principals feel driven to produce high test scores on standardized tests. Teachers may want their students to look good so that they look good as well. Since it has become common practice to publish school-by-school test results in the media and to grade and fund schools based on their scores, added pressure on students, teachers, and administrators is causing concern.

In Walker County, Georgia, the Naomi Elementary School participated in a National Study of School Evaluation (NSSE) parent and student opinion survey on honesty and cheating. The survey indicated that cheating was a possible problem area for Naomi. An alarming 33.9 percent of students and 29.4 percent of parents felt that cheating occurred frequently at Naomi, while 61 percent of students admitted that they were only somewhat honest, fair, and responsible.

To tackle this issue, the school community established a goal (with performance indicators) that students would make a commitment to creating quality work and striving for excellence while demonstrating that they are self-motivated to act with honesty and put forth their best effort in the pursuit of learning goals and tasks.

The Naomi School community then created a series of "action steps" to reach their goal. They established a Project Action Team consisting of school staff, parents, community members, and students to establish an academic integrity policy that includes a clearly defined honor code for students and a verifiable contract to be utilized during the 2003–2004 school year. They implemented a curriculum that focuses on the ethical traits of honesty, responsibility, self-discipline, citizenship, integrity, honor, and determination. They commissioned students to create and present drama skits for PTO programs to be presented throughout the year on themes of fairness, integrity, responsibility, and work ethics. They conducted seminars for parents and community members to introduce the goal and to open dialogue concerning cheating. They developed a program to assist students, parents, and staff in the recognition and demonstration of character and ethical traits with emphasis on honesty, fairness, and integrity.

Naomi School set up an assessment plan that included the use of surveys to be distributed yearly to teachers, students, and parents to determine the perception of progress toward improvement in student demonstration of honesty, integrity, and fairness. Grade-level and schoolwide reviews and evaluations of student progress in relation to work study habits would be recorded on student progress reports and permanent records. Administration would review discipline referrals to determine any existing or developing trends in relation to honesty, integrity, and fairness.

Naomi School then published the project with its goals, action plan, and assessment plan at www.myschoolonline.com. Go online and see what progress the school has made since this book was published.

Confronting School Bullies

"Most children know when there's bullying," say Pepler and Craig (1997) of the LaMarsh Centre for Research on Violence and Conflict Resolution, "but they don't report it." The Centre's research points out that bullying problems tend to fester under the surface. Michael Thompson (2001) reports that peer rejection is more likely to cause a child to leave school than academic difficulties.

A study of Toronto schools found that a bullying act occurred every 7 seconds, but teachers were aware of only 4 percent of the incidents. Teachers may believe that they are withit enough to be aware of bullying behavior in their classroom, but Pepler and Craig (1997) found that while 7 of 10 teachers reported that they always intervene, their students disagree. Only one in four students says that teachers almost always intervene, and 75 percent of the students believe that teachers are either unaware or unwilling to get involved in the situation. Parents are not always seen as mediators either. Close to 40 percent of victims say they have not talked to their parents about the problem. They suffer in silence on the playground or in the classroom, observed only by their peers, who are also reluctant to report the behavior.

Lack of intervention implies that bullying is acceptable and can be done without fear of consequences. Bullies and their accomplices need to understand that they cause harm and that their behavior will not be tolerated at school. They can change.

Ask any child what a bully looks like, and he or she is likely to describe someone who is bigger and stronger. Bullies certainly are known for their ability to overpower others physically, but mental, psychological, or verbal bullying can be just as damaging to children. The advent of new technologies has brought with it new forms of bullying known as *cyberbullying*. This occurs when a student is harassed or otherwise targeted by other students using the Internet, interactive and digital technologies, or mobile phones. Although schools may be limited by legal restrictions as to their level of involvement or intervention, they can be very effective brokers in working with the parents to stop and remedy cyberbullying. They may also want to add the issue of cyberbullying to educational programs they institute to control bullying schoolwide. Recent reports of victims of cyberbullying who have taken their own lives should serve as a strong reminder of the power of this medium. Dr. Thomas Lickona (2004) reminds us that schools that embark on implementing antibullying education programs should be careful to seek out programs that are research based. He points out that researchers who investigated over 500 such programs found only 4 school-based programs with proven effectiveness. One such study of schools that created their own programs rather than using tested approaches showed a 35 percent increase in bullying behavior.

EFFECTIVE ANTIBULLYING PROGRAMS. Norwegian psychologist Dr. Dan Olweus (2001), who for the past 30 years has been involved in research and intervention work in the area of bully/victim problems among schoolchildren and youth, offers perhaps the best known of the effective programs in his Olweus Bullying Prevention Program. His program was selected as one of 10 "model programs" approved to be used in a national violence prevention initiative in the United States. This program has been shown to reduce bullying by 50 percent or more in schools where it is fully implemented. It also has demonstrated major reductions in vandalizing, stealing, and fighting while improving classroom climate and positive student attitudes toward schooling (Black, 2003; Olweus, 2004). For a more comprehensive look at the Olweus program, visit the public website at www.olweus.org/public/index.page.

When bullies are allowed to torment other students, many feel the need to suffer in silence for fear that speaking up will provoke further torture, but bullying is not a problem that usually just takes care of itself. Action needs to be taken

As a reflective teacher using withitness to prevent bullying, you can take the following steps:

Use withitness to respond to bullying. Tell your students that you want to know when they feel bullied. When a bullying act is reported, have a frank discussion with the bully. Try to connect with him or her and find out what he or she wants or needs to feel happier and more successful without the need to bully other students.

Teach communication skills. If young primary-age students are reluctant to discuss the subject, allow them to role-play bullying behavior with puppets or dolls. For intermediate and middle school students, hold a classroom meeting on the subject of bullying. Ask the class to suggest ways for children to express their feelings in a positive way. Practice methods that children can use to resolve problems firmly and fairly.

Identify ways to distinguish between teasing and bullying. Teach children how to ignore routine teasing. Not all provocative behavior must be acknowledged. Help children identify acts of aggression, bossiness, or discrimination. Encourage children not to give up objects or territory to bullies. This discourages bullying behavior.

In March 2004, Health and Human Services Secretary Tommy G. Thompson announced a national campaign to educate Americans about bullying and youth violence, both of which have an extremely negative impact on children's success in school and their overall well-being.

"Bullying is something we cannot ignore," Secretary Thompson said. "From the schoolrooms to the schoolyards we must nurture a healthy environment for our children. By engaging the entire community in preventing bullying we can promote a more peaceful and safe place for children to grow."

According to the U.S. Department of Education, one in four children who act as bullies will have a criminal record by the age of 30. These same students are much more likely to smoke, drink alcohol, and have lower grades in school. While we tend to think of the impact of bullying on the victims, we must not ignore the bully. These students are also our responsibility.

The U.S. Health and Human Services campaign against bullying is called "Take a Stand, Lend a Hand. Stop Bullying Now!" The campaign includes a web-based animated story, along with many other resources for teachers, administrators, and parents. See their website at www.stopbullyingnow.hrsa.gov.

TEACHING STUDENTS HOW TO RESOLVE CONFLICTS. In many schools, conflicts have escalated to violent confrontations. Students bicker, threaten, and harass one another. Conflicts among racial and ethnic groups are on the rise. Truancy is epidemic in some areas. Traditional discipline programs involving scolding and suspensions do not appear to improve such situations. What can we do? What will you do when you are confronted with these situations? In some learning communities, teachers are instructing students on how to be peacemakers and to resolve conflicts for themselves and their peers. Johnson and Johnson (1995) provide a curriculum for such programs in their book, *Teaching Students to Be Peacemakers*. Through the use of role plays and other learning opportunities to practice conflict resolution skills, students learn how to negotiate and mediate when conflicts arise.

Many teachers are finding that teaching conflict resolution skills is a necessary part of helping students to get along with one another. David Stewart teaches fifth grade in Cocoa, Florida. He includes the teaching of speaking and listening standards as a part of a unit on resolving conflicts.

Effective communication between teacher and student is based on mutual trust that grows from the basic moral principles of caring, consideration, and honesty. Reflective teachers who are guided by these moral principles express them in the classroom by listening empathetically. Listening is one of the most important ways of gathering information about students' needs in order to make informed judgments about why students behave the way they do.

Discussions between teacher and student must be guided by consideration for the child's feelings and fragile, developing self-concept. There is also a great need for honest, open exchanges of feelings and information among all members of a classroom. A sense of community and shared purpose grows from a realistic understanding of each other's perceptions and needs.

Scheduling Time for Active Learning

Daily and Weekly Schedules

Teachers at all levels believe they cannot fit everything they want to teach into the school day. Charles (2002) cites "dealing with the trivial" as one of teachers' greatest time robbers (p. 243). When teachers simply try to fit everything into the day, they are as likely to include trivial matters as important ones. A reflective teacher weighs the relative importance of each element of the school program and allocates time accordingly. This may mean eliminating certain items entirely and carefully scheduling the minutes of the day to meet students' most important needs.

Schedules differ from grade to grade, depending on the relative importance the subject has at that grade level and the way the school is structured and organized. The most frequently used structure in elementary schools is to place students in grade-level, self-contained

Reflective Action Case Study

TEACHING LANGUAGE ARTS STANDARDS IN CONJUNCTION WITH A CONFLICT RESOLUTION UNIT

David Stewart
Fifth-Grade Teacher

Teacher Begins to Plan

I was concerned that my students didn't seem to have the vocabulary and speaking skills necessary to discuss conflicts that arose in the classroom and on the playground. I began to plan by reviewing the state language arts standards related to speaking and listening. I located two standards that could easily be integrated into a unit on conflict resolution:

- The student will use new vocabulary that is introduced and taught directly.
- The student will listen and speak to gain information for a variety of purposes.

Teacher Considers What Students Already Know

I listened to my students as they talked about problems in the classroom and heard a lot of blame words but not many problem-solving words. I decided to start my unit by introducing and practicing some words and phrases that help communicate feelings.

Reflective Teacher Uses Withitness and Reflects on the Event

As I listened to my students talking about classroom conflicts and assigning blame, I began to list some of their words on the board. I reflected on their feelings and tone of voice as they spoke and assigned feelings to their verbalizations. After I thought about feelings and noted their words, I began a discussion by asking the speakers how they were feeling as they spoke the words. I made a list of feelings on the board. Their ability to name feelings was interesting. They chose words like *bad*, *mad*, and *sad*.

Teacher Does Research and Invites Feedback

I talked to my teammates and told them about the event. They suggested that I look at lessons on vocabulary while researching programs for conflict resolution. I went to the Internet and found several good resources:

- www.scoe.net/pass—A resource that describes school-based conflict resolution programs in California
- *Conflict Resolution in the Schools: A Manual for Educators*—A book that I ordered online that would help me plan my program

I read the information on the website and began reading the book. I shared some of the ideas for my unit with my teammates and asked for feedback. Several of them wanted to join me in teaching this unit since they saw the need in their classrooms as well.

Teacher Reflects Again, Using Feedback, Research, and Creativity

I decided to begin my unit by teaching peaceful vocabulary and having the students brainstorm words they could use to express their feelings while solving problems by interacting peacefully. I made a video of the students' interactions so I could share it with my teammates and get their feedback on how it went and where to go next.

I started by reviewing the discussion we had in class and building on the words they had used. I set up some simulations where I gave the students a situation and had them use verbal interactions to determine:

- What happened?

- Exactly what words were spoken?

- How did those words make you feel?

As they answered the questions, I noted their responses on the board. After the activity, we discussed other vocabulary they might use, and I introduced feeling words: *frustrated, angry, embarrassed, disappointed*, and *furious*. As we explored each of these words, we talked about their meanings, discussed times when they had felt like that, and acted out the words.

My teammates and I watched the video of this first lesson and discussed plans for continuing the unit. All of them agreed to teach the unit in their classrooms as well.

Teacher Creates a New Action Plan

I began the unit by teaching active listening and making I statements. I challenged the students to build a new vocabulary of peaceful words, and we practiced using conflict resolution strategies. I was heartened by the students' responses and their stories of how they were using their new vocabulary with their siblings at home.

Because the entire fifth grade was using this conflict resolution unit, the principal asked us to share what we were doing at a faculty meeting. We showed some of the video we had made, and the faculty voted to make this project a schoolwide activity.

Several parents have commented on their children's knowledge of respectful words and the impact of this project on interactions in their homes. Teaching conflict resolution is now a schoolwide commitment.

classrooms in which one teacher has the responsibility for teaching all academic subjects. In other cases, students may have a homeroom, but their academic subjects are departmentalized, meaning that teachers specialize in one academic area and students move from class to class during the day.

For example, the primary grades are usually structured as self-contained classrooms, and primary teachers often schedule reading and language arts activities for up to one-half of the school day. The intermediate grades may be self-contained or departmentalized, but in either case, math, science, and social studies activities are usually given more time than they are in the primary grades. In junior high school, the schedules are likely to be departmentalized, meaning that each teacher specializes in one subject and teaches it to several classes of students during the day.

No two schedules are alike. Teachers in self-contained classrooms are usually allowed great discretion in how they allocate time. Typically, state requirements mandate how many minutes per week are to be allocated to each of several subjects, but teachers make varied plans within those prescriptions. For example, the state may require a minimum of 150 minutes of math per week: Teacher A may schedule 30 minutes per day; teacher B may schedule 40 minutes for 4 days; teacher C may schedule 45 minutes of Mondays, Wednesdays, and Fridays with brief review periods on other days.

Elementary class schedules may be rigid or flexible, they may be the same every day or vary greatly, and they may be governed by bells or by the teacher's own inner clock. Regardless of how a schedule is determined, Charles (2002) recommends that "the daily classroom schedule should be explained in such a manner that students know what activities are to occur at each part of the day and how they are to work and behave during those activities" (p. 10). When students know the schedule, they can learn to manage their own time more efficiently. A teacher who uses a consistent schedule may create a permanent display of the schedule on a bulletin board; a teacher who varies the schedule from day to day can write the current schedule on the chalkboard each morning.

The conventional wisdom of teachers is that the most difficult subjects should be scheduled early in the day when students are most likely to be attentive. Reading and language arts are often the first subjects of the day in a self-contained classroom, followed by math. Science, social studies, art, computers, and music compose the afternoons. This may be the preferred schedule, but often school constraints make it difficult to achieve. Physical education, art, computers, and music may be taught by other teachers in separate classrooms, so the schedule for these special classes may affect the classroom teacher's schedule. Some groups must be scheduled for special classes in the morning, causing classroom teachers to adjust their plans.

Planning Time

Teachers may be annoyed when special classes interrupt their scheduled lessons, but they appreciate one important side effect: When the class leaves for art, computers, music, or physical education, the classroom teacher often has a planning period. Planning time is generally part of the teacher's contract and is designed to provide opportunities for individual or collegial planning. Teachers of self-contained classrooms usually have complete discretion over their planning time, but departmentalized teachers frequently hold meetings during their planning time to discuss how they will plan and deliver their shared curricula.

Teachers use planning time in various ways, some productive and others less so. Charles (2002) recommends that teachers use this time as efficiently as possible by "prioritizing tasks, giving attention to those that are absolutely necessary, such as planning, scoring papers, preparing for conferences, and preparing instructional materials and activities. Also high on the list should come those tasks that are difficult or boring, leaving for later those that are most enjoyable" (p. 244). Less efficient teachers may use the time for socializing, complaining, smoking, eating, reading magazines, or making personal telephone calls. Later they complain that the school day is too short and that they have too much work to do at home.

Charles (2002) recommends that routine tasks such as watering plants, cleaning the room, feeding animals, and distributing materials should not be done during planning time or even be done by the teacher at all. The teacher who is an efficient time manager delegates as many of these routine tasks as possible to student helpers. This has two effects that contribute to a healthy classroom environment: (1) It reduces the stress teachers feel about time, and (2) it provides a sense of responsibility and meaningful accomplishment for the student helpers.

Most reflective teachers want to create a classroom in which students can meet their basic human needs for belonging and achievement. To accomplish this, they consider every aspect of the environment as it relates to children's needs: They arrange the furniture to meet students' needs for a sense of belonging; they create rules and schedule time to meet students' needs for security; they provide opportunities for students to write about and discuss their other feelings and needs. They do this because they want to create a nurturing sense of community in their classroom as a means of enhancing successful achievement.

Involving the Larger Educational Community

In Chapter One, we emphasized the importance of sharing your philosophy of education with parents, colleagues, and administrators. This is important in helping them understand the methodology and underlying reasoning for the approaches used in your classroom. This communication is especially vital when it comes to classroom management and the rules and expectations in your class. Once you and the students have mutually established the classroom rules and procedures, these should be shared with your larger educational community. This might be done through a class newsletter, website, or verbally at back-to-school night.

Parents and administrators should always feel that they are kept up-to-date with what is happening in the classroom. If a student is having adjustment difficulties or is having problems following classroom rules, parents need to be aware of these problems. If you are able to communicate regularly with your educational community, they feel more a part of the learning team. When you and the parents can begin to align the expectations at home and at school, students will find them easier to understand and meet.

Group Focus Activity

Your professor may involve you in this activity to explore room arrangements and teaching philosophies.

1. You will work in small groups.
2. Each group will match the room arrangements (Figures 2.1, 2.2, 2.3, and 2.4) with the scenarios of the first day of school found in Figure 2.5.
3. Each group will then read the excerpts from the philosophies of education (Figure 2.6) and decide which of the teachers in the scenarios from the first day of school (Figure 2.5) wrote each of the excerpts.
4. The class will meet back together to discuss how they made their selections and decisions.

Figure 2.6   Excerpts from the educational philosophies of teachers.

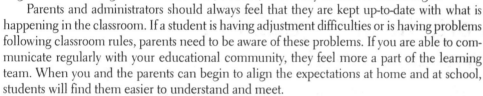

I believe that teaching consists of making students aware of the responsibilities of a member of a free society. An effective classroom runs by having everyone aware of the rules and expecting everyone to do their part. Cooperative learning has a place in my classroom, but I believe that I, the teacher, am the person responsible for planning instruction that meets the needs of each child.

I believe in discipline and hard work. I believe that students need to view school as their place of work. As a student, I was motivated and dedicated, and I want to pass that work ethic along to my students. I feel that most of today's children are given entirely too much freedom and are not learning any self-discipline. Teaching these attitudes and skills is a major part of my responsibility as a teacher.

I believe that it is my responsibility as a teacher to help each child discover the wonders of learning. I want my students to be an active part of all decisions in the classroom. Of course, I am ultimately responsible for the major decisions, but I want my students to learn to make good decisions, and I feel they won't be able to do that without practice in weighing different possibilities.

I believe that teaching consists of presenting material in an interesting way and then getting out of the way so that students can experiment and discover learning. I want my students to display their individual interests and strengths; I, as the teacher, should not impose my preferences on them. I encourage my students to read widely and respond to the writing through their preferred mode—writing or drawing or discussing.

Preparing for Your Licensure Exam

In this chapter you read about many elements that contribute to a safe, healthy, and happy classroom. Reread "A View into the Classroom" at the beginning of the chapter, and think about it as a case study you might encounter on your licensure exam. Answer the following questions to demonstrate your understanding of the teacher's role in creating a supportive learning environment:

1. What evidence do you find in Jennifer's story that shows her use of reflective action?
2. What considerations did Jennifer give to the differentiation of instruction?
3. What do you know about Jennifer's philosophy of education from reading her story?

Portfolio of Professional Practices Activity

There are actions you can take to demonstrate that you are a person who is committed to your students and their learning. What can teachers do to demonstrate concern with their students' self-concept? What actions can teachers take to demonstrate their willingness to help students develop good character and civic virtues?

Observations of Classroom Management

1. Select a classroom to visit to focus on the classroom management strategies of the teacher you observe. Ask the classroom teacher if you can lead a 30-minute discussion with the students on the classroom rules and consequences for breaking or following the rules. Retell what happened during your discussion. For example, describe the rules of the classroom and tell how they are documented. Are they clearly written for all students to see or are they simply "understood" to be the rules. Do the rules seem to be constant or change from situation to situation? What are the consequences of breaking rules? Are the consequences clearly documented or merely "understood"? You must be able to describe all important elements and features of how the rules were created, how the teacher presents the rules to the students, and how the students respond. Include enough detail in your description that would allow an outsider to see what you saw as you observed the situation.

2. The next step is to write an *analysis* of this classroom teacher's rules and consequences. Analysis deals with reasons, motives, and interpretation and is grounded in the concrete evidence of the situation. What are the reasons the teacher gives for choosing these rules? What are the reasons for the teacher's selection of consequences? What do you think motivated the teacher to choose how to present and document these rules to the students? How does the student response to these rules and consequences give evidence of their effectiveness?

3. Finally it is time for *reflection* on the entire process you observed. How would you approach the rule making and presentation process if this were your classroom? What would you do the same way as you observed this classroom teacher do, and why? What would you do differently, and why? Provide enough detail in your reflection to show assessors what you have learned from this experience, and how it will inform and improve your own teaching and classroom management practices in the future.

Connections between Your Teaching Philosophy and Your Teaching Environment

Revisit the draft of the philosophy of education you began in the previous chapter.

1. Reflect on your philosophy and relate it to the type of classroom environment you will need to set up in order to implement your philosophy of teaching.

2. Using the blank Classroom Activity Sheet, design a classroom furniture arrangement that would support the types of groupings and activities you may choose to implement in your approach to teaching.

References

Black, S. (2003). *An ongoing evaluation of the bullying prevention program in Philadelphia schools: Student survey and student observation data.* Paper presented at Centers for Disease Control's Safety in Numbers Conference, Atlanta, GA.

Charles, C. (2002). *Elementary classroom management* (3rd ed.). Boston, MA: Allyn & Bacon.

Evertson, C., & Harris, A. (2002). *Classroom management for elementary teachers* (6th ed.). Boston, MA: Allyn & Bacon.

Glasser, W. (1969). *Schools without failure.* New York: Harper & Row.

Glasser, W. (2001). *Every student can succeed.* Los Angeles, CA: William Glasser Institute.

Johnson, D., & Johnson, R. (1995). *Teaching students to be peacemakers.* Minneapolis, MN: Burgess Publishing Co.

Jones, F. (2000). *Tools for teaching.* Washington, DC: Frederic H. Jones and Associates.

Lickona, T. (1992). *Educating for character.* New York, NY: Bantam Books.

Lickona, T. (2004). *Character matters: How to help our children develop good judgment, integrity, and other essential virtues.* New York, NY: Bantam Books.

Marzano, R. (2003). *What works in schools.* Alexandria, VA: Association for Supervision and Curriculum Development.

Maslow, A. (1954). *Motivation and personality.* New York, NY: Harper & Row.

Noddings, N. (2005). *The challenge to care in schools* (2nd ed.). New York, NY: Teachers College Press.

Olweus, D. (2001). *Olweus' core program against bullying and antisocial behavior: A teacher handbook.* Bergen, Norway: Research Center for Health Promotion (Hemil Center). (This can be ordered from Dan Olweus at Olweus@psyhp.uib.no.)

Olweus, D. (2004). The Olweus Bullying Prevention Programme: Design and implementation issues and a new national initiative in Norway. In P. K. Smith, D. Pepler, & K. Rigby (Eds.), *Bullying in schools: How successful can interventions be?* (pp. 13–36). Cambridge, UK: Cambridge University Press.

Pepler, D., & Craig, W. (1997). *Bullying: Research and interventions.* Toronto, Canada: Institute for the Study of Antisocial Youth.

Thompson, M. (2001). *Best friends, worst enemies.* New York, NY: Ballantine Books.

Blank Classroom Activity Sheet

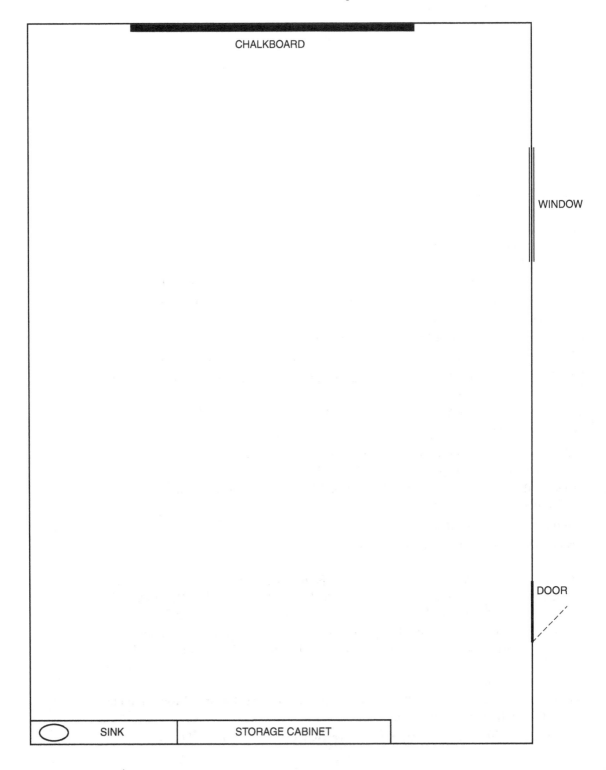

Lesson Planning and Sequencing

"A journey of a thousand miles begins with a single step."
Lao-Tze

This chapter is designed to further demystify the process of writing your first lesson plans. We will describe ways to use the reflective action processes to envision and then describe on paper the goals and objectives you want to achieve, the materials you will need to gather, the step-by-step procedures you will use to teach your lesson, and the assessment devices you will employ to measure what your students have achieved.

Questions for Reflection as You Read the Chapter

1. What considerations must teachers address as they plan lessons and lesson sequences?
2. What elements are vital in a good lesson plan?
3. What is the role of mandated standards in planning lessons?

A View into the Classroom

Vince Michaels teaches fourth grade in a suburb of Minneapolis, Minnesota. His students come from a variety of cultures and socioeconomic levels. Four of his students speak Spanish at home. Vince has set up a website for his class and wants to involve his students in writing articles for an online classroom newsletter.

Vince shares his story of how he planned a sequence of lessons to prepare his students to become news reporters:

As I began to plan the lessons introducing my students to news reporting and using computers to write and post articles on the class website, I realized that this project would involve a sequence of lessons. My students were not all familiar with computers, and none of them had strong keyboarding skills.

I looked at the Minnesota Language Arts Standards and noted that this project addressed the following standards:

- *Media literacy. Critically analyzing information found in electronic media and using a variety of these sources about a topic and representing ideas.*

- *Media literacy. Using print, pictures, audio, and video to express ideas and knowledge gleaned from media sources.*

- *Writing. Composing various pieces of writing using the writing process (prewriting, drafting, editing, etc.).*

- *Technology. Using technology to learn.*

I began this project with a lesson on newspapers. I brought in copies of the local newspaper, and we looked at the features in the paper. The students identified sections such as Sports, Local News, National News, Feature Articles, Comics, and Advice. We talked about writing a class newspaper and which sections they would like to include in their paper. Students were asked to identify the section of the paper they would like to work on, and they were allowed to join the staff for the section to which they wanted to contribute. I introduced them to the website for the local newspaper. They were to use that as a model for the class online paper and examine previous articles in their chosen section.

We selected one of the articles from the newspaper to examine its structure. I introduced the concept of the Five W's (and one H). I told them about Rudyard Kipling's (1902) memorialization of the concept in a poem he wrote to accompany his tale of "The Elephant's Child." They all learned the piece:

I keep six honest serving-men
(They taught me all I knew);
Their names are What and Why and When
And How and Where and Who.

   I taught a minilesson on news writing and modeled the process using the SMART Board so that the students could observe how I wrote the article on the computer, highlighting the Five W's (and one H) and displayed it on the SMART Board. We then rewrote it together (shared writing) to make it flow better using the students' input and suggestions.

   I set up keyboarding stations on the three computers in my classroom and taught a minilesson on keyboarding. I assigned some practice texts for them to use in learning to use the keyboard effectively. I tried to choose texts using the majority of the keys that would be interesting to them as they practiced. I think it is important to consider the interests and skills of your students in any of the tasks you assign.

   After several sessions of keyboarding practice, each "news staff" group was asked to choose a topic for an article. I taught a minilesson on brainstorming and decision making that demonstrated how to work as a group to decide on a topic and begin the writing process. Each group chose a typist to enter the article into the computer. They chose someone to keep track of the Five W's (and one H) and to make sure they were including all pertinent information. They also chose an editing team who reviewed the article and suggested corrections or changes. We brainstormed some of the following guidelines for their articles:

- The article should be about something that happens in our class or school.

- The article should include references to people in our class, their families, or people in the school.

- The article should help the reader learn more about our classroom or school.

   At this point, they used their classroom writing time to work in teams to write their first article, enter the article into the computer, and perform a first edit. I asked one staff's permission to use their article for a minilesson on editing. The members of the sports staff were eager for me to use their article, and using the SMART Board, I taught a minilesson on editing. The students read the article with me, we identified the Five W's (and one H) in the article, and the students suggested changes in wording as well as information that was not included that they felt was important. In every case, the sports staff members were consulted and asked whether or not they agreed with the changes; agreed-upon changes were made.

   Once the editing was completed, I demonstrated how the staff could post the article to the website and displayed a chart that walked them through the posting process. We chose a class editing staff of three students who would do a final read of each article and approve it before anything was officially posted.

   The next minilesson I taught was on the use of a digital camera to add photos and/or video to their articles. The sports staff posted some photos of the soccer game they had reported on, and they taped an interview with the team goalie who made the game-saving move. We enjoyed watching the video and making the choices of pictures to add to the website.

   As a result of this project, my students now participate in the writing and editing of an article for the class website each week. We make the website available to our parents, school and district administrators, and the general public. We also run hard copies each week for the students who do not have computers at home. One of our bilingual students translates some of the articles into Spanish. I always like to verify the translation, and we include it in the newsletter.

This project is a good example of the multitude of standards that can be addressed using an interactive project approach. The students are no longer reluctant writers because they are excited about seeing their writing in print and enjoy adding their art and photos to the newsletter. They are also getting a lot of attention due to the sharing of their efforts with their whole community. Parents are excited about the project because they get more information about what is happening in their child's classroom. School administrators are impressed with the way the students are excited and motivated about writing and with the number of state standards that are obviously being addressed by this type of ongoing project.

Our articles have included discussions of content in all the curricular areas. As the students grew more confident in their writing abilities and skills in online publishing, we also began to include some of their creative writing and art activities. We added interviews with school personnel and local celebrities, movie and television show reviews, and an advice column. The advice column often deals with tender topics of particular interest to our students, such as bullying. One of the other teachers in my school has now begun a class blog based on our model, which serves many of the same objectives as our website.

REFLECTING ON THE CLASSROOM EXPERIENCE

Vince's story demonstrates ways in which a reflective teacher plans and sequences lessons to support student learning. Vince obviously values the differences, interests, and strengths of his students and makes an effort to keep their parents informed. What evidence did you find that identify this teacher as reflective and withit?

Lesson Planning

When you think of the term *lesson plans*, what comes to mind? Perhaps you think of a piece of paper containing detailed directions that describe how to teach something to a class of students, or perhaps you envision a weekly plan book with brief notations that serve to remind experienced teachers what they have planned to accomplish each period in the school day.

Beginning teachers often want to find examples of excellent lesson plans so they can see how other, more experienced teachers have organized their teaching. How do they write meaningful learning objectives? How do they think of every detailed instruction? How do they write out a way to assess what students have gained from the lesson? It can seem like a mystery to many new teachers.

Looking at Leaders in Lesson Planning

Two major leaders in the process of developing meaningful lesson plans and curriculum are Ralph Tyler and Benjamin Bloom. You will see references to their research and methodology throughout the following chapters. Tyler's (1949) basic principles on curriculum development were extended by Bloom in a most useful way. (A fuller discussion of Tyler's groundbreaking curriculum planning method follows in Chapter Four.) Bloom was a notable student of Tyler, and Bloom and his colleagues (1956) attempted to respond to Tyler's first question of "determining the educational purposes that a school should seek to attain" (p. 61) as completely as possible. In meetings with other teachers, they brainstormed and listed all the possible purposes of education—all the possible educational objectives that they could think of or had observed during their many years of classroom experiences. Then they attempted to organize and classify all of these possible objectives into what is now known as the *taxonomy of educational objectives*. Their intent was to provide teachers with a ready source of possible objectives so that teachers could select the ones that fit the needs of their own students and circumstances. They also intended to help teachers clarify for themselves how to achieve their educational goals. A third purpose for the taxonomy was to help teachers communicate more precisely with one another. Bloom's taxonomy has been widely used in education for more than 50 years.

During the 1990s, a former student of Bloom's, Lorin Anderson, led an assembly that met for the purpose of updating the taxonomy, hoping to make it more relevant for the twenty-first century. Representatives of three groups, cognitive psychologists, curriculum theorists, and instructional researchers, worked together to revise the taxonomy (Anderson & Krathwohl, 2001).

Bloom's taxonomy first subdivides educational purposes into three domains of learning: cognitive, affective, and psychomotor. The *cognitive domain* deals with "the recall or recognition of knowledge and the development of intellectual abilities and skills"; the *affective domain* deals with "interests, attitudes, and values"; and the *psychomotor domain* concerns the development of manipulative and motor skills (Bloom et al., 1956, p. 7). The revised taxonomy (Anderson & Krathwohl, 2001) updates the cognitive domain, the main focus of educational objectives. It further divides this domain into *factual knowledge, conceptual knowledge, procedural knowledge*, and *metacognitive knowledge*. "These categories are assumed to lie along a continuum from concrete (*factual*) to abstract (*metacognitive*). The *conceptual* and *procedural* categories overlap in terms of abstractness, with some procedural knowledge being more concrete than the most abstract conceptual knowledge" (Anderson & Krathwohl, 2001, p. 5). Based on Anderson and Krathwohl's (2001) work, these are the definitions of the four categories:

1. *Factual knowledge*. This refers to the basic elements students must know to be familiar with a discipline or to solve problems within a discipline.

2. *Conceptual knowledge*. This covers the interrelationships among the basic elements that enable them to work together.

3. *Procedural knowledge*. This references ways to *do* something: methods of inquiry, criteria for using skills, algorithms, techniques, and methods.

4. *Metacognitive knowledge*. This encompasses knowledge of learning in general as well as knowledge of a person's own way of learning.

Clarifying Educational Goals and Outcomes

Bloom's three domains (cognitive, affective, and psychomotor) are considered to be important in the curriculum because together they support the growth and development of the whole student. Educators used to begin writing curriculum documents by carefully wording their educational goals. An *educational goal* is a general long-term statement of an important aim or purpose of an educational program. For example, most schools have a goal of teaching students how to read and write, another to ensure that they understand the cultural heritage of the United States, and another to help them develop attitudes and habits of good citizenship.

Although standards-based education is relatively recent, it is based on an approach that has been in place for a number of years. In the past, goals translated into operational plans were specified as *outcomes*. Teachers thought about what outcomes were expected as a consequence of being in school and taking part in the planned curriculum. Educators need to be aware that goals express intentions but that other factors may occur that alter the expectations in the educational process. Standards and outcomes are statements that describe what students will demonstrate as a culmination of their learning. Spady (1994) proposes that outcomes must specify "high quality, culminating demonstrations of significant learning in context" (p. 18). A high-quality demonstration means one that is thorough and complete, showing the important new learning the student has gained or demonstrating the mastery of a new skill or process. Outcomes are designed to be assessed at or near the end of a learning period.

Written outcome statements are used to translate goals into actions. They describe what students will be able to do as a result of their educational program. If educators can envision what they want students to be able to do or know after a series of learning experiences, then they can plan with that outcome in mind. Learning outcomes generally describe actions, processes, and products that the student will accomplish or produce in a given period.

Cognitive outcomes are expressed in terms of students' mastery of content or subject-matter knowledge. For example, kindergartners are expected to master the alphabet, third graders are expected to master multiplication facts, and sixth graders are expected to show knowledge of the history of ancient civilizations.

Most teachers view affective outcomes as being related to the development of character. Typically, schools highlight the affective outcomes by emphasizing good citizenship, self-esteem, respect for individual and racial differences, and appreciation of art, music, and other aspects of our cultural heritage. Positive affective outcomes are major goals in character education programs and have been shown to improve academic achievement (as noted in Chapter Two).

Educators also write many psychomotor outcomes, including strategies, processes, and skills that involve both the mind and the body in the psychomotor domain. Note that some of these psychomotor outcomes might also be categorized as *procedural knowledge*. For example, elementary students are expected to learn how to decode symbols to read, write, calculate, solve problems, observe, experiment, research, interpret, make maps, and create works of art, music, and other crafts. These skills are successfully honed and practiced using similar methods at the secondary level.

Individual teachers may write outcome statements for their own classes, but when they work collectively to clarify a set of schoolwide outcome statements, the effect on students is likely to be much more powerful and result in greater growth and change. This enhanced growth is a result of the consistency of experiences that students have in every classroom and with every adult in the school. Many school districts have statements of philosophy (often called *mission statements*) and outcome statements written in policy documents, but they may or may not be articulated and applied in the schools themselves. For effective change to take place, the school faculty must consider their educational purposes each year, articulate them together, and communicate them to the students through words and deeds.

In a classroom, each teacher has the right and the responsibility to articulate a set of educational outcomes for his or her students. Working alone or with teammates at the same grade level or subject area, the classroom teacher may want to articulate approximately two to four yearly outcome statements in each of the three domains. Tyler (1949) encourages teachers to select a small number of highly important goals "since time is required to change the behavior patterns of human beings. An educational program is not effective if so much is attempted that little is accomplished" (p. 33).

Writing Useful and Appropriate Outcome Statements

The wording of standards or outcome statements must be general but not vague—a subtle but important distinction. Some school documents contain goals such as "to develop the full potential of each individual." What does this mean to you? Can you interpret it in a meaningful way in your classroom? Can you translate it into programs? Probably not. This goal statement is so general and vague that it cannot be put into operation, and it would be difficult to determine whether it is being attained.

An outcome statement should be general, in keeping with its long-term effects. It should also describe, clearly and precisely, how you want your students to change and what you want them to be able to do at the end of the term of study.

Following are some examples of useful *cognitive* outcome statements:

Kindergarten students will be able to recognize and name all the counting numbers from 1 to 20.

Fifth-grade students will demonstrate that they understand how technology has changed the world by creating a time line, graph, chart, or set of models to show the effects of technology on human experience.

Following are examples of *affective* outcome statements:

Second-grade students will demonstrate that they enjoy reading by selecting books and other reading materials and spending time reading in class and at home.

Students at all grade levels will demonstrate that they tolerate, accept, and prize cultural, ethnic, and other individual differences in human beings by working cooperatively and productively with students of various ethnic groups.

Following are a couple of examples of *psychomotor* (sometimes referred to as skill or process) outcome statements:

Third-grade students will measure and compare a variety of common objects using metric units of measurement of length, weight, and volume.

Sixth-grade students will compose and edit written works using a word processing program on a computer.

In many school programs, outcome statements are intended to be accomplished over the course of a school year. Yearly outcome statements can be written for one subject or across several disciplines. Outcome statements can also be written for a shorter period, such as a term or a month. They are used as guides for planning curriculum and learning experiences for that length of time. At the end of a given time, the teacher assesses whether students have successfully demonstrated the outcome. If not, the teacher may need to repeat or restate the outcome statement to ensure that it can be met.

Some outcome statements may need to be modified because they are too vague. In the following example, compare the first vague statement with the improved second statement:

Original *outcome statement*. Students will demonstrate that they understand the U.S. Constitution.

Improved *outcome statement*. Students will describe the key concepts in the articles of the U.S. Constitution and give examples of how they are applied in American life today.

Other outcome statements may need to be modified because they are too difficult for the students. Compare the following examples:

Original *outcome statement*. Fourth-grade students will demonstrate that they know the key concepts of the Bill of Rights by creating a time line showing how each has evolved over the past 200 years.

Improved *outcome statement*. Fourth-grade students will create an illustrated mural showing pictorial representations of each of the articles in the Bill of Rights.

Some outcome statements may need to be improved by adding learning opportunities that will stimulate student interest and motivation to learn the material. Consider the following examples:

Original *outcome statement*. Students will recite the Bill of Rights.

Improved *outcome statement*. Students will work in cooperative groups to plan and perform skits comparing how life in the United States would differ with and without the constitutional amendments known as the Bill of Rights.

Standards and outcome statements are useful guides for educational planning but must be adapted to fit the needs of a particular teacher and class. For this reason, curriculum planning is an evolving process. A curriculum is never a finished product; it is constantly being changed and improved from day to day and year to year.

FORMATS FOR STANDARDS. Standards might appear in one of three formats. Some standards are *procedural*: They refer to what procedures the students will be able to perform. Others are *declarative*: They state what broad concepts students will be able to understand. Still others are *contextual*: They refer to the ways and contexts in which the knowledge will be used (Kendall & Marzano, 2000). For example, a procedural standard might state that students will locate mountain ranges and rivers on a state map. A declarative standard might state that students will explain the concept of regional weather conditions. The contextual standard might state that students will determine when to use a map and when to use a globe to locate needed information.

An obvious contrast between more reflective and less reflective teachers is that after teaching for 20 years, a reflective teacher has accumulated 20 years of experience and uses that experience to shape and improve curricular decisions. A less reflective teacher is likely to have simply repeated his or her year of experience 20 times. Reflective teachers want to have an active role in the decision-making processes in their schools, and curricular decisions are the ones that count the most. They also display a strong sense of responsibility for making good curriculum choices and decisions, ones that will ultimately result in valuable growth and learning for their students.

Writing Objectives to Fit Goals and Outcome Statements

Goals are long-term broad descriptions of how you want your students to grow and develop; *outcome statements* refer to what you want students to know, understand, and be able to do during a given time. As you try to visualize your students accomplishing these goals and outcomes, it is useful to envision a sequence of events that will lead to successful accomplishment of the goal. Teachers often find it useful to write these sequential steps as a series of objectives that work together to accomplish the goal or outcome. Reflective teachers rarely plan a lesson in isolation; rather, they consider each lesson in relation to what students already know as well as what they hope students will be able to do at a later time. This big picture thinking characterizes reflective teachers, who realize that larger goals guide the selection of small daily tasks.

EDUCATIONAL OBJECTIVES. Educational objectives are specific short-term descriptions of what teachers are expected to teach and/or what students are expected to learn. As described by Bloom and colleagues (1956) in the *Taxonomy of Educational Objectives*, they are intended to be used as an organizational framework for selecting and sequencing learning experiences. Embedded in any large goal (such as teaching children to read) are hundreds of possible specific objectives. One teacher may have an objective of teaching students how to decode an unfamiliar word using phonics and another objective of teaching students how to decode an unfamiliar word using context clues; another teacher may select and emphasize the objectives of decoding unfamiliar words by using syllabication or linguistic patterns to meet the same overall goal.

The most commonly used model for writing behavioral objectives is based on the work of Tyler (1949), which required the statement of a *behavior* and the content to be addressed, thus the term *behavioral objective*. Anderson and Krathwohl (2001) have revised these elements slightly, calling them *cognitive processes* instead of *behaviors* and addressing *knowledge* in place of *content*. Part of the reasoning behind these changes is the alignment of the writing of behavioral objectives with current knowledge in cognitive psychology rather than the assumed (although not intended) alignment with a more fundamental definition of behaviorism popular in Tyler's time (Anderson & Krathwohl, 2001).

Objectives are used to describe the sequence of learning events a teacher believes will help students achieve a given outcome. They also allow teachers to assess and chart group or individual progress. Teachers can ascertain students' needs more accurately if they have established a guideline of normal progress with which to compare each student's achievement.

BEHAVIORAL OBJECTIVES.   Teachers who prefer to be specific about their lesson planning choose to write behavioral objectives. Behavioral objectives can have a very positive effect on teaching effectiveness; teachers who use them become better organized and more efficient in teaching and in measuring the growth of students' basic skills. When following a planned sequence of behavioral objectives, the teacher knows what to do and how to judge students' success. This system of planning also allows the teacher to better explain to students exactly what is expected of them and how to succeed.

There are six steps in writing behavioral objectives:

1. Identify the standard or standards to be addressed by this objective.

2. Identify exactly what you want your students to be able to do as a result of the lesson. For example, "The students will learn to pluralize nouns" doesn't tell what the students will be able to do, whereas "The students will demonstrate their understanding of the pluralization of regular nouns by adding *-s* or *-es* to singular regular nouns as appropriate" states specifically what they are expected to be able to do.

3. Identify the conditions under which the students will demonstrate their understanding. For example, adding "given a list of 10 singular regular nouns" clarifies the conditions you will present the students while at the same time setting up how you will assess the students' learning.

4. Identify the criteria for success. This establishes the expectation as to how well the task must be completed to consider that students have achieved the objective. For example you might expect that each student attain 90 percent mastery; this objective would require that a student correctly pluralize the noun 9 times out of 10.

5. Put the three sections of the objective together and create a statement that tells what the students will be able to do, under what conditions, and to what degree. Note that it's common to state the conditions first. For example, "Given a list of 10 singular nouns, the student will pluralize the nouns appropriately with 90 percent accuracy."

6. Reread your objective to determine if you can easily identify what the students will do, under what conditions, and to what degree. If any one of these pieces is missing, rewrite the objective to include the missing element.

Levels of behavioral objectives.   Anderson and Krathwohl (2001) identify three levels of objectives that can be used for different purposes in educational planning. *Global objectives* are broad and cover one or more years. They provide a vision for successful planning and can be used to plan a multiyear curriculum such as reading. *Educational objectives* have a more moderate scope, covering weeks or months and can be used to design curriculum and plan units of instruction. *Instructional objectives* have a much more focused scope, covering just hours or days; they are used to prepare lesson plans, daily activities, and experiences. All three of these types of objectives are vital in planning and implementing curriculum and instruction to meet the needs of all students. The use of multiple levels of objectives helps to overcome some of the challenges and criticisms of the use of behavioral objectives in general.

Critics of behavioral objectives believe that when curriculum planning is reduced to rigid behavioral prescriptions, much of what is important to teaching and learning can be overlooked or lost. Thus, reflective teachers use behavioral objectives in their lesson planning for those learning events and activities that warrant them and rely on other less rigid objectives when appropriate.

PROBLEM-SOLVING OBJECTIVES.   As an alternative form for learning that cannot be predicted and calibrated, Eisner (1985) suggests the *problem-solving objective*:

> In a problem-solving objective, students are given a problem to solve—say, to find out how deterrents to smoking might be made more effective, how to design a paper structure that will hold two bricks 16 inches above a table, or how the variety and quality of the food served in

the cafeteria could be increased within the existing budget. In each of these examples, the problem is posed and the criteria necessary to resolve the problem are clear. But the forms of its solution are virtually infinite. (pp. 117–118)

Eisner (1985) points out that behavioral objectives "have both the form and the content defined in advance. There is, after all, only one way to spell *aardvark*." The teacher using behavioral objectives is successful if all the children display the identical behavior at the end of the instructional period. "This is not the case with problem-solving objectives. The solutions individual students or groups of students reach may be just as much a surprise for the teacher as they are for the students who created them" (Eisner, 1985, p. 119).

As an example, a problem-solving objective might state: "When given a battery, a light-bulb, and a piece of copper wire, the student will figure out how to make the bulb light." This objective describes the conditions and the problem that is to be solved but does not specify the actual behaviors the student is to use. The criterion for success is straightforward but is not quantifiable, and in fact, some of the most important results of this experience are only implied. The teacher's primary aim is to cause the student to experiment, hypothesize, and test methods of solving the problem. This cannot be quantified and reported as a percentage. Problem-solving objectives, then, are appropriate when teachers are planning learning events that allow and encourage students to think, make decisions, and create solutions. For that reason, they are frequently employed when teachers plan lessons that are designed to develop critical, creative thinking. They are especially valuable when teachers are planning learning events at the higher levels of the revised Bloom's taxonomy (2001).

Planning Lessons for Higher-Level Thinking

Many teachers now use the revised *Taxonomy for Learning, Teaching, and Assessing* (Anderson & Krathwohl, 2001) as the basis for organizing instructional objectives into coherent, connected learning experiences. The term *Bloom's revised taxonomy* (as commonly used by teachers) refers to the six levels of the cognitive domain described here. Any curriculum project such as a year-long plan, a unit, or a lesson plan can be enriched by the conscious planning of learning events at all six levels of the taxonomy.

Higher-level objectives	Level 6. Creating
	Level 5. Evaluating
	Level 4. Analyzing
	Level 3. Applying
Lower-level objectives	Level 2. Understanding
	Level 1. Remembering

Remembering objectives can be planned to ensure that students have the ability to retrieve, recognize, and recall relevant knowledge from their long-term memory. *Understanding objectives* support students as they construct meaning from oral, written, and graphic messages through interpretation. Behavioral objectives are very useful and appropriate at the remembering and understanding levels.

With *applying objectives*, problem-solving objectives or expressive outcomes can be written that ask students to apply what they have learned to other cases or to their own lives, thereby causing them to transfer what they have learned in the classroom to other arenas. *Analyzing objectives* and their outcomes call on students to look for motives, assumptions, and relationships such as cause and effect, differences and similarities, hypotheses and conclusions. When analysis outcomes are planned, the students are likely to be engaged in critical thinking about the subject matter. Because *evaluating objectives* require students to make judgments based on criteria and standards, activities that involve research and critiquing are appropriate. Activities involving *creating objectives* require that students use their knowledge and skills to put elements together to form a functional whole and offer students opportunities to use creative thinking as they combine elements in new ways, plan original experiments, and create original solutions to problems.

For higher-level objectives, problem-solving situations and expressive outcomes are likely to be the most appropriate planning devices. For example, in planning a series of learning events on metric measurement, the teacher may formulate the following objectives and outcome statements:

Remembering-level behavioral objective. When given a meter stick, students will point to the length of a meter, a decimeter, and a centimeter with no errors.

Understanding-level behavioral objective. When asked to state a purpose or use for each of the following units of measure, the student will write a short response for meter, centimeter, liter, milliliter, gram, and kilogram, with no more than one error.

Applying-level problem-solving objective. Using a unit of measure of their choice, students will measure the length and width of the classroom and compute the area.

Analyzing-level problem-solving objective. Students will create a chart showing five logical uses or purposes for each measuring unit in the metric family.

Evaluating-level judgment-making objective. A group of four students will work together to judge the effectiveness of written arguments for the adoption of the metric system in the United States.

Creating-level expressive objective. Students will create a reader's theater performance to illustrate ways in which the United States would be more globally viable if we adopted the metric system of measurement.

When we review the six objectives and outcomes for metric measurement, we see clearly that the first two differ from the others in that they specify exactly what students will do or write to get a correct answer; in addition, the criteria for success are not ambiguous. These two qualities are useful to ensure successful teaching and learning at the knowledge and comprehension levels. After successfully completing these first two objectives, students will have developed a knowledge base for metric measurement that they will need to do the higher-level activities. In the problem-solving types of objectives, students are given greater discretion in determining the methods they use and the form of their final product. In the expressive outcome statements, discretionary power is necessary if students are to be empowered to think critically and creatively to solve problems for themselves.

Although the taxonomy was originally envisioned as a hierarchy, and although it was believed that students should be introduced to a topic beginning with level 1 (remembering) and working upward through level 6 (creating), most educators have found that the objectives and learning experiences can be successfully taught in any order. For example, a teacher may introduce the topic of nutrition and health by asking students to discuss their opinions or attitudes about smoking (an evaluating-level objective). The teacher may then provide the students with data about the contents of tobacco smoke and work back up to the evaluating level. When students are asked their opinions again at the end of the lesson, their judgments are likely to be stronger and better informed.

As in the example about smoking and health, it is often desirable to begin with objectives that call on students to do, think, find, question, or create something and thereby instill in them a desire to know more about the topic. Remembering- and understanding-level objectives can then be designed to provide the students with the facts, data, and main ideas they need to further apply, analyze, and evaluate the ideas that interest them. Figure 3.1 shows a planning device offering teachers ideas for learning events that correspond to each level of the taxonomy.

Planning Lessons for Active Learning

Teachers can use their reflective actions to ensure a high-quality learning experience for their students. They begin by using withitness when they write the first draft of their lesson plan.

Figure 3.1 Using the revised Bloom's taxonomy for planning lessons.

Level	Action Verbs for Lesson Objectives	Appropriate Questions
1. Remembering	Choose, define, find, label, list, match, name, select, show, tell	What is . . . ? How would you show . . . ? How would you define . . . ?
2. Understanding	Classify, compare, contrast, demonstrate, explain, interpret, outline, relate, rephrase, summarize	How would you classify the type of . . . ? How would you state or interpret in your own words . . . ? What facts or ideas demonstrate . . . ?
3. Applying	Apply, build, construct, develop, interview, make use of, model, organize, plan, solve, utilize	How would you apply . . . ? What examples can you construct to . . . ? How would you model your understanding of . . . ? What would develop if . . . ?
4. Analyzing	Analyze, assume, categorize, dissect, distinguish, examine, simplify, test for	How would you analyze the parts or features of . . . ? How is ____ distinguished from . . . ? What inference can you assume . . . ? What evidence can you test for . . . ?
5. Evaluating	Appraise, criticize, deduct, defend, dispute, estimate, evaluate, interpret, justify, prioritize	How would you defend . . . ? Dispute . . . ? How would you prioritize . . . ? What would you cite to defend the actions of . . . ? Based on what you know, how would you interpret . . . ?
6. Creating	Adapt, change, combine, compile, compose, create, design, elaborate, formulate, improve, invent, modify, originate	What would you change to solve . . . ? Can you elaborate on the reason . . . ? How would you adapt ___ to create a different . . . ? Can you formulate a theory for . . . ?

Source: Adapted from Anderson, L. W., & Krathwohl, D. R. (Eds.). (2001). *A taxonomy for learning, teaching, and assessing: A revision of Bloom's taxonomy of educational objectives.* Boston, MA: Allyn & Bacon.

Reflective teachers try to picture in their minds what a lesson will look like in real life. They try to anticipate what their students need, what they can do easily, and where they will need the most guidance and positive feedback.

Reflective teachers recognize that students are more motivated to learn when they understand why this learning is important. For this reason, they explain the reason for each lesson. When describing your objectives, use words and examples that are easily understood by the students at your grade level. For example, during a science lesson, a reflective teacher might say:

> We are doing this experiment today to help you see for yourselves how solids can literally disappear in a liquid. The procedures we are going to use are the same type of procedures that real scientists use when they want to discover something new about the laws of science.

After this initial explanation, students are likely to be eager to begin. They want to get on with the experiment and see for themselves what happens. They enjoy acting as scientists do during the process.

To make learning tasks even more inviting, reflective teachers know that it is important to model the physical behaviors or mental processes needed to do the work: Kindergarten teachers model how to write a capital letter A, elementary teachers demonstrate how to divide a pizza into equal fractions, middle school teachers show students how to place their hands on the keyboard of the computer, and high school teachers do a sample algebra problem on the board. After modeling, reflective teachers stay just as active on the sidelines, encouraging and guiding students as they begin the active process of finding out how things work.

Another role that the most effective teachers take while teaching a new skill is to model internal behaviors (such as problem solving) by thinking aloud while they model the first example for their students. By telling the students verbally what they are thinking when they work on a problem, teachers provide real-life examples of how learning occurs. Thinking aloud is particularly helpful when asking students to comprehend an unfamiliar skill or a difficult concept.

At all stages of lesson planning and presentation, reflective teachers carefully observe and interact with their students—learning what students already know and where they need extra help. This observation and assessment are critical to the success of any given lesson as well as to the planning and sequencing of future lessons. It also helps to think again about this process when things happen during a lesson that surprise you or upset your plans.

Planning Assessments Tailored to Lesson Objectives

How does a teacher measure success? Chapter Ten covers in detail the topic of assessing students' needs and accomplishments, with a focus on creating authentic assessment systems that describe students' progress over time. In designing lesson plans, however, it is useful to consider some options for assessing students' accomplishments during a single lesson.

Traditionally, the methods used to assess individual achievement are either written or oral quizzes, tests, and essays. When elementary teachers want to determine whether the class as a whole has understood what was taught in a lesson, they frequently use oral responses to questions that usually begin with "Who can tell me . . . ?" These are useful and efficient ways to assess student achievement at the remembering and understanding levels of Bloom's taxonomy, but reflective teachers are seldom satisfied with these measures alone. They seek other methods that are less frequently used but more appropriate in evaluating learning at the higher levels.

Remembering-level objectives are tested by determining if the student can remember or recognize accurate statements or facts. Multiple-choice and matching tests are the most frequently used measuring devices.

Understanding-level objectives are often tested by asking students to define terms in their own words. (Only memory would be tested if the students were asked to write a definition from memory.) Another frequently used testing device is a question requiring a short-answer response, either oral or written, showing that the student understands the main idea. Essays that ask students to summarize or interpret are also appropriate. Multiple-choice tests are used as a test of comprehension, but the questions call on the students to do more than recall a fact from memory; they ask students to read a selection and choose the best response from among several choices.

At the applying level, students are usually asked to apply what was learned in the classroom to a new situation. For that reason, applying-level objectives are usually assessed by presenting an unfamiliar problem that requires the student to transfer what has been learned to the unfamiliar situation. Essays in which the students describe what they would do to solve an unfamiliar problem can be used. In classrooms where students are encouraged to use manipulative materials and experiment with methods to solve problems, teachers assess the processes used by the student and the end product such as a hand-drawn or computer-generated design of a new device, a written plan for solving a problem, or a model of a new product. These products may or may not be graded, depending on the teacher's need to quantify or qualify students' success.

Analyzing-level objectives may also require that the teacher present unfamiliar material and ask the student to analyze it according to some specified criteria. But in these situations, students may also be asked to analyze various elements, relationships, or organizational principles, such as the categorization of elements, differences and similarities, cause and effect, logical conclusions, or relevant and irrelevant data.

Again, essays may be used to assess analytical behavior, but the essays must do more than tell the main idea (comprehension) or describe how the student would apply previously learned knowledge. Analytical essays must clarify relationships, compare and contrast, show cause and effect, and provide evidence for conclusions. Other student products that are appropriate for assessing analysis are time lines; charts that compare, contrast, or categorize data; and a variety of graphs that show relationships.

The types of student products that demonstrate evaluating-level objectives are infinitely variable. They might include activities for creating and using an evaluation standard or using one to compare and contrast the relative worth of products, written analyses, or practical applications.

The ways for students to demonstrate creating-level objectives might include such things as creative essays, stories, poems, plays, books, and articles, which are all appropriate for assessing language arts objectives. Performances are just as useful and can include original speeches, drama, poems, and musical compositions. Student-created products may also be original plans, blueprints, artwork, computer programs, and models of proposed inventions. Student work may be collected in portfolios to demonstrate growth and achievement in a subject area.

Assessing the relative success of higher-level student products is more difficult. No objective criteria may exist for judging the value or worth of a student's original work. When student products are entered in a contest or submitted for publication, outside judges with expertise in the subject area provide feedback and may even make judgments that the classroom teacher cannot make. Many elementary teachers simply record whether a finished product was turned in by the student rather than attempt to evaluate or grade it.

Evaluating-level objectives call on students to make a judgment. To test a student's ability to make a judgment, the teacher must provide all of the needed data, perhaps in the form of charts or graphs, and ask the student to draw certain conclusions from these data. Another form of assessment is to ask students to state their opinions on a work of art or to judge the validity of a political theory, offering evidence to support their opinions. The types of products that students create at this level are critical essays, discussions, speeches, letters to the editor, debates, drama, videotapes, and other forms that allow them to express their points of view.

Evaluation outcomes and objectives are difficult to grade. A teacher who offers students an opportunity to express their own views usually places high value on independent thinking and freedom of expression. Therefore, the teacher cannot grade a student response as right or wrong but can, however, assess whether the student has used accurate, sufficient, and appropriate criteria in defending a personal opinion. Student work that has cited inaccurate, insufficient, or inappropriate evidence should probably be returned to the student with suggestions for revision.

In summary, assessment of student accomplishments should be directly linked to the lesson's objectives. To assess basic knowledge and skills, behavioral objectives are useful because they state exactly what the student will be able to do and specify the criteria for success. For higher-level objectives, problem-solving objectives may be less precise but still should describe the type of student behavior or expected product and give some general criteria for success.

When teachers plan by writing clear behavioral, problem-solving, and expressive objectives for their lessons, they are clarifying their expectations regarding what students will gain from the lesson and their criteria for success. The assessment section of a lesson plan is then usually a restatement of the criteria expressed in the objectives. You will see an example of this in the sample lesson plans in this chapter.

Predicting Possible Outcomes of Lesson Plans

Imagine that you have written your first lesson plan and decide to show it to some experienced teachers, asking them what they think about it. Congratulations! You are using the very important reflective action of inviting feedback. You hope that the veteran teachers will read your plan and look up with huge smiles to tell you that you have done a great job.

What is more likely is that one of the teachers will begin the discussion with, "What if . . .?" Another might say, "Have you thought about . . .?" Another might even laugh and tell a story about the "perfect lesson plan" that turned into a disaster in the classroom. When Judy Eby was a student teacher at the University of Illinois in Urbana, she planned just such a perfect lesson. Within a unit on animal behavior, she planned a series of lessons in which students were allowed to conduct experiments on live animals. Following her written lesson plan, she asked students to bring in small animal cages from home to house the animals. The students brought in leftover gerbil cages, bird cages, and other small containers. On the first day of the new unit, Judy went to the university and got one white mouse per student and put the mice in the students' cages. The mice were smaller and more agile than expected, however, and they quickly squeezed out of the cages and began running around the classroom. Chaos ensued. She asked the students to help catch the mice and put them all into a glass-walled aquarium. Although planned objectives were not met that day, there were certainly many opportunities for problem solving and "unintended" outcomes.

Judy and her master teacher spent the afternoon rethinking the entire lesson plan. They decided to identify individual mice by using different colors and patterns of ink dots so that students could tell their mice apart. Having done this, they went home for the night. When they returned the next morning, the mice had disrupted the plan again. Baby mice had been born during the night, and some of the adult mice were dead or wounded by attacks from other mice. The third revision of this lesson plan called for mealworms instead of mice to be used as the experimental animals.

Most veteran teachers have experienced this type of scenario more than once. Even the best plans can go wrong. Indeed, part of the nervousness many teachers feel before teaching a lesson comes from this very realization. It is hard to prepare for the unexpected.

Even when the basic lesson plan runs smoothly, it is almost a given that in any lesson, some students will require different experiences or explanations to understand the new concept or skill being taught. Some teachers can think on their feet and address student confusion on the spot, but this can be a challenge for a new teacher. We suggest that you consistently plan a second way of introducing or extending any given concept just in case you need it! We think you'll often be glad you did. Relational teachers are aware that students learn differently and that some may need a second strategy to achieve the lesson objective.

As we observe new teachers presenting lessons, one thing we notice is that discipline and management problems rarely occur when the lesson content is focused slightly above students' current knowledge base. This is probably due to the fact that students feel challenged but not overwhelmed by the experience, so they are engaged in learning and feel happy to cooperate. In contrast, problems seem to arise when a teacher prepares a lesson that covers content the students already know. They act restless and may become disruptive when they feel that the teacher is babying them or talking down to them. What should you do when you arrive in a setting, materials in hand, and find out the students have already mastered the content you planned to teach? Should you press bravely on, working your way through the lesson because it is what you worked so hard to prepare? To do so is to ignore the learning needs of your students. We have often seen this and believe that the biggest reason for this choice is a simple one—the teacher has nothing else prepared and has yet to think through the next steps in the learning sequence.

Adapting Activities for Differentiated Instruction

Often teachers plan their lessons with a set of objectives for the students in their class whose knowledge and skills are at grade level. The term *at grade level* means the average or typical level of understanding or skill that most children are able to achieve at that age and in that grade. As teachers gain experience teaching at a grade level, they are able to describe what the typical learner at that grade level can accomplish. Because most children in the class will have skills and knowledge near the average, it makes sense for teachers to plan lessons with difficulty levels conforming to that average.

Reflective teachers realize that in any classroom, there is likely to be a wide range of student achievement and experience. There are bound to be students who have already learned and mastered the concepts being taught. Many kindergarten students come to school knowing the entire alphabet and how to count to 100. Some students may be capable of acting as a "classroom expert" in using the computer. Planning for ways to extend the knowledge of these students is just as important to the success of your lesson as planning for ways to help students who do not understand something right away. When you enter a classroom with a plan for extending a lesson's concepts and content, you will feel more confident and will enhance the learning experiences of more of your students.

There are also likely to be students who appear to be completely bewildered during a lesson, whereas others give no readable cues for you to tell whether or not they understand the lesson concepts. Some students may sit quietly but refuse to try the learning task you have assigned to them. Reflective teachers accept that there are many reasons students may fail to respond in the ways they hope and plan for. For example, a student may be hungry, tired, or preoccupied with a concern (outside or inside of school) that is more compelling than this lesson (Maslow, 1954). Students may doubt their ability to succeed at the task and avoid it in an attempt to save face, or they may feel that the task is far too easy and therefore not worth the effort to complete. Students may also need more experience with new or unfamiliar vocabulary.

If you consider reasons a student may not respond appropriately to your lesson, you can begin to write variations in your lesson plan to accommodate these students. For example, if you realize that some students may feel threatened by a particular task, such as reading aloud to the entire class from their book report, you can plan an alternate task, such as allowing students to work in pairs and discuss their book reports with a peer. By having a backup plan, you will know what to do when a student stares blankly instead of working. By visualizing and trying to predict the possible outcomes of your lesson plan, you can avoid these uncomfortable situations, maintain the flow of the lesson, and involve all your students more productively. See Figure 3.2 for some troubleshooting guidelines related to student lack of responsiveness.

Writing a Well-Organized Lesson Plan

When teachers plan for day-to-day learning experiences, they are creating lesson plans. Usually a lesson plan is created for a single subject or topic for one day, although some experiential, hands-on lessons may be continued for several days in a row. Teachers in self-contained classrooms must devise several different lesson plans each day, one for each subject they teach, unless they choose to use multidisciplinary units. Teachers in the upper grades who work in departmentalized settings where students travel from class to class for various subjects must still create different lesson plans for each grade or group of students they teach.

In the university or college courses designed to prepare teachers, the lesson plan is an important teaching or learning device. Both college professors and experienced classroom teachers can provide the aspiring teacher with models of good lesson plans. Students can look on the Internet or purchase books that contain well-written lesson plans, but it is only by actively creating their own plans that they are able to demonstrate the extent to which they understand and can apply the theories and principles they have learned about reflective thinking and planning.

For that reason, many university and college programs require students to create a number of precise and detailed lesson plans. Sometimes students observe that the classroom teachers they know do not write such extensive plans for every lesson. Instead, these teachers write their lesson plans in large weekly planning books, and a single lesson plan may consist of cryptic notations, such as "Math: Review p. 108; Social studies: Review Chap. 7; Science: Continue nutrition." Although experienced teachers may record their lesson plans with such brief notes, novice teachers need to write lessons in great detail. They need to develop the mental skills and facilities to see each lesson in its entirety and in its attention to detail prior to presenting it to their students. This ability to think ahead and predict the lesson design related to expected outcomes comes after years of practice and lesson planning. Every good teacher

Figure **3.2** Troubleshooting guidelines related to student lack of responsiveness.

Behavior	Possible Causes	Possible Remedies
Student is not doing assigned work.	Student does not understand directions. Work is too difficult. Work is too easy. Student is distracted by other students. Student has poor work habits.	Give guided practice by creating visual for support. Provide additional guided practice before asking student to work independently. Add challenge to assignment, preferably with practical application. Move student to study carrel or quiet area of room, facing away from others. Create contract with student.
Student gets into conflicts with teacher or other students.	Student may be avoiding work in certain curriculum areas. Conflict involves same students regularly. Student may have had negative experiences with former teachers or other adults.	Use active listening to see how confident student is in curriculum in question. Use conflict resolution strategies. If necessary, separate students to ease tension between them. Monitor your reactions to student to detect any negative body language on your part. Use active listening and try to reserve judgment until you hear all facts.
Student calls out/interjects answers or information at inappropriate times.	It may be family pattern of communication. Student feels need for recognition. Student lacks understanding of established classroom procedures.	Use one-on-one discussion to establish that student understands need for respectful classroom interaction. Establish acceptable signal to show student you recognize he knows the answer and you need to hear from others in group as well. (The key to success of this strategy is consistency. Do not permit student to gain the floor by "calling out.")
Student gets up and wanders around classroom.	Student needs to move around. Student may be avoiding work because it's inappropriate. There is change in teacher expectations from previous year.	Build activity breaks into or between your lessons. Provide planned movement to help address student's need to move about. (See "Student is not doing assigned work" above.) Use one-on-one conference to review this year's expectations. Create behavior contract if necessary.
Student takes long time to complete written work.	Student has poor fine-motor skills. Task is too difficult. Student is distracted.	Shorten the task; as student's skills improve, begin to lengthen task. Allow student to use word processor for lengthy writing tasks. (See "Student is not doing assigned work" above.)

has gone through this same process and recognizes the importance of good, clear planning in order to provide the greatest benefit for students. Writing detailed lesson plans also enables novice teachers to communicate their plans to the professor or mentor teacher, who can provide feedback on the plan before the lesson is taught. Experienced mentor teachers can easily see how the lesson is organized and may be able to offer suggestions for improving the presentation or, at the least, for avoiding predictable pitfalls.

Well-written lesson plans have additional value in that they can be shared. A teacher's shorthand notes that serve as a personal reminder can rarely be interpreted by an outsider. If a substitute teacher is called in to replace a classroom teacher for a day or longer, the substitute needs to see the daily plans in language he or she can understand and use. Teams of teachers often write lesson plans together or for each other, so they need to have a common understanding of the lesson objectives, procedures, assessment, and resources.

The form may vary, but most lesson plans share a number of common elements. Three essential features of a complete, well-organized lesson plan are the objectives, procedures, and assessment. These correspond to the four questions of curriculum planning formulated by Tyler (1949). Lesson objectives specify the "educational purposes" of the lesson, the procedures section describes both "what educational experiences can be provided" and the way they can be "effectively organized," and the assessment section describes the way the teacher has planned in advance to determine "whether these purposes are being attained" (Tyler, 1949, p. 1).

The description, another feature in a lesson plan, is used to identify it and give the reader a quick overview of its purpose or description. A lesson plan also often contains information about the resources teachers need as background preparation for teaching the lesson as well as any materials necessary for actual execution of the lesson.

A suggestion for teachers in this age of computers is to create a basic outline of a lesson plan on a word processor and save it on a disk. Then, when you wish to write a lesson plan, you can put the outline on the screen and fill in the spaces. You may also want to take some time to access the Internet and look at various lesson plans posted there; many sites are available through commercial publishers as well as through groups of teachers at local and state levels.

The Internet provides some new clues and models that can inform and enliven your teaching. Almost any search engine on the World Wide Web has a category called *education* and a subcategory called K–12 *education*. Type "K–12 Lesson Plans" into Google to find web pages filled with real-life examples of teachers' lesson plans in every subject at every grade level. Other exciting materials and suggestions can be found at http://k6educators.about.com.

For example, Ask Eric Virtual Library can be accessed at http://ericir.syr.edu. This web page contains a library of lesson plans created by teachers and submitted to the Educational Resources International Clearinghouse (ERIC). The Gateway to Educational Materials is another source of ready-to-use lesson plans at www.thegateway.org. Once you have located these web pages, you can bookmark them and refer to them frequently. When you have mastered the art of writing your own lesson plans, you can submit one of your best to these types of organizations for others to see.

LESSON PLAN FORMATS.   Including all of the ideas discussed in this chapter in one lesson plan can sound pretty daunting, but it is something that will become second nature to you with experience. To help you remember the important aspects of a lesson, we offer you two different models of lesson plan formats in Figures 3.3 and 3.4. Figure 3.3 is a lesson plan format that you might use when teaching a specific skill or strategy that you intend to model and give the students practice in. Figure 3.4 offers a format for use in a lesson where the students will be problem solving or "discovering" knowledge without direct teaching. Take some time to review them and see if you can explain why each part has been included and how the two formats differ. These formats can be copied on your computer disk for use in writing lesson plans both in college and for the rest of your teaching career.

For the lesson plan format using direct teaching (Figure 3.3), begin by putting in the title, subject area, grade level, and lesson duration. Using clear and specific objectives for each lesson will help you maintain focus and avoid overwhelming students with too many ideas at once. Once you have established your basic objectives for the lesson, think about some of the students in your class who have special needs. Write notes to yourself to describe how you will scaffold the lesson for students who do not understand or who are learning to speak English. Write notes about enriching the lesson for students who have mastered the concept you are teaching and need a more challenging curriculum.

By listing the materials you need ahead of time, you avoid getting halfway through the lesson and missing something you need. Each step of the procedure in our model may help you to think through what you will do to prepare for and teach the lesson. The preassessment

Figure 3.3   Annotated reflective action lesson plan format.

Title of Lesson:

Subject Area: **Lesson Duration:** (What is your estimate of time?)

Standards Addressed: (What state or national standards are addressed?)

Materials and Resources:
Teacher Materials: (What materials will you need to teach the lesson?)

Student Materials: (What materials will students need to use to complete the lesson?)

Objective: (What will students be able to do at the conclusion of the lesson?)

Reflective Action Procedures:
Pretesting: (How will you assess students' prior knowledge and skills related to this lesson?)

Adaptations for Students with Special Needs: (What adjustments will you make for special needs students or English language learners?)

Motivation: (What will you say or do to get students interested in the lesson?)

Teacher Explanation: (How will you explain what students will be learning and why learning it is important?)

Teacher Modeling: (How will you demonstrate what students will do?)

Guided Practice: (How will you take students step-by-step through the lesson?)

Check for Understanding: (How will you determine if students are ready to practice on their own?)

Independent Practice: (What will students do to practice what you have taught them?)

Closure: (How will you review or celebrate the learning that has taken place?)

Assessment: (How will you know that your objective has been met? How will you determine which students need further instruction?)

Plan for Further Instruction for Students Who Need It: (How will you provide additional instruction for students who did not meet the objective or for those who need enrichment activities?)

step refers to the process of finding out what your students already know prior to teaching a new lesson. Reflective teachers use this strategy to avoid behavior problems from students who do not have a clue what you are talking about as well as from those who are bored. This strategy also helps you to build the background for the day's lesson. For example, if you were preassessing students' knowledge of metric measurement, you might want to show a meter stick to your students and ask if they know what it is and what it is used for.

After you have written a draft of your lesson plan, imagine yourself teaching it and consider the possible outcomes that may result. Think through what you will do if students do not understand or appear to be bored because they have already mastered the concept. What can you predict about the reaction of students in your classroom who are learning English? What will they need from you and their classmates to be successful in this lesson? You can see that the outcome prediction is a vital aspect of withitness and reflective action in teaching.

Figure 3.4 Annotated problem-solving lesson format.

Title of Lesson:

Subject Area:

Lesson Duration: (How long will it take to teach this lesson?)

Standards Addressed: (What content/standards will be addressed in the lesson?)

Materials and Resources:

Teacher Materials: (What materials will you will need to prepare for and present the lesson?)

Student Materials: (What materials will students need to complete the activity?)

Objective: (What will students be able to do at the conclusion of the lesson? In a problem-solving lesson, the focus should be on the process and use of problem-solving strategies.)

Reflective Action Procedures: (What steps will you follow in teaching the lesson?)

Pretesting: (How will you assess students' prior knowledge and skills related to this lesson?)

Adaptations for Students with Special Needs: (What adjustments will you make for students who need additional support, who have additional challenges, or who are English language learners?)

Motivation: (What will you say or do to get students interested in the lesson?)

Teacher Explanation: (How will you explain the process of problem solving as it relates to the activity to be completed?)

Teacher Modeling: (How will you demonstrate what students will do to use problem-solving strategies to complete the assignment?)

Guided Practice: (What will students do to start the process while you monitor, make suggestions, and refocus their efforts?)

Check for Understanding: (How will you determine if students used problem-solving strategies such as analyzing, evaluating evidence and alternative points of view, interpreting, and drawing conclusions?)

Independent Practice: (What will students do to complete the project using problem-solving strategies?)

Closure: (How will you review or celebrate the learning that has taken place?)

Debriefing: (How will you encourage students to discuss the processes used in problem solving?)

Assessment: (How will you know that your objective has been met? How will you determine which students need further instruction?)

Plan for Further Instruction for Students Who Need It: (How will you provide additional instruction for students who did not meet the objective or for those ready for enrichment?)

In the active learning experience with the lightbulb described earlier, the teacher could aid the students in comprehending what they learned by having them share what they did that worked and did not work. Concepts can be developed by articulating and generalizing what they learned about electricity. Such a teacher-led discussion is an essential part of active, hands-on learning. It provides a sense of closure.

Every lesson or presentation can benefit from some thoughtful consideration of its ending. It is important to allow time for closure. You may use this time to ask questions that check for understanding so that you will know what to plan for the lesson that follows. You may allow the students to close the lesson with their own conclusions and new insights. A few moments spent summarizing what was learned is valuable in any form. Insight will probably occur in this period. At the close of one lesson, you can also indicate what will follow in the next lesson so that your students know what to expect and how to prepare for it.

Planning Problem-Solving Lessons

Problem-solving lessons require a slightly different approach. In teaching students to solve problems, you are focusing on the processes of evaluating, analyzing, testing solutions, and seeing results. The parts of the lesson plan are similar to the skills lesson plan, but the emphasis is very different.

In a problem-solving lesson, you still address content standards, but the students will be acquiring the mastery of the standards deductively. In other words, you will not teach the standards directly but will allow the students access to materials, resources, and experiences that will help them to discover the concepts related to the standards.

Problem-solving lessons emphasize the process of using reasoning to solve problems, explore varying points of view, and make connections between information and conclusions. Problem solving involves critical thinking and provides opportunities for students to be involved in different processes:

- Analyzing parts of a whole to see how they interact with one another
- Analyzing and evaluating evidence
- Synthesizing and making connections between information and possible solutions
- Interpreting information and drawing conclusions
- Reflecting critically on learning experiences and processes
- Identifying and asking significant questions

Because of the differences between teaching a skills-based lesson plan and a problem-solving lesson plan, the teacher focuses on explaining and modeling the use of the processes. It is also vital to add a debriefing section to the problem-solving lesson. Students must learn to verbalize and analyze the processes they use to solve problems so that the steps become a part of their metacognitive learning scenarios.

Sequencing

Sequencing Objectives in Mathematics

Some subjects are very sequential in nature. Mathematics is the best example in the elementary curriculum because its concepts and operations can be readily ordered from simple to complex. Teachers can effectively organize the teaching of computational skills in the basic operations of addition, subtraction, multiplication, and division very easily. For example, outcome statement 1 describes a possible sequence for teaching an essential understanding about the concept of numbers:

Outcome statement 1 (mathematics). Primary students will be able to show how addition and subtraction are related to one another.

To accomplish this outcome, primary teachers will introduce the students to the concept of numbers and give them concrete manipulative experiences in adding and subtracting one-digit numbers. Students may act out stories in which children are added and subtracted from a group. They may make up stories about animals or objects that are taken away and then brought back to demonstrate subtraction and addition.

Math textbooks offer a sequence of learning activities and practice of math facts, but reflective teachers find that math textbooks must be used flexibly and supplemented with other learning experiences. Before planning math lessons for a particular group of students, the teacher must pretest their entry-level knowledge and skills. Pretests will reveal that some children have already mastered some of the skills in the sequence and do not need to spend valuable time redoing what they already know; they need enriched math activities to allow them to progress. Other children may not have the conceptual understanding of number relationships to succeed on the first step. For them, preliminary concrete experiences with manipulative materials are essential for success.

To achieve outcome statement 1, students could be asked to meet these sample math objectives:

1. Use blocks to show addition of two single-digit integers.
2. Use blocks to show subtraction of two single-digit integers.
3. Use pennies and dimes to show place value of 1s and 10s.
4. Subtract pennies without regrouping.
5. Add pennies and exchange 10 pennies for a dime.
6. Subtract pennies by making change for a dime to show regrouping.
7. Tell how subtraction is related to addition using coins as an example.

These sample objectives are representative of the basic remembering- and understanding-level skills needed to accomplish the outcome statement. They can be written in the behavioral objective form, specifying what percentage of correct answers must be attained to demonstrate mastery.

These objectives emphasize basic computational skills that all students need to learn. However, in keeping with the National Council of Teachers of Mathematics' recommendations to emphasize problem solving over computation, reflective teachers are likely to plan lessons that allow students to explore the relationships between addition and subtraction and that include many additional math outcomes and objectives at the higher levels of Bloom's revised taxonomy (as found in Anderson & Krathwohl, 2001) to teach students how to apply the math facts and computation skills they are learning to actual problem-solving situations. However, this example does illustrate the importance of matching objectives to outcome statements in a logical sequence. Each of the objectives builds on the one before it. As students master each objective, they are continually progressing toward mastering the outcome statement.

Sequencing Objectives in Language Arts

Not all subjects in the elementary curriculum are as sequential as mathematics. Language arts consists of knowledge, skills, and abilities that develop children's understanding and use of language. Reading, writing, speaking, listening, visually representing, and interpreting visual information are all part of the language arts curriculum, and each one can and should have its own outcome statement(s). Outcome statement 2 suggests one illustration of how the language arts curriculum is designed:

Outcome statement 2 (language arts). Students will write standard English with correct spelling, accurate grammar, and well-organized meaning and form.

This outcome statement will take years to accomplish, but teachers at every grade level are responsible for providing learning experiences that build toward the ultimate goal. The objectives to reach this goal may be similar each year for several years but written in increasing levels of difficulty. This is known as a *spiral curriculum*.

To achieve outcome statement 2, students could be asked to meet these sample language arts objectives by the end of grade two:

1. Write a sentence containing a subject and a verb.
2. Use a capital letter at the beginning of a sentence.
3. Use a period or question mark at the end of a sentence.
4. Review and edit sentences for complete meaning.

By the end of grade four, students will be able to:

1. Write a paragraph that focuses on one central idea.
2. Spell common words correctly in writing samples.
3. Use capitalization and end punctuation correctly.
4. Review and edit a paragraph to improve the organization of ideas.

By the end of grade six, students will be able to:

1. Write several paragraphs that explain one concept or theme.
2. Use a dictionary to spell all words in a paper correctly.
3. Use correct punctuation, including end marks, comma, apostrophe, quotation marks, and colon.
4. Review and edit papers to correct spelling, punctuation, grammar, and organization of ideas.

By the end of grade eight, students will be able to:

1. Write papers with an introductory paragraph, logical reasons, data to support the main idea, and a closing statement.
2. Use a dictionary to spell all words in a paper correctly; use a thesaurus to add to vocabulary of the paper.
3. Eliminate fragments and run-on sentences.
4. Review and edit papers to correct spelling, punctuation, grammar, organization of ideas, and appropriateness for the purpose.

When teachers have curriculum guidelines such as these, they must still translate the outcome statements and objectives into actual learning experiences that are appropriate and motivating for their students. To pretest how well your students can use written language when they enter your classroom, plan a writing experience in the first week. Analyzing these writing samples will allow you to plan suitably challenging activities for your students. In this example, the second-grade teacher must decide what topics to have students write about and when to limit students to copying teacher-made examples or allow them to begin writing their own sentences. The fourth-grade teacher knows that students will not learn all of these skills in just one writing lesson. It is necessary to provide many interesting classroom experiences so that students will have ideas to express in their writing. The sixth-grade teacher has to plan a series of research and writing experiences so that students will have ample opportunities to synthesize all of the skills required at that grade level. The eighth-grade teacher must plan a series of lessons to provide opportunities for students to proofread their pages to ensure they have integrated introductory and closing statements, as well as self-editing to meet grade-level standards.

Curriculum planning of subjects such as language arts is a complex undertaking because it contains so many varied outcomes and objectives. The previous example illustrates only a single outcome for teaching students how to write. Teachers must also plan outcome statements and objectives for reading, listening, speaking, visually representing, and interpreting visual methods.

Sequencing Objectives in Science

The science curriculum should inform students of the basic facts and concepts of science topics, but it should also allow students opportunities to experience how scientists work. These dual goals of the science curriculum are often expressed as teaching both content and process. An example of an outcome statement in science that covers both content and process follows:

> *Outcome statement 3 (science).* Students will demonstrate the properties of electricity and magnetism and show how their energy can be used to benefit mankind.

If the teacher were planning a series of lesson plans to accomplish this outcome, she would use a sequence of process-oriented learning experiences that allow students to discover some important properties of electricity and magnetism, followed by a few content-oriented lessons to review and articulate what they discovered. As a culmination, she would allow students to apply what they have learned and synthesize their own inventions using the energy from batteries and magnets. Many teachers have also found that the incorporation of simulation software like Virtual Labs: Electricity (www.riverdeep.com) provides an exciting opportunity for her students to experience the results of their choices and decisions.

To achieve outcome statement 3, students could be asked to meet these sample science objectives by the end of the unit on electricity and magnetism:

1. Demonstrate how electricity travels in a closed circuit.
2. Demonstrate how magnetism attracts and repels certain metals.
3. Investigate the basic properties of electricity and magnetism.
4. Be able to compare and contrast electricity and magnetism and identify key properties of each.
5. Invent some beneficial ways to use electricity and magnetism.

Using this approach, the first lesson plan would involve hands-on experiences using batteries, copper wire, and lightbulbs so that students can demonstrate to themselves how electricity travels in a closed circuit. On subsequent days, lessons would be planned to allow students to investigate the properties of magnets and electricity. Then the teacher would plan a lesson in which students created charts comparing the two, and there would be a lesson in which students discussed the properties and learned to use terminology correctly. They might then each take a written test on these properties and terms. Finally, there would be several days for students to work on their inventions and present them to classmates and parents.

Sequencing Objectives in Social Studies

Reflective elementary teachers can also see the need for both content and process in their social studies curriculum. They attempt to help their students build a knowledge base in history and geography but also give attention and time to teaching students how to acquire information on their own.

An example of an outcome statement in social studies that covers both content and process follows:

> *Outcome statement 4 (social studies).* Students will use a map and a globe to find place names and locations. They will then create a chart listing the countries, major cities, rivers, and mountain ranges in each continent.

To achieve outcome statement 4, students could be asked to meet these sample social studies objectives at the end of the map and globe unit:

1. Identify the seven continents on a world map and a globe.
2. Interpret the country boundaries with a map legend.
3. List the countries in each continent.
4. Interpret the symbol for rivers on the map legend.
5. List the major rivers in each continent.
6. Interpret the symbol for mountain ranges on the map legend.
7. List the mountain ranges in each continent.
8. Create a chart showing the countries, cities, rivers, and mountain ranges in each continent.

In this example, the teacher has planned a set of learning activities that will add to the students' knowledge base about world geography. This set of activities also equips students to be able to find and interpret information on maps and globes with up-to-date Internet information such as Google Earth (www.google.com/earth/index.html). This social studies curriculum demonstrates that by employing hands-on learning experiences, students are able to learn both content and processes simultaneously and that they are active rather than passive learners throughout the entire set of activities. An oral or written pretest might consist of having students name or point to certain geographic locations and read and interpret a map legend. The information from the pretest is valuable in planning lessons that use students' existing knowledge and add to it.

Sample Lesson Plans

Lesson plans are written scripts that teachers use so they can present a well-organized set of learning experiences for their students. The objectives of the lesson specify the teacher's expectations for what the students will learn or be able to do as a result of the lesson. When teachers plan objectives that specify the criteria for success, they are clarifying for themselves what the students must be able to do to demonstrate mastery of the skill or understanding of the lesson's concepts.

To plan the procedures of a lesson in advance, many reflective teachers visualize themselves teaching the lesson. They write what they must do to teach the lesson successfully and what the students must do to learn the material. Teachers who can visualize the entire process of teaching and learning can write richly detailed lesson plans. When they begin to teach the lesson, they have a supportive script to follow.

As teachers become more proficient and experienced at planning and teaching, their written lesson plans are likely to become less detailed. For beginning teachers, however, a thorough, richly detailed plan is an essential element for a successful lesson.

Sample Writing Lesson Plan

Diane Leonard teaches in a first-grade classroom in Fresno, California. To support her students, many of whom are learning English as a second language, Diane does a lot of modeling before she asks her students to work independently. She also plans guided practice activities to help her students understand exactly what she expects them to do. When she has her students work independently, Diane often uses the time to teach an additional guided practice lesson to students who need extra help in order to be successful.

Diane begins the lesson with all of the children sitting in front of a chart. They sing a song about a turkey, the topic of their writing. Diane then reads an informational book about turkeys, which helps the students gain information about their topic. She then leads the class in labeling the parts of a turkey and adding descriptive words to their labels. This exercise provides a model for students to use as they return to their desks to complete the prewriting activity, drawing and labeling a picture of a turkey. See Diane's lesson plan (Figure 3.5) for this prewriting activity.

Figure 3.5   Sample first-grade writing lesson plan.

Title of Lesson: Writing about Turkeys

Subject Area: Language arts   **Lesson duration:**   30 minutes

Standards Addressed: Writing: Students will write short descriptive paragraphs.

Materials and Resources:

Teacher Materials: Chart paper, markers, informational book about turkeys (Schug's *Turkeys on the Farm*, 2006)

Student Materials: Writing paper (with room for drawing at the top), pencils, crayons

Objective: After teacher explanation, modeling, and guided practice, students will draw and label a picture of a turkey and add a descriptive word for each of the labels in preparation for writing a descriptive paragraph.

Adaptations for Students with Special Needs: While other students are working independently, I will provide additional guided practice for students who are not ready to work on their own as the others are working independently.

Reflective Action Procedures:

Pretesting: I will show a picture of a turkey and ask students to identify its parts (feathers, tail, wattle, beak, legs, claws).

Motivation: "We have been talking about turkeys, and today we are going to learn more about them so we can write a story about turkeys. We will sing a song about turkeys (to the tune of Bingo). I will write the word *turkey* on the chart paper as we sing the song."

Teacher Explanation: "We are going to learn a good prewriting strategy. After I read a story about turkeys, we will draw a picture of a turkey; then we will label the parts so that we will have the words we need to write our own story." I will then read the book *Turkeys on the Farm* (2006) and show students the labeled picture in the book.

Teacher Modeling: I will show students how to use their hands to form the outline of the turkey by modeling using my hand and the chart paper, and we will label each part on the chart.

Guided Practice: I will ask students to help me write a descriptive word for each part we labeled. As students suggest descriptive words, we will spell them together as I write the words on the chart.

Check for Understanding: I will go back through the process we have used: (1) drawing the turkey, (2) labeling the turkey, and (3) writing a descriptive word for each label. I will then ask students to read each of the labels and descriptive words we have written on the chart.

Independent Practice: Students will go back to their seats to draw and label their turkeys.

Closure: Students will bring their labeled drawings to the celebration circle and share what they have done.

Assessment: During circle time, I will observe the work students have done and keep a list of students who will need additional instruction before they are ready to continue the writing.

Plan for Further Instruction for Students Who Need It: I will work with students who need help in getting their drawings completed with labels and descriptive words while other students work in learning centers later in the morning.

Diane will follow up this prewriting lesson with a lesson on drafting the story, following the same approach: explaining, modeling, providing guided practice, and supporting the students who need it with additional instruction while the majority of the class works independently. See Figure 3.6 for an example of one of the stories the children wrote.

Figure 3.6   First-grade writing sample about turkeys.

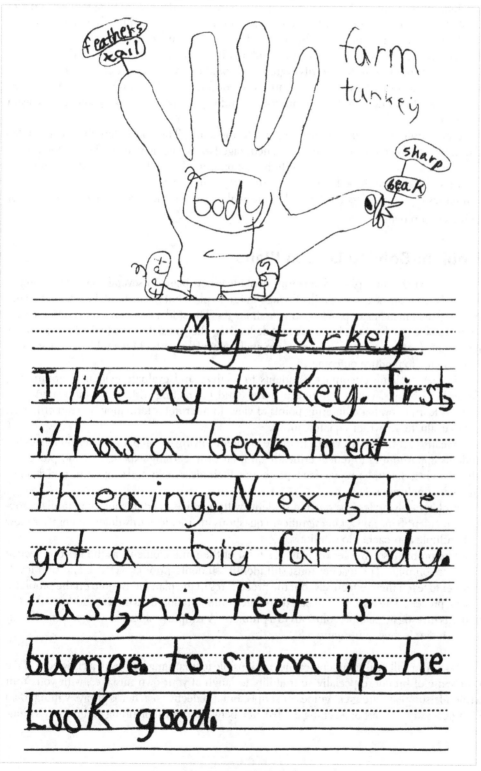

Sample Science Lesson Plan

Jeffrey Butler uses a website about butterfly migration to teach science lessons in observations, describing change, and collecting and reporting scientific data. Using the website http://www.learner.org/jnorth/tm/monarch/jr/IntroMig1.html, Jeffrey employs the slide presentations and activities to encourage his students to become citizen scientists.

Jeffrey introduces the unit by showing several slideshows from the website to introduce the students to monarch butterfly migrations, show the students how to observe and document observations, and demonstrate methods to examine the habitat needs of butterflies.

To teach his students the value of careful observation, Jeffrey uses photos from the butterfly migration site to support the students in acquiring observation skills. The students look at the photos to identify signs of seasonal change: They look for hints to identifying the season by carefully examining the condition of the plants and other clues as to the time of year depicted in the photos, including changes that take place from season to season.

Opportunities to write are embedded into the study. The vocabulary they learn is displayed in the classroom and students are encouraged to use the new vocabulary in documenting their observations. Because the butterfly site posts weekly updates and photos of butterfly sightings, the students have frequent opportunities to update their migration maps and write summaries of the progress the butterflies are making in their migration. See Figure 3.7 for Jeffrey's lesson plan.

Problem-Solving Lesson Plans

Problem-solving lesson plans differ from content lesson plans in several ways. The content standards are addressed, as in a reflective action lesson plan, but the focus of the lesson is on the teaching and practicing of problem-solving strategies. The students are encouraged to use various types of reasoning, both inductive and deductive. They must decide which of these types is appropriate for the problem; they must also analyze how the parts of the problem interact with each another to produce outcomes.

Problem solving encourages students to analyze and evaluate evidence, arguments, claims, and beliefs. Using resource materials and interacting with peers and experts, the students learn to evaluate differing points of view, to interpret information, to read critically, and to evaluate the writer's qualifications.

Because debriefing is a vital part of the problem-solving lesson plan, the teacher gives the students opportunities to reflect critically on their own learning experiences and processes. This also gives the students practice is presenting their ideas orally and supporting and defending their conclusions.

Problem-solving lessons provide students with practice in addressing nonfamiliar problems and identifying and asking significant questions in order to clarify different points of view and multiple approaches to solutions.

The problem-solving lesson plan has most of the same elements as the basic reflective action lesson plan. The teacher must still identify students' prior knowledge and skill levels in order to teach them effectively, but the procedures in the plan focus more on the problem-solving process. The lesson is still based on state content standards, which are addressed as the students investigate possible solutions to a problem. A sample problem-solving lesson plan for social studies is shown in Figure 3.8.

Soon you will be the student teacher responsible for planning lessons in a classroom. Take your sense of humor, especially your ability to laugh at your own mistakes, with you. Your written lesson plans are great guides or scripts, but a reflective teacher is always willing to ad lib if necessary. The art of teaching is a balance between careful planning and improvisation.

***Figure* 3.7**   Science lesson plan.

Title of Lesson: Writing summary paragraphs from science data

Subject Areas: Science and Language Arts   **Lesson duration:**   One hour

Standards Addressed:

Materials and Resources:

Teacher Materials: Clue cards related to butterfly migration (available on the butterfly site), butterfly books, migration maps, vocabulary charts

Student Materials: Paper and pencils

Objective: Students will use posted new vocabulary and migration maps to document their understanding of butterfly migration, vocabulary, and effective summarization.

Reflective Action Procedure:

Pretesting: Before I begin the teacher explanation I will ask students to identify vocabulary words on the chart that correspond to the definitions I give verbally.

Adaptations for Students with special needs: Students who struggle with the vocabulary, writing, or understanding English will be allowed to work with a partner.

Teacher Explanation: I will review the definition of the word *fact* and explain the assignment: writing fact sentences summarizing butterfly migration using vocabulary on the vocabulary charts.

Teacher Modeling: I will demonstrate using words from the vocabulary chart and checking facts in the butterfly books or on the butterfly site to summarize the progress the butterflies are making on the migration maps.

Guided Practice: I will invite students to share some sentences that they might write. The sentences should include words from the vocabulary chart relating to the migration maps. I will provide them with practice in documenting their facts using the resource materials.

Independent Practice: Students will be given time to write summary sentences related to weekly migration progress based on the migration maps. They will document their facts using the migration maps and the website.

Closure: Students read one of their summary sentences and then post it on a sentence strip next to the weekly migration progress map it describes.

Assessment: I will use observation during the process, including the writing and reading of summary sentences, to identify any students who need additional guided practice.

Plan for Further Instruction for Students Who Need It or Enrichment for Students Needing More Advanced Instruction: Students needing further instruction will work with me individually or in small groups to practice with my guidance. Students ready to move onto more advanced activities will be given an opportunity to create booklets summarizing the butterfly migration with maps replicating the migration maps.

Figure 3.8 Sample problem-solving lesson plan: sixth-grade social studies.

Title of Lesson: Why do we live here?   **Subject Area:** Social studies

Lesson duration: Two or three 45-minute blocks

Standards Addressed: Use the history/social sciences framework for California public schools as a guide to the eras and civilizations to study. These standards require students not only to acquire core knowledge in history and social sciences but also to develop critical thinking skills that historians and social scientists employ to study the past and its relationship to the present.

Materials and Resources:

Teacher Materials: Use a variety of maps and documents to identify physical and cultural features of neighborhoods, cities, states, and countries and to explain the historical migration of people, the expansion and disintegration of empires, and the growth of economic systems.

Student Materials: Students will have use of teacher materials as well as additional library resources, Internet access, and a variety of building materials including cloth, twine, glue, and various papers.

Objectives: Using problem-solving methodology and a variety of resources and materials, students in grade six will create a dwelling and make a presentation demonstrating their understanding of how and why people choose the place in which they live and the impact of the physical environment on how people construct their homes and live their daily lives.

Reflective Action Procedures:

Pretesting: Conduct a class discussion on what kinds of things determine where people choose to live. Observe students' responses to identify areas to include in the teacher explanation and modeling.

Adaptations for Students with Special Needs: Provide appropriate reading and resource materials for students at all levels and capabilities as needed. Remove physical barriers that might interfere with student interactions. Provide extension materials and activities for advanced students.

Motivation: Continue and expand the pretesting discussion on why students' families moved to where they live now. Ask students to interview parents or grandparents about their reasons for moving to where they live and what attracted them to that locale.

Teacher Explanation: Inform students that they will be divided into groups and provided with a variety of materials for building a model of a dwelling in an appropriate surrounding environment. Each group must choose from a list of locales provided and also prepare an enticing travel brochure encouraging others to live there. Explain that they must examine and evaluate the resource materials before making their decisions.

Teacher Modeling: Choose a few resource materials for a specific locale (not one from the list students choose from), and demonstrate how information can be gathered before planning and building the dwelling and environment can begin. Verbalize your thought process to students to demonstrate your analysis and decision-making strategies.

Guided Practice: Place students in groups, and monitor their progress as they make decisions and preparations for the presentations. Offer suggestions and guidance based on student input only as necessary to keep the process moving forward and focused.

Check for understanding: Ask each group a series of questions on how and why they made decisions relating to the project. Focus on the process as well as the cognitive outcomes.

Independent practice: Groups create dwellings, environments, and presentations.

Closure: Hold a class discussion on the process required in each group related to reaching decisions on the completion of the project. Include discussion on problems in the process and how those areas were addressed in the group. Also discuss how the groups analyzed and evaluated information to make decisions.

Figure 3.8 (continued)

> **Assessment:** Students will write a letter home describing what their living conditions are, how they came to be there, what their life is like there, and where they might go if they were to leave that location. Create a scoring rubric for evaluating the letters to see if students included pertinent information on the locale, environment, and process of decision making. Be sure to share your rubric with students before having them write the letters.
>
> **Plan for further instruction for students who need it:** Through observation, identify students who exhibit a lack of understanding of the process and/or development of the presentations. Provide opportunities for students to work on computerized simulations of decision-making processes.

Involving the Larger Educational Community

It is important that you communicate with parents about the state standards for the grade you are teaching. This should be done early in the school year through a newsletter or parent meeting. This doesn't have to be a lengthy or in-depth discussion, but it is vital that parents understand how the standards change as their children move along in the grades.

The first requirement for this responsibility is that you understand exactly what is required at your grade level. Review the standards carefully and compare them to the grade-level standards for the year before and after. You can use a few key standards to help parents understand both the ways that student requirements will be different in this new school year and the ways that you will be supporting their children's growth.

This is also a good opportunity to involve the parents as members of the learning team. Provide them with various ways in which they can support their children:

- Providing a set time and place for homework to be done each night
- Encouraging their children when they get discouraged
- Providing their children with reading and writing materials at home
- Providing their children with an example by reading and having time to interact with the television turned off
- Limiting television time and engaging in family conversation, game time, and reading

Group Focus Activity

Your professor may involve you in a group activity to explore lesson objectives.

1. Work in a small group to identify the missing parts in each of these objectives. Rewrite each of the objectives to include all necessary elements.
2. Come back to the large group and share your discussion and rewrites.

Incomplete Objectives Activity

Identify the three elements of a learning objective in each of the following examples. If an element is missing, rewrite the objective to include all necessary elements. The three required elements are:

1. The conditions under which the learning will take place. Ask yourself, "Do I identify the instruction or condition under which the students will be working?"

2. The action or behavior that will provide evidence of the learning. Ask yourself, "Do I identify what the student will do to demonstrate the learning that has taken place?"

3. The criteria for success. Ask yourself, "What level of mastery do I expect in order to determine the success of the lesson?"

Objectives

1. After teacher explanation, modeling, and guided practice, students will alphabetize a list of 10 words.

2. Given a set of 20 math problems, students will score at least 80 percent.

3. Students will write complete sentences with 90 percent accuracy.

4. Given a list of 20 prepositions, students will demonstrate their meaning.

5. Students will define their spelling words.

6. After guided practice, students will learn the names of the continents.

7. Students will complete a timed multiplication worksheet.

8. After reading chapter 10 in their social studies books, students will know the contents of the chapter.

9. Students will write a descriptive paragraph.

10. After playing a game of opposites, students will identify the opposites of 10 words by correctly matching them.

4. Return to your small group to sort the following group of objectives into Bloom's levels of the cognitive domain.

Sorting Objectives

Read these learning objectives and sort them into levels according to Bloom's revised taxonomy. After they are sorted, refer to Figure 3.1 to check for accuracy.

- Level 6. Creating
- Level 4. Analyzing
- Level 2. Understanding
- Level 5. Evaluating
- Level 3. Applying
- Level 1. Remembering

Objectives

1. Given a list of similes, students will generate a list of alternate examples they could use to complete each simile with 80 percent accuracy.

2. Given 5 descriptive paragraphs, students will rank them according to their use of description and verbally defend their ranking with examples.

3. After reading an essay promoting recycling, the students will develop a visual to represent the author's ideas with at least 80 percent of the essay's points demonstrated.

4. After reading poems by Shel Silverstein, students will memorize and recite 1 poem with 100 percent accuracy.

5. After reading Martin Luther King Jr.'s "I have a dream" speech, students will paraphrase his ideas with 80 percent accuracy.

5. Come back to the large group to explain and defend your sorting.

Preparing for Your Licensure Exam

In this chapter, you read about lesson planning and sequencing. Reread "A View into the Classroom" at the beginning of the chapter, and think about it as a case study you might encounter on your licensure exam. Answer the following questions to demonstrate your understanding of lesson planning and sequencing:

1. What considerations did Vince give to the individual needs of his students?
2. How did Vince interest his students in the writing project?
3. How did Vince use grouping strategies to support his students' learning and their individual interests?

Portfolio of Professional Practices Activity

Using the reflective action lesson plan format, write a lesson plan that you might teach in your own classroom. Be sure to include all the required elements; assume that you have one student with auditory deficits (learning disability) and another student who is just beginning to speak English for whom you need to plan adaptations.

References

Anderson, L. W., & Krathwohl, D. R. (Eds.). (2001). *A taxonomy for learning, teaching, and assessing: A revision of Bloom's taxonomy of educational objectives*. Boston, MA: Allyn & Bacon.

Bloom, B., Engelhart, M., Furst, E., Hill, W., & Krathwohl, D. (1956). *Taxonomy of educational objectives: Cognitive domain*. New York, NY: Longman Publishers.

Eisner, E. (1985). *Educational imagination* (2nd ed.). Upper Saddle River, NJ: Merrill/Prentice Hall.

Kendall, J., & Marzano, R. (2000). *Content knowledge: A compendium of standards and benchmarks for K–12 education*. Aurora, CO: Mid-Continent Regional Educational Laboratory.

Kipling, R. (1902). *Just so stories: The elephant's child*. New York: Oxford University Press.

Maslow, A. (1954). *Motivation and personality*. New York, NY: Harper & Row.

Schug, M. (2006). *Turkeys on the farm*. Mandato, MN: Capstone Press.

Spady, W. (1994). Choosing outcomes of significance. *Educational Leadership, 51*(6), 18–22.

Tyler, R. (1949). *Basic principles of curriculum and instruction*. Chicago, IL: University of Chicago Press.

Blank Problem-Solving Lesson Plan Format

Title of lesson:

Subject area:

Lesson duration:

Standards addressed:

Materials and resources:

Teacher materials:

Student materials:

Objective:

Reflective Action Procedures

Pretesting:

Adaptations for students with special needs:

Motivation:

Teacher explanation:

Teacher modeling:

Guided practice:

Check for understanding:

Independent practice:

Closure:

Debriefing:

Assessment:

Plan for further instruction for students who need it:

Planning Curriculum Units

"Would you tell me which way I ought to go from here?" asked Alice.
"That depends a good deal on where you want to get," said the Cat.
"I really don't care where," replied Alice.
"Then it doesn't much matter which way you go," said the Cat.

Lewis Carroll, *Alice's Adventures in Wonderland* (1865)

D o you have a vision of yourself teaching a roomful of students who are excitedly investigating, experimenting, discussing, and reporting on what they are learning? Beginning teachers and student teachers often report that what they want to do most is create a learning environment that motivates their students to want to come to school and want to learn as much as they can about important matters.

Current national standards and state curriculum guides are also the products of the vision of experienced teachers, working in collaboration to provide beginning teachers with guidelines for what to teach and how to teach it. These documents encourage teachers to create programs that develop students' deeper understandings of a few important subjects rather than provide them with superficial surveys of data. At the local school district level, teachers are responsible for translating the curricular visions described in national and state standards into practical classroom learning experiences. The word vision is carefully chosen in this discussion because at the local level, teachers and principals are often encouraged to develop a common vision and create a mental image of what they want to accomplish with students.

One of the most natural and authentic ways to translate a vision of core curriculum goals into practical classroom experiences is by planning thematic units of study that engage students in actively seeking information on a topic that has meaning in their lives. Many teachers use a series of thematic units for their long-term planning. There is something refreshing and inherently motivating for both teachers and students using this plan. A unit of study lasts a specified number of days or weeks, during which everyone is motivated to investigate and find out everything they can about the topic. Then, during an exciting culmination, the students proudly display what they have learned. After a brief period devoted to assessment, this unit ends and a new one begins. When this rhythm is established in a classroom, complaints of boredom or repetition are rare from students or the teacher. The pace is quick, the goals are clear, and the expectations are high when everyone is involved in a thematic unit on an interesting, challenging topic.

Questions for Reflection as You Read the Chapter

1. How can teachers integrate the teaching of curriculum units into standards-based education?

2. How can teachers utilize reflective action in creating curriculum units?

3. How does collaboration with colleagues enhance curriculum planning and use of resources?

A View into the Classroom

One of classroom teachers' most important responsibilities is to plan the curriculum, the course of events and learning experiences for their students. To illustrate the complexity of the planning process, here is a brief first-person account of some issues that Diane Leonard faced during her first 3 months at Balderas Elementary School in Fresno, California.

When I first walked into my second-grade classroom in July, I encountered a large empty room with piles of textbooks on every counter. I knew that I had the freedom to create my own curriculum using the texts, but I also knew that I had to address the state-mandated standards in reading, writing, math, science, social studies, visual and performing arts, and physical education. I also understood that most of my second graders were just learning English and that I would have to address the English language development standards with them.

I didn't know my students yet, so I didn't want to presume to plan an entire year's curriculum until I had met them and determined their needs. I knew I wanted to plan integrated units and collaboratively build the group into a learning community. I found my answer in the state history/social science standards. Standard 2.1 speaks of students identifying things that occurred in the distant past as opposed to things that occurred yesterday. The standard suggests activities such as tracing family histories, conducting family interviews, making time lines, and mapping family travel and relocations. I thought, "What a perfect way to get to know my students while addressing the social studies standards." I began to think of all the other grade-level standards that could be addressed in the process of a family history study. Students would be practicing oral English as they interviewed their parents and grandparents, and they would be addressing writing standards as they wrote the stories they learned from their families.

I began to collect family-related literature to read to the students. I found stories about families and things they did together, stories of grandparents and how they had lived long ago, and folktales that had the different ethnic backgrounds represented by my students. I looked through the soft-back leveled readers I would be using for my guided reading groups to find family stories. I found short poems about families that I printed onto charts for daily choral reading; I also made copies of the poems so the children could illustrate them and practice reading them for their homework.

Because we were housed in a brand-new school, none of the children had been in our school building the previous year, so we began the year with a short map-making activity where we created a map of our new school. We took walks around the school and practiced our oral English by interviewing the secretary, cafeteria manager, librarian, custodian, and principal. We placed their offices on our school map and used shared writing to create their stories. We learned how to ask questions and how to transfer our newfound knowledge into stories about our school. We talked about the new school becoming a community and wrote a class book about our school. I used the big book I Went Walking (Williams, 1990) as a shared reading; I read it aloud, and we reread the repetitive text together and related the story to our walk around the school. We re-created the book, writing our own big book using our newfound school friends in place of the animals seen in the original story.

During this same time, we were generating questions to ask our parents and grandparents. We were preparing for our family history unit. The students began to interview their parents and grandparents, focusing on questions about what life and school were like a long time ago when the parents and grandparents were 7 years old. The students brought their stories back to the classroom, and we began to write our family history books. Some of the children brought in photographs and crafts to add to the discussion. We used roll-type fax paper and created family time lines; when possible, we invited parents and grandparents to demonstrate the art, crafts, cooking, dances, or music of their cultures. Whenever we had guests, we asked questions about how things had changed since the guests were children.

Our culminating activity was a family covered-dish dinner where we shared the family books, time lines, and oral reports. Since my students come from many different cultures, we couldn't always communicate in English, but the older siblings served as translators. There were many tears shed as the students shared their family history books that evening. We had electronically scanned some of the photos so we could include them in the family books, and the parents were excited about the new family treasures created by the children.

We were able to incorporate math into our study as we created the time lines and determined the number of years between events. We also used math in creating the maps showing the travels of the families and the great numbers of miles they had traveled to come to Fresno. We incorporated science as we compared the way things were done in the past—for example, the types of machines used to get work done when the parents and grandparents were young. We even discovered simple levers and pulleys in some of the modern machines we use today. We learned a lot about the visual and performing arts as we examined the various arts and crafts work done by the different cultural groups. We even practiced several types of dances taught by our fellow students or their parents. One grandfather came to school and taught tai chi as a physical exercise; some of the boys thought it rather silly until they tried it for 20 minutes. We also learned a number of new playground games from the different cultures.

The morning after the family history dinner, the children were very excited about how well the families had received their books. They had also discovered a number of new foods they liked and were ready to plan a new unit of study. Many of them had been very interested in the folktales we had read and wanted to do more of that. Several of them had been told traditional folktales by their parents and grandparents in the course of the family history interviews and wanted to write and illustrate the stories to create storybooks for their younger brothers and sisters. So began our second unit, writing and telling folktales. I immediately began to find ways to integrate other content areas into the study so I could address multiple content standards.

REFLECTING ON THE CLASSROOM EXPERIENCE

As Diane's account shows, teachers face a multitude of complex issues and judgments in their own classrooms regarding curriculum. As a teacher, Diane has a great deal of freedom (and responsibility) to decide what to teach and when to teach it, but her decisions are influenced by many forces, both past and present. We all tend to focus on the way federal, state, and local standards are being used as the basis for educational decision making, but we should also be aware of how history and tradition exert powerful influences over what is taught in schools. The "three Rs" have served as the basis for planning in U.S. schools for more than a century, and there are active and vocal groups of citizens who believe that the primary goal of K–12 schools should be to instill these basic skills in their students.

Regarding the role of education, some groups believe that schools are the custodians of the culture and that the primary goal should be to develop good citizenship and understanding of the great ideas and literature produced by Western civilization. Others believe strongly that the primary goal of a modern education is to teach students how to use reasoning, problem-solving, and communication skills as a means of learning how to learn so that they are able to gather the information they will need in their lives. Still others hold that the new wave of computer technology available to this generation makes older forms of learning obsolete, and they call for an emphasis on the use of technology in K–12 schools to prepare students for a future that will be vastly different from the present. There is also a growing trend toward creating school programs that are multidisciplinary and multicultural by design, with a new emphasis on investigation, inquiry, research, experimentation, and conflict resolution.

Diane discovered how difficult it is to plan so many different types of school programs all at once. Like many beginning teachers, she wanted to incorporate the best ideas from all of the influential groups she had read about in her teacher education program. At times, the responsibility seemed so overwhelming that she wished there was just one standard curriculum for all teachers to follow. Her task was made easier, however, because she could refer to the content standards for which she was responsible and choose activities that would help move her students toward meeting those standards.

How School Curricula Are Planned

National Standards and Federal Mandates for Curricula

Many nations have uniform standards for school curricula. When these standards exist, individual teachers plan their daily programs to coincide precisely with national expectations. In some countries, if you were able to visit several schools in various cities at the same time of the school year, you would find the students using the same textbooks and working on the same chapter as students both in other cities and in rural areas. Periodically, all children attending the schools take national examinations as a means of testing whether they have learned the requisite material and, at the same time, whether schools are accomplishing their mission of teaching the national curriculum.

Some countries, including the United States, have no such tradition of a uniform mandated national curriculum. Historically, the regulation and supervision of K–12 curriculums in the United States have resided with the states. Although many states have established curriculum guidelines and examinations, there has also been a strong public sense that the best curriculum is the one planned at the local level based on local interests, values, and resources as well as the needs of a particular group of students in each school district.

Recently, however, some school districts have been criticized by the media or by citizen watchdog groups because their students have performed badly on a variety of tests and measurements of academic progress. As a result of the public's perception that some school districts prepare students for the world much better than other school districts do, a debate is growing over the value of establishing national standards for student performance. Recently, several movements to establish national standards for the preparation of teachers and for teaching effectiveness have fostered the debate.

An initial step in improving the quality of teaching and learning was the passage of federally legislated mandates in the No Child Left Behind Act of 2001 (http://en.wikipedia. org/wiki/No Child Left Behind), which required that any school receiving federal education funding employ highly qualified teachers. The federal definition of *highly qualified teacher* does not simply mean that the teacher holds a teaching credential but that the teacher also has passed a standardized test that documents the mastery of all the subject matter he or she will teach. For elementary school teachers, this means they must demonstrate mastery of reading, writing, science, social studies, and health and physical education. A variety of national standardized assessments are being used across the states to document teachers' subject-matter competency for credentialing.

In response to the public's desire to be able to measure and compare the progress of students across the nation, Congress mandated that the U.S. Department of Education provide a set of assessment tools to measure K–12 students' subject-matter knowledge in five areas in addition to the testing of teacher candidates. The Department of Education produced a document known as the National Assessment of Educational Progress (NAEP), which is commonly referred to as the nation's report card. NAEP provides benchmarks for each subject area, describing what students should be able to do or demonstrate at various grade levels.

In July 2009, a new program, Race to the Top, was announced by President Barack Obama. This program, funded by the Department of Education's ED Recovery Act, is designed to encourage school reform. Race to the Top emphasizes the following reform areas:

- **Standards and assessments**—It encourages states to set and assess rigorous standards that prepare students for college and career. This must include standards and assessments for critical knowledge and higher-level thinking skills.

- **Teachers and leaders**—It encourages states to develop plans for attracting, supporting, and monitoring the progress of teachers and leaders in education. This includes plans both for reforming and improving teacher preparation and teacher evaluation and for rewarding effectiveness. Teacher placement is an area to be addressed, as well. The best and most talented teachers should be placed in the schools where they are most needed.

- **Effective data systems**—States are encouraged to implement integrated data systems to be used in making key decisions and improving instruction.

- **Struggling schools**—States are required to give high priority to the identification and transformation of struggling schools. Innovation and identification of effective practices are to be used in this process.

- *Education reform*. States are required to promote collaboration between educators and other stakeholders to raise student achievement and close achievement gaps. The establishment and the expansion of support for high-performing public charter schools are encouraged, as are programs for improving math and science education and for promoting other innovation and reform on an ongoing basis.

For more information about Race to the Top, go to http://racetotop.com/about-rttt.

Discussion about National Curriculum Standards

As is often the case in a vigorous multicultural democracy such as the United States, there is little agreement about the form that educational standards should take or how they should be used. Subject-area specialists, for example, argue that their disciplines are so different from each other that standardizing performance expectations across the disciplines would be impossible (Viadero, 1993).

Many other philosophical debates concern the purpose of national standards in education. Before establishing one set of universally accepted standards, educators will need to agree on issues such as whether the national standards and benchmarks ought to describe basic or minimal competency in each subject area or whether they ought to describe higher-level expectations. A national debate continues over the value of emphasizing content versus process knowledge in most subject areas, and this causes the authors of standards and benchmarks to disagree about whether to assess content knowledge or performance standards.

State Standards as Basis for Curriculum Planning

In the United States, each state has a department of education that has traditionally taken responsibility for establishing guidelines for curriculum development. Recently, these state departments of education have become much more interested in measuring achievement as well.

Currently, 49 of the 50 states have adopted content standards in K–12 programs. This movement is not without its critics, however, Brooks and Brooks (1999) observe that most standards-based reform efforts are illogical because they ignore the differences in the way that students learn and the diversity of experiences that students bring from their multicultural backgrounds. Assessing state standards for many states depends on constructing or buying standardized assessments that equate test results with student learning. These types of systems tend to reward schools whose students score well on the assessments and sanction schools whose students do not. Brooks and Brooks (1999) decry the "un-deviating, one-size-fits-all approach to teaching and assessment in states that have crowned accountability king. Requiring all students to take the same courses and pass the same tests may hold political capital for legislators and state-level educational policymakers, but it contravenes what years of painstaking research tells us about student learning" (p. 20).

Constructivists such as Brooks and Brooks (1999) believe that only by analyzing students' understandings and ways of learning and then customizing our teaching approaches to each student's cognitive processes can we hope to increase student achievement. This constructivist approach to learning and assessment of learning is closely aligned with the concept of reflective action in teaching that we propose in this textbook. Reflective action in teaching calls for teachers to use their withitness to perceive students' needs—individual student needs in this case that vary widely depending on background experiences, multiple intelligences, and physical development of the brain and nervous system. Diane's approach to the planning of units based on content standards while taking into account the needs and functioning levels of her students, described in the beginning of this chapter, is a reasonable way of addressing both sides of the debate.

Another role of state departments of education is to publish curriculum guidelines for all of the subject areas in public K–12 education. Many states revise their curriculum guidelines by inviting representative teachers and administrators from all areas of the state to form a committee responsible for considering ways to incorporate both state and subject-matter standards into meaningful curriculum outlines. The resulting documents are then published as "curriculum frameworks" and distributed to all of the school districts they serve.

Curriculum frameworks at the state level change frequently based on the latest research in education. They are also heavily influenced by political pressure and interest groups within the state. As a beginning teacher, you will be expected to become familiar with the latest curriculum frameworks for your state and implement them in your classroom.

Textbooks and Curriculum Planning

School textbooks have an enormous impact on the curriculum. Elementary school textbooks are undergoing major revisions to meet the demand for updated, active, student-centered learning rather than the older emphasis on receptive rote learning. Many of these changes are controversial, reflecting the often divisive issues that are hot topics among adults in our society.

One of the greatest controversies regarding textbooks today is the rewriting of social studies textbooks to include multiple perspectives on history. Critics of traditional textbooks suggest that they are written solely from the perspective of the white European male, and they believe students should learn history from multiple perspectives. Traditionalists believe that eliminating or ignoring content in traditional textbooks will misrepresent history and that the subject will become diluted in an effort to please every interest group. Reflective teachers attempt to clarify their own values and their own curriculum orientations and beliefs as they make decisions about the curriculum they teach.

When first-year teachers move into their classrooms, the textbooks are already there, placed in formidable rows or piled in cumbersome stacks. Novice teachers have been told about the importance of individualizing education and meeting the needs of all students in their professional preparation programs. When reality sets in, they realize that many of the materials they need to plan a highly creative program that meets the students' individual needs are not in the classroom. A less reflective teacher will, without thinking, distribute the textbooks and begin teaching on page 1, perhaps emulating former teachers, with the intent of plowing through the entire book by the end of the year.

Reflective teachers, however, are more inquisitive and more independent in their use of textbooks. They ask questions of other teachers: "How long have you been using these textbooks? How were they chosen? Which parts match the school or district curriculum guides? Which parts are most interesting to the students? What other resources are available? Where do you go to get your ideas to supplement the textbook? In your first year of teaching, how did you meet the individual needs of your students when you had only textbooks available to you?"

Less reflective teachers tend to assume without question that the "approved" or "correct" curriculum is the one found in textbooks because it is written by "experts." They attempt to deliver the curriculum as written, without questioning its effects or adapting it to the students' needs and interests.

More reflective teachers consider decisions about curriculum planning to be within their jurisdiction, their domain of decision making. They consult with others, but they take responsibility for deciding which parts of a textbook to use to meet the needs of their own particular class and to match the goals and learning outcomes their state and local curriculum committees establish.

Reflective teachers are seldom satisfied to use textbooks alone. They know that students must have a motivation to search for meaning and create their own understanding of the world of ideas. "When students want to know more about an idea, a topic, or an entire discipline, they put more cognitive energy into classroom investigations and discussions and study more on their own," state Brooks and Brooks (1999, p. 22). Fortunately, there are many *trade books*, books not written as textbooks, now available on many topics related to science, social studies, mathematics, and literature that are written at a variety of reading levels. Many of these are beautifully illustrated, sometimes with full-color photographs, and add much depth to any study in the classroom. Some schools have a fund that can be used for the purchase of these types of books. Teachers often collect *text sets*, sets of books on one topic or by one author, that can be used to add multiple perspectives to the unit studies.

Other Influences Affecting Curriculum Development

The notion that the learner's needs must be satisfied in order to be a successful teacher is not a new idea. Ralph Tyler (1949) observed this in his earliest work. Since then, there has been consistent support for Tyler's elegant (simple but not simplistic) curriculum planning method. He proposed four fundamental questions that should be considered in planning any curriculum (1949, p. 1):

1. What educational purposes should the school seek to attain?
2. What educational experiences are likely to attain these purposes?
3. How can these educational experiences be effectively organized?
4. How can we determine whether these purposes are being attained?

Reflective educators are likely to use Tyler's basic principles in planning, organizing, and evaluating their programs because the principles are remarkably similar to the process of reflective thinking. Essentially, he suggests that teachers begin curriculum planning by perceiving the needs of students, gathering information, making a judgment about an educational purpose, selecting and organizing the strategies to be used, and then evaluating the effectiveness of their curriculum plan by perceiving its effects on their students. These are very similar processes to those outlined in the model of reflective action presented in Chapter One.

Although reflective teachers are not likely to memorize Tyler's four questions word for word, they are likely to carry with them the fundamental notion of each:

1. What shall we teach?
2. How shall we teach it?
3. How shall we organize it?
4. How shall we evaluate it?

With the adoption of state-mandated standards, question 1 is answered for us. However, reflective teachers must still address questions 2 through 4 with respect to the needs and functioning levels of their students. Reflective teachers ask themselves these questions each year because they have probably noticed subtle or dramatic changes in their communities, subject-matter materials, students, or themselves from year to year that cause them to reexamine their curricula. On reexamination, they may confirm that they want to continue to teach the same curriculum in the same way or that they want to modify some aspects of it. As teachers grow in experience and skills, most greet each new year as an opportunity to improve on what they accomplished the previous year. Rather than continue to teach the same subjects in the same ways year after year, reflective teachers often experiment with new ways of teaching and organizing the curriculum.

An obvious contrast between more reflective and less reflective teachers is that after teaching for 20 years, a reflective teacher has accumulated 20 years of experience, whereas a less reflective teacher is likely to have repeated 1 year of experience 20 times. Reflective teachers want to have an active role in the decision-making processes in their schools, and curricular decisions are the ones that count the most. They also display a strong sense of responsibility for making good curriculum choices and decisions, ones that will ultimately result in valuable growth and learning. The advent of the use of more and more technology in the classroom has also added immeasurably to the resources available for educating and motivating students. Teachers now have a myriad of technological options literally at their fingertips to address the wide variety of student learning styles, student interests, and educational requirements in their classrooms.

Planning Units to Fit Your Curriculum

No other model of curriculum development involves teachers in a more active and professional capacity than the planning, teaching, and evaluation of thematic curriculum units. They appeal greatly to reflective teachers who want to be part of the decision-making process and to use their own creative ideas and methods. However, planning thematic curriculum units also adds greatly to the responsibility of classroom teachers. To create a successful unit, teachers must be willing to explore the state-mandated standards, gather a wide variety of information, and create an excellent knowledge base about the topics they have chosen so that the learning experiences they plan will be based on accurate and interesting information. They must also be willing to work with their colleagues to make sure that their curriculum units do not repeat or skip over important material in the elementary curriculum. Care must be taken to align their units with what was covered in earlier grades and what their students will learn in subsequent years.

Even when teachers decide to create their own thematic curriculum units to translate curricular visions into actual classroom experiences, many are not certain how to do that or what to cover in each unit. In this chapter, we examine how teachers decide what units to teach and how they organize the learning experiences in a curriculum unit to ensure that students acquire the knowledge, skills, and processes that are intended.

Building Units Based on State Standards: Backward Mapping

The term *backward mapping* describes the reversal of traditional curriculum planning in which the teacher starts with textbook-driven activities and concludes with a wide range of learning outcomes. With backward mapping, the teacher begins with the state standards—what she wants the students to accomplish—and builds the lessons, activities, and assessments based on those standards. Backward mapping follows a sequence of steps that supports the teacher's decision-making process:

Step 1. Select and analyze the standards(s) to be met.

Step 2. Select or design an assessment to use so that students can demonstrate mastery of the standard(s). This assessment can be determined by having the students participate in an activity that can be observed to determine their performance levels.

Step 3. Identify what students must know and be able to do in order to perform well on the assessment.

Step 4. Plan lessons and implement them, providing all students with opportunities to acquire and practice the skills and knowledge needed to succeed on the planned assessment.

Step 5. Assess students and plan further instruction or individual support, as needed.

As you will see, these steps in backward mapping fit well with the steps of reflective action planning, which also begins with examining the state curriculum standards.

Deciding on Unit Topics

A single teacher can work alone or with colleagues to translate state and local curriculum standards into units of study. Working alone, a single teacher analyzes state and local standards to be implemented at that grade level in math, science, social studies, language arts, and fine arts, and he or she also examines the curriculum materials supplied by the school district, looking for a theme. The teacher may choose to look for unit topics within a subject, such as a math unit on fractions, a science unit on magnets and electricity, or a social studies unit on the electoral process. Other units may be interdisciplinary, that is, designed to include information and materials from several subjects at one time. For example, a theme titled "Change" may include learning experiences in science, math, social studies, and literature.

When teachers opt to collaborate with colleagues, such as those at the same grade level, their combined knowledge and ideas are likely to result in a much more comprehensive set of units and a greater variety of learning experiences. Whether a teacher works alone or with a team, the first step remains deciding on a series of curriculum units that corresponds to the major educational goals for that grade level.

When a unit topic to teach comes to your mind, you need to reflect on whether it is appropriate according to several criteria. Roberts and Kellough (2000) suggest that you consider the following questions: Is this theme one that has a proper length (not too short or too long)? Will you be able to find good materials and resources on this subject? Does the theme have a broad real-life application? Does the theme have substance? Is it worth spending time on this topic? Will the students be interested in this topic and be motivated to learn about it?

Wiggins and McTighe (2005) recommend using a backward design for unit planning. What are the goals or standards that you want to accomplish, and how can your unit plan achieve these goals and meet these standards? As previously stated, this approach also requires you to think about the evidence that will prove that your students have met the standards. Evidence of achievement is usually gathered through some type of assessment of learning or understanding. Therefore, using the backward mapping approach for your unit plan, you will want to (1) identify the desired results, (2) determine what evidence can measure or assess the accomplishment of these results by your students, and (3) plan the learning experiences and methods of instruction you will use in your unit plan.

When teachers select unit topics, Wiggins and McTighe (2005) recommend that the focus be on a topic that will result in students gaining "enduring big ideas [about the subject] that have lasting value beyond the classroom" rather than students simply learning facts or skills (p. 78). For example, if you want to plan a unit on nutrition, they suggest that you create a unit that will result in students learning that a balanced diet contributes to both physical and mental health throughout their lifetime. Learning this "enduring big idea" is more important than simply having students learn which foods fit into the various food groups.

Creating a Curriculum Unit Using Reflective Actions

To create a curriculum unit based on reflective actions, you should consult your state standards for the subjects that you want to include in your unit. When reflective teachers approach the development of a curriculum unit, they consider their long-term goals for that subject or subjects. By consulting the state standards for the subjects to be included in the unit, you can be confident that your long-term goals and those in the standards are congruent. In social studies, for example, you may begin with some questions: "What are my major social studies goals this year? What are the state standards in social studies that support and coincide with my goals? What should I include in this unit of study to accomplish these goals?" Or you may begin by considering the core outcomes your students are expected to achieve during the year and then plan curriculum units that will encourage your students to learn the content and enhance the skills that make up those outcomes. Regardless of the area of study, there are several steps in planning a curriculum unit based on reflective action.

CONSIDER WHAT STUDENTS ALREADY KNOW.   As a reflective teacher, you consider and reflect on the skills and knowledge the students will need to bring to the unit to be successful in learning new material. Pretest your students to assess their present knowledge and skills. Some may have already mastered most of the content you intend to teach, so consider ways to challenge them by compacting the curriculum so that they can go on to more challenging material. Other students may have serious gaps in their knowledge or may lack background experiences or language structures necessary to successfully participate in the planned activities; consider how you will scaffold the new material to make it accessible to them.

Teachers who think and plan using the reflective actions described in Chapter One are likely to consider the cues they perceive from their students' interests and talents when planning thematic units. As they plan curriculum, teachers tend to ask themselves: "What do my students need to learn? How do they enjoy working? What learning experiences will motivate my students to become actively engaged in the learning process? What language skills and vocabulary will need to be taught so that students can express their newly acquired knowledge?"

CREATE AN INITIAL PLAN FOR THE UNIT. Once they have decided on a topic, teachers who use reflective actions then sketch out a preliminary draft of a unit and begin to consider some interesting ways to teach it. The first draft may resemble a concept web, or it may be based on something they have read in a curriculum guide, seen online, or recalled from their own school experiences.

REFLECT ON THE INITIAL PLAN AND WORK TO MAKE IT FIT THE NEEDS OF STUDENTS. Reflective teachers are likely to begin to establish some criteria for selecting certain content or methods while omitting others. As a reflective teacher, you consider what to include and what to exclude by asking yourself: "What knowledge and skills am I responsible for teaching at my grade level, and how can I help my students understand the application of this content to their success in school or in life? How can this curriculum assist them in developing what they need most? What attitudes do I want to instill in my students? How can this unit help them attain those attitudes? What values do I want to model for my students during this curriculum unit? How can I best model those values for them?"

RESEARCH AND CONFER WITH COLLEAGUES. At many points along the way, reflective teachers are likely to do additional research on the subject or on teaching methods they can include in their new unit. They are also likely to talk with other trusted colleagues about how they have taught the same subject. Many teachers share their unit plans with others, but most agree that sharing a unit plan is very much like sharing their recipes for making spaghetti sauce—no two sauces or units are identical. Still, a trusted colleague can point out things for the beginning teacher to consider, share strategies for motivating student interest, and suggest new materials to include in the unit.

REVISE THE UNIT. As a reflective teacher who has researched the topic and conferred with colleagues, you might then ask: "What changes have occurred to me as a result of my interactions with colleagues? Do I have a new and original way to approach the topic? Have my basic goals changed?" Teachers who use reflective action tend to enjoy the process of combining all the content materials and methods they have learned during planning into an original set of learning experiences that fits their own teaching style and the needs of their students. No two thematic units are ever alike. Even when teachers plan together up to this point, they are likely to interpret the materials they have gathered differently and add their own unique spin to the way they teach the unit.

Throughout the process of planning and teaching the unit, teachers who use reflective action are likely to be asking themselves: "How can I adapt the materials I have available to meet my goals? What new instructional materials shall I create to teach this material effectively? What risks are possible if I try to teach this unit in my own way? Which risks am I willing to take? What gains are possible if I take risks? Do the possible gains outweigh the risks?"

During a thematic unit, reflective teachers create original bulletin boards, group activities, work or activity sheets, processes for promoting student interaction, methods to assess student accomplishments, and ways to allow their students to perform or display what they have learned. These teachers are also carefully examining standards across disciplines. In planning a social studies unit, for example, many standards in reading and writing, science and mathematics, visual and performing arts, and so on can be infused into the planned unit activities. If there are English language learners in the class, then language objectives must be included in each of the activities to ensure their full participation and success. For many reflective teachers, these opportunities for creativity are some of the most important sources of pride and are often cited as some of the most significant perks of their careers.

CONSIDER ALTERNATE PLANS. All teachers encounter challenges in teaching and managing their classrooms. Teachers who use reflective actions are able to prevent some of these challenges because they try to imagine the consequences of their plans before putting them into action. For example, if you are planning to introduce innovative learning materials to motivate students, you will want to consider what types of management procedures will be needed for distributing and using these materials. The introduction of new and interesting materials may need to include time for the students to explore the materials before they are asked to implement their use in activities.

Teachers who use reflective actions in their thinking and planning anticipate the students' need to explore. Making your expectations very clear will assist in arriving at a positive outcome in student interactions with materials. If an unexpected problem arises, teachers use withitness in the midst of the problem to observe what is happening and respond appropriately. Afterward, they talk both with the students and with their colleagues to reframe the problem and create a new plan, if necessary.

PUT THE PLAN INTO ACTION AND GET STUDENT FEEDBACK. As a reflective teacher, the day you present your new unit plan to your students is an exciting day for you and your class. There is a sense of heightened expectations as you reveal the plan. Students may have a lot of questions, and you may be able to answer some, but not all, of their questions right away. You use withitness during the initial presentation to get feedback from your most important critics: your students. They will give you cues as they react to the plan with excitement, confusion, fear, or increased motivation to learn. You can also discuss the first day's presentation with your colleagues and get ideas about how to reframe the plan for yourself or for your students. After the first day, you will be even better equipped to rethink and adjust certain parts of the plan. If your students react with fear or confusion, you can make changes now, before it is too late. If they react with excitement, you can consider adding even more challenging materials to the plan.

Reflective teachers are also able to laugh at their own mistakes and learn from their errors in judgment without an overwhelming fear of the consequences or feelings of guilt. As they plan their thematic units, they are likely to encounter difficulties in locating suitable materials. When this happens, they become very good at scrounging for the materials they need, or they substitute other materials and go on teaching.

When they begin to teach their units, some of the lessons they planned are likely to turn out quite differently than they expected, but they simply assess, regroup, and reteach as needed. As the unit nears completion, they may discover that, due to their students' choices and actions, some unplanned effects have occurred. These are simply accounted for and evaluated along with the outcomes that were planned.

Throughout the process of planning, organizing, teaching, and evaluating a thematic unit, good communication skills are necessary. Reflective teachers must often persuade their colleagues or administrators to allow them to take time, spend money, take certain risks, and establish certain priorities to teach their thematic units the way they want. Assertiveness is a very important trait in curriculum development, especially considering the different curriculum orientations that various members of the faculty adopt. The ability to clearly connect the unit and its outcomes to established and mandated standards continues to be a powerful influence on these types of decisions.

Conflicts may arise with students as well. When reflective teachers introduce a creative new way to learn a difficult subject, some students may react by stating their own preferences. When this occurs, teachers who use reflective actions simply explore new ideas with the students and attempt to address the needs of the students and the possibility of working those needs into revised approaches and activities within the unit plan.

Sequencing Learning Experiences in a Curriculum Unit

Practically speaking, the process of developing a curriculum unit includes the following eight tasks:

1. Defining the topics and subject matter to be covered in the unit
2. Defining the cognitive processes and affective goals or outcomes that tell what students will gain and be able to do as a result
3. Outlining the major concepts that will be covered
4. Gathering resources that can be used in planning and teaching
5. Brainstorming learning activities and experiences that can be used in the unit
6. Organizing the ideas and activities into a meaningful sequence
7. Planning lesson plans that follow the sequence
8. Planning evaluation processes that will be used to measure student achievement and satisfaction

Analysis will reveal that these statements correspond to Tyler's (1949) four questions. Tasks 1, 2, and 3 pertain to his question, "What shall we teach?" Tasks 4 and 5 relate to his question, "How shall we teach it?" Tasks 6 and 7 respond to his question, "How shall we organize it?" Task 8 answers his question, "How shall we evaluate it?"

When seen in print, these eight tasks appear to depict an orderly process, but curriculum planning is rarely such a linear activity. Instead, teachers find themselves starting at various points in this process. They skip or go back and forth between these tasks as ideas occur to them. For example, a team member may begin a discussion by showing a resource book with a particular learning activity that could be taught as part of the new unit. Discussions may skip from activities to goals to concepts to evaluation to organization. Nothing is wrong with this nonlinear process as long as teachers are responsible enough to reflect on the overall plan to determine if all of Tyler's questions have been addressed fully and adequately. When the plan is complete, it is important to review it and ask yourself: "What are the outcomes I expect from this unit? Are the learning experiences directly related to the outcomes? Is my organization of activities going to make it possible for my students to achieve my outcomes? Are the assessment systems I've established going to measure the extent to which the students have accomplished the outcomes?"

Thematic units vary in types of learning experiences and in organization. Some subjects, such as math, are organized sequentially, but others are not. The types of learning experiences also vary greatly depending on the subject, the resources available, and the creativity or risk taking of the teacher.

Most teachers use the textbook or a district curriculum guide as the basis for planning and as an important resource. *Do not limit yourself to a single textbook as the source of all information in planning your unit or in teaching it.* A good textbook can be a valuable resource for you as you plan and for your students as they learn about the topic, but a rich and motivating unit plan will contain many other elements.

Supplemental reading materials from libraries or bookstores might include biographies, histories, novels, short stories, plays, poems, newspapers, magazines, how-to books, and a myriad of other printed materials. Other resources to consider are films, videotapes, audiotapes, and computer programs on topics that relate to your unit. Many interesting student-centered computer programs allow your students to have simulated experiences, solve problems, and make decisions as if they were involved in the event themselves. A good example is the computer game Oregon Trail II, distributed by Softkey International, Boston, in which the student travels along the Oregon Trail, making decisions about what supplies to buy, when and where to stop along the way, and how to handle emergencies. This program can enrich a unit on

westward expansion by providing more experiences involving problem solving and critical thinking than reading and discussion could ever yield.

Many educational games also provide students with simulated experiences. Some are board games that can be purchased in a good toy store or bookstore; others are more specialized learning games sold by educational publishers or distributors. Your school district probably receives hundreds of catalogs from educational publishers. Locate them and find out about the many manipulative and simulation games available on your topic.

Consider field trips that will provide your students with experiences beyond the four walls of the classroom. Which museums have exhibits related to your topic? A simple walk through a neighborhood to look for evidence of pollution or to view variations in architecture can add depth to your unit. If you cannot travel, consider inviting a guest to speak to your students about the topic. Sometimes parents are excellent resources and are willing to talk about their careers or other interests.

In thinking about how to organize a unit, many reflective teachers prefer to begin with a highly motivating activity such as a field trip, a guest speaker, a simulation game, a hands-on experiment, or a film. They know that when the students' initial experience with a topic is stimulating and involving, interest and curiosity are aroused. The next several lessons in the unit are frequently planned at the knowledge and comprehension levels of Bloom's taxonomy to provide students with basic facts and concepts so that they can build a substantial knowledge base and understanding of the topic. After establishing the knowledge base, further learning experiences can be designed at the application, analysis, synthesis, and evaluation levels to ensure that the students are able to think critically and creatively about the subject. This model of unit planning is not universal, nor is it the only logical sequence, but it can be adapted to fit many topics and subjects with excellent results.

Designing the Curriculum to Reflect Multicultural Values

One of the enduring controversies in curriculum planning is how to design a curriculum that accurately reflects and honors the wide variety of cultural values represented by students in our schools and communities. James Banks, director of the Center for Multicultural Education at the University of Washington, has similar goals when he advises teachers to redesign their curricula to promote "cultural excellence."

Banks (1992) believes that the redesigned curriculum should describe the needs and contributions of all Americans and include their struggles, hopes, and dreams. It should not be an add-on to the existing curriculum but should be an integral part of every subject taught. Ask students to reflect on these areas; explain that when students can answer these questions, they will be better equipped to function in their own world as well as in the larger community that may be populated by people who answer the same questions very differently.

To develop a multicultural curriculum for your classroom regardless of what subject you teach, plan learning experiences that reflect the concerns of the diverse cultural groups that make up the class, using questions such as, "Who am I? Where have I been? What do I hope for?" Banks believes that the school and the community provide important opportunities for students, parents, and teachers to learn about differing views. Encourage students to share their different perspectives and opinions; show them that you value the different ways they solve problems and view the world around them.

Reissman (1994) recommends that as you assign learning tasks, consider how each assignment can be used to strengthen intergroup understandings, respect for each other's cultures, and the development of skills that will later be needed in community, national, and global citizenship. Her book, titled *The Evolving Multicultural Classroom*, may be a valuable resource in your curriculum planning. According to Sleeter and Grant, students "develop knowledge by interacting mentally and to some extent physically with people and objects around them. This interaction requires active involvement. Knowledge that is poured into a passive mind is quickly forgotten" (1994, p. 218).

Another benefit of the multidisciplinary curriculum is that it leads teachers to share what they are doing and work together to plan learning experiences. Teachers who come to school, close the doors of their classrooms, and teach in isolation are becoming a thing of the past. For example, when doing curriculum planning, many districts team beginning teachers with experienced teachers to develop and share curriculum materials.

This new trend has created an environment in which teachers do not structure their curricula into separate blocks of time. As Beane (1991) points out, when confronted with a problem, individuals do not say, "Now which part of this is science and which part of this is language arts?" Instead, people address problems with a multidisciplinary approach and use whatever resources and content they need to resolve them.

In his analysis of subject-matter teaching, Brophy (1992) emphasizes the importance of teaching fewer topics with more depth, a practice that allows students to have a greater understanding of each topic and lets teachers emphasize higher-order applications. Brophy indicates that state curriculum guides and textbooks should be modified to accomplish this task, and in many cases they are being revised to include a greater emphasis on integrated curricula.

Planning Curriculum for a Multicultural, Bilingual Classroom

Maria Cortes teaches fifth grade in Madera, California. Her students are all native Spanish speakers, and most speak Spanish at home. Maria takes an unusual approach in her bilingual classroom. Because most of her students speak Spanish at home, she begins the day in Spanish at the beginning of the year. She gradually transitions to English as the day progresses until she's teaching mostly in English, with occasional explanations in Spanish when she wants to clear up some confusion in her students or when she wants to make comparisons between the way something is expressed in the two languages.

Maria chose her year-long theme, "Making a New Nation," from the history/social sciences standards and infuses her instruction in reading, language arts, math, and science. Maria feels that this theme is especially appropriate for her students since they are all first- or second-generation immigrants from Mexico. Following is Maria's discussion of her social studies unit.

I chose to base my year-long theme on the social studies standards because social studies is my personal passion and also because my students can relate to the motivations and problems of immigrants as they move into a new culture. I can also find many literature selections published in both English and Spanish that relate to this social studies topic.

One of my main objectives is to make sure that my students maintain their Spanish fluency and literacy while gaining English fluency and literacy. By the end of the fifth grade, most of my students are truly bilingual and biliterate. Our class library has an equal number of books in Spanish and English.

Many of my colleagues teach one day in Spanish and alternate days in English. We begin our day in Spanish and switch to English after lunch at the beginning of the year. By Christmas, I have gradually moved to more English in the morning and tend to do introductory lessons in Spanish and follow-up lessons in English. I always review English vocabulary as part of lessons taught in Spanish.

A number of the standards in fifth grade lend themselves to class simulation activities. We relate some of the concepts taught to personal experiences:

- *When we study immigrant patterns, we interview our parents and grandparents to document the when, how, and why they came to Madera.*
- *When we study conflict and cooperation with Native Americans, we explore conflicts in culture they and their families have experienced.*
- *When we study town meetings and assemblies, we replicate them by having class meetings to resolve some class problems.*
- *When we study the writing of the Constitution, we actually write a class constitution.*

- *When we study Mexican settlement of the west, we actually plot the information we gained from our families onto the maps used in our study.*
- *When we study states and capitals, we write letters to students in different states and compare what we are studying to what they study in their states. We exchange digital photographs of our schools and cities and take a virtual tour of their capital cities whenever one is available online.*

Students in my class can choose to read books in English or Spanish but must read in both languages. They tend to alternate languages for both their reading and their book reports. We have lessons in both English and Spanish grammar. I find that the comparison of the two tends to help them understand and remember the rules for both. Most of my students are most comfortable writing in English, but they are required to complete a Spanish writing piece at least once a week. I keep reminding them about how marketable they will be as completely bilingual, biliterate adults. They are opening up many job opportunities by improving their Spanish literacy.

I have developed an online relationship with two elementary teachers in Mexico, and we discuss what students are reading in fifth grade there. I find books in Spanish for my students that are recommended by my online Mexican teacher friends. This serves to open conversations between students comparing Mexican culture to American culture and has led to some research in how things are different in other cultures, as well.

Tailoring Curricular Time Lines to Fit Goals and Outcome Statements

Time is the scarcest resource in school. Reflective teachers who organize time wisely are more successful in delivering the curriculum they have planned than teachers who fail to take time into consideration. Teachers who simply start each subject on page 1 of every textbook and hope to finish the text by June are frequently surprised by the lack of time. In some cases, they finish a text early in the year, but more often the school year ends without students ever getting to the subjects at the back of the textbook. In mathematics, some classes never cover geometry year after year; in social studies, history after the Civil War is often crammed into a few short lessons at the end of the year.

Will you be satisfied if this happens in your classroom? If not, you can prevent it by preplanning the time you will give to each element or subtopic of each subject area you are going to teach. This may seem like an overwhelming task at first, but it can be less threatening if you understand that you are not required to plan every outcome and objective for every subject before the year begins. You need to give the entire curriculum an overview and determine the number of days or weeks you will allot to each element.

Begin by examining the standards for your grade level and comparing them to the textbooks in your classroom, looking at the way in which they are organized. Most books are divided into units, each covering a single topic or collection of related topics within the academic subject. Mathematics books are likely to contain units such as place value, operations, measuring, and geometry; history books are divided into units on exploring, settling the new frontier, and creating government; and English books contain units such as listening, writing, and speaking.

Curriculum units are excellent planning devices because they show students how facts, skills, concepts, and applications of ideas are related. The alternatives to planning with units are either planning a single continuous yearlong sequence of experiences or planning unconnected and unrelated daily experiences. Units will be used as the basis for planning throughout the rest of this book.

Decide if the units in your school's textbooks are valuable and important as well as whether you agree with the way they are organized and the quality of learning experiences they contain. Consider whether using a particular textbook will result in achieving the state-mandated standards. Will it result in achieving the goals and outcomes you have for your class? If the textbook learning experiences match your outcomes and the state standards, you can plan the year to coincide with the sequence of units in the book.

If the textbook does not coincide with your planned outcomes or if you disagree with the quality or the organizational pattern of the book, you have several options. In reviewing the textbooks, you must also decide if the textbooks fit your students and whether they respond to the learning needs of your students. You can plan to use the book but present the units in a different order. You can delete units, or you can use some units in the book as they are written but supplement with other materials for additional units not covered or inadequately covered in the book. The most adventuresome and creative teachers may even decide to use the textbook only as a resource and plan original teaching units for the subject. They then search bookstores and the Internet for resources.

In any case, you should carefully consider the amount of time you want to allot to each unit you plan to teach. Create a time line, chart, or calendar for each subject, and use it as you judge how much time to spend on each subtopic. For time line planning, you can divide the school year into weeks, months, or quarters. For a subject such as mathematics, you may think about the year as a total of 36 weeks and allot varying numbers of weeks to each math topic you want to cover during the year. For a subject such as language arts, you might think of the school year as 8 months long and create eight different units that involve students in listening, speaking, writing, and reading activities. You may divide the year into four quarters for subjects such as science or social studies, with four major units planned for the year. These examples are only suggestions. Each subject can be subdivided into any time segments, or you may combine subjects into interdisciplinary units that involve students in mathematics, science, and language arts activities under one combined topic for a longer period of time.

Making reasonable and professional judgments about time line planning depends on having information about your students' prior knowledge and their history of success or failure before the year begins. The pace of your curriculum depends to some degree on the skills and knowledge your students have acquired before you meet them. But your own expectation for their success is also important. You want to avoid the trap many teachers fall into of reviewing basic skills all year because a majority of their students have been unsuccessful in the past. If you expect them to succeed in your curriculum and be ready to move on to new challenges, then you should provide them with new challenges. They are much more likely to respond to your positive expectations.

The time lines you create at the beginning of the year need not be rigid and unchanging. They are guidelines based on the best knowledge you have at the time. As the year progresses, you will undoubtedly have reasons to change your original time line. Students' needs, interests, and successes will cause you to alter the pace of the original plan. Current events in the country, your local community, or your classroom may cause you to add a new unit to your plan. Interactions with other faculty members may bring you fresh insights about how you want to organize the way you allocate time in your classroom.

Using Long-Term Curriculum Planning

Long-term curriculum planning, either individually or collectively, is an important job for teachers. If you are teaching in a self-contained classroom, you have the freedom to write your own curriculum as long as it relates to the district and state standards and responds to the learning needs of your students. If you are working in a team-teaching school, you will need to articulate your vision of curriculum to your teammates and adjust yours to include their ideas as well as your own. In either case, the curriculum you create will improve with experience. As you see the effects of your original planning and assess your students' mastery of the standards, you will reflect on your planning and find ways to improve it with each succeeding year.

Hayes-Jacobs (1997) recommends that faculty members in a school work together to map the curriculum so that everyone on the staff knows what is actually going on in classrooms. This strategy requires teachers to meet and create the maps for each subject area or grade level. The maps include a brief description of the content to be covered, a description of the processes and skills to be emphasized, and the type of assessments to be used to demonstrate that students have achieved the goals and met the standards that apply.

When you begin teaching, you may be assigned to a curriculum task force or planning committee. In discussions with your colleagues, you are likely to gain new insights and information, but you may also experience frustration with points of view that differ from your own ideas, which come from a different perspective. Be prepared to speak assertively about your own ideas and beliefs. You may be the one to suggest innovative ways of dividing the curriculum into units. Although your ideas may meet skepticism or resistance from some teachers, it is quite appropriate for you to articulate them, because schools rely on fresh ideas from faculty members with the most recent college or university training to enhance the curriculum and to create positive innovations and change.

Example of Long-Term Curriculum Planning

LANGUAGE ARTS PLANNING FOR THE PRIMARY GRADES. The language arts curriculum of the twenty-first century places roughly equal emphasis on cognitive, affective, and psychomotor outcomes. Teachers now tend to believe that the best environment for learning is one that enhances a child's love of reading, writing, speaking, listening, and being creative. Teachers also know that students must master the basic skills of phonics, sentence construction, and word usage to be proficient readers and writers. In an integrated language arts curriculum, students listen to or read literary works, write in journals, participate in editing groups, and speak for a variety of purposes. They also have skills lessons to master the proper grammar, punctuation, spelling, and other conventions of the English language.

As a primary-grade teacher in Charlestown, West Virginia, Jenny Bishop and her colleagues planned this integrated curriculum together. Jenny offers the following explanation.

> We began our plan by deciding that we would use thematic units to accomplish the state outcomes. We quickly discovered that language arts cannot be separated from science, social studies, and mathematics when you use a unit approach, so we incorporated those areas into our planning. All of us had attended numerous classes and workshops on using thematic units and had read every book we could find on the subject of using an integrated language arts curriculum in the classroom. But now it was time to sit down and make our plan for the coming school year. We began by going through the science, mathematics, and social studies curriculum guides to familiarize ourselves with what had to be covered in those areas at our grade level. We then studied the language arts standards. We chose to teach one or two thematic units a month depending on the length of the units.

Examples of Thematic Units

The following sections illustrate the processes teachers use as they select, order, and create unit plans in several subjects from the elementary curriculum. Because each teacher has a personal curriculum orientation and philosophy, the process of decision making is more complex when teachers plan together than when they plan alone. The following examples demonstrate how teachers create their own curriculum units and what they put down on paper to record their plans for teaching. You will notice many variations in the way units are created and what they contain depending on what their purposes are and what philosophies and values the teachers who create them have.

Multidisciplinary Primary Unit

Adams (1999) suggests that multidisciplinary units are the way to develop literacy across the curriculum. Literacy is much more than reading in today's educational environment; it is also concerned with promoting mathematical, historical, social, and scientific literacy.

To create such units, teachers frequently choose themes or topics and plan learning experiences that involve students in reading, writing, speaking, doing science investigations, solving math problems, enjoying music, and experiencing art. A single teacher can certainly plan and teach a multidisciplinary unit, but we have found that the units planned by two to four teachers are often more exciting because they incorporate each teacher's different perspectives and strengths. For example, at Eastside Elementary in Charleston, West Virginia, primary-grade teachers often plan their language thematic units together. Jenny, along with Doris Mathis and Karen Knox, recently planned an interdisciplinary unit titled "Fall," highlighting the life cycles of plants and animals.

They begin with State of West Virginia language arts standards that ask students to use reading strategies to aid comprehension and fluency. The standards ask teacher to address setting purposes for reading, making predictions, and making personal connections to text. The standards also ask teachers to create opportunities to infer meanings and interpret them.

Jenny, Doris, and Karen also know that teachers often have difficulty fitting in all the subjects of their busy curricula. They find that by using a thematic unit, they can teach several subjects simultaneously. To plan a unit, these teachers use a graphic organizer known as a *planning web*. They sit down with a large piece of paper and write the thematic topic in the middle of the page. They add the various disciplines they want to cover at different positions on the paper and then brainstorm learning experiences that fit the topic under the appropriate subject areas. One of their planning webs is shown in Figure 4.1.

Through their observations of the students they teach, the three teachers learned that, in the minds of primary-grade students, reading and writing are closely related. Their interdisciplinary thematic units allow students to read, write, and investigate interesting topics such as caterpillars, cookies, and planets. In each unit, they select appropriate topic-specific children's books of fiction, nonfiction, and poetry and locate songs on the topics whenever possible. Skill teaching is embedded in the unit within the context of literature, poetry, or music. The science and social studies facts and concepts are easily mastered by students when they are presented in the context of hands-on experiments and are reinforced by illustrated stories, poems, and songs. Math concepts are introduced by counting, measuring, sequencing, and patterning games and activities appropriate to each unit. Figure 4.2 shows a written plan for the unit on changes describing some of the specific learning experiences and how the unit is evaluated.

Figure 4.1   Planning web for a thematic unit.

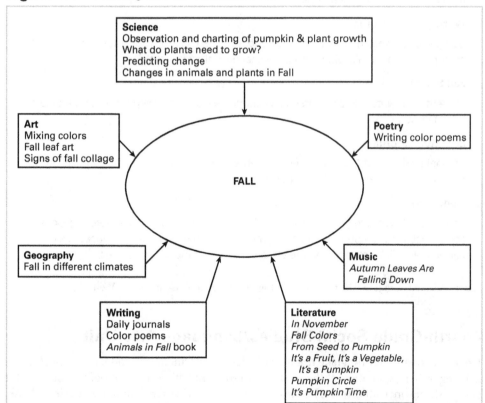

Source: Adapted from Jenny Bishop, Eastside Elementary School, Charlestown, West Virginia.

Figure 4.2 A multidisciplinary primary unit titled "Fall."

Description. This unit was planned for a group of students ages 5 to 7 years. The purpose of the unit was to further the students' understanding of the changes in climate, plants, and animals in fall.

- **Cognitive goal.** Students will demonstrate understanding of the changes that take place when seasons change and how geography makes a difference in climate.
- **Affective goal.** Students will accept the integration of learning and change as natural parts of their lives.
- **Psychomotor goal.** Students will use observations skills as part of learning. They will use reading and writing to document their observations and express their creativity.

Activity: Planting and Observing the Growth of Pumpkin Vines

Students will plant pumpkin seeds and document the growth of the vines and pumpkins through observation journals. They will also experience the removal of seeds from a pumpkin so that they understand where we get the seeds.

Children's Literature

A collection of books on fall will be used in this unit. Some books can be read by the students. Others will be read aloud by the teacher.

Art Activities

Students will collect pictures from magazines that show things related to fall and fall scenes. They will create fall collages with their pictures.

Students will create fall pictures with fall colors after an activity where they mix a variety of colors for their pictures.

Students will collect fall leaves on a nature walk around the school grounds and then use the leaves to create pictures.

Writing Color Poems

Using examples from *Hailstones and Halibut Bones* (O'Neill, 1989), students will write color poems about fall colors, using fall scenes in their poems.

Fall Songs

Students will write and sing verses of Autumn Leaves Are Falling Down to the tune of London Bridge.

Literature Journals

Students will collect facts about fall and write about them in their daily journals based on reading and hearing books about fall.

Geography

Students will gain understanding of the effects of weather on fall in different geographic areas. Websites will be viewed on the interactive whiteboard, and the locations of the fall pictures will be mapped on the classroom map of the United States.

Source: Adapted from Jenny Bishop, Eastside Elementary School, Charlestown, West Virginia.

Fourth-Grade Social Studies/Language Arts Unit

Janet Gengosian, a fourth-grade teacher at Greenberg Elementary School in Fresno, California, begins her exploration of the westward movement with a series of books related to the gold rush era in California. The first of the books, *Nine for California* (Levitin, 1996), describes a family's trip across the broad expanse of middle and western America on a stagecoach to join their father, who was already working in the goldfields of California. The second in the series, *Boom Town* (Levitin, 1998), takes a look at the growth of a small town centered on the mining activities, taking into account the ideas of supply and demand and a variety of economic interests. The third book in the series, *Taking Charge* (Levitin, 1999), gives an account of the responsibilities of maintaining a family in the early days of a boom-town. It provides an opportunity to contrast children's lives of the past with those of today. Janet chose this series of books because she can use them to explore a great variety of the content contained in the history/social studies standards in the context of high-interest stories. They also provide opportunities for active learning strategies for the children through simulations, active vocabulary role play, reader's theater, and so forth.

Janet's planning begins with reviewing both the history/social science standards and the reading/language arts standards for the fourth grade. She then begins to gather support materials for her California history unit, which will begin with simulation based on *Nine for California*. She plans to come dressed as the character of the mother in the book. The students will begin simulation journals by writing a daily entry as the story unfolds day by day during the 21-day stagecoach trip to California. She also includes activities such as mapping the family's route across the country; these maps will include topographic features encountered in their journey. Janet plans to integrate a number of the history/social science standards related to the westward movement, the gold rush, and basic economics into this study.

Under the reading/language arts standards, Janet addresses a number of standards related to comparing and contrasting information from several sources and writing narratives based on experiences and simulations, with a focus on descriptive writing. Because her students are second language learners, she plans to focus on vocabulary development and comprehension through the writing and multiple readings of reader's theater scripts.

Janet begins the unit with the reading and simulation activities. She quickly grabs the students' interest and creates a heightened level of excitement by using *Nine for California*, a book that tells the story through the eyes of children who are relatively the same age as her students. In talking about the gold rush, it becomes evident to Janet that there are some gaping misconceptions about certain terms related to the study, for example, *gold fever*. The students relate this to an illness that the miners had, based on the students' understanding of what having a fever means to them. Janet sees the need for an activity to help clarify this term. She paints some rocks with gold paint and plans a simulated "gold fever" activity. While the students are out of the room, Janet hides the gold rocks throughout the room. She greets her students at the door and explains that the room has been turned into a goldfield. Before she allows them to enter the room, she gives them each a length of yarn with which to mark their "claim" area. Janet has set up a video camera to capture the actions of the children as they search for gold and "stake their claims" around the room. Once started, the activity is quite frenzied as the children rush from place to place within the room, discovering gold and staking their claims. The video camera captures all the action, and when Janet reviews the tape with the students at the end of the activity, they are quite surprised at how frantic their actions appeared. The discussion following the viewing of the videotape allows Janet to clarify the term *gold fever*. She follows this activity with a writing prompt, leading the children to write descriptive entries in their simulation journals telling how they felt when they suffered from gold fever.

In the exploration of *Boom Town*, they set up a mock frontier town, including needed businesses, to stimulate discussion about the economy and concepts of supply and demand. As students begin to choose businesses to open, they prepare to deliver an oral presentation to the "town council" with supporting reasons as to why they should be allowed to bring their businesses to the town. They continue adding to their simulation journals, describing how the town is growing and developing.

Taking Charge, the third book in the series, leads the class into a study of the way of life in the boomtown and the responsibilities of adults and children. It gives Janet an opportunity to engage her students in a comparative analysis of life in the gold rush days versus life today. She also takes this opportunity to challenge the students to investigate the differences in the types of information that might be gained from different types of texts, that is, narrative texts versus informational texts versus expository texts.

Janet's culminating activity for the unit is the writing of a class poem using a format called "I used to think, but now I know." She starts the poem off for the children with the line, "I used to think gold fever was a disease, but now I know it describes the way the miners rushed to search for gold and stake their claims." The students then continue adding their own verses to the poem, stating new things they learned or correcting misconceptions they had prior to the unit study.

Janet also includes a variety of activities in the unit that address other content standards. Math is covered by having the students make maps, document distances traveled, carry out economic transactions in the mock village, measure products to be sold, and so forth. Science standards are involved through investigations of machines, geology, and navigation. Visual and performing arts standards are addressed in the simulations and dramatic representations, illustrations, and songs produced by the students during their "travels" across the country; physical education standards are incorporated in a variety of games and dances the children re-create from the period.

Janet utilized California's standards in history/social sciences and language arts to prepare her unit plan using the set of procedures shown in Figure 4.3 as a guide for making certain that the standards were adequately addressed. Then she used her imagination and creativity to make sure the unit engaged her students in active learning.

Upper-Elementary Mathematics Unit

Mathematics is generally thought of as a subject that does not lend itself to multidisciplinary planning, but recently many teachers have been experimenting with ways to connect

Figure 4.3   Integrating standards into a history/social studies unit plan.

To plan her California history unit, Janet identified the following standards and then put them into a sequence of learning experiences as described in the text:

California Fourth Grade History/Social Science Standards

Identify physical geographic features.

Use maps, charts, and pictures to describe how communities vary.

Compare how and why people traveled to California and the routes they traveled.

Analyze the effects of the gold rush on settlements, daily life, politics, and the physical environment.

Study the lives of women who helped build California.

Explain how the gold rush transformed the economy of California.

Discuss immigration and migration to California and its effects on diversity.

Describe the daily lives of the people.

California Reading/Language Arts Content Standards

Read and understand grade-level-appropriate material using predictions and comparing information from several sources.

Identify sequential and chronological order to strengthen comprehension.

Compare and contrast information on the same topic from several sources.

Create multiple-paragraph compositions.

Write compositions that describe and explain events and experiences using concrete sensory details.

Ask thoughtful questions and respond to relevant questions with appropriate elaboration in oral settings.

Summarize major ideas and supporting evidence in effective oral presentations.

mathematics to other subject areas and life experiences. As Piaget demonstrated, mathematics is a subject that requires early experiences with concrete examples and hands-on experiences that allow students to manipulate materials to understand mathematical relationships. Later, upper-intermediate-grade students can be expected to understand these same relationships at a more abstract level without the need to see them in a concrete way. Many teachers like to plan their mathematics curriculum using thematic units so that students have multiple opportunities to experience and investigate the mathematical relationships they are learning.

Mathematics is also a subject that requires lateral thinking, reasoning, and problem-solving strategies that cannot be taught in a sequential series of lessons. Current mathematics units encourage students to explore mathematical relationships and select from a variety of strategies to set up and solve problems. Skillful computation is no longer sufficient as an outcome or performance expectation; it is also important that students be able to apply mathematical operations to real-life problems and tasks.

Based on these organizational principles, an effective curriculum unit in math is likely to (1) present new skills and concepts in order of difficulty; (2) initiate new learning with concrete manipulative experiences so that students can understand the concepts involved; (3) teach students a variety of problem-solving strategies; and (4) provide examples, tasks, and problems that call on students to apply their newly learned skills and strategies in lifelike situations to problems they can relate to and want to solve.

Mathematics is an example of a spiral curriculum. This means that certain concepts and skills are taught every year but in an upward spiral of difficulty. Each year begins with a review of skills from previous years followed by an introduction of new skills and concepts. For this reason, the topics of mathematics units are likely to be similar from year to year, but the way these topics are addressed and the complexity of the concepts vary greatly. Mathematics education now emphasizes problem solving and investigating as means of developing mathematical powers. When possible, real situations and problems are becoming the basis for the curriculum.

California Mathematics Standards for the upper elementary grades ask teachers to provide learning experiences that will challenge students to "use data samples of a population and describe the characteristics and limitations of the samples." A good example of a mathematics unit that involves students in realistic data collection and interpretation is presented in Figure 4.4. Marvin Howard created this unit, titled "Exercise Habits," for his sixth-grade students. He uses it at the beginning of the school year to engage his students' interest in mathematics, to help them develop a sense of confidence in their mathematical powers, and to show the students how useful and important mathematics can be in their everyday lives.

Fifth-Grade Science Unit

Joanne Vinetta teaches fifth grade in Eagan, Minnesota. Joanne takes her class to Eagle Bluff Environmental Education Center each January for a three-day outdoor learning experience. The curriculum included during this trip is planned to address Minnesota Science Standards and Scientific Inquiry Standards. The inquiry standards addressed relate to the learning of scientific questioning, comparing, categorizing, and reporting. The fifth graders take part in many problem-solving and team-building activities that address standards related to personal growth in the development of positive attitudes toward nature and participation in outdoor activities.

The main focus of the Eagle Bluff activity is related to the science standards theme titled "Passport to Weather and Climate." Joanne's goals for her students include their understanding of the following:

- Differences between weather and climate
- Safety and preparation for outdoor winter activities
- Flora and fauna identification and survival

Figure 4.4   Exercise patterns of sixth graders.

Description

This unit functions as both a mathematics unit and an exercise in collecting data for research. Hopefully, it will also make students and their parents aware of how much, or little, exercise is being done. The types of exercises will also be explored and data collected for specific types of exercises.

Cognitive and Skill Outcome Statements

1. Students will collect and record data accurately.
2. Students will create bar and circle graphs representing the data collected.
3. Students will evaluate the data they collected about their own exercise patterns.
4. Students will combine data from all members of the class to make generalizations and interpretations about exercise patterns of students their age.
5. Working in small groups, students will create an oral presentation to report their findings and recommendations.

Affective Outcome Statement

Students will become aware of the amount of time they spend in active activity and make judgments about whether this amount of time is sufficient to gain and maintain physical fitness.

Time Line for Project

Week one. Discussions of data collection, how to gather data, how specific data must be, what types of activities to include in data collection.

Weeks one and two. Data collection.

Weeks three and four. Data interpretation, creation of bar and circle graphs, group work to create oral presentations.

Week five. Oral presentations and unit evaluation. Collaborative creation of scoring rubric for oral presentations.

Source: Adapted from Marvin Howard, sixth-grade teacher, Hidalgo Elementary School, Fresno, California.

Before the trip to Eagle Bluff, Joanne uses a number of the activities available on the Eagle Bluff website to prepare her students for their experiences at the Environmental Education Center (www.eagle-bluff.org/in-the-classroom.html). One of the activities involves charting the length of the daylight hours, temperature, and solar elevation over a period of time. To allow her students to truly understand the changing of seasons, Joanne starts this activity at the beginning of the year so that her students can see the gradual changes and the relationship of the number of daylight hours and position of the sun to the temperatures across the school year.

This classroom activity provides background knowledge for a class titled "Big Freeze" at the Eagle Bluff Environmental Education Center. The class explores how plants and animals survive the harsh winters in Minnesota as well as materials in nature that provide insulation for them. The students also learn how to use some of these same materials to provide shelter for themselves in case they might ever need to survive outdoors in winter.

After the Eagle Bluff trip, Joanne expands on the students' experiences and addresses science standards in her classroom. The students continue to observe seasonal changes in their community; using online connections to other sections of the country, they also monitor seasonal changes in New Mexico, Oregon, South Florida, and Virginia. In addition, students observe and research the ways in which plants and animals respond to changes in weather, and they are always surprised that their online friends tend to define their spring and summer seasons' weather experiences differently than they do in Minnesota.

The first day at the Eagle Bluff Environmental Education Center begins with classroom activities to prepare the students for their morning outdoor exploration. They then venture out to observe and take notes and photographs. Returning to the classroom, they warm up, examine specimens they've gathered, discuss their observations, and view photographs taken by the Eagle Bluff staff. Day one begins with the "Big Freeze" study, where the students explore how animals and plants survive the winter. After they observe things in nature, they go back to the classroom to conduct experiments exploring different natural materials and how well they insulate.

After lunch on the first day, the students examine different characteristics and identification keys of the approximately 40 native tree species of Minnesota. Working in teams, participants learn to use a dichotomous key to identify distinguishing characteristics of some of Eagle Bluff's trees and discover the many uses people have for trees. They prepare for the outdoor activity by learning how to identify trees, how to investigate the trees, and how to work in groups to identify them. When they return to the classroom, they learn more about the attributes of and the uses for different trees.

Evenings are spent participating in group challenges designed to foster team cooperation and personal character development. Communication, trust, problem solving, and cooperation are essential ingredients to each group's success in challenge activities.

On the second day, the students hike to a secluded site to experience a day in the life of the Oneota Native Americans. This includes practicing skills such as starting fires with friction, grinding corn for bread, making twine, playing Native American games, and sharing stories in the "longhouse." They actually prepare and eat foods similar to those the Oneota would have eaten and do the work children of the tribe would have performed.

On the third day, students explore the dynamic interrelationships of wildlife populations and their habitats. Through interactive demonstrations and explorations, they learn about components of habitats, limiting factors, and biodiversity; then they see examples of these concepts at work in surrounding natural areas.

Using all their senses, students work to unravel the mysterious lives of Eagle Bluff's wildlife and discover the local food chains. They spend time exploring and interpreting animal signs, acting out a sample food chain, and working together to create a demonstration of one large food web. After the afternoon classroom activity, the students study winter safety. Then they go back outside to observe and climb rock formations, returning to camp by riding on a "zip-line." Appropriate classroom activities always precede outdoor explorations of the winter forest. Once again, the evening is spent in team-building and problem-solving activities.

After three days, the students "return to civilization" much more confident in their understating of nature and in their own personal abilities and survival skills. To quote Megan Bateman, one of Joanne's students, "I learned that I could climb a mountain and ride a zip-line. I had a lot of fun, but I also learned a lot about nature and Indians and working with a group to solve problems. I gained a lot of self-confidence because I found out I could do things all the other kids can do even though I'm smaller" (personal communication, January 28, 2011).

Joanne continues to use this activity each year because she sees her students gaining so much understanding of nature, weather, and climate, as well as how to work with others. "I know the parents of my students thought I'd lost my mind the first year I planned an outdoor experience in January in Minnesota, but now they all want to know when we're going. I never lack for volunteers to chaperone."

We hope that these unit plans will inspire you to think outside the box when you have your own classroom and are able to plan curriculum. The state standards that you must meet are easily incorporated into highly creative and motivating thematic units. Your students will experience the thrill of researching and investigating topics of high interest, and you will experience the pride and success that come when the whole class is engaged in active learning for a real-life purpose.

Involving the Larger Educational Community

When you plan to spend an extended amount of time on a study such as a thematic unit, it is important to convey your plans to the parents of your students. Explain the purpose of the unit and the goals and standards to be addressed. Let them know what will be expected of the students, especially if you will be requiring long-term projects. Keep parents informed of the time lines, due dates, and any special events that they will want to attend. You may find that you have parents with expertise or access to resources that will be very helpful in your planning. Make sure that parents know that you welcome any help, support, or resources they can provide.

Thematic units lend themselves well to the use of community resources. Very often there are people in the community who can serve as experts, providing demonstrations, slide shows, or hands-on activities for your students. Reflective teachers create resource files identifying local experts, places to visit, and creative activities available in the area. They explore their communities with learning opportunities in mind. They enjoy talking to local merchants and people they meet with the idea of introducing their students to the wide variety of people who live and work nearby.

Group Focus Activity

The following six-step activity points out the viability of a spiraling curriculum in which knowledge is built on knowledge in an additive process of reviewing and expanding learning.

1. The class is divided into groups, one group for each grade level.

2. Each group searches the appropriate Department of Education website for a list of state standards and chooses one overarching concept that is taught at all grade levels (for example, government, American symbols, heroes, mechanics of writing). For an example from the California Social Studies Standards, see Figure 4.5.

Figure 4.5 Overarching concepts for guided exploration.

> **Mapping Skills**
>
> *Kindergarten* – Distinguish between land and water on maps and globes, and locate general area references in legends and stories.
>
> *First grade* – Locate on maps and globes their local community, their state, the United States, the seven continents, the four oceans.
>
> *Second grade* – Locate on a simple letter-number grid system the specific locations and geographic features in their neighborhood or community.
>
> *Third grade* – Identify and locate on a map geographic features in their local region (deserts, mountains, valleys, hills, coastal areas, oceans, lakes).
>
> *Fourth grade* – Explain and use the coordinate grid system of latitude and longitude to determine the absolute location of places in their state and on Earth.
>
> *Fifth grade* – Trace the routes of the major land explorers of the United States, the distances traveled by explorers, and the Atlantic trade routes that linked Africa, the West Indies, the British colonies, and Europe.

Source: Adapted from California Social Science Standards.

3. On a large piece of chart paper, each group writes the grade-level standard related to the selected overarching concept.

4. Each group then generates a list of grade-appropriate activities related to the overarching concept and writes the suggested activities on the chart below the standard (they might be added using different colors).

5. The groups post their charts around the classroom in grade-level sequence, and each group makes a short oral presentation, discussing the standard and explaining how the suggested activities relate to the standard.

6. Each group also points out how the grade-level standard expands on and adds to knowledge gained in the previous grade level.

Preparing for Your Licensure Exam

In this chapter you read about the elements of curriculum planning. Reread "A View into the Classroom" at the beginning of the chapter, and think about it as a case study you might encounter on your licensure exam. Answer the following questions to demonstrate your understanding of the ways in which teachers gather information about their students and plan curriculum units to meet the needs of their students while addressing the state standards for the grade level:

1. What methods did Diane use to gather information about her students in order to plan effective instruction?

2. How did Diane involve parents in her curriculum planning?

3. How many curricular areas (reading, writing, math, etc.) were included in Diane's unit? How could she have included more areas?

Portfolio of Professional Practices Activity

To give evidence of your reflection on long-term curriculum planning, do the following:

1. Choose one state standard that you will be expected to use in your curriculum planning for student teaching.

2. Write the standard.

3. Write a brief paragraph on what you think are the reasons and motives that resulted in this state standard being adopted, including what this standard is going to accomplish and why it was adopted by your state.

4. Explain how this standard will affect the way you create curriculum in this subject area. How will this standard make your planning easier than if you had no standard to follow? How will it make your planning more difficult?

5. Imagine that you are beginning to plan a yearlong curriculum for this subject area. How would you use this state standard to begin planning? Write a general long-term plan to achieve this standard. Will you teach it continuously for a period of time or come back to this subject matter every week or so during the year?

6. Explain how you will assess your students' accomplishment of this standard. How will you prove to yourself that your students have successfully mastered this standard? How will you prove this to your school administrators?

7. Reflection always requires self-analysis. Reflect on the difficulties you had in planning this simple curriculum. How will you improve this process when you are called on to plan a real curriculum?

References

Adams, D. (1999). *Literacy today: New standards across the curriculum.* New York, NY: Garland Publishing.

Banks, J. (1992). Multicultural education: For freedom's sake. *Educational Leadership, 49*(4), 12–15.

Beane, J. (1991). Middle school: The natural home of the integrated curriculum. *Educational Leadership, 49*(2), 9–13.

Brooks, J., & Brooks, M. G. (1999). In search of understanding: The case for constructivist classrooms. *Educational Leadership, 57*(3), 18–24. Alexandria, VA: Association of Supervision and Curriculum Development.

Brophy, J. (1992). Probing the subtleties of subject-matter teaching. *Educational Leadership, 49*(7), 4–8.

Fowler, A. (1995). *It's a fruit, it's a vegetable, it's a pumpkin.* Chicago, IL: Children's Press.

Hall, Z. (1999). *It's pumpkin time!* New York, NY: Scholastic.

Hayes-Jacobs, H. (1997). *Mapping the big picture.* Alexandria, VA: Association of Supervision and Curriculum Development.

Kottke, J. (2000). *From seed to pumpkin.* Chicago, IL: Children's Press.

Levenson, G. (1999). *Pumpkin circle.* Berkeley, CA: Tricycle Press.

Levitin, S. (1996). *Nine for California.* New York, NY: Orchard Books.

Levitin, S. (1998). *Boom town.* New York, NY: Orchard Books.

Levitin, S. (1999). *Taking charge.* New York, NY: Orchard Books.

O'Neill, M. (1989). *Hailstones and halibut bones: Adventures in color.* Garden City, NJ: Doubleday.

Reissman, R. (1994). *The evolving multicultural classroom.* Alexandria, VA: Association for Supervision and Curriculum Development.

Roberts, P., & Kellough, R. (2000). *A guide for developing interdisciplinary thematic units* (2nd ed.). Upper Saddle River, NJ: Merrill/Prentice Hall.

Rylant, C. (2000). *In November.* Orlando, FL: Harcourt.

Sleeter, C., & Grant, C. (1994). *Making choices for multicultural education.* Upper Saddle River, NJ: Merrill/Prentice Hall.

Tyler, R. (1949). *Basic principles of curriculum and instruction.* Chicago, IL: University of Chicago Press.

Viadero, D. (1993). Standards deviation: Benchmark-setting is marked by diversity. *Education Week,* June 16, pp. 14–17.

Walsh, R. (1997). *Fall colors.* New York, NY: Troll.

Wiggins, J., & McTighe, G. (2005). *Understanding by design handbook* (2nd ed.). Alexandria, VA: Association of Supervision and Curriculum Development.

Williams, S. (1990). *I went walking.* Boston, MA: Red Wagon Books.

Differentiating Instruction

"Don't try to fix the students, fix ourselves first. The good teacher makes the poor student good and the good student superior. When your students fail, we, as teachers, too have failed."

Marva Collins, American educator and founder of Westside Preparatory School, Chicago, Illinois

In 1975, Marva Collins (from whom the above quote is taken) established Chicago's Westside Preparatory School, which was famous for successfully providing classical education for impoverished students, many of whom had been wrongly labeled as learning disabled by public schools. Today's classrooms are also extremely diverse. With the infusion of exceptional education students into the mainstream classroom, the growth of multicultural groups across the United States, and the recognition that students learn in a great variety of ways, teachers must address a wide variety of individual needs whenever they plan lessons, units, or any learning experience for their students. A differentiated classroom is easy to recognize (Tomlinson, 2005):

- Teachers know what their students know and can do, and they begin instruction at the students' level.
- Teachers provide ways for individual students to succeed. This may involve offering a range of approaches in teaching, a range of ways for students to interact or work, and even a range of differing assignments for students to accomplish.
- Teachers hold all students to high standards but accept that they will not all follow the same road to learning.
- Teachers actively diagnose their students' needs and learning styles and prescribe the best approaches for their students.
- Teachers use time effectively and flexibly and rarely teach whole-group lessons because they recognize the wide range of interests and abilities within their classes.

Questions for Reflection as You Read the Chapter

1. How does one teacher meet the many needs of all the students?
2. In what ways does the teacher differentiate instruction?
3. Which differentiations are appropriate for students of varying needs?

A View into the Classroom

Marcy Lennon is a third-grade teacher in Miami, Florida. Her classroom of 23 students includes 3 children diagnosed with attention deficit disorder (ADD), 1 child with a profound hearing loss, 2 students co-enrolled in the gifted program, 1 child in a wheelchair, and 5 students at different levels of English language development who speak Spanish at home. Marcy's students range in reading levels from 1.3 to 5.7 (first grade, third month to fifth grade, seventh month). As Marcy prepares her lessons, she begins with the state standards for third grade and then looks at the levels of functioning of her students. She knows she has to teach them at their levels but support them to achieve mastery of the third-grade standards by the end of the school year. Marcy uses learning centers to provide meaningful activities for her students while she works with small groups or individuals, teaching them at their levels. Marcy says, "I plan learning centers so that students can work at their own levels and simultaneously move toward achievement of grade-level standards. Students have a learning plan that tells them what they are responsible to accomplish each day. They work in centers, on computers, in small groups, and individually. Using this approach allows me to meet their needs while they are learning responsibility for their own actions and, to a large degree, some of their own learning."

When Marcy teaches a lesson, she has to plan instructional differentiations for her students. For her ADD students, Marcy sits them close to her and involves them by having them answer questions, hold and pass out materials, and have reasons to move around the classroom periodically. She breaks up lessons into short segments and stops to check for understanding before moving to the next section of the lesson.

Her hearing-impaired student has a listening device but also reads lips, so Marcy makes sure he is looking directly at her as she gives directions. The student in the wheelchair sits in a place in the classroom where she can move to the bookshelves, bathroom, and other areas without being blocked in by furniture; there is always a place left at learning centers that she can access, and several students are assigned to assist this student in the event of a fire drill or other emergency exit.

Planning for the English language learners (ELLs) in the classroom requires that Marcy know their English development levels and use many visuals, gestures, and other props so that they can better understand the instruction. She gives these students additional guided practice when the other students begin follow-up activities at learning centers. Because all of her ELLs speak Spanish at home, Marcy translates some English words into Spanish for key concepts to use when she works with these students.

Marcy sets up her learning centers with color-coded folders: The red-level activities provide more practice in the basic skills taught, the yellow-level activities move the students to the next level of functioning in the skill, and the green-level activities serve as enrichment for students who have mastered the skill taught. Students know which color folder to use at the centers, although they can always attempt another level if they are motivated to do so. Marcy often plans learning centers as follow-up activities for lessons she teaches. For example, after teaching a lesson on writing beginning, middle, and end (BME) stories, Marcy sets up a BME Story Center:

- *For students who are just beginning to understand the concept (red level), Marcy provides an activity sheet for the students to identify the elements found in the beginning, middle, and end of stories the students read at the center. The stories have been selected to represent the various levels at which the students read. This activity is a repeat of the same activity used in the lesson Marcy taught while providing additional practice using different books.*

- *At the yellow level, students will be provided with a variety of books and asked to identify at least two books that conform to the BME format. They will complete an activity sheet showing how the book follows that format.*

- *Students who are ready to move to the green level get to write their own BME books using a graphic displayed at the center that lists the elements to be included in each section of the book and using a planning activity sheet where they plan their story before writing.*

Marcy knows that there are several ways to differentiate instruction. Choosing effective differentiations requires that the teacher know her students well—what they know, how they learn best, what special needs they possess, and what approaches motivate them. As each year passes, Marcy develops new ways to differentiate in appropriate ways. Following are some of Marcy's approaches:

- *Shortening assignments to give students just the appropriate amount of practice without overwhelming them*

- *Providing extra guided practice for students who need it*

- *Giving instruction to provide background experience and knowledge to equip them to be successful in lessons to be taught*

- *Providing vocabulary instruction prior to teaching lessons to enable students to better understand concepts being taught*
- *Providing leveled instruction to introduce concepts, and giving differentiated amounts of guided practice and enrichment activities to meet the needs of all students*
- *Considering differing needs for movement, quiet, visual support, and kinesthetic activities to support learning, and planning for these differing needs before teaching the lesson*
- *Considering differing needs for seating to maintain attention and to limit distractions*

All of these differentiations require that teachers know their students well, observe them daily, and adjust lessons based on student observations and achievement levels.

REFLECTING ON THE CLASSROOM EXPERIENCE

Teachers in today's classrooms quickly realize that their students come to them with a wide variety of background experiences, learning styles, and educational levels. Meeting the needs of all the students requires organization and excellent observation skills.

In order to meet individual needs, a teacher first must identify those needs and then develop a number of teaching strategies to address them. One of the most challenging responsibilities of teaching is finding the time to individualize instruction, meet with small groups, and monitor learning. Marcy demonstrates a number of approaches to address this challenge; other teachers may address this challenge in different ways. As a beginning teacher, it is vital that you become aware of the ways in which teachers adapt instruction and use grouping to meet the needs of all students.

Starting the School Year

As soon as they succeed in getting a teaching position, most teachers are eager to get into their classrooms to arrange furniture, establish schedules, put up bulletin boards, consider rules and consequences, and plan major units of study. However, surprises are inevitable when school starts and the classroom is filled with students from many different backgrounds who have a variety of abilities, talents, and needs.

The first day of school can be a daunting experience for a teacher who has spent a lot of time and energy planning the perfect beginning for the school year. Some students may appear to be totally disinterested while others appear to be intent on disrupting the teacher's plans. In many classrooms today, there are likely to be some students who are struggling to understand and speak English. New teachers often find themselves sitting at their desks thinking, "What ever made me think I could do this?" Even experienced teachers find themselves comparing their new class to last year's class, thinking, "These students have so many more needs than last year's group!" They may be forgetting that last year's class had made a whole school year's worth of progress when they parted at the end of the school year.

Teaching today's diverse student population is most definitely a challenge. Students bring a wealth of different perspectives to the classroom, whether they are from mainstream American homes or homes with multiple languages. We believe that all students are teachable, and we hope you agree. Teachers who have faith in their students' abilities to learn are the ones who are able to make the most significant and positive differences in their students' lives. Stephanie Collom, a resource teacher in Fresno, California, at Hidalgo Elementary School, where native English speakers are rare, observed: "All the children come to school with faith in me as their teacher. I have to find ways to support their learning so that their faith is justified. I also have to believe in their abilities as learners and find a way to make sure that they succeed."

Many teachers begin their teaching careers expecting the students in their classes and the curriculum they teach to resemble the students and curriculum they experienced when they were in school. It is sometimes a big shock to realize how much has changed in education in a very short time. The students in today's classrooms come to school from diverse backgrounds, not only in experiences but also in language exposure and perceptions of school. To add complexity to the issue, it seems that at the same time as the student body is becoming more diverse, the state-mandated curricula are becoming more focused on meeting a single set of standards for all.

Teachers in today's schools are expected to be able to teach the traditional skills to a very nontraditional group of students. In addition, teachers are expected to diversify their instructional methods in ways that support students' self-esteem, knowledge of technology, and ethnic and language backgrounds. An added challenge in working with diverse populations is the different expectations that parents from different cultures bring to the school setting.

Celebrating diversity is vastly different than tolerating diversity. At the end of the twentieth century, the goal seemed to be for teachers in multicultural settings to show acceptance of students' differences. In the twenty-first (and hopefully more enlightened) century, teachers have the goal of finding ways to encourage all students to value their own cultural heritage and appreciate the contributions of their classmates from a range of diverse backgrounds.

One major difference that affects learning is that of language. In order to teach effectively, teachers must understand how language is acquired and know how to adjust their assessment, curriculum, and planning to take advantage of the multiple language-centered perspectives contained within almost every classroom.

Language Acquisition and the Classroom Teacher

The research into language acquisition issues is rich and productive. Linguists and educators working together have discovered effective ways to support students in their acquisition of new languages and content knowledge. It is vital that classroom teachers understand the implications of language acquisition theory so that they can provide the scaffolding necessary for their students to be successful in the classroom (Krashen, 1996).

In his study of language acquisition, Krashen (1996) makes a distinction between language acquisition and language learning that is vital to the support of students in the classroom in their gradual acquisition of fluency in a new language. Krashen's research demonstrates that language acquisition is a natural process; he observes how easily and readily young children acquire their home language without formal teaching and without drill and practice! Natural language acquisition is a gradual interactive process based on receiving and understanding messages, building a listening (receptive) vocabulary, and slowly attempting verbal production of the language in a highly supportive, nonstressful environment.

Krashen (1996) explains to teachers that it is necessary to duplicate these conditions as much as possible in a classroom in order to foster the acquisition of a second language. According to this theory, teachers will be most successful in teaching English if they plan interactive learning activities and speak or write in words selected carefully to match their students' level of understanding. This concept is termed *understandable language* or *comprehensible input*, and it incorporates the use of props, gestures, pictures, and other strategies that contribute to each child's acquisition and eventual production of the language.

Language Scaffolding

Scaffolding is a term used in teaching that involves modeling and demonstrating a new skill. It requires a highly interactive relationship between the teacher and the student while new learning occurs. Bruner's (1997) work with mothers and children led him to recommend such a relationship. As a mother reads aloud to a toddler, she may simplify the book to meet the attention span and interests of her child, calling the child's attention to material that is appropriate and eliminating material that is beyond the child's present level of understanding; she is also likely to allow the child to interact with her as they read and discuss the words and pictures on each page. This flexible and simplified interaction between mother and child allows the child to connect new ideas to existing schemata at his or her own level.

Teachers can apply scaffolding in the classroom by reducing complex tasks to manageable steps: helping students concentrate on one task at a time; being explicit about what is expected; interpreting the task for the student; and coaching the student using familiar, supportive words and actions. When a teacher coaches the student through a difficult task, he or she must provide sufficient scaffolding through the use of hints and cues so that the student can succeed. As the student becomes more skillful, the scaffolding can be reduced and finally eliminated.

Scaffolding is an especially valuable technique for the primary teacher because most young students require supportive interactions and accommodations to their existing vocabularies to learn new skills. Scaffolding is also appropriate for upper-level students when the tasks are complex or when the students have difficulty with the language.

For some beginning teachers, scaffolding may not come naturally because they may not have experienced scaffolded learning in their own school experiences. This technique can be learned only by reflecting on the needs of students, gathering the latest information on such techniques from reading and talking to experienced teachers who have used the techniques successfully, and gradually adding such strategies to personal repertoires.

Scaffolding academic language supports students' successful participation in content-area instruction. Academic language is associated with school subjects such as mathematics, science, and social studies. It places a higher cognitive demand on the speaker and listener.

Cummins (1986) identifies two types of language that students acquire. The first, Basic Interpersonal Communication Skills (BICS)—or social language—is learned more quickly and easily than the second, Cognitive Academic Language Proficiency (CALP)—or academic language. Academic language scaffolding supports the student in CALP, the language necessary for the student to participate successfully in classroom learning opportunities.

In order for students to participate successfully in academic lessons in the classroom, teachers use a series of scaffolding strategies that include modeling academic language; contextualizing academic language using visuals, gestures, and demonstrations; and supporting the students in the use of academic language through active learning activities.

Susan McCloskey, a kindergarten and first-grade teacher at Viking Elementary School in Fresno, California, provides a perfect example of language scaffolding as she teaches her students the concepts of same and different. She begins her lesson by modeling. She takes two large teddy bears and holds them up for the students to see: "These are the same," she says. She puts one bear down and picks up a stuffed bunny: "These are different," she states. She asks students to come to the front of the class and hold two stuffed animals. The other students repeat the words, saying "Same" and "Different," depending on the animals the child is holding. Susan then has the students draw pictures of their favorite foods. They show their pictures and talk about the fact that some children like the same foods and others like different foods; during recess, she photocopies some of their pictures onto a large sheet of copy paper. When they return to the classroom, she arranges the students into pairs, carefully placing them together so that each pair has a relatively strong English speaker. All of her students are ELLs, so she does not have the advantage of strong English models, other than herself and classroom volunteers and aides.

As she gives the instructions for the activity, Susan demonstrates. She tells them to cut out the pictures as she models cutting out the pictures. She tells them to paste together the pictures that are the same. As she says this, she models choosing two pictures of hamburgers and placing them together on a large sheet of construction paper. She repeats, "These are the same," as she points to the two hamburgers she has pasted onto the construction paper. The students work together, some talking in English, some in Hmong, their native language. Susan moves around the room supporting the students, asking questions about the concepts of same and different. To anyone observing, the lesson is obviously a success.

However, it is at the end of the lesson that Susan adds the piece that scaffolds the students into new levels of language. As each pair of students completes the task, they bring the paper to Susan. She points to one group of pictures on the construction paper and asks, "Why did you put these together?"

The first child says, "Same."

"Yes," confirms Susan, "they are all the same. This is a hamburger. This is a hamburger. This is a hamburger. This is a hamburger. They are all the same," she says as she points to each hamburger on the page. She then continues to ask the same child, "Why did you put these together?" as she points to the hot dogs.

The child responds, "This is hot dog. This is hot dog. This is hot dog. This is hot dog," as he points to each one. "They all same."

Susan then asks the other child in the pair the same questions. Because this child has been watching and listening, she responds in phrases just as Susan has modeled. With just a few minutes of the teacher's language scaffolding, these two children have moved from one-word responses to responses in simple sentences. Many teachers would have been pleased that the students had completed the task correctly and would have put a smiley face or star at the top of the page without utilizing the teachable moment and providing the vital language scaffolding as part of the lesson. Knowing how children acquire language is a necessary part of effective teaching with ELLs.

Stages in Language Acquisition

When students are acquiring a new language, they go through predictable stages. The stages begin with students listening to language: They are taking in (or receiving) language at this stage, often referred to as the silent period. Teachers should be aware that students are processing the language they are hearing and should know that it is important for language to be contextualized so that it is understandable. After this silent (or preproduction) period, students move into the early production stage, where they can give one- or two-word responses. They then move into speech emergence, where they are attempting to speak phrases and short sentences but are still making grammatical errors. They move gradually into intermediate fluency, where their sentences lengthen and their errors are fewer. Finally, over time, they become fluent in English.

Teachers need to be aware of these stages so that they can adapt their questioning strategies and expectations to support students' progress to higher language stages. It is especially important that teachers actively seek ways to keep ELLs involved in the classroom community. Allowing students to sit idly, not engaged or processing the instruction that is going on in a classroom, is never acceptable, so teachers must be armed with strategies to use in engaging students.

Leveled questions are used when teachers adapt the way they ask questions so that students can answer or respond to them according to their language acquisition stage. The use of leveled questions enables a teacher to include ELLs in the classroom activities and support their active engagement, which in turn supports their language acquisition. To level the questions, the teacher must observe the students as they interact in English. Once the teacher knows the level at which the students interact in English, the questions the teacher poses to the students can be adjusted to ensure their success in answering. The teacher may use gestures or visuals or slow his or her speech slightly while asking the questions. The teacher asks the questions in a way that encourages each student to answer by pointing to a visual or giving a one-word response, complete sentence, or explanation depending on the level of the student's language acquisition. The teacher's role in using this strategy involves knowing each student's level of English acquisition and providing enough context in the question so that each student can respond, either verbally or nonverbally, with understanding and confidence.

Optimal Levels of Instruction

Reflective teachers who want to encourage each student to function at the highest level of achievement monitor each student's level of understanding closely to see what interventions are needed. Lev Vygotsky, a Russian cognitive psychologist, called the optimal level of instruction for each student the "zone of proximal development" (zpd). The zpd for each student is based on the level at which the student can no longer solve problems on his or her own but must be supported by a teacher or a more knowledgeable peer (Dixon-Kraus, 1996). In order for the teacher to provide instruction for each student at an optimal learning level, or zpd, the teacher must use reflective actions to gain an understanding of the student's needs. This is especially vital for students who have special needs or who are learning English as a second language. For suggestions on identifying language levels and adapting instruction for the different levels, see Figure 5.1.

Figure 5.1   Adapting instruction for different language development levels.

Level	Description	Appropriate Questions	Ways to Adapt Instruction
Preproduction	Student is not yet producing English words or phrases. (It is also called the silent period.) He/she *is* developing receptive language.	Show me . . . Is this the ____ one? (Use a picture or graph.)	1. Add pictures or realia (real objects) to develop vocabulary. 2. Give multiple examples. 3. Always accompany verbalizations with gestures, visuals, or realia. 4 Keep sentences short. 5. Smile and nod a lot to give encouragement.
Early production	Student is beginning to say a few words or short phrases.	Is it ____ or ____? (Give choices so student just has to repeat one of the words or phrases.)	1. Label things with both English and native language labels. 2. Show, don't just tell. 3. Always accompany verbalizations with gestures, visuals, or realia.
Speech emergence	Student is beginning to produce simple sentences but is still making a lot of pronunciation and grammar errors. He/she can now ask questions that require short sentences in response.	Did this happen at the beginning or the end? Where did you find this answer?	1. Written assignments may still need to be shortened. 2. He/she may need a little more time to complete assignments. 3. Reading texts may still need to be simplified. (Just rewrite science and social studies texts using shorter sentences and simpler words.) 4. He/she will need vocabulary instruction, especially in science and social studies.
Intermediate fluency	Student is producing longer sentences and is less reluctant to speak English, but he/she is still making some errors in pronunciation and grammar.	How did you . . . ? What was the character trying to do?	5. He/she should be able to participate in regular lessons with success as long as you add visuals, gestures, and realia. 6. He/she may still need direct instruction related to higher-level vocabulary.

Source: Adapted from Herrell & Jordan, 2012.

Five Factors in Differentiating Classroom Instruction

Whether a student is learning English as a second (or third) language or having difficulty absorbing academic content, there are five factors that reflective teachers consider when planning and implementing instruction. Although these factors were identified as important when teaching ELLs, Herrell and Jordan (2012) found them equally effective with English-only students in the classroom.

The first factor is *comprehensible input*. The teacher looks at the lesson and asks, "Is the instruction I am giving understandable to my students?" If the students are experiencing confusion or simply not getting it, the teacher must consider ways in which the instruction can be made more understandable. It is important to consider how to give explanations while demonstrating something. The teacher may want to ask, "Am I just talking, or am I modeling, using pictures, gestures, real objects to demonstrate the concepts I am trying to get across? Am I using words that I have defined and demonstrated? Am I relating new concepts to past experiences, giving examples, showing instead of telling?"

Good explanations require a lot of thought. Giving multiple examples supports understanding, and giving nonexamples is also very helpful. For example, when teaching about the characteristics of mammals, a teacher might say, "A zebra and an elephant are both examples of mammals; fish and birds are not examples of mammals."

The second factor is the *quality of verbal interactions* with and among your students. Ask yourself, "Am I providing opportunities for the students to interact with one another? Do the students have an opportunity to use hands-on materials? Are they given a chance to see the practical importance of what they are being asked to learn?"

The third factor is the *contextualization of the language experiences* you provide for your students. In other words, are new words and ideas presented within a context so the students have an opportunity to link the vocabulary and concepts to a bigger picture? One of the biggest factors in a student's ability to comprehend language is how well that language is supported by context. The direction, "Take out your science book," when spoken while holding up the science book is easily understood even by a student who knows no English or a student who cannot hear well. Just getting in the habit of supporting instruction by using gestures and visuals and by showing while telling is highly supportive of language acquisition and student understanding.

The fourth factor is the *selection of teaching and grouping strategies that reduce student anxiety*, not aggravate it. Students who are anxious about being called on or being asked to speak in front of their peers often have difficulty processing information or even listening attentively. Krashen (1996) calls this the *affective filter*, an emotional process that prevents the learner from hearing or processing new information. Teachers who want to be able to diminish or eliminate the likelihood of triggering a student's affective filter must find ways to create a classroom climate that encourages and motivates each student while at the same time reducing anxiety. One important consideration for you to reflect on is the way you ask questions and respond to errors. If students know that making an error is not going to cause them to be ridiculed in front of the class, they feel much freer to answer questions and take risks. It is not enough to refrain from embarrassing students, however. There should be a consistent monitoring of the verbal interactions among students as well. A "no tolerance rule" related to student ridicule provides a healthy classroom climate conducive to learning. This happens only when the teacher models it, discusses it openly, and tolerates no negative verbal interactions among the students.

The fifth factor to be considered is the *opportunities to increase the level of active student involvement* within the classroom. Opportunities to actively engage in classroom activities designed to practice and gradually master the skills being taught are as vital to language acquisition as they are to other aspects of student learning. Activities that provide students with opportunities to work in small groups on a project that requires the use of new skills and problem-solving strategies also require the students to engage in verbal interactions and contextualize the language they are using, and these activities generally serve to reduce anxiety.

When all five of these factors are considered in scheduling the school day and planning individual lessons and activities, the classroom becomes a community of learners. The reflective teacher observes the classroom climate and uses withitness to perceive any indications of discord or anxiety that may be standing in the way of learning. Planning time for purposeful student interactions is a vital building block for developing a strong sense of community. Students need time to interact and get to know one another. As they know more about each other, they will begin to value the diversity and uniqueness of the individuals who make up the community.

Two of these important factors can be achieved by using cooperative group activities as a strategy for teaching in your classroom. Language acquisition for ELLs is enhanced by their taking part in a cooperative group effort where communication skills are required to complete an assigned task, and increased understanding and appreciation of diversity occur as well.

Slavin (1995) reports that cooperative groups may actually improve race relations within a classroom. When students participate in multiracial teams, studies show that they choose one another for friends more often than do students in control groups. Researchers attribute this effect to the fact that working together in a group as part of a team causes students to promote more differentiated, dynamic, and realistic views (and therefore less stereotyped and static views) of other students (including peers with special needs or those from different ethnic groups) than do competitive and individualistic learning experiences (Johnson & Johnson, 1993).

You must remember that it is you, as teacher, who are responsible for providing comprehensible instruction for all of your students and adjusting that instruction for their individual needs. Don't rely on students to provide the adjustments for you. For instance, it might be tempting to seat ELLs or students who need additional attention next to stronger students and ask the stronger ones to provide scaffolding for the ELLs. Although this is sometimes helpful, it should never take the place of adapted instruction by the teacher. Try to add visuals, gestures, realia, and multiple examples to your instruction to support those students who need a little extra help. You may even have to rewrite some of the more difficult texts using shorter sentences and less complex vocabulary. This is not as difficult as it sounds and has been found to benefit all struggling students (Herrell & Jordan, 2012).

Addressing the Needs of All Students

Needs of Gifted Students

You may have students in your classroom who are very bright or who work at a higher level than the others. These students are often overlooked and not challenged because they are able to participate with success or even find other activities to fill their time, like reading library books or drawing pictures. Make it a habit to plan some extension activities for those students who appear to be just filling time once their work is done. These students can become the class experts or be given the task of using the Internet to find additional information about topics the class is studying.

Using learning centers in your classroom provides a unique opportunity to provide assignments on several levels so that your struggling students can do a basic task and others can complete a "challenge" task. You may even be surprised at the students who choose to attempt the challenge task. The results of their challenges will enhance everyone's understanding if you give them a chance to share their research with the class in some way. We will explore additional ways of challenging your most able students in Chapter Eleven. See Figure 5.2 for examples of ways to create challenge activities based on the revised Bloom's taxonomy (Anderson & Krathwohl, 2001).

Needs of Exceptional Education Students

As a classroom teacher, you will have a wide variety of students in your classroom. Some students may have already been identified as eligible for exceptional education (sometimes called special

Figure 5.2 Creating challenge activities based on Bloom's revised taxonomy (Anderson & Krathwohl, 2001).

Bloom's Level	Objective	Description of Activity
Remembering	Given cards with the elements of beginning, middle, and end (BME) format books on them, students will sort the elements into stacks showing whether they occur in the beginning, middle, or end of the book with ____ percent accuracy.	Students are provided with a sorting mat labeled B, M, and E. They are given cards with the elements of BME stories on them to sort into the place in the story where they occur. When they have completed the activity, they self-check their work using the answer key available from the class helper (who checks to make sure the activity was completed prior to self-checking). (Elements: Characters are introduced, problem is identified, problem gets worse or more interesting, problem is solved.)
Understanding	Given examples of excerpts from familiar texts, students will identify them by selecting those that relate to each of the elements of BME format with ____ percent accuracy.	Students are given a story mat listing the elements of BME format stories and a handout containing excerpts from familiar stories that they will sort onto the story mat, demonstrating their understanding of the elements of BME stories. (Example: "Grandpa woke up and his teeth were missing." Child would place this sentence under Problem is identified.) After the activity has been completed, students self-check using the answer key available from the class helper.
Applying	Given a variety of books, students will identify the ones that follow the BME format with ____ percent accuracy.	Books are available to students at their reading levels. A visual showing the elements of BME book format is displayed at the center. Students are asked to identify two books in the group that follow the BME format. (This requires them to scan or read several of the books.)
Analyzing	Given statements of motivation, students will contrast them with characters in familiar BME stories and identify how the change in motivation might change the outcome of the story with ____ percent accuracy.	Students are given statements of motivation for characters in familiar stories. They then write a sentence or two describing how the motivation is different than that of the character in the story and how the outcome of the story might change if the main character had acted on the different motivation. Their results will be shared and discussed in a sharing circle after center time. (Example: What would have happened if Grandpa had blamed his grandkids for stealing his teeth?)
Evaluating	Given a variety of books at their reading levels, students will explain why one of the books does not follow the BME format with ____ percent accuracy.	Students are provided with a variety of books at their reading levels and a chart showing the elements of a BME story format. They must choose a book that they decide does not qualify as a BME book and justify their choice by writing a statement defending their decision. They will then present their book to the sharing circle and explain why they decided the book was not a BME format story.
Creating	Students will write a story following the BME format and include all the elements in the correct places with ____ percent accuracy.	Students are given time to write their own stories using the BME format. They use a planning sheet that contains the elements of the BME format to use as a prewriting activity.

Source: Some examples are adapted from *Grandpa's Teeth* by R. Clement (1997).

education). Others may be struggling with achieving grade-level standards and may require that you refer them for testing to determine whether they qualify for special programs.

If a child has identified disabilities of any type (physical, mental, or emotional), you are required to adapt your classroom instruction for this child in appropriate ways.

There are two types of written plans that are used with students who are identified as needing adaptations: the 504 plan and the Individual Education Plan. The *504 plan* is written for students who can function in the regular classroom with adaptation without being included in an exceptional education program. This plan is written by a school committee, usually consisting of the student's classroom teacher, the student's parent/guardian, and a guidance counselor; an exceptional education teacher is not part of this committee. In order for the plan to be effectively written, the classroom teacher must be able to provide examples of the student's work and behaviors over a period of time. This requires that the teacher make observations, collect work samples, and write anecdotal records documenting ways in which the student learns best and pinpointing areas of the curriculum in which the student experiences difficulty.

For students who are identified as qualifying for special assistance from an exceptional education teacher, an *Individual Education Plan (IEP)* is written. This plan is also written by a similar committee, but this time the committee includes an exceptional education teacher. The plan identifies learning goals and specifies the personnel responsible for addressing those goals. For example, a student struggling with reading may have reading instruction with both the classroom teacher and the exceptional education teacher, speech instruction with a speech clinician, and possibly other interventions with other specialists. These specifics would all be included in the IEP.

Both 504 plans and IEPs must be updated at least once a year. The classroom teacher plays an important role in the documentation of the interventions used in the classroom, providing work samples and anecdotal records of classroom observations and student/parent conferences. Effective updates of the plans are only possible when strong evidence is provided by the classroom teacher.

Interventions provided in the classroom must be documented by the classroom teacher for a period of 4 to 6 weeks, and the student's Response to Intervention (RTI) must be documented. In other words, the committee wants to know what intervention strategies are being used with the student, what the lengths of the interventions are, and what resultant learning takes place through the use of the interventions. This type of information is mandatory and necessary before changes in the plan are implemented to improve the student's learning and before a student can be referred for exceptional education programs. Figure 5.3 offers examples of interventions that might be used in the classroom.

Electronic record keeping is extremely important in tracking the interventions used, the length of each intervention, and the results obtained. This provides for efficient and timely updating of information and easy access to records for conferencing and planning. There are also computer programs available to assist the teacher in the following:

- Writing 504 plans and IEPs
- Cataloguing intervention strategies
- Sharing information among teachers and parents on a web-based system with limited access codes (such as SPEDASSIST)
- Creating yearly reports required by each district

Teachers in today's schools must be organized and reflective in order to maintain the types of records needed when serving diverse student populations. It is not at all unusual to have students with several different types of special needs in one classroom.

Needs of Students Not Working at Grade Level

You may discover that some of your students have not met the grade-level standards during their previous schooling. You are, of course, responsible for teaching the grade-level standards

Figure 5.3 Examples of classroom interventions.

Student Behavior	Sample Objective	Examples of Interventions
Does not demonstrate problem-solving skills	The student will solve problems by asking for clarification of information not understood ___ out of ___ occasions.	• Have the student repeat instructions and answer questions about what is expected of him/her. • Set aside time each day for problem-solving games and practicing clarifying questions. • Model the asking of clarifying questions when interacting with students.
Has difficulty with short-term and long-term memory	The student will recall information at intervals of 10–15 minutes on ___ out of ___ occasions.	• Assign one task at a time. Give the student adequate time to complete it. • Have the student develop a flow chart of the steps necessary to complete a task. • Use sentence dictation to develop the student's short-term memory skills. Begin with three-word sentences, and increase sentence length as the student demonstrates success. • Be sure to have the student's hearing tested if it has not been checked recently.
Is unprepared for tests	The student will study and perform classroom tests with ___ percent accuracy.	• Teach the student note-taking formats and ways to use the notes when preparing for a test. • Provide time and instruction in class to prepare for tests. Have the student chart his/her success, and provide incentives such as free reading time as his/her scores improve. • Reduce the number/length of tests and quizzes, and increase them gradually as the student demonstrates success.
Requires repeated drill and practice to learn what other students master easily Does not perform or complete classroom assignments during allotted class time	The student will use visual and auditory cues to practice concepts ___ percent of the time. The student will complete classroom assignments within the allotted time ___ percent of the time.	• Use wall charts to introduce a new concept; include visual images such as pictures for the student to associate with previously learned concepts. • Teach and practice a list of key vocabulary words to learn for each new concept. • Review concepts orally and write short sentences for the student to review when studying the concept. Provide review time each day for the student to review these sentences. • Reduce assignment directions to individual steps. Require that one step be completed before beginning the next step. • Have the student use a timer to complete tasks within a given time. Chart the time needed for completion so that he/she can see progress. • Follow a less desirable assignment with a highly desirable assignment. Require that the first assignment be completed before starting the second.
Does not remain on task	The student will remain on task until the task is completed ___ out of ___ times.	• Monitor the student's on-task time, and place a star on a small chart on his/her desk each time you walk by and the student is on task. Have him/her chart his/her stars each day to document progress. • Provide the student with a carrel or divider at his/her desk to reduce auditory and visual stimuli. • Provide the student with a predetermined signal (hand signal, verbal cue, etc.) when he/she begins to display off-task behaviors.

for the grade you are assigned. The students who are behind will need support so that they can move forward and hopefully catch up. You have several responsibilities to these children:

1. You must assess their skills and determine exactly what they know and can do.
2. You must plan lessons based on their present levels that are designed to move them forward.
3. You must provide additional instruction to help them achieve the missing skills.
4. You must continue to include them in the activities of the class and provide support so that they can be as successful as possible while they are catching up.
5. You must provide all this support in a way that encourages them, motivates them, and validates their efforts.

If this sounds like a lot of responsibility, it is. This is one of the most challenging of a teacher's assignments. You are responsible for all your students, and you must take them where they are and move them forward. This requires careful planning. In order to have time to play catch up with the students who require it, you have to have some time during the day when the majority of your students are working independently so that you can provide additional instruction to those who need it.

One natural way of providing this type of differentiated instruction is to work with small groups. By grouping your students for instruction, you can provide expanded opportunities for students who are ready to move more quickly and also provide catch-up instruction for those who are behind. Grouping also keeps the catch-up groups from feeling that they are being singled out or punished.

When providing whole-group instruction, consider using the following four-step instructional model:

1. *Teacher explanation.* You present the material to be learned and the reason for learning it.
2. *Teacher modeling.* You demonstrate what is to be done.
3. *Guided practice.* You walk the students through the skill or task to be performed with guidance.
4. *Independent practice.* The students practice the skill or task independently.

The beauty of this model is that it provides a natural time for additional guided practice for those who need it. The majority of the class will be ready to go to independent practice after some limited guided practice. While they work independently, the teacher can gather the students who need additional instruction and engage in additional guided practice.

Student Learning Styles

Learning styles are identifiable preferences that students exhibit that serve to improve their ability to learn. There has been much speculation over the past 30 years related to determining the importance of learning styles, identifying learning styles, and adapting teaching methods to individual learning styles. Dunn and Dunn (1992) in their book, *Teaching Elementary Students through Their Individual Learning Styles: Practical Approaches for Grades 3–8*, address ways in which students are affected by elements in the classroom and identify four elements:

1. The student's immediate environment (sound, light, temperature, and design)
2. The student's emotionality (motivation, persistence, responsibility, and need for structure or flexibility)

3. The student's sociological needs (working by oneself, in pairs, with peers, with an adult, or varied)

4. The student's physical needs (perceptual needs, intake, time, and mobility)

Dunn and Dunn (1992) also make several recommendations for teachers planning to address differing learning styles in their students:

- Make changes in the classroom arrangement that will benefit all students, such as redesigning the classroom to allow for easy movement, developing small-group techniques, and using contracts to motivate students to work at their best level.

- Use dividers for students in the classroom to provide learning stations with limited noise and movement as distractions.

- Use multisensory resources, including auditory, visual, tactile (the need to use the sense of touch in order to learn), and kinesthetic (the need to move the body in space in order to learn), to teach the required curricular content.

Marilee Sprenger in her book, *Differentiation through Learning Styles and Memory* (2003), gives suggestions for approaches to be used for students with perceptual needs—visual, auditory, tactile, kinesthetic. She stresses the use of a variety of approaches to meet the needs of all learners:

- Methods for visual learners include ensuring that students can see words written down, using pictures to clarify concepts and vocabulary, drawing time lines for events in history, writing assignments on the board, and using overhead transparencies or SMART Boards to display visuals, instructions, etc.

- Methods for auditory learners include repeating difficult words and concepts aloud, incorporating small-group discussions, organizing debates, listening to books on tape or CD, writing and presenting oral reports, and encouraging oral interpretations.

- Methods for tactile learners include using realia (concrete representations) and allowing students to touch the models; encouraging students to use whiteboards or chalkboards to write information in large print; teaching student to trace letters, pictures, and numbers; and teaching students note-taking strategies.

- Methods for kinesthetic learners include dramatic reenactments, role playing, movement activities, and opportunities for movement between classroom activities.

Planning for different learning styles in your classroom involves observing your students. If you provide a variety of activities in your classroom and allow students to choose among them, you will get some important information about their learning preferences. If you have students who are having difficulty completing their work in the classroom, moving them to a quieter area of the classroom where there are fewer distractions and observing the results will help you decide if these are students who need a quieter learning environment. It is important that you recognize the possibilities of these differences ahead of time so that you can plan quiet areas, areas nearer the windows with better light, places away from the high-traffic areas of the classroom. A class discussion of learning styles will also provide information because many students are aware of their learning styles and needs. There are several inventories of learning styles available online, and it is interesting to have the students complete one of these inventories and then compare the results to your observations:

www.learning-styles-online.com/inventory/questions.asp

http://people.usd.edu/~bwjames/tut/learning-style/stylest.html

www.personal.psu.edu/bxb11/LSI/LSI.htm

www.engr.ncsu.edu/learningstyles/ilsweb.html

http://ttc.coe.uga.edu/surveys/LearningStyleInv.html

Interactive Goal Setting

Teachers can support the growth of their students' levels of performance by using interactive goal setting as a natural forum for celebrating growth and setting goals for the future. Vince Workman, a fifth-grade teacher in Fresno, California, sets aside time to discuss his students' accomplishments with them during each of the six grading periods in the school year. He schedules these student conferences throughout the year, recycling back through his class in approximately the same order so that students can expect to meet with him for goal setting every 6 weeks. Since Vince and his students work together to select work samples for student portfolios, he begins the conferences by asking the students to talk about the work they have accomplished since their last student–teacher conference. Students talk about the work they have chosen to share; then together, the teacher and the student look at the grade-level standards and decide which of the standards have been met or are in the process of being met. They decide together on an appropriate challenge for the next week.

For example, Alberto, an ELL who is reading at approximately the third-grade level, has set a goal of reading two library books a week. He is keeping a reading journal and a vocabulary notebook to monitor his own understanding of the books he is reading and to focus on building his English vocabulary. Vince encourages Alberto to use the new words he is learning every day and often calls on Alberto in class to share some of the new words he is practicing. Because vocabulary study is one of Alberto's self-selected goals, he is much more motivated to keep working on his vocabulary journal. Vince talks to him briefly almost every day about new words he is exploring and celebrates Alberto's growing word knowledge with him frequently by simple responses such as, "That's a great word for that, Alberto. Explain where you first found that word and some of the ways you have found to use it." Alberto's first vocabulary goal was to learn two new words a day. He has increased his goal every 6 weeks so that he is now focusing on six new words each day. His vocabulary journal helps both Alberto and Vince to track the progress he is making. A sample page from Alberto's vocabulary journal is shown in Figure 5.4.

Self-Esteem and Intrinsic Motivation

A student's ability to learn is greatly enhanced when self-esteem and self-perception are strong and the student has a high degree of motivation. Krashen (1996) suggests that students who feel valued, who feel like the tasks they are being asked to accomplish are "doable," and who feel they can make mistakes without recrimination are more open to instructional processes. When students think the work is too difficult or they are afraid to ask questions and to seek help, their "affective filter" is raised, impeding the educational processes. This means that

Figure 5.4   Alberto's vocabulary journal.

Week 1—Goal: Learn two new words each day.

Day 1:   Words from *Stellaluna*

Clutched   I told my mom that I clutched my bookbag so I would not lose it.

Clambered   I clambered onto the school bus after school.

Day 2:   Words from science class

Explored   We explored drops of water. We looked at them very closely.

Process   When water changes from water to steam, that is called a process of evaporation.

students' emotional needs are screening out any information being presented by the task or the text being read so that they are unable to absorb or thoroughly understand the educational input.

Raths (1998) also identifies eight emotional needs that people strive to satisfy. These are the need for love, achievement, belonging, self-respect, freedom from guilt, freedom from fear, economic security, and self-understanding. Raths believes that children whose needs are not satisfied exhibit negative, self-defeating behaviors such as aggressiveness, withdrawal, submissiveness, regressiveness, and psychosomatic illness.

Raths (1998) recognizes that teachers cannot expect to satisfy the many unmet needs experienced by all the students in their classrooms. However, he does believe that "children cannot check their emotions at the door and we should not expect them to. If unmet needs are getting in the way of a child's growth and development, his learning and his maturing, I insist that it is your obligation to try to meet his needs" (p. 141). Raths's (1998) book, *Meeting the Needs of Children*, contains many pages of specific suggestions about what teachers can do to help meet children's emotional needs so that they are free to learn.

Enhancing Effects of Student Success

All individuals want to win or succeed. Virtually all the students who walk into a classroom on the first day of school hope that this year will be *the* year, that this grade will be the grade, and that this teacher will be the teacher who will make it possible for them to succeed. Some enter secure in the knowledge that they have succeeded before, but they are still anxious to determine whether they can duplicate that success in this new situation. Others enter with a history of failure and harbor no more than a dim, hidden hope that maybe they can succeed if only they can overcome their bad habits and learn how to succeed.

Winning and success are two powerful motivators for future effort and achievement. In *Schools without Failure*, Glasser (1969) notes:

> As a psychiatrist, I have worked many years with people who are failing. I have struggled with each of them as they try to find a way to a more successful life. From these struggles I have discovered an important fact: regardless of his background, his culture, his color, or his economic level, *he will not succeed in general until he can in some way first experience success in one important part of his life.* Given the first success to build upon, the negative factors . . . mean little. (p. 5)

It is possible to restate Glasser's message as a significant principle of teaching and learning: When an individual experiences success in one important part of life, that person can succeed in life regardless of background, culture, color, or economic level. Glasser's (1998) *Choice Theory in the Classroom* is a practical guide to assist teachers as they reflect on the fundamental goals of education and begin to establish an environment where students can learn to make positive, productive choices that lead to success.

It is especially important for children who have been raised in culturally different settings to experience success in their new school environments. Caring, reflective teachers are quick to perceive that children who are new to the school or the community need to experience success quickly in order to adjust well to their new surroundings. Assign new students a task that you are sure is well within their capability, and then show your acceptance and satisfaction with the work they accomplish.

The same is true for students who may appear indifferent or even resentful of school and teachers. Try to understand that they may have a history of being unfairly treated by other, less caring teachers. Students who have faced failure over and over again often develop very negative attitudes toward schoolwork and frequently mask their need for approval with defensive and disruptive behaviors in an effort to hide their hurt and shame. You can be the teacher who helps them change their behavior by perceiving their need for success and structuring some tasks to fit their unique talents and abilities so that they can experience the true and lasting joy of succeeding and being productive.

Classrooms as Communities

How does a class of strangers or competitive individuals develop into a community? As with all other important classroom effects discussed in this chapter, the teacher has the power to create a positive, healthy, mutually supportive, productive classroom environment from the first day of school. Through furniture arrangement, schedules, body language, words of welcome, rules, consequences, and interactions with the class, the teacher demonstrates a unique leadership or teaching style to the students. A sense of community is also achieved through honest, open communication of needs and feelings among students and their teachers.

But it takes more than talk to create a classroom community. Students need to be taught to work together in obtaining mutually agreed-upon goals. These goals can be related to content standards such as supporting one another in learning multiplication tables, working together to complete a community-based project, or writing a collaborative reader's theater script to present at back-to-school night.

Communities of learners grow throughout the school year. They grow from roots established at the very beginning by a classroom teacher who accepts children's suggestions and builds on those ideas, integrating content into related studies based on students' unique interests. Communities recognize that diversity among its members is a positive factor. Cultural diversity tends to enrich the classroom communities when reflective teachers choose to celebrate differences among students rather than seek to make all students adapt to one standard.

Using Assessment Devices to Identify Students' Needs

In many ways, the teacher's role in diagnosing students' needs is quite similar to the role of a medical doctor in diagnosing disease. Doctors get information from observing and talking with patients about their medical histories. Similarly, teachers observe and talk with their students to assess their learning histories. But some important information needed for an accurate diagnosis cannot be observed or discussed. Just as doctors may find that laboratory tests provide them with valuable information about the patient, so teachers may find that achievement tests and other assessment procedures can provide them with valuable data about their students.

Many school districts use nationally normed standardized tests to assess the academic achievement their students make from year to year. The typical standardized test consists of reading, spelling, English, mathematics, science, and social studies exams given over a period of several days. The teacher does not write the questions or establish the criteria to fit a particular classroom; instead, the tests are created by nationally recognized testing companies, and the items are written to approximate what is taught across the nation in each subject area at each grade level.

Statistical calculations of test scores provide information about a student's performance. The score may be translated into a percentile or a grade-equivalent score. These interpretations are done by comparing the student's raw score with the raw scores of the sample population. A *percentile rank* tells you what percentage of the students tested scored below a given score; for example, if Joe receives a percentile rank of 78, this means that 78 percent of the students at Joe's grade level scored lower than he did.

Grade-equivalent scores were created by test publishers especially for use in schools. The results are reported as a function of grade level; for example, if Sally receives a grade-equivalent score of 4.2, this means that her performance is similar to that of students who are in the second month of fourth grade. If Sally is in the fourth grade, her score tells the teacher that Sally is doing about as well as she is supposed to be doing. If Sally is in the second grade, the score tells the teacher that Sally is capable of functioning like students who are 2 years above her present grade level, but if Sally is in sixth grade, her score alerts the teacher that Sally is functioning like students who are 2 years below her present grade level.

When used well to inform teachers about students' academic needs, standardized tests provide numerical scores that can be used to document the growth of students in their abilities to read, work math problems, and answer questions about academic subjects such as science, social studies, English grammar, and spelling.

Assessment strategies appropriate for ELLs and exceptional education students include the use of *observation and anecdotal records* (Rhodes & Nathenson-Mejia, 1993) by the classroom teacher and paraprofessionals, who watch these students' reactions and responses and document their growth. In addition, *performance sampling*, where students are asked to perform certain tasks while teachers observe and document their responses, is effective in monitoring and documenting student growth. The third assessment strategy, *portfolio assessment*, is a way of maintaining records of observations, performance sampling, and ongoing growth. These three assessment strategies, when combined, provide a rich store of information about ELLs and exceptional education learners and give a more complete picture of their individual growth and learning development (Herrell & Jordan, 2012).

The use of standardized tests varies widely from district to district. In some schools, they are used to diagnose learning difficulties of individuals so that corrective measures can be taken. In some school systems, the test results are published in local newspapers to compare how well students from different schools are doing in the basic skills. This practice is a controversial issue among educators because the tests were not designed to be used as a measure of excellence among schools, but the public and the press have come to believe that they can be used that way.

Interpreting Data from Students' Cumulative Files

Standardized test scores are recorded in a permanent record for each student. This record of information, called the *cumulative file* (often referred to as a *cume file*), is kept on each student in a school. Each year, the classroom teacher records in each student's file such data as information about the student's family, standardized test scores, reading levels, samples of written work, grades, and notes on parent–teacher conferences. At the end of a school year, the cume files are stored in the school or district office until the next year, when they are redistributed to the students' new teachers.

Obviously, these files contain much information for teachers to use in preliminary planning. By studying them, a teacher can make judgments about placement in reading, math, or other study groups before meeting the students. Alert teachers may discover information about a student's home environment, such as a recent divorce or remarriage, that can help them in communicating with the student. Some files may reveal little about the students; others may be overflowing with records of conferences or staffing signaling which students have exhibited a special need or difficulty.

Yet many teachers resist looking at their students' cume files before meeting the class. Kidder's (1989) *Among Schoolchildren* provides a realistic look at the entire school year of a fifth-grade class in upstate New York. In the opening chapter, which describes the beginning of the school year, the teacher, Chris Zajac, reflects on the value of cume files as she ponders what to do with a student named Clarence, whose negative attitudes toward school have become apparent on the first day of school:

> Chris had received the students' cumulative records which were stuffed inside salmon-colored folders known as "cumes." For now she checked only addresses and phone numbers and resisted looking into histories. It was usually better at first to let her own opinions form. But she couldn't help noticing the thickness of some cumes. "The thicker the cume, the more trouble," she told Miss Hunt. "If it looks like *War and Peace*. . . ." Clarence's cume was about as thick as the Boston phone book. And Chris couldn't help having heard what some colleagues had insisted on telling her about Clarence. One teacher whom Chris trusted had described him as probably the most difficult child in all of last year's fourth-grade class. Chris wished she hadn't heard that. (pp. 8–9)

Although data and observations about students made by former teachers may be a valuable resource for planning, many reflective teachers, like Chris, are aware of the power of the self-fulfilling prophecy, in which their own expectations may influence the way their students behave or achieve in school. Teacher expectations can lead to self-fulfilling prophecies; in other words, what you expect from a student may interfere with your ability to make objective observations. If you expect Janie to fail, you may only see the mistakes or misbehaviors she displays and may overlook or discount her attempts to show improvement. In this way, your expectations can discourage Janie from trying very hard because you fail to notice when she does her work well, and she may give up her efforts and live "down" to your expectations.

When cume files contain data and descriptions of low academic achievement or misbehavior, nonreflective teachers may assume that the students are unteachable or unmanageable. On the first day of school, the teacher may place such students at desks set apart from the rest of the class or hand them textbooks from a lower grade. These teacher behaviors tell the students how the teacher expects them to behave and perform in this class. If these expectations are consistent over time, they are likely to affect the students' self-concept and motivation in such a way that they achieve poorly and behave badly. In contrast, consider the possible effects of warm and encouraging teacher behavior on these students. If the teacher builds rapport with these students, includes them in all classroom activities from the first day, and works with them to establish their achievement levels and needs, it is likely that their behavior and achievement will improve during the year.

Reflective teachers who understand the great influence of their expectations on their students prefer to assess the strengths and needs of each student independently in the first few weeks of class; then they may read the cume folders at the end of September to see how their assessments fit with those of the students' previous teachers.

A good case can be made for either point of view: using cume folders for preliminary planning, or waiting to read them until the students are well known to you. This is an issue that you will need to consider and decide for yourself. Perhaps if you understand the power of teacher expectations, you can find a way to use the information in the files to establish positive expectations and resist the tendency to establish negative ones.

Avoiding Labels for Students

Tests and other recorded information about a student can sometimes cause teachers and parents to think about students in oversimplified terms, or labels. Whether you gain information about your students through formal assessments or informal interactions, it is important to avoid the temptation to categorize or stereotype particular students. You can probably recall a time in your own life when you were burdened with a label you resented. Perhaps you dealt with a nickname that you detested or an academic designation that failed to capture your real potential. Learning about your students and acting in their best interests without labeling require a great deal of care and reflection. How often a quick perusal of a cumulative file, a glance at a standardized test score, or a few days of observation in the classroom have led a teacher to label a student as a *slow learner*, a *behavior-disordered student*, or an *underachiever*. These labels can stick for life! When communicated to a student and his or her family (whether indirectly or directly), such labels can have disabling effects all by themselves. Many labels imply that a student is deficient in some way and contribute to a self-fulfilling prophecy, where further erosion of self-concept and self-confidence causes even more severe learning difficulties.

Students with excellent school performance can also suffer from labeling. Some teachers refer to their most capable and willing students as overachievers. This pseudoscientific term is attached to students whose tests scores are only moderate but whose grades and work habits are excellent. The implication is that these students are working beyond their capacity, and this is somehow seen as a negative characteristic by some teachers (and some peers).

Students with high test scores on standardized tests, especially IQ or achievement tests, are frequently labeled *as gifted students*. At first glance, this label may appear very positive; certainly many parents seek it for their children. Careful reflection, however, reveals that this label can be as damaging as any other. Rimm (2008) notes that "any label that unrealistically narrows prospects for performance by a student may be damaging" (p. 84). Being labeled a *gifted student* tends to narrow the expectations for performance for that student to a constant state of excellence, so any performance less than excellent can be interpreted by the student and/or the parent as unacceptable.

The *gifted* label also has other negative implications. Eby and Smutny (1990) ask a question: If 2–5 percent of the students in a given school are labeled as *gifted*, then what are the other 95–98 percent of the students? Not gifted? What is the hidden consequence for a sibling or a very good friend of a so-called gifted student? What happens to the student who scores a few percentage points below the cutoff score for a particular gifted program? What do we call him, *almost gifted*?

Broader labels also carry damaging consequences. The term minority carries a connotation of being somehow less than other groups with respect to power, status, and treatment. Terms such as *economically disadvantaged, culturally deprived*, and *underprivileged* may also create stress and anxiety among those to whom they are applied. These may be especially insidious because they fail to acknowledge the value and unique contributions of various individuals or groups.

As you become aware of the various strengths and needs among your students, you can work to address them without relying on labels. Students who are learning English can be joyfully released to work with a special tutor and be warmly welcomed back to the classroom. Children who encounter difficulty working in large-group settings can spend part of their day in small groups and build interaction skills in larger groups under carefully designed conditions. Children who learn more quickly can be challenged to extend their thinking through engaging inquiry projects. No matter what their needs, our students can be welcomed to our classrooms as unique and valued individuals—labeled only as *important, cared for*, and *wanted*.

Using Pretests to Diagnose Students' Needs

Pretests are assessment devices designed to gather useful information to plan what students need to learn and what teachers need to teach. At the beginning of a term or a unit of study, teachers use pretests to determine what skills and knowledge pertaining to the subject students already have mastered. Pretests can take the form of brief short-answer quizzes, or teachers may ask students to write a paragraph or two telling what they already know about a topic to be studied. Students may also describe any prior studying they have done in another year or another class and any experiences they have had on family trips or elsewhere that relate to the topic about to be explored.

The best use of pretests occurs when the teacher and the students discuss the results together and share their insights into what the students need to do next. For example, a pretest may reveal a pattern of correctable mistakes in a mathematics operation. The teacher may be able to reteach the process quickly, and the student will be able to proceed successfully. In another instance, the pretest may reveal that a student has mastered the material already, and the conference may then focus on an enriched or accelerated learning opportunity for that student while the others are learning the material.

Making Placement and Grouping Decisions

In the past, standardized tests were frequently used to qualify students for special programs such as exceptional education, classes for the gifted, or bilingual education. In most cases, these types of placements are no longer made solely on the basis of test results but also include opportunities for the parents and teachers involved in students' education to provide information and share in the decisions. Currently a 504 plan that documents classroom interventions and a student's response to the interventions is required prior to placing a student in any exceptional education program.

For many years, teachers used pretests and standardized test scores to determine students' placement in reading groups for instructional purposes. In more recent years, teachers have began using more authentic types of reading assessments such as Clay's (2006) observation survey and reading observations called *running records* to document students' reading abilities, use of strategies, and cueing systems. In kindergarten and first-grade classes, students are grouped in flexible reading groups for guided reading instruction. They read short paperback books for this instruction so that the groups can remain flexible. The short books can be read in one reading group period, and then students can be regrouped when they show the need. This practice is helping to eliminate the old traditional "speedboats, sailboats, and rowboats" reading groups that were set in concrete; that served to convince students that they were poor readers because they were always placed in the low (rowboats) reading group; and that kept them there for their entire elementary school careers. Teachers today are finding that grouping can help students to learn if the grouping is done with careful reflection. Heterogeneous groups where each student has a special function are being used frequently in classrooms because each student gets more opportunities to interact, work together to solve problems, and discuss the task to be done.

Teachers may also use data from pretests, observations, and running records to create cooperative groups and partners for peer tutoring. To strengthen student motivation and interaction, many teachers employ the cooperative team concept. Cooperative groups typically consist of three to five students who are assigned a set of tasks to complete by cooperating with and assisting one another. Each student in the group has an assigned function, and the group members must work together to complete the assignment. Cooperative groups are extremely effective when they are given instruction in working together to achieve their goals. In some classrooms, teachers use pretest data to decide which students to assign to each team. Often teachers use cooperative groups to promote peer coaching and interactive assistance among their students. In this case, a team of four students may consist of one student with very strong performance, two with moderate performance, and one with relatively weak performance in the subject area. Similarly, peer tutoring dyads may consist of one student who is skilled and one who is less skilled or one student who has little English vocabulary and another student who speaks the same home language but can speak English at a higher level. These are simply examples; other types of cooperative group placement decisions, for different purposes, are also possible.

Using Performance Sampling and Portfolio Assessment

Performance sampling is a type of authentic assessment where a student is observed in the process of accomplishing academic tasks and is evaluated on the way in which the tasks are done. Performance sampling is well named because the teacher observes a sample of the student's performance in given academic tasks. Following are examples of the types of tasks used in performance sampling:

- Working math problems
- Responding to a writing prompt by creating a prewriting activity, writing a draft paper, and then revising the paper
- Researching a topic in science or social studies and creating a poster or overhead transparency to demonstrate the main concepts that were researched

Performance sampling is particularly appropriate for assessing ELLs and exceptional education students and for documenting students' responses to interventions. This is true because the degree of achievement they can demonstrate is based on their ability to perform the task (Hernandez, 2001).

Portfolio assessment is a term that refers to a system for gathering observations, performance samples, and work samples in a folder or portfolio; analyzing the contents of the portfolio on a regular basis; and summarizing the students' progress as documented by the contents of the portfolio (Herrell & Jordan, 2012). Often, students are involved in making selections of work to be kept in the portfolio. Students are also involved in reviewing and summarizing the work, setting goals for future work, and sharing the contents of their portfolios with parents (Farr & Tone, 1994).

This approach to assessment is particularly appropriate for ELLs and exceptional education students because it allows assessment based on actual sampling of the students' work and their growth, with less dependence on scores on standardized tests, which are often difficult for these students to understand (Hernandez, 2001). Portfolio assessment allows students to demonstrate their content knowledge without being so dependent on English fluency or reading ability. The strength of this approach to assessment is its celebration of progress rather than a focus on weaknesses.

Involving the Larger Educational Community

If planning for and providing differentiated instruction seems like an overwhelming task, there is good news. You, as the classroom teacher, don't have to do it all yourself. Your school and community are full of resources that you can employ to help you.

Following the reflective action model involves conferring with other professionals to solve challenges in your classroom. You have specialists in your school or district who can help you identify resources and plan ways to redesign your classroom to meet the needs of your students. For example, your library media specialist can help you locate books at a variety of reading levels, resource materials (maps, visuals, computer programs) for teaching units of study, computer programs for providing extra practice for students who need remediation in such things as math facts or vocabulary.

Your technology specialist—if you are lucky enough to have one—can help you design ways of using technology to better meet the needs of your visual and tactile learners. These specialists can also help you learn to use available technology and integrate computers, SMART Boards, overhead projectors, and other technologies such as a Global Positioning System (GPS) or a handheld computer.

Exceptional education teachers will be able to suggest interventions for students who are experiencing difficulty in the classroom. They can help you to devise approaches to documenting the success of any interventions you implement.

Community resources, including public libraries, museums, nature programs such as zoos and nature preserves, and arts programs, are all available to teachers to enrich their curriculum. Many of these resources will bring programs into the classroom to support your unit plans and help to meet the differing needs of your students.

Communicating with parents sometimes becomes challenging when the parents don't speak or read English fluently. It is important to make sure that all your parents are receiving information in a form that they can use. Most schools have someone on staff who can translate notes and newsletters so that parents can be aware of the needs that their children have or the important events that take place at the school. Using these services requires some advance planning, however. Translation takes time. If there is no one available to provide this important service, there are several reliable translation sites online. Before you use these online services for translation, though, it is very helpful to have a native speaker read through the translation to make sure you are saying what you want to say. Go to www.world.altavista.com to try out the translation service.

Many businesses allow their employees flex time to volunteer in schools. If you are planning a unit of study that relates to a business in your community, you can contact the business and ask if they have someone who could come to work with your students: Banks could have someone to explain how to use automatic teller machines (ATMs) or how to write checks or balance a checkbook; restaurants could send someone to demonstrate

sanitary food preparation or different ways to prepare vegetables to make them more appealing; and engineering firms might offer to have someone teach a lesson on the importance of building strong foundations.

The list of possibilities is endless. The key to using community resources is, of course, to know your community and establish good lines of communication with possible resources. Most businesses recognize that supporting their local schools is good business and are often open to supporting your students' needs.

Group Focus Activity

This exercise provides practice in recognizing different levels of English language development.

1. Divide the class into small groups. One student in each group serves as the recorder, and another serves as the reader.

2. Each group reader reads aloud each of the scenarios provided in Figure 5.5.

3. Using Figure 5.1 as a resource, each group identifies the English language development level for each student described in the scenarios. They should also give an explanation as to how they determined the language development level for each student. The recorder will be taking notes so that the group can report back to the class.

4. Bring the groups back to together to share, compare notes, and discuss their findings.

Preparing for Your Licensure Exam

In this chapter you read about ways to differentiate instruction to meet the varying needs of students. Reread "A View into the Classroom" at the beginning of the chapter, and think about it as a case study you might encounter on your licensure exam. Answer the following questions to demonstrate your understanding of the process of unit planning:

1. In what ways did Marcy differentiate instruction in her classroom?

2. What methods are recommended to identify individual needs of students?

3. How can a teacher use learning centers to provide differentiated instruction?

Portfolio of Professional Practices Activity

You need to show evidence of your ability to use analysis in a student needs assessment plan. Providing appropriate instruction requires that you have a plan for truly getting to know your students. To practice ways of gaining knowledge of your students, we suggest that you interview a student to determine that student's academic needs at this point in time. Select a student whose culture is different from yours. Talk with the student about what is important and valued in his or her family.

Ask questions to learn about how this student prefers to learn. Sample questions are provided here, but you may want to make up your own as well:

Do you learn easily by reading about something?

Do you learn well by listening to a teacher explain something?

Do you need the teacher to write examples on the board?

Figure 5.5 Scenarios for the group focus activity.

1. Juan is 8 years old, and his family speaks Spanish at home. He seems to be fluent in English on the playground. He has an accent and makes grammatical errors but has no problem making himself understood. In the classroom, however, he has great difficulty reading the textbooks, although he can read the third-grade reading text with some mispronunciations. He is not able to answer questions about what he has read and also has difficulty understanding the meanings of the words he reads.

2. Maria is a quiet 5-year-old with big brown eyes. She doesn't speak at all but watches everything that is going on around her. She seems to understand what is being said to her because she lines up with the other students, comes to circle time when the signal is given, and follows oral directions. On the playground, she plays with the other girls, but they always converse in Spanish.

3. Chan is the most popular fellow on the playground. He is a great soccer player and shouts instructions to his teammates in English. In the classroom, he is fairly successful and can complete most assignments, although he sometimes needs extra guidance in following directions. He often asks, "What's that word mean, teacher?" when class discussion involves science or social studies concepts. His pronunciation is fairly accurate, but he often omits articles in his reading, speaking, and writing.

4. Ivan is one of the most verbal students in the classroom. His oral delivery is rapid, although he often mispronounces words. He leaves off plurals and other endings, but it doesn't seem to slow him down. He has a wealth of background knowledge in his native language, Russian. He's eager to share this information and wants the teacher to help him perfect his English.

5. Ming is just beginning to put together English sentences. She listens attentively and tries to imitate English pronunciation. She gets confused when you give her more than one direction at a time, but she always tries to do what she is asked. She has developed a habit of watching the other students before she responds to directions because she doesn't want to do the wrong thing. She is most comfortable in activities where she can reply with a formula sentence like, "I would like red one, please."

Do you learn best by having somebody show you something or by working alone?

Do you need a quiet room, or can you work when others are talking or when the television is on?

Does it bother you when there is movement around you?

After your interview, write an initial description of which conditions this student needs in order to learn and feel safe and comfortable in your classroom. Ask yourself what else you need to know in order to make a thorough assessment of this student's needs. What information can you find on the Internet that relates to needs assessment? Talk to an experienced teacher or try a chat with other teachers on the Merrill Methods Cluster page or on www. Schoolnotes.com. If possible, try to meet this student's family and learn what the parents' hopes and expectations are for their child.

Write an analysis of this student's academic and social/emotional needs in the classroom. What do you think motivates this student to learn? Why does this student have certain strengths and weaknesses? Give evidence to support your analysis and conclusions. Then write a brief action plan describing the classroom conditions that you believe to be important for this student to learn effectively. Include in your plan ideas for encouraging this student to feel safe and comfortable in your classroom.

References

Anderson, L., & Krathwohl, D. (Eds.). (2001). *A taxonomy for learning, teaching, and assessing: A revision of Bloom's taxonomy of educational objectives.* Boston, MA: Allyn & Bacon.

Bruner, J. (1997). *The culture of education.* Cambridge, MA: Harvard University Press.

Clay, M. (2006). *An observation survey: Of early literacy abilities* (revised 2nd ed.). Portsmouth, NH: Heinemann.

Clement, R. (1997). *Grandpa's teeth.* Sydney, NSW, Australia: HarperCollins Publishers Pty Limited.

Cummins, J. (1986). Empowering minority students: A framework for interaction. *Harvard Review, 56,* 18–36.

Dixon-Kraus, L. (1996). *Vygotsky in the classroom: Mediated literacy instruction and assessment.* White Plains , NY: Longman.

Dunn, R., & Dunn, K. (1992). *Teaching elementary students through their individual learning styles: Practical approaches for grades 3–8.* Boston, MA: Allyn & Bacon.

Eby, J., & Smutny, J. (1990). *A thoughtful overview of gifted education.* White Plains, NY: Longman.

Farr, R., & Tone, B. (1994). *Portfolio performance assessments.* Fort Worth, TX: Harcourt Brace.

Glasser, W. (1969). *Schools without failure.* New York, NY: Harper & Row.

Glasser, W. (1998). *Choice theory in the classroom.* New York, NY: Perennial.

Hernandez, H. (2001). *Teaching in multilingual classrooms.* Upper Saddle River, NJ: Merrill/ Prentice Hall.

Herrell, A., & Jordan, M. (2012). *Fifty strategies for teaching English language learners* (4th ed.). Upper Saddle River, NJ: Merrill/Prentice Hall/Pearson.

Johnson, D., & Johnson, R. (1993). *Circles of learning: Cooperation in the classroom.* Alexandria, VA: Association for Supervision and Curriculum Development.

Kidder, T. (1989). *Among schoolchildren.* Boston, MA: Houghton Mifflin.

Krashen, S. (1996). *The natural approach: Language acquisition in the classroom.* Upper Saddle River, NJ: Prentice Hall.

Raths, L. (1998). *Meeting the needs of children.* New York: Educator's International Press.

Rhodes, L., & Nathenson-Mejia, S. (1993). Anecdotal records: A powerful tool for ongoing literacy assessment. *The Reading Teacher, 15,* 503–509.

Rimm, S. (2008). *Why bright children get poor grades.* Scottsdale, AZ: Great Potential Press.

Slavin, R. (1995). *Cooperative learning* (2nd ed.). Boston, MA: Allyn & Bacon.

Sprenger, M. (2003). *Differentiation through learning styles and memory.* Thousand Oaks, CA: Corwin Press.

Tomlinson, C. (2005). *The differentiated classroom: Responding to the needs of all learners.* Upper Saddle River, NJ: Pearson Education.

Using Teaching Strategies That Engage Students in Active, Authentic Learning

Frances Roberts/Alamy

"Learners need time and opportunities to use and practice new learning in realistic ways."

Brian Cambourne, author of *The Whole Story: Natural Learning and the Acquisition of Literacy in the Classroom* (1993)

The mission of teachers is to be knowledgeable about the subjects they teach and about how they teach those subjects to students. The knowledge of subject matter, while essential, is not enough to become a master teacher. Certified teachers must also be able to demonstrate the knowledge and skills needed to present the subject matter to students effectively. Teachers need to employ a variety of teaching methods, including analogies, metaphors, experiments, demonstrations, and illustrations. In this chapter, we describe these methods and many more that you can learn how to use in your classroom.

Teachers are also responsible for managing and monitoring student learning. They should place a premium on student engagement. Our model of reflective action in teaching also makes active student engagement a priority. Facilitating student learning is not simply a matter of placing young people in educative environments; teachers must also motivate them, capturing their minds and hearts and engaging them actively in learning.

Teachers need to use multiple methods to meet their goals. Accomplished teachers should know how to employ a variety of instructional skills: how to conduct Socratic dialogues, how to lecture, how to oversee small cooperative learning groups. The ensuing sections of this chapter will provide you with the basic ideas of these and many other teaching strategies. As a reflective teacher, you know that the information in this textbook is just a starting place. You will need to do more research on each strategy to become proficient in it.

Questions for Reflection as You Read the Chapter

1. What is authentic learning?
2. How does a teacher meet standards and provide authentic learning?
3. What teaching skills and approaches enhance student learning?

A View into the Classroom

Jeff Butler teaches a fifth-grade classroom in Fayetteville, Arkansas. His students enter his classroom each morning bursting with energy and ready to be fully engaged in their own learning. Jeff states that he had an exciting teacher in his elementary years, so he wanted to become a teacher who motivated his students to enjoy learning.

"I thought back to my year in sixth grade," Jeff explains. "I remember that Mr. Bowen was enthusiastic about learning. He would often say things like, 'Watch this! This is so neat!' when he was demonstrating science principles. He also planned hands-on learning every day. We didn't just read about things. We experimented with things, we wrote stories and books, we visited local museums and then created our own museum to show the history of our little town. We wrote grant proposals and got funding from the local city government for our museum. This wasn't simulation; this was real. That's the kind of classroom I want to create for my students."

When you enter Jeff's classroom, a student guide welcomes you. The guide has obviously been trained to explain what is going on in the classroom at the time, the displays that are on the bulletin boards, and the standards that are currently being addressed. The guide also proudly shows the shelves of student-written books in the library corner and explains how the students publish their own books using the word processing program on the classroom computer and binding the books in various ways they have learned as part of their writing program.

Jeff uses his language arts time each day to conduct a reading/writing workshop in which his students work through the stages of writing and publishing just as if they were "real authors."

The reading workshop is aligned with the writing workshop. The students read examples of writing of the genre they are studying at the time, which gives them examples of the formats they are using in their writing. For example, when they are writing poetry, they read great poetry and talk about the different forms that poetry can take.

Jeff's math program requires that he teach a series of math concepts assigned to his grade level. To make this curriculum more meaningful to his students, Jeff designs projects that require the students to actually use the math concepts in order to complete their project. The students can complete individual projects or work in small groups to complete larger projects. Jeff encourages his students to plan projects to benefit their school or community. For example, one spring his students planned a community garden, designed the plot using their geometry skills, researched the types of plants to plant at the correct time of year, figured out the amounts of water and fertilizer needed, and calculated the cost of the vegetable yield based on their expenditures. Just for fun, they kept track of the time they invested in planting, weeding, and harvesting and how much the vegetables would have cost if they had been paid employees. The families in the community kept the garden going over the summer and enjoyed the fresh vegetables. This project was funded by a local bank through a grant proposal Jeff and his students wrote jointly. One of his students wrote a book about the project illustrated with photographs showing each of the steps they took in completing the project. The student titled the book If You Plant It, They Will Eat!

Jeff uses a number of strategies to differentiate instruction in his classroom. He plans tiered assignments so that his students can begin a study at a basic level and gradually move up until they can complete challenge activities. The walls of the classroom display a number of charts that the students complete to celebrate their own progress. The charts show the levels of the activities completed and the dates of completion.

Jeff encourages his students to select their best work to add to their personal growth portfolio. When they add an assignment or written product to their portfolio, they write a brief statement telling what new skill the product represents. At the end of the school year, the portfolio contents are bound into a book titled My Fifth-Grade Memory Book. Jeff takes a lot of pictures during the year, and these photos are also included in the memory books.

REFLECTING ON THE CLASSROOM EXPERIENCE

Jeff was inspired by a creative teacher in his youth and approaches his curriculum and lesson planning with the intention of involving his students in memorable experiences. By providing an example of excellence to his students, Jeff offers them opportunities for authentic learning and celebrates their growing excellence with them. In education, we often refer to this type of teacher as "one who makes a difference."

As a beginning teacher, sometimes it's difficult to think of yourself as making a difference, but being a reflective teacher helps you to focus on improving your teaching every day. Planning authentic learning experiences isn't always easy, but it is well worth the effort if students develop skills, strategies, and attitudes that enable them to be more successful both in school and in life.

Authentic Learning

The term *authentic learning* is used to distinguish between the achievement of significant, meaningful, and useful knowledge and skills from that which is trivial and unrelated to students' lives. The Wisconsin Center on Organizing and Restructuring of Schools has concentrated on defining standards of authentic instruction. Its studies have led to the conclusion that many conventional instructional methods do not allow students to use their minds well and result in learning that has little or no intrinsic meaning or value to them beyond achieving success in school.

These studies recommend establishing standards for teachers to use as guidelines in selecting and learning to use teaching strategies that promote authentic learning. According to their research, the standards for authentic instructional methods should emphasize higher-order thinking, depth of knowledge, connectedness to the world, and substantive conversation and should provide social support for student achievement (Newman & Wehlage, 1993).

As a learner, you may have had teachers who used teaching strategies that stimulated you to use higher-level thinking and problem-solving skills. You may recall learning experiences that encouraged you to delve deeply into a subject that had real meaning to your life or class discussions that sparkled with enthusiastic exchanges of ideas and opinions within a social system that encouraged you to challenge yourself to make more and more meaningful accomplishments. If you recall school experiences such as these, you have experienced authentic learning.

You may have had other teachers who relied on conventional methods that required rote memorization of facts and dates or other content. You may recall learning a lot about a little or participating in boring recitations in which students were expected to parrot what they had memorized. You may remember competitive social systems that rewarded those students who were able to memorize and recite quickly and those who were able to figure out what the teacher wanted to hear. If you recall school experiences such as these, you will need to overcome the natural tendency to repeat learned patterns and challenge yourself to learn to use many new and exciting instructional strategies.

Your personal conception of the teaching and learning processes is drawn from your own experiences as a learner, but for reflective teachers, it is also drawn from the values and beliefs they hold about what students need to know and how students ought to behave, from perceptions and reflections about the theories and practices of other classroom teachers they observe. To become a reflective teacher, you must make yourself aware of the emerging research and knowledge base about teaching and learning. Gathering information from research is an important attribute of a reflective thinker and teacher.

Retrieval Process

Schema Theory

The retrieval process is obviously a critical factor in being able to use stored information. Knowledge, concepts, and skills that are learned must be stored in the brain until they are needed. According to Piaget's *schema theory* (1970), each subset of knowledge is stored in a *schema,* an outline or organized network of knowledge about a single concept or subject. It is believed that young children develop *schemata* (the plural form of schema) made up of visual or other sensory images; as their language skills increase, verbal imagery replaces sensory images.

For example, an infant stores sensual images in the schemata for his or her mother, bottle, bed, and bath; later the verbal labels are added. A schema grows, expands, or otherwise changes due to new experiences. If the infant sees and touches a large, round, blue rubber ball, he or she can store sensory images of its size, shape, color, and rubbery feel. At a later encounter, the infant may experience its bounce, and he or she can store these images in the same schema. A year later, when the child learns to say the word *ball,* the label is acted on in working memory and stored in long-term memory within the schema for ball.

Students come to school with varied schemata. Some students who have had many experiences at home, in parks, at zoos, in museums, and in other circumstances may enter kindergarten with complex schemata for hundreds of topics and experiences. Other students, whose experiences have been severely limited by poverty or other circumstances, are likely to have very different schemata, and some of these may not match the prevailing culture's values or verbal labels. Similarly, if students come from highly verbal homes where parents talk with them frequently, their schemata are likely to contain accurate verbal labels for stored sensory experiences and phenomena; students who are raised in less verbal homes, however, will have fewer verbal components to their schemata. This theory complements Piaget's observations of stages of development and helps us to understand how a child's vocabulary develops.

Schemata also vary according to their organizational patterns. As children mature, each schema expands to include many more facts, ideas, and examples. In cases of healthy development, the schemata are frequently clarified and reorganized. Learning new information or observing unfamiliar examples often causes a schema to be renamed or otherwise altered. For example, very young children have a schema labeled *doggy* that includes all four-legged, furry creatures. As they see new examples of animals and hear the appropriate labels for each type, the original schema labeled *doggy* is reorganized to become simply a subset of the schema *animal*. New patterns and relationships among schemata are forming every day of a child's life when the environment is full of unfamiliar concepts and experiences.

Schema theory helps to explain why some students are able to retrieve knowledge better than others. Students who have many accurately labeled schemata are more likely to have the background knowledge needed to learn an unfamiliar concept. Students whose schemata are richly detailed and well organized into patterns and hierarchies are much more likely to be able to retrieve useful information on request than are students whose schemata are vague and sparse.

Reflective teachers who believe that it is in their power to help their students improve their cognitive processing recognize that one of the best ways to do this is to stimulate students to actively create more well-developed, accurately labeled, and better organized schemata.

At the elementary grade levels, teachers recognize that one of their most important responsibilities is to aid students in schema development with accurate verbal labels. In the earliest grades (especially kindergarten), teachers emphasize spoken labels, teaching students to recognize and to name objects and concepts such as numbers, letters of the alphabet, and colors. In the primary grades, teachers emphasize the recognition and decoding of written labels as an integral part of the reading program. When students exhibit difficulties learning to read, the reflective teacher is likely to plan learning experiences that assist the students in developing schemata that are prerequisites for reading.

Students who have been raised in environments characterized by few experiences with books are likely to have an underdeveloped schema for reading and books. This may also prove true for English language learners, who may not have access to text material in the home or whose parents are reluctant to read books to them, even in their first language. Reflective teachers who consider the needs of the whole individual are likely to provide their students with many opportunities to hear stories read aloud, to choose from a tempting array of books, and to write their own stories as a means of developing a rich and positive schema for the concept of reading.

Advance Organizers

When teachers want to assist students in retrieving information from their schemata, they provide verbal cues that help the students access the appropriate information efficiently. In the case of English language learners, this may require multisensory cues, gestures, and visual cues as well. Teachers can also provide cues to assist students in accurately and efficiently processing and storing what they read, see, or hear. Ausubel (1960) proposed that learners can comprehend new material better when, in advance of the lesson, the teacher provides a clear statement about the purpose of the lesson and the type of information that learners should look or listen for. This introductory statement is known as an *advance organizer*. English language learners benefit from a similar teaching strategy called *preview/review*, in which they are given an advance organizer prior to the lesson and a review following the lesson, both in their native language. This allows them to be prepared for the information they are about to receive and to clear up any questions or misunderstandings they have following the lesson.

When we relate this theory to the information processing theory, it is apparent that the advance organizer provides the learner with an important cue as to which schema will incorporate this new knowledge. The learner can be more efficient in processing the information in working memory and transferring it to the appropriate schema in long-term memory than if no advance information was presented. For example, consider what is likely to happen when a third-grade teacher introduces a lesson on long division with no advance organizer. Some students will simply reject the new knowledge as incomprehensible. Using an advance organizer, the teacher might begin by writing an example on the board of a large number such as 100 and then ask students to subtract 10 from that number. Students will compute the subtraction problem as 100 minus 10 and get 90. Then they will compute 90 minus 10, 80 minus 10, and so on until they reach 0. In this way, students can use a previously learned skill of subtraction to organize their thoughts and make division more comprehensible. When the teacher asks how many 10s are in 100, the students can look at their subtraction problems and count the number of 10s they subtracted from 100. When the teacher then tells the students that division is a short way to solve this problem, it provides students with the cues they need to retrieve their subtraction schema in advance of the new learning.

In Chapter Three we read about Jeff Butler's unit of study of the migration of butterflies. The students learned to collect data and track the movement of butterflies using communication with students across the nation via the Internet. Had Jeff tried to lecture his students on the topic, many would have been bored and nonresponsive. Others may have been overwhelmed by the amount of data available. Students were motivated to learn because of the advance organizer Jeff used, explaining the migration concepts supported by visuals from the Internet and the students' personal experiences with butterflies. They were excited about using new technology in the project.

In follow-up studies of Ausubel's hypothesis, many educational researchers designed experiments that showed the same effects. Therefore, this knowledge has been added to our growing common knowledge base about teaching and learning. In fact, this particular study demonstrates the way in which the knowledge base grows. The original hypothesis and study conducted by Ausubel (1960) led others to apply the principle to different types of students and environments. As the hypothesis was confirmed in subsequent studies, the knowledge was gradually accepted as a reliable principle of effective teaching. You probably experience the beneficial effects of advance organizers when your teachers tell you in advance what to listen for in a lecture or what to study for an exam. Now you can learn how to use this principle in your teaching career for the benefit of your students.

Differentiated Instructional Strategies for Authentic Learning

As we discussed in Chapter Five, one size does not fit all. This commonsense idea is used as a metaphor for learning by Gregory and Chapman (2002) as they describe methods teachers can use to respond to students' individual differences. It is possible to differentiate your school program in four important ways: content, assessment tools, performance tasks, and instructional strategies.

The first requirement for a differentiated curriculum is the creation of a safe and nurturing classroom environment much as we described in Chapter Two. For students to be able to express needs and acknowledge differences, there needs to be a climate of warmth, safety, and nurturance. Students need to be encouraged to take risks and to recognize that what is a safe and easy task for one student may pose a risk for others. The classroom environment must be collaborative and inclusive of all ranges of abilities, talents, interests, and special needs without making a big point about it, without calling attention to it. This can frequently be accomplished by the creation of cooperative groups, which are called *tribes* by Gibbs (2001). Tribes are communities, and communities tend to be inclusive and collaborative. In addition, there needs to be a sense of heightened interest, challenge, and stimulation in the classroom so that all students feel suitably challenged.

In every class and for almost every assignment, there are likely to be students who have great difficulty achieving the objective. They are not likely to succeed unless the teacher modifies the initial lesson plan to provide them with individual or small-group lessons to reteach the skills they lack. For some children to achieve successful growth of skills and understanding, the teacher must be willing to alter the pace of the lessons, the difficulty of the material, and the criteria for success.

For students who learn more slowly, one modification that is needed is to reduce the volume of material in a lesson. If the grade-level lesson calls for the students to complete 20 problems in one class period, the teacher may reduce this requirement to 10 or 15 problems for a student who works slowly. If 20 problems were expected of this child, there would be little chance for success, resulting in frustration for both teacher and student. When the requirement is lowered, the student has an opportunity to succeed and is likely to show the increased motivation that accompanies success.

A child may have missed or not learned some important basic skills in previous grades for a variety of reasons. Illness, family problems, emotional difficulties, inferior teaching, or frequent moves may have prevented a child from learning the skills that most students his or her age have attained. For students who have not attained the basic skills necessary for a grade-level task, the modification needed is to teach the prerequisite skills before introducing the new material. When these prerequisite skills have been successfully mastered, the student may proceed at the same pace as the rest of the class.

One or more children in your classroom may be identified as having *learning disabilities*, which usually means that a child has one or more of a variety of learning disorders, some physical and others social or emotional in origin. When a student has been labeled *learning disabled*, a teacher who specializes in working with such students will be called on to create an Individual Education Plan (IEP) for that student; you, as the classroom teacher, will receive some guidance from the IEP on how to modify your lessons for that student.

In some schools, many students come from backgrounds where the primary language of the home is not English. This has implications for instruction and lesson planning. Although these students may be able to understand the content of the lessons, the teacher may need to vary the delivery of the content in order to make it comprehensible to them. English as a second language (ESL) or sheltered English programs may be available for students learning this new language. When this is the case, the ESL teacher can assist other teachers in assigning appropriate materials, adjusting teaching styles, and helping students acquire language skills that will help them to succeed. For students learning the language, it is necessary to offer contextualized learning experiences—lessons that provide context clues using props, visuals, graphs, and real objects. Teachers may need to speak more slowly and enunciate more clearly while encouraging their other students to do so as well.

Children with hearing impairments need lessons that are modified to provide directions and instruction using visual aids. Similarly, children who have sight impairments may require extra auditory learning aids. Less obviously, some children may have strong auditory, visual, or kinesthetic learning style preferences. To meet the needs of these children, teachers must modify their lessons to accommodate all three types of learning styles. For visual learners, this is usually accomplished by providing instructions and examples using visual aids such as the chalkboard, books, and written handouts. For auditory learners, the teacher may allow students to use tape recorders to record the instructions and examples given in class. Kinesthetic learners require manipulative materials and hands-on experience to make sense of unfamiliar material. When a teacher provides visual, auditory, and kinesthetic learning aids and experiences, students may modify their own lessons by taking in the needed information in the form that fits their own learning style preferences.

Acceleration and Enrichment Strategies

For students who work unusually rapidly and accurately on grade-level material, the task is to provide appropriately challenging learning experiences so that these students are able to continue to make gains even though they have mastered the grade-level requirements. Two standard methods serve the needs of highly able learners: *acceleration* and *enrichment*.

Although both strategies are valuable modifications, acceleration is appropriate for sequential subjects such as math, and enrichment is appropriate for other subject areas. An inappropriate modification is to give the child more work at the same level. For example, if 20 math problems are required of the students working at grade level, an inappropriate modification is to require the highly able learner to do 40 problems. This practice is common but does not serve the student's real need to be challenged to gain new skills and understanding.

Some acceleration strategies that teachers can choose from include ability grouping, curriculum compacting, and mastery learning. *Ability grouping* requires the teacher to modify the curriculum to correspond to three different groups in the classroom: High, middle, and low groups are created, with variations in materials and expectations for success. Reflective teachers must consider the possible negative consequences of lowered self-esteem and the possible positive benefits of academic fit and organizational efficiency when deciding whether or how to use ability grouping in the classroom.

In some schools, ability grouping may be organized across several grade levels. Subjects such as math and language arts may be scheduled at the same time of day, allowing students who work above or below grade level to leave their own classrooms and travel to other classrooms where the instruction is geared to their learning level.

Curriculum compacting can occur in a single classroom. This strategy requires the teacher to pretest students in various subject areas. Those children who demonstrate mastery at the time of the pretest are allowed to skip the subsequent lessons altogether, a strategy which compacts the grade-level curriculum for them. The teacher then provides materials at a higher level of difficulty for these students, who typically work on their own through the more difficult material with little assistance from the teacher, who is busy instructing the students at grade level.

Mastery learning is a highly individualized teaching strategy designed to allow students to work at their own pace on material at their own difficulty level. Pretests are used to place students at the appropriate difficulty level; as each new skill is learned, a posttest demonstrates mastery. This technique is described in more detail in Chapter Seven.

Enrichment strategies vary according to the imagination of the teacher who creates them. The teacher provides students who demonstrate mastery of a basic skill with a challenging application of that skill. Objectives and learning experiences at the higher levels of Bloom's taxonomy are often used as the basis for enrichment activities. A child who easily masters grade-level material is frequently allowed to investigate or research the topic in greater depth. For outcomes of enriched activities, students typically create an original product, perform an original skit, or teach the class something they have learned from research.

Modification of lessons is a continual challenge for teachers. It is not easy to decide whether a student needs a modified lesson, and reflective teachers struggle with this decision because they know that when they lower their expectations for a student, one of the effects may be lower self-esteem, creating the conditions for a self-fulfilling prophecy that the student cannot achieve at grade level. But they also know that when adult expectations are too high, students experience little or no success, leading to a similar downward spiral. For beginning teachers, it is wise to consult with other teachers in the school, especially teachers who specialize in working with children who have special needs. Talk over your concerns with these specialists, and make informed decisions about lesson modifications.

Presentation Skills

Teaching is more than telling. You have been on the receiving end of teachers' lectures, discussions, and other forms of lessons for many years, and you know from your own experiences that the way teachers teach or present material has an effect on student interest and motivation, which are both integral aspects of the classroom climate. You may have been unable to understand the beginning of a lesson taught by a teacher who failed to get the full attention of a class before speaking. You have probably experienced sinking feelings when a teacher droned on in a monotonous voice during a lecture, or you may have experienced frustration when a teacher explained a concept once and hurried on, ignoring questions or comments from the class. Reflective teachers are not likely to be satisfied with a dull, repetitive, or unresponsive presentation style. Most of them are anxious to improve their presentation skills to stimulate interest and motivate student achievement. Presentation skills that you can learn to use systematically in your lessons include the following: attention-getting beginning, enthusiasm, clarity, smooth transitions, timing, variation, interaction, and closure.

GETTING STUDENTS' ATTENTION.   To systematically consider the way you present a lesson, think about the beginning. The introduction to a lesson is very important, whether it is the first lesson of the day or a transition from one lesson to another. As Kounin (1977) found in his study of well-functioning classrooms, transitions and lesson beginnings start with a clear, straightforward message or cue signaling that the teacher is ready to begin teaching and stating exactly what students should do to prepare themselves for the lesson. To accomplish this when you teach, you need to tell your students to get ready for a certain lesson and to give you their full attention. Some teachers use a visual cue, such as a finger on the lips or a raised arm, for this purpose; others may strike a chime or turn off the lights to cue the students that it is time to listen.

It is unlikely that students will become quiet instantly. It will probably take a few moments to get the attention of every student in the class. While you are waiting, stand up straight and make direct eye contact with those who are slow to respond. Watch quietly as the students get their desks, pencils, books, and other needed materials ready for the lesson. The waiting may seem uncomfortable at first, and you may be tempted to begin before they are ready because you will think that time is being wasted. Do not give in to this feeling. Wait until every voice is quiet, every chair stops scraping, every desk top stops banging, and every pencil stops tapping. Wait for a moment of pure undisturbed silence; then quietly begin your lesson. You will have the attention of every student.

Some teachers use a bit of drama to begin a lesson. They may pose a question or describe a condition that will interest their students. Richard Klein, a teacher at the Ericson School on Chicago's West Side, begins teaching a unit on aviation by asking students what they know about the Wright brothers. The students' replies are seldom very enthusiastic, so he unexpectedly asks them, "Then what do you know about the Wrong brothers?" They show a bit more interest but are still unable to provide many informed responses. So Richard turns off the lights and turns on a videotape of the Three Stooges in a skit called "The Wrong Brothers." Afterward, partly in appreciation of Richard's humor, the students show a greater willingness to learn about the real historical events.

Often teachers begin with a statement of purpose, describing how this particular lesson will help their students to make an important gain in skills or knowledge. Still others begin by doing a demonstration or distributing some interesting manipulative materials. This technique is called providing an *anticipatory set*, both to gain attention and to motivate students to be interested in the lesson. Your presentation skills can benefit by using a variety of anticipatory sets appropriate to the lesson content and objective.

In contrast, less reflective teachers begin almost every lesson the same way: "Open your books to page _____. David, read the first paragraph aloud." This example employs no presentation skills. This nonmethod relies on the material itself to whet the students' interest in the topic. Although some materials may be stimulating and appealing, most are not. The message the teacher gives to the students is, "I don't care much about anything; let's just get through this." The students' motivation to learn drops to the same level as this message and can best be expressed as "Why bother?"

Teachers often display a greater degree of excitement and interest for material they themselves enjoyed learning, and they pass that excitement about learning on to the students. A teacher who reads aloud with enthusiasm conveys the message that reading is fun; a teacher who plunges into a science investigation with delight causes students to look forward to science. After you gain your students' attention and inspire them to want to know more, you move on to the lesson itself.

ENTHUSIASM.   Enthusiasm is the inner experience of a teacher's interest in his or her students and subject, and animation is its outward sign. There are at least two major aspects of enthusiasm. The first is sincere interest in the subject; the other aspect is vigor or dynamics, and both are related to getting and maintaining student attention. Outwardly, the teacher displays enthusiasm by using a bright, lively voice; open, expansive gestures; and facial expressions showing interest and pleasure. Salespeople who use animated, enthusiastic behavior could sell beach umbrellas in the Yukon in January. Why shouldn't teachers employ these techniques as well? You can "sell" long division better with an enthusiastic voice, you can convince your students that recycling is important with a look of commitment on your own face, and you can encourage students' participation in a discussion with welcoming gestures and a warm smile.

Is animation something you can control? Absolutely. You can practice presenting information on a topic with your classmates, using an animated voice and gestures. They can give you feedback, which you can use to improve your presentation. Have yourself videotaped as you make a presentation. When you view yourself, you can be your own best teacher. Redo your presentation with new gestures and a different voice. Repeat this procedure several times, if necessary. Gradually, you will notice a change in your presentation style, and you can add these new techniques to your growing repertoire of effective presentation skills.

CLARITY.   The clarity of the teacher's presentation of lesson directions and content is a critical factor in student success. Good and Brophy (2002) list the importance of teacher clarity as a consistent finding in studies of teacher effectiveness. Their review of research on teacher clarity describes negative teacher behaviors that detract from clarity, which include using vague terms, mazes, and discontinuity and saying "uh" repeatedly.

As an example of vague terms, consider how you would expect students to respond to a lesson introduced this way:

> See if you can find page 76, and look at this division problem. This example might help you to understand a little more about how this all works. Maybe if you read this, you can even get some idea of how to do these problems.

The vague terms such as *if, might, maybe,* and *how this all works* in this example have the effect of making the teacher sound tentative and unsure of the content. As an introduction to a lesson, it is not likely to capture students' attention or interest. Clarity can be improved in this example by exchanging the vague terms for specific ones, resulting in a simple, straightforward statement:

> Turn to page 76 and look at the long division problem at the top of the page. We will work through this example together until you are confident that you know how to do this type of problem.

Clarity also suffers from what Good and Brophy (2002) call *mazes,* which are false starts or halts in the teacher's speech, redundancy, and tangled words:

> Okay now, let's turn to page . . . um, just a minute. Okay, I've got it now. This chapter, er, section in the book lesson *will hopefully, um it better or we're both in trouble,* get you to understand multiplication, *uh,* facts . . . I mean the patterns behind, underlying the facts.

Even when students attempt to pay attention, they may be unable to decipher the meaning of the teachers' words if the presentation is characterized by the false starts in this example. It is obvious that the way to improve this statement is to eliminate the redundant words. Clarity is also reduced when the teacher begins to present a lesson, is interrupted by a knock at the door or a student's misbehavior, and then begins the lesson again. Kounin (1977) notes that the most effective teachers are able to *overlap* teaching with other classroom management actions, that is, they are able to continue with the primary task—presenting the lesson to the class—while at the same time opening the classroom door or stopping misbehavior with a glance or a touch on the shoulder. When teachers can overlap their presentations, the clarity of their lessons is greatly enhanced.

The third teacher behavior that detracts from clarity is discontinuity, in which the teacher interrupts the flow of the lesson by interjecting irrelevant content (Good & Brophy, 2002). This is why lesson planning is so important. Without a plan, teachers may simply begin a lesson by reading from a textbook. As they or the students are reading, the teacher (or a student) may be reminded of something that is interesting and may discuss the related topic for quite some time before returning to the original lesson. This side discussion may or may not be interesting or important, but it is likely to detract from the clarity of the original lesson.

The fourth detractor from clarity is the teacher repeatedly saying "uh." Other repetitive speech patterns, such as "you know," are probably just as annoying. For the beginning teacher, it is likely that some of these teacher behaviors will occur simply as a result of nervousness or unfamiliarity with the content being taught; these four detracting behaviors usually decrease as a result of teaching experience. In other words, as a teacher gains experience, the four detracting behaviors subside and clarity increases. Another teacher behavior found to enhance clarity is an emphasis on key aspects of the content to be learned.

SMOOTH TRANSITIONS.   Just as lesson introductions are important to gain students' attention, smooth transitions are essential to maintaining that attention and making the classroom a productive working environment. Transitions occur within a lesson as the teacher guides students from one activity to another. They also occur between lessons as students put away what they were working on in one lesson and get ready for a different subject.

Good and Brophy (2002) note that knowing when to terminate a lesson is an important element of teacher withitness. When the group is having difficulty maintaining attention, it is better to end the lesson early than to doggedly continue. This is especially important for younger students, whose attention span for even the best lesson is limited. When lessons go on after the point where they should have been terminated, more of the teacher's time is spent compelling attention and less of the students' time is spent thinking about the material.

In addition to moving students to another classroom, transitions between activities and lessons may require that students move from place to place in the room, such as having one group come to the reading circle while another group returns to their seats; usually students are also required to exchange one set of books and materials for another. These movements and exchanges have high potential for noise in the form of banging desk tops, scraping chairs, dropped equipment, and students' voices as they move from lesson to lesson.

Jerky, chaotic transitions result when the teacher gives incomplete directions or vague expectations about student behavior. "Take out your math books" is incomplete in that the teacher does not first specify that the students should put away other materials they have been working with. The result may be that the students begin to work on desks cluttered with unnecessary materials.

Often, inexperienced teachers begin to give directions for a transition, and the students start to get up and move around while the teacher is still speaking. When this happens, a teacher may attempt to talk louder so that he or she can be heard over the din. A way to prevent this from occurring is to inform students clearly that they are to wait until all directions have been given before they begin to move.

Smooth transitions are characterized by clear directions from the teacher about what is to be put away and what is to be taken out, who is to move and where they are to go. Clear statements of behavioral expectations are also important. The same techniques for getting attention that were described previously apply to the beginning of each new lesson. After a noisy transition between lessons, it is essential for the teacher to have the students' complete attention before beginning the new lesson, so the teacher should wait until all students move into their new positions and get all their materials ready before trying to introduce the lesson.

The teacher can use a signal to indicate that the new lesson is about to begin. Raising a hand, turning lights off and on, or giving a simple verbal statement such as "I am ready to begin" can signal to the students that they should be ready for the next lesson. After giving the signal, the teacher should wait until the students have all complied and are silent before beginning the new lesson.

In considering strategies that result in smooth transitions, teachers do well to reflect on the students' needs for physical activity. In a junior high or high school, students can move between periods. At the elementary school or in a block of time in the middle school, it is unrealistic to expect students to be able to sit still through one lesson after another. Some teachers take 5 to 10 minutes to lead students in singing or movement games between two working periods; other teachers allow students to have a few moments of free time in which they may talk to friends, go to the restroom, or get a drink of water. Some transitions are good opportunities for teachers to read aloud from a storybook or challenge students to solve a brain teaser or puzzling mathematics problem. Reflective teachers find that when they allow students a respite and a change of pace during a brief transition period, the work periods are more productive and motivation to learn is enhanced.

TIMING. Actors, speakers, and comedians give considerable attention to improving the timing of their presentations because good timing engages the attention of an audience, emphasizes major points, and sometimes creates a laugh. Teachers also work in front of an audience, and class presentations can be improved by considering timing and pacing as means of getting attention and keeping it. Pausing for a moment of complete silence before you begin teaching is a good example of a way to incorporate timing into your presentation.

In most instances, students respond best to teachers who use a brisk pace of delivering information and instructions. Kounin's (1977) research on the most effective classroom managers demonstrated that students are best able to focus on the subject when the lesson has continuity and momentum and that interruptions result in confusion. When teachers forget to bring a prop, pause to consult a teacher's manual, or backtrack to present material that should have been presented earlier, inattention and disruptive behavior are likely to occur. Jones (1987) found that students' attention improved when teachers gave them efficient help, allocating 20 seconds or less to each request for individual help or reteaching. When this time was lengthened, the result was restlessness and dependency on the part of students.

At times, a pause in instruction can improve your presentation. Researchers (Grobecker, 1999; Lerner, 2003) have found that it is important to present new information in small steps, with a pause after the initial explanation to check for understanding. Students may not respond immediately during this pause because they need a moment to put their thoughts into words. Wait for them to do so. Then encourage questions and comments, and ask for examples or illustrations of the fact or concept being discussed. The initial pause allows your students to reflect on the new material before you test their understanding.

VARIATION. Variation is an essential lesson presentation skill for teachers who want to develop a healthy, vital classroom climate. In analyzing classroom videotapes, Kounin (1977) noticed that satiation results in boredom and inattentiveness. If presentations are monotonous, students will find a way to introduce their own variations by daydreaming, sleeping, fiddling with objects, doodling, or poking their neighbors.

Planning for variation is important when you present a lesson of 30 minutes or longer. Divide your lesson into several segments, using lecture for only part of the time. For example, include segments of discussion, independent practice, small-group interaction, and application activities. If you cannot break a single lesson into segments, plan to use a variety of strategies during the course of a day: Use quiet independent work for one subject, group interaction for another, lecture for a third, and hands-on activities for a fourth. In this way, your students will always be expectant and eager for each new lesson of the day and will feel fresh and highly motivated to learn because of the variations in the way you choose to present material. If teachers attempt to address different learning styles in each lesson, they cannot help but provide variation in the classroom. All lessons should be checked for activities that address the different learning modalities, something that is discussed in more detail later in the chapter.

INTERACTION.   Students thrive on interaction with the teacher and with their classmates. Rather than employing a traditional teacher-to-student, student-to-teacher communication pattern, open up your classroom to a variety of interactive experiences: Pushing the desks into a large circle encourages open-ended discussion from all students, arranging the desks in small groups encourages highly interactive problem solving, moving the desks aside leaves a lot of space in the middle of the room for activities, and pairing the desks provides opportunities for peer teaching or partnerships of other kinds. Your presentations can include all these types of activities, and you will find that it is motivating not only to your students but also to you. You will feel a sense of expectant excitement as you say, "All right, students, let's rearrange the desks."

The need for interaction derives from the powerful motivational need for belonging described by Maslow (1954) and Glasser (2001). When these needs are frustrated or denied, disruptive behavior is likely to occur as a means of satisfying them. When teachers consciously plan interactive learning experiences, they allow students to satisfy their important desires for interaction and belonging and thereby prevent unnecessary discipline problems.

CLOSURE.   At the end of most learning experiences, the teacher can ensure that students have mastered the objectives of the lesson or have integrated the new concepts into their existing schemata by having them either share what they did that worked and didn't work or articulate and generalize what they have learned about a new concept. For example, after a period of independent investigation about how batteries and lightbulbs work, the teacher may ask students what they could do to make a lightbulb give off more light. Such a teacher-led discussion is an essential part of active hands-on-learning and provides a sense of closure.

Every lesson or presentation can benefit from some thoughtful consideration of its ending. It is important to allow time for closure when you plan your lessons. You may use this time to ask questions that check for understanding so that you will know what to plan for the lesson that follows. You may also allow the students to close the lesson with their own conclusions and new insights by asking them an open-ended question such as "What did you discover today?" If insight is to occur, it is likely to occur during this summary experience. At the close of one lesson, you can also indicate what will follow in the next lesson so that your students know what to expect and how elements of the lessons fit together to make a whole concept.

To review all the elements of an effective lesson presentation, see Figure 6.1.

Active, Authentic Learning Experiences

Teachers who value authentic learning present material in ways that engage their students in active rather than passive learning by including many verbal, visual, or hands-on activities. Consider a lecture on a topic such as the closed circuit in electricity. Ho-hum. Add a visual aid such as a poster or an overhead projection, and students sit up in their seats to see better. Now add a demonstration: Turn off the lights; hold up a battery, some copper wire, and a lightbulb. Your students watch expectantly with a new sense of interest. Turn on the lights again.

All these techniques are adequate to teach the students a concept, but none is as valuable as a hands-on experience for in-depth learning and understanding. Picture this scene instead. After lunch, the students come into their classroom to find a battery, a flashlight bulb, and a piece of copper wire on each desk. After getting their attention, the teacher simply says, "Working independently, try to get your bulb to light up." Lights go on all over the room as well as in children's eyes and in their minds as they struggle with this problem. The motivation to succeed is intense and intrinsic, not tied to any exterior reward. Each individual has a sense of power and a need to know.

Figure 6.1 Elements of an effective teaching presentation.

Attention-getting	• Arousing them with novelty, uncertainty, surprise • Posing questions to the learners • Having the learners pose questions to be answered by the lesson
Enthusiasm	• Showing your interest in the students and the topic • Demonstrating ways that the knowledge is valuable and exciting
Clarity	• Stating the purpose of the lesson clearly • Presenting the information or directions in an organized manner • Making connections between and among the elements of the lesson • Relating the lesson to prior knowledge
Smooth transitions	• Giving clear instructions and providing a visual for support before moving students into activities • Using a plan for moving students in an organized manner • Providing clear expectations for behavior and products to be produced
Timing	• Using pauses and visuals in a timely manner to support learner understanding • Providing instructions prior to asking students to perform
Interaction	• Providing opportunities for students to discuss ideas among themselves • Providing verbal support for students' verbal responses
Variation	• Planning lessons in segments to maintain interest • Using a variety of approaches in every lesson (lecture, discussion, hands-on activities, individual practice, etc.) • Providing a variety of response activities that consider differing intelligences (visual, oral, written, group discussion, etc.)
Closure	• Planning a brief celebration of learning or way to summarize the main points of the lesson • Giving the students an opportunity to share their efforts and new knowledge • Checking for understanding

The key to authentic learning is allowing your students to encounter and master situations that resemble real life. Simulated experiences are often just as valuable as real life for elementary school students and are much safer and more manageable for the beginning teacher. While your students may never invent a marketable product, you can simulate this type of exploration by inventing products that are needed in your classroom. You can simulate the debate and communication skills necessary to solve international crises by creating a mini United Nations in your room in which each student studies one country in depth and engages in substantive conversations about the varied needs and strengths of that country.

Brian Cambourne is a researcher from New Zealand who was curious about the conditions needed for students to become thoroughly engaged in the learning process. He visited classrooms of highly effective teachers and observed how they provided authentic literacy learning. In the classrooms he visited, he saw highly motivated primary students reading books and then eagerly writing their own books, poems, and plays. From this research, Cambourne (1993) summarized the conditions for learning that he saw demonstrated in these exciting classrooms. He identified these conditions as exemplifying authentic learning:

- The students were immersed in text. The classrooms were full of books, posters, and charts, and the teachers read aloud several times during the day.

- Demonstrations were very common. Teachers didn't just talk, they showed.

- The teachers expected certain responses from the students and the students knew what was expected of them.

- The students had responsibilities for the use of materials, maintenance of the classroom environment, and the proofreading and submission of work.

- The teachers provided authentic opportunities for the students to actually use the skills they were acquiring.

- The teachers understood approximation and its place in development. Small steps toward the standard were recognized and celebrated.

- The teachers provided feedback and responses to the students in the form of both verbal and written comments, as well as visual responses, such as smiling, nodding, and giving signals of support.

Systematic Classroom Instruction

Providing Direct Instruction of New Knowledge and Skills

The curriculum contains a high proportion of basic knowledge and skills that learners must master thoroughly to succeed in the upper grades. Basic language concepts such as recognizing letters, using phonics, decoding words, writing letters and words, and using conventions of sentence and paragraph construction must be mastered. Basic mathematical concepts such as number recognition, quantity, order, measurement, and the operations used in computation must be learned.

Many models of direct instruction are appropriate for teaching this type of material. They are often known as five-step or seven-step lessons because they are described in a chronological sequence of steps that results in getting students' attention; reviewing what has been learned up to the current lesson; systematically teaching, modeling, and practicing the new material; and then demonstrating individual and independent mastery of what was taught.

The direct instruction model includes the following seven steps:

1. Create an anticipatory set to interest your students in the lesson by asking a thought-provoking question, providing an interesting visual aid, or using a puzzling and intriguing opening statement about the topic.

2. Connect this lesson with what has come before by providing a short review of previous prerequisite learning or otherwise describing relationships between the current lesson and other subjects being studied by the class.

3. Offer a short statement of the purpose for learning this new information to convince your students that this lesson has a meaning to their lives beyond just achieving well in school. Tell them what they are going to learn and why it is important.

4. Present new, unfamiliar, and complex material in small steps, modeling each step by doing an example yourself. Give clear and detailed instructions and explanations as you model each process.

5. Provide a high level of active practice for all students. After you model a step, allow every student to practice the example on his or her own or with a learning partner.

6. Monitor students as they practice each new step. Walk around and look at their work as they do their sample problems. Ask a large number of questions to check for student understanding, and try to obtain responses from many different students so that you know the concept is clearly understood by the class. Provide systematic feedback and corrections as you see the needs arise.

7. Provide an opportunity at the end of each practice session for independent student work that synthesizes the many steps students have practiced during the lesson. This may be assigned as seat work or homework. It is important to check this work and return it to students quickly, offering assistance to those who have not demonstrated independent mastery of the new material.

When these seven strategies are reviewed, many readers may respond, "But isn't that what all teachers do? What is new about these methods?" It is true that many teachers have used these strategies throughout the history of education; unfortunately, many other teachers have not. We have all observed classroom teachers who take a much less active role than these systematic procedures call for. They assign work, have students exchange papers and correct each other's work, and collect the papers.

On close examination, these seven steps describe methods that would be used by a teacher who takes an active role in helping students process the new information being taught. These methods are also highly compatible with the concept of authentic learning because students are encouraged to think about what they are learning, construct the new knowledge in a meaningful context, and respond to substantive discussion in a supportive environment for learning. Although direct instruction is frequently associated in people's minds with whole-class instruction, you can readily see that these systematic steps can be used during small-group instruction as well.

In selecting appropriate teaching methods and strategies, reflective teachers are likely to look for and discover relationships among various theories of learning and methods of teaching. One such relationship exists between this direct instruction model of systematic teaching and the process of thinking and learning known as *information processing*.

The first step is to begin a lesson with a short review of previous prerequisite learning. This strategy is a signal to the learner to call up an existing schema that will be expanded and altered in the new lesson. Beginning a lesson with a short statement of goals provides the student with an advance organizer that allows more efficient processing. In practice, these first two steps are often presented together and can be interchangeable with no ill effects.

Information processing theories suggest that there are limits to the amount of new information a learner can process effectively at one time (Gagne, 1985). When too much information is presented at one time, the working memory becomes overloaded, causing the learner to become confused, to omit data, or to process new data incorrectly. This overload can be eliminated when teachers present new material in small steps, with student practice after each step. This allows learners to concentrate their somewhat limited attention on processing manageably sized pieces of information or new skills.

Teachers who give clear and detailed instructions and explanations and who model new skills are likely to provide students with the support they need while they are processing new information in their working memories.

Providing students with a high level of active practice after each step and again at the conclusion of a series of steps is important because the practice enhances the likelihood that the new information will be transferred from working memory to long-term memory, where it can be stored for future use. Each time a new skill is practiced, its position in long-term memory is strengthened.

As teachers guide students during initial practice and ask a large number of questions, as they check for student understanding and obtain responses from all students, teachers are also encouraging their students to process the information accurately. Learning occurs when schemata stored in long-term memory are expanded, enriched, and reorganized. Effective teacher questions and checks for understanding cause students to think about new ideas from a variety of perspectives and to update their existing schemata accordingly. Providing systematic feedback and corrections and monitoring students during seat work also increase the likelihood that students will process the important points and practice the new skills in the most efficient manner.

Using Teacher Modeling and Demonstration

When teachers present new information to students, they must carefully consider the method they will use to introduce it. For students, it is rarely sufficient for teachers simply to talk about a new idea or skill. A much more powerful method of instruction is to model or demonstrate it first and then give students an opportunity to practice the new learning themselves.

A simple example of this technique occurs in the primary grades when teachers say, "First, I will say the word; then you will say it with me." In the middle grades, the teacher may first demonstrate the procedures used in measuring with a metric ruler and then ask students to repeat them. In the upper grades, teachers may write an outline of a paragraph and then ask students to outline the next one.

Teacher demonstration and modeling are effective instructional techniques for almost every area of the curriculum. It is useful in teaching music: "Clap the same rhythm that I do." It is vital in teaching mathematics: "Watch as I do the first problem on the chalkboard." It can be easily applied to the teaching of creative writing: "I'll read you the poem that I wrote about this topic, and then you will write your own."

When a teacher circulates in the classroom to monitor students as they practice or create their own work, it is efficient for him or her to use modeling and demonstration on a one-to-one basis to assist students in getting started or in correcting mistakes.

Structuring Tasks for Success

Researchers have found that the degree of success students have on school tasks correlates highly with achievement in the subject area. This supports the widely known maxim "Success breeds success." Both formal research and informal discussions with students reveal that when students experience success on a given task, they are motivated to continue working at it or to tackle another one. The number and type of successful learning experiences that students have affect their self-knowledge, leading them to have expectations regarding probable success or failure in future tasks.

To structure tasks for success, a teacher must create a good fit among his or her expectations, student abilities, and difficulty of the task. Rimm (1995), who has specialized in assisting underachieving students reach their potential, states:

> [Students] must learn early that there is a relationship between their effort and the outcome. If their schoolwork is too hard, their efforts do not lead to successful outcomes but only to failures. If their work is too easy, they learn that it takes very little to succeed. Either is inappropriate and provides a pattern which fosters underachievement.
>
> When teachers select and present academic tasks to their students, they need to reflect continually on how well the task fits the students' present needs and capacities. (p. 73)

Glasser (1969) has been committed to improving schools throughout his career. As a psychiatrist, he strongly believes that a person cannot be successful in life "until he can in some way first experience success in one important part of his life" (p. 5). Glasser recognizes that children have only two places in which to experience success: home and school. If they are lucky enough to experience success in both settings, they are likely to be successful in their adult lives. If they achieve success at home, they can succeed despite a lackluster school experience. But many students come from homes and neighborhoods where failure is pervasive; for these students especially, it is critical that they experience success in school. Glasser's (1969) book, *Schools without Failure*, offers many realistic and practical methods to help teachers develop a classroom environment that breeds success. His newer book (2001), *Every Child Can Succeed*, updates this classic and valuable philosophy for your classroom.

Matching Learning Styles and Teaching Styles

Each person has a particular pattern of needs or preferences that allows for optimal learning. Some students learn best in quiet rooms; others prefer a certain level of noise in the room. Students have individual preferences for degrees of light and dark, temperature, and seating arrangements.

Learning styles of enormous variety have been described and include preferences for the structure of tasks and the best time of day for learning. Although you cannot accommodate the needs of every student, you will want to be aware of the many variations in learning styles so that when a student with an unusual sensitivity or a severe impediment to learning appears in your classroom (and this will happen), you will be able to reflect on the student's particular needs and provide a learning environment or restructure your teaching style to better match the student's learning style. A set of learning styles based on sensory preferences is especially useful to reflective teachers. Eight studies in the 1980s examined preferences for visual, auditory, and kinesthetic learning. Most learners were found to prefer receiving information either visually (by viewing or reading), aurally (by hearing), or kinesthetically (by touching, working with, or otherwise manipulating materials).

Teachers have a strong tendency to teach using the modality they prefer as a learning modality. Specifically, visual learners who rely on reading and viewing material to learn tend to rely on reading and other visual aids as teachers. Similarly, if you learn best by hearing, you may assume that others do also; as a result, you may teach primarily using lecture and discussion. Kinesthetic learners who enjoy hands-on activities as students tend to provide many of these active learning materials in their own classrooms. Currently, two major approaches (one requiring schoolwide cooperation) exist for solving this educational dilemma.

In the first (schoolwide) approach, teachers at each grade level may be identified as having visual, auditory, or kinesthetic preferences, and students are then tested and placed in the classroom with the teacher whose style matches their own. But this approach offers few opportunities for learners to improve their weaker learning modalities. The other approach is for each teacher to conscientiously plan to teach using all three modalities. For example, when presenting a lesson, the teacher will provide visual aids in the form of pictures and reading material; auditory aids in the form of lecture, discussion, or tape-recorded material; and kinesthetic aids in the form of models or other manipulative materials. Studies show that providing all three types of learning experiences to all students is likely to result in higher achievement than simply matching learning styles.

Designing Learning Experiences for Multiple Intelligences

For students to experience success in school, it is necessary for teachers to understand that each individual perceives the world differently and that there is not just one way to learn or one way to teach. Prior to the emergence of this theory, most people were convinced that there was just one type of intelligence and that all human beings had an intelligence quotient (IQ) that ranged from 0 to approximately 200, with the great majority of individuals in the average range near 100, plus or minus 16 points.

Gardner's (2000) theory of multiple intelligences disputes that old belief system, and he proposes the alternate theory that humans have more than one type of intelligence. He originally described seven different intelligences: verbal-linguistic (word smart), logical-mathematical (logic and math smart), visual-spatial (art smart), musical (music smart), bodily-kinesthetic (body and movement smart), interpersonal (people smart), and intrapersonal (self-awareness smart). Later, he added an eighth intelligence known as naturalist, describing people who are very smart about nature and natural phenomena, and a ninth intelligence called existentialist, describing a curiosity about life and death and famous philosophers. Other researchers have suggested additional intelligences. In her teaching and curriculum planning, Eby (1990) proposes an intelligence related to mechanical and technical inventiveness, and her curriculum projects encourage students to be inventive and to expand their technical and mechanical skills.

Teachers who wish to acknowledge and support the varied intelligences of their students try to provide learning experiences that allow students to use their special strengths in learning a subject or skill. For example, when teachers present new material to a class, they are likely to describe it in words and ask for verbal feedback for linguistically talented students. They attempt to provide problem-solving activities related to the subject for logical-mathematical students. They give spatially talented students visual cues and allow them to react to the new material with drawings or diagrams. They may encourage musically talented students to commit the new material to memory via a song or allow them to create a musical response to what they have learned. Teachers set aside time and space for bodily-kinesthetic gifted students to learn with their bodies by modeling, acting out, or pantomiming the material they are learning. For students with a special facility for interpersonal communication, teachers plan stimulating classroom discussions; for students who are especially good at intrapersonal examination, they provide opportunities for written or oral responses related to how the new material relates to their own sense of self.

Kagan and Kagan (1998) provide a teacher's guide to using the multiple intelligences, which they abbreviate *MI*, in their classrooms, titled *Multiple Intelligences: The Complete MI Book*. This resource suggests three MI visions: matching, stretching, and celebrating. The first vision describes methods teachers can use to match instructional strategies with their students' varied intelligences. The second vision encourages teachers to stretch each student's capacities in his or her nondominant intelligence as well as use his or her dominant intelligence. The third vision suggests ways of celebrating and respecting one another's differences and unique patterns of learning.

By incorporating the concept of multiple intelligences into your curriculum planning, you are taking a large positive step toward accomplishing the goal of differentiated instruction. One size does not fit all, and neither does one teaching strategy. Lesson plans that take advantage of the various strengths, talents, and intelligences of students are much richer and more interesting to everyone: Give visual-spatial learners the opportunity to do a visual presentation of what they learn, ask bodily-kinesthetic learners to do an activity to demonstrate the concept, let musicians create a musical response. Your classroom will hum with activity and enthusiasm.

Armstrong (2000) explores ways that teachers can apply this concept to K–12 educational experiences. He describes the intelligences as follows:

Linguistic intelligence ("word smart")

Logical-mathematical intelligence ("number/reasoning smart")

Spatial intelligence ("picture smart")

Bodily-kinesthetic intelligence ("body smart")

Musical intelligence ("music smart")

Interpersonal intelligence ("people smart")

Intrapersonal intelligence ("self smart")

Naturalist intelligence ("nature smart")

Instead of a single IQ number, each individual has a different profile of strengths and talents using these eight domains. One child might have a very high spike in logical-mathematical intelligence and low levels of the seven other intelligences. Another student may have two or three high peaks on her profile, and some students may have relatively high levels for six or seven of the intelligences. In fact, it is our belief that people who choose elementary education as their field of study and career are often people who have relatively high levels of many intelligences; for example, they are good (but not great) at math, language arts, sports, music, and art. This profile may predispose a person to consider being a teacher at the elementary level, where he or she is able to use different talents and interests in creating curriculum and teaching the many varied subjects in the elementary curriculum. Reflective teachers are those who also embody high levels of interpersonal and intrapersonal intelligence. They know themselves, and they want to know and understand others. These teachers are likely to acknowledge and support the varied intelligences of their students by providing learning experiences that allow students to access their special strengths in learning a subject or skill.

Armstrong (2003) describes methods for using multiple intelligences to promote literacy. He retells the story of the blind men who touch various parts of an elephant and then report that an elephant is like a rope or a wall or a tree stump based on their individual experiences. Armstrong suggests that the concept of *literacy* is just as complex as an elephant and hence is not easily described by any single individual. If a king were to ask several blind educators in his village to examine the concept of literacy, one educator might respond that literacy is made up of words—whole words. The second educator might return to the king saying, "Literacy isn't made of whole words! It's made up of sounds! All kinds of sounds! Sounds like 'thhhh' and 'buh' and 'ahhhhh' and 'ayyyyy' and 'juh' and many more. In fact, I counted all the sounds, and there are exactly 44!" A third educator might examine the concept and claim that it isn't made up of sounds or whole words at all; it's constructed out of stories, fables, songs, chants, poems, and books. A fourth educator might return saying, "They're all wrong! Literacy is made up of whole cultures. It's about understanding who we are, and what we're capable of, and how each of us can speak, and read, and write with our own voices, and in this way contribute to the good of all" (Armstrong, 2003, pp. 5–6).

Involving the Larger Educational Community

Reflective, caring teachers are likely to confer with their colleagues and try to understand concepts as complex as literacy with open minds and hearts. They will try to see one perspective and then look for other perspectives or sides to each issue. They search and reflect, search and reflect, actively trying to improve their own understanding of educational dilemmas. They are not threatened by the complexity or ambiguities inherent in their chosen profession; rather, they become excited by the opportunities to learn more about each student's learning style and preferred intelligence patterns. They can use this information to create original unit plans or lesson plan activities that encourage their students to become active searchers and interpreters of knowledge rather than passive recipients of knowledge. With this philosophy, reflective teachers attempt to plan varied and interesting lessons, which their students view as authentic, meaningful, and purposeful learning experiences

As you are making plans to involve your students in active, authentic learning experiences, it is important to include parents in the learning team. When you design class newsletters or parent meetings, explain the types of activities you will be exploring in the classroom, and help parents to find ways to include activities at home that will reinforce some of the same learning. Parents can be very helpful in finding different ways for their children to apply skills in real-life activities:

- Doing the math involved in planning a party, measuring a room for paint or wallpaper, or doubling a recipe
- Writing a letter to a friend or relative
- Reading to younger brothers, sisters, or cousins
- Drawing a plan for new flower beds
- Designing a cake for a relative's birthday
- Composing a poem or song for a special family occasion
- Designing a crossword puzzle to help a sibling learn spelling words

Group Focus Activity

This exercise provides practice in using multiple intelligences in a teaching activity.

1. Your professor will divide the class into several groups.

2. Each group will be given a specific task to teach in a given subject area.

3. Each group will design three teaching activities for their task or concept using three different intelligences from Gardner's work on multiple intelligences.

4. Each group will discuss their task and activities.

5. Suggested tasks:

   Introduction to subtraction
   Rhyming words
   Irregular verbs
   Condensation
   Color wheel
   Rules for playground game
   Rhythm

Preparing for Your Licensure Exam

In this chapter you read about ways to engage your students in authentic learnng. Reread "A View into the Classroom" at the beginning of the chapter, and think about it as a case study you might encounter on your licensure exam. Answer the following questions to demonstrate your understanding of the process of planning and teaching lessons for authentic learning:

1. How does teaching for authentic learning differ from more traditional models of teaching?

2. What approaches does Jeff employ in his classroom? What makes them authentic?

3. What presentation skills are needed by the teacher in order to engage students in meaningful learning?

Portfolio of Professional Practices Activity

Teachers command specialized knowledge of how to convey a subject to students. Accomplished teachers learn the most appropriate ways to present subject matter to students through analogies, metaphors, experiments, demonstrations, and illustrations. Teachers must be able to make well-reasoned and careful decisions about what aspects of the subject matter to emphasize, what types of presentation skills to employ, and which ways to pace their instruction.

In this chapter, we describe many presentation skills that increase clarity and student motivation. To assess your own teaching performance, it is important to see yourself in action, so videotape one of your teaching lessons. As you observe the video of your own teaching, assess your presentation skills, rating your attention-getting beginning, enthusiasm, clarity, smooth transitions, timing, variation, interaction, and closure. If possible, teach the lesson again, making improvements based on your self-evaluation.

As you observe your video, notice your strengths and weaknesses. What does your body language say? How does your voice sound? Do you make false starts in your phrasing, such as "Here is an example . . . I mean . . . look at this. . . ." Do you have eye contact with your students? What facial expressions and gestures do you want to work on? Choose one of the presentation skills described in this chapter that you want to improve in your own teaching. For example, you may choose enthusiasm if you feel that your presentation style is too low key. For the next four occasions when you work with students, focus on that skill and attempt to improve it. Ask the classroom teacher for feedback, and work to refine and master this skill to your own satisfaction.

Record the lesson again to see if the presentation skill you worked on has improved. Decide which are your strongest presentation skills at this point in time. Write a one- to two-page description, analysis, and reflection of your videotaped lesson to include in your portfolio to give evidence of your ability to learn from experience.

References

Armstrong, T. (2000). *Multiple intelligences in the classroom* (2nd ed.). Alexandria, VA: Association of Supervision and Curriculum Development.

Armstrong, T. (2003). *The multiple intelligences of reading and writing: Making the words come alive*. Alexandria, VA: Association of Supervision and Curriculum Development.

Ausubel, D. P. (1960). The use of advance organizers in the learning and retention of meaningful verbal material. *Journal of Educational Psychology, 51,* 267–272.

Cambourne, B. (1993). *The whole story: Natural learning and the acquisition of literacy in the classroom*. New York, NY: Scholastic.

Eby, J. (1990) *Gifted Behavior Index*. Buffalo, NY: Dok Publications.

Gagne, E. (1985). *The cognitive psychology of school learning*. Boston, MA: Little, Brown.

Gardner, H. (2000). *Intelligences reframed*. New York, NY: Basic Books.

Gibbs, J. (2001). *Tribes*. Windsor, CA: CenterSource Systems.

Glasser, W. (1969). *Schools without failure*. New York, NY: Harper & Row.

Glassser, W. (2001). *Every child can succeed*. Los Angeles, CA: William Glasser Institute.

Good, T., & Brophy, J. (2002). *Looking in classrooms* (9th ed.). Boston, MA: Allyn & Bacon.

Gregory, G., & Chapman, C. (2002). *Differentiated instructional strategies: One size doesn't fit all*. Thousand Oaks, CA: Corwin Press.

Grobecker, B. (1999). Mathematics reform and learning disabilities. *Learning Disability Quarterly, 22,* 43–58.

Jones, F. (1987). *Positive classroom discipline*. New York, NY: McGraw-Hill.

Kagan, S., & Kagan, M. (1998) *Multiple intelligences: The complete MI Book*. San Clemente , CA: Kagan Cooperative Learning.

Kounin, J. (1977). *Discipline and group management in classrooms*. New York, NY: Kreiger.

Lerner, J. (2003). *Learning disabilities: Theories, diagnosis, and teaching practices*. Boston, MA: Houghton Mifflin Company.

Maslow, A. (1954). *Motivation and personality*. New York, NY: Harper & Row.

Newman, F., & Wehlage, G. (1993). Five standards of authentic instruction. *Educational Leadership, 50*(7), 8–12.

Piaget, J. (1970). *Science of education and the psychology of the child*. New York, NY: Viking Compass Book.

Rimm, S. (2005). *Why bright children get poor grades*. Tucson, AZ: Great Potential Press.

chapter seven

Developing a Repertoire of Teaching Strategies

Gabe Palmer/Alamy

"A teacher who is attempting to teach without inspiring the pupil with a desire to learn is hammering on cold iron."

Horace Mann (1989, p. 11)

School experiences should be enjoyable for both teachers and students. One way of heightening the enjoyment, as we mentioned in Chapter Six, is by using a variety of teaching strategies and activities. When learning experiences are varied and purposeful, students are more likely to become actively engaged in the learning process. Their intrinsic motivation to learn is also likely to improve if the skill or knowledge they are learning is presented in an interesting format. To promote the enjoyment of teaching and learning, many reflective teachers are continuously searching for new methods and strategies to motivate and engage their students in the learning process. Developing a repertoire of teaching strategies is also necessary because students' needs and learning styles are diverse; for this reason, teachers must be ready to modify lesson plans and present information in more than one way.

The purpose of this chapter is to introduce you to a variety of teaching strategies and encourage you to plan engaging lessons and learning experiences for your students. As you consider each strategy, you will quickly recognize that the descriptions in this chapter are not sufficiently detailed for you to become proficient in using each new strategy. This book can provide only an overview of the descriptions, illustrations, and examples you will need to employ these methods successfully. For strategies that you wish to implement in your classroom, you will need to use the reflective action of initiating an active search for more detailed descriptions of these strategies in books and journal articles or through observations of experienced teachers.

As you read about or select a strategy to try in a laboratory setting or classroom, you will find that some of them work for you while others do not. You will need to reflect about what works for you and your students and why. As you think about what works for you, it is quite acceptable for you to combine, adapt, modify, and add your own unique strategies to the ones you read about or observe. Through this process of practice and reflection, you will discover, create, and refine your own unique teaching style.

Questions for Reflection as You Read the Chapter

1. What benefits do students receive from each of the different learning strategies?
2. How can a teacher develop a repertoire of different teaching strategies?
3. What resources are available to teachers to help them acquire new teaching approaches?

A View into the Classroom

Celeste Natum teaches sixth grade in a small town in Oklahoma. Because her students live in a rural area, they have limited experiences with cultural events, museums, and zoos that most city children enjoy. Celeste has been teaching for 12 years and has gradually developed a rich repertoire of teaching strategies to engage her students in activities that will both inspire them to enjoy learning and give them a taste of some things they miss by living far away from the city.

One of the role-playing activities that Celeste has developed involves the students in planning and constructing models of skyscrapers. The students research construction techniques on the Internet, form construction companies, and build skyscrapers to scale, using their math and science skills. They research building materials, costs, and safety requirements; they also delve into requirements for buildings in earthquake zones and the extra cost of building them to withstand earthquakes.

As the students form their construction companies, they identify the roles of different workers in the company, and they learn to write proposals, which must be approved by the teacher and a building code committee before any building begins. The students locate materials to simulate actual building materials used in skyscrapers and design their buildings to scale.

When the buildings are complete, the groups set them up to simulate a city and prepare models of people, in the same scale, to simulate the difference in size between people and skyscrapers. The construction companies explain their processes and the features of each building, providing students with opportunities for oral presentations.

In social studies, Celeste's students engage in simulations related to the history they are studying, creating a language and graphics to demonstrate ways of writing similar to those of ancient civilizations. They create a civilization in their classroom and begin to make decisions without the benefit of modern-day technologies, weapons, or tools. They are often heard to say, "You can't use that. It wasn't invented until 19–." As a result of this study, the class creates a time line of inventions, showing when each new development occurred in history.

Recently, Celeste discovered a website that allows students to create a "fake" Facebook page. By using this tool, www.myfakewall.com, she and her students can assemble interactive Facebook pages for historical figures and events. To create a fake wall, she needed to register for a My Fake Wall account. She was then able to upload images, write wall posts, even create "likes" and make comments on fake posts. Celeste found this to be an engaging way for students to publish biographical information about historical figures; they could also use My Fake Wall to create fake Facebook pages about characters in the novels they read. She's thinking of using this for her end-of-year project for her class. They would be placed in small groups, with each group creating a Facebook page for several historical and/or literary characters.

Celeste uses the Smithsonian website (www.si.edu) to provide her students with simulated field trips, and the students often visit the Smithsonian by Internet in conjunction with their studies. Celeste uses a SMART Board (an interactive electronic display board) to display the videos from the Smithsonian so that she can engage her students in discussions related to their studies and the exhibits at the Smithsonian. As a result of her use of this website, a number of families with students in her classes have taken family vacations to Washington, D.C., to visit the Smithsonian because of their children's interest in the museum.

REFLECTING ON THE CLASSROOM EXPERIENCE

As you observe in classrooms, you will want to note the varying approaches that teachers use. If you see teachers repeatedly using the same strategies, challenge yourself to think of different approaches you could use to address the same topics. Celeste's classroom provides an outstanding model of students who are actively involved in their own learning.

One measure of student involvement and engagement is the amount of teacher talk that takes place as compared to the amount of student talk that is encouraged. Students who are engaged in discussion and verbal explorations of the topic being studies provide the teacher with rich feedback on their learning experiences, possible misconceptions, and interest levels. A reflective teacher uses this feedback to identify student needs, areas of growth, and ideas for expansion and enrichment.

Examples of Teaching Strategies in Action

Discovery Learning

The philosophy underlying what is called *discovery learning* is that students will become more active and responsible for their own learning in an environment that allows them to make choices and encourages them to take initiative. To accomplish this goal, many teachers like to arrange their classrooms to provide as much space as possible for activity and learning centers. They enjoy creating curriculum units and lessons that allow students to choose from among many alternatives. The main principle of discovery learning is that students learn best by doing rather than just by hearing or reading about a concept. Teachers find this strategy an excellent addition to their repertoire, and it can be used occasionally to provide real (rather than vicarious) experiences in a classroom.

In employing discovery learning, the teacher gathers and provides equipment and materials related to a concept that the students are to learn. Sufficient materials should be available so that every student or pair of students has immediate access to them. Materials that are unfamiliar, interesting, and stimulating are especially important to a successful discovery learning experience. After providing the materials, the teacher may ask a question or offer a challenge that causes students to discover the properties of the materials. As the students begin to work with the materials, the teacher's role is to monitor and observe as the students discover the properties and relationships inherent in the materials, asking occasional questions or making suggestions that will guide the students in seeing the relationships and understanding the concepts. The period of manipulation and discovery is then followed by a discussion in which students report on what they have observed and learned from the experience.

A simple example at the primary level is the use of discovery learning to teach the concept of colors and their relationship to one another. Rather than telling students that blue and yellow make green or demonstrating that they do while students watch, the teacher using discovery learning provides all the students with a brush and two small puddles of blue and yellow paint on white paper and allows them to discover it for themselves. In this case, the opening question may simply be, "What happens when you mix blue and yellow together?" When this relationship becomes apparent and students verbalize it, the teacher can then provide additional puddles of red and white paint and challenge students to "create as many different colors as you can." Discovery learning experiences can be designed to allow students to find out how and why some things float, what makes a lightbulb light, how electricity travels in circuits, and what differences exist between solutions and mixtures.

Math relationships also can be discovered. Beans, buttons, coins, dice, straws, and toothpicks can be sorted according to size, shape, color, and other attributes; objects can be weighed, measured, and compared. The concept of multiplication can be discovered when students make sets of objects in rows and columns. Many resources in the form of math curriculum projects involving discovery learning are presently being developed for schools because discovery is a part of the problem-solving process, currently a hot topic in education.

To view multiple examples of discovery lessons, go to http://edcommunity.apple.com/ali. This site also offers a large collection of teacher demonstrations of a variety of active learning strategies discussed in this chapter; choose other descriptors from the table of contents to learn more.

Inquiry Training

Closely linked to discovery learning is a strategy known as *inquiry training*. Teachers who believe that their students must learn how to ask questions and carry out other types of investigations to become active learners often plan lessons that stimulate their students' curiosity and then train them in asking productive questions and using critical thinking, observation skills, and variations of the scientific method to gather information, make informed estimates or predictions, and design investigations to test their hypotheses.

As an example, a classroom teacher wanted to train her students to think like scientists, using the skills of observation, inquiry, prediction, hypothesis testing, and experimental design to find out what they need to know. She grouped her students into pairs and distributed a clear plastic glass and five raisins to each dyad. She asked them to predict what would happen to the raisins if they were dropped into a glass of water. Most students correctly guessed that the raisins would sink to the bottom of the glass. The teacher then discussed with her students the need to keep an open mind and not jump to easy conclusions based on prior knowledge. She poured a carbonated lemon-lime beverage into the students' glasses and asked them to predict whether the raisins would sink or float. Each pair of students wrote down their prediction; the teacher generated a chart on the board showing the class predictions.

After recording the predictions, the teacher allowed the students to drop the raisins into their glasses. At first, it appeared that the students who predicted the raisins would sink were correct when the raisins fell to the bottom of the glasses, but as the students watched, several raisins began to rise to the top. In the next few minutes, the students observed a puzzling phenomenon: Raisins moved up and down in the glasses, each at its own pace.

At this stage in the lesson, the teacher encouraged the students to ask questions of her and of each other as they all tried to make sense out of what they were observing. The teacher answered their questions with either *yes* or *no*, giving her students the responsibility of articulating the questions and gathering the information they needed to make meaning out of the situation. Soon they began to generate new investigations that they would have to undertake to discover why some raisins moved up and down more quickly and why some settled to the bottom.

To stimulate your own curiosity and encourage you to use the reflective actions of gathering information, being creative, and being persistent in solving problems, we will not disclose the reasons for the raisins' movement. Attempt the experiment yourself, and try to think like a scientist. If you have opportunities to learn like this yourself, you will be better able to provide your students with the encouragement and support they need without rushing to provide them with answers. You will allow them to take the time they need to inquire and experiment so that they can succeed and fully experience the "aha" moment, just as scientists do when their inquiries lead them to new understandings. See Figure 7.1 for a step-by-step model for inquiry training.

Role Playing

When problems or issues involving human relationships are part of the curriculum, teachers may choose to use *role playing* to help students explore and understand the whole range of human feelings that surround any issue as they act out roles. This strategy is frequently used to resolve personal problems or dilemmas, but it can also be employed to gain understanding about the feelings and values of groups outside the classroom.

For example, to help students understand the depth of emotions experienced by immigrants coming to a new and unfamiliar country, the teacher may ask students to role-play the interactions among family members who are separated or the dilemmas of the Cubans who set off for America in a leaky boat or others who want to immigrate to the United States but are stopped by immigration quotas.

Successful and meaningful role playing has two major phases: the role playing itself and the subsequent discussion and evaluation period. In the first phase, the teacher's responsibility is to give students an overview of both phases of role playing so that they know what to expect. The teacher then introduces and describes a problem or dilemma, identifies the roles to be taken, assigns the roles, and begins the action by setting the stage and describing the immediate problem the actors must confront. Roles must be assigned carefully. Usually teachers select students who are involved in the problem to play the role. In an academic dilemma, the roles

Figure 7.1 Inquiry training model.

This model is designed to promote thinking, inquiry skills (such as observing, collecting, and organizing data), active learning, verbal expression, tolerance of ambiguity, and logical thinking (Joyce, Weil, & Showers, 2008).

1. Identification of the problem
2. Data gathering and verification
3. Data gathering and experimentation
4. Organization, formulation, and explanation
5. Analysis of the process

may be assigned to students who most need to expand their experience with and understanding of the issue. Students who are not assigned roles are expected to be careful observers.

To set up the role-playing situation, the teacher can arrange some chairs to suggest the setting of the event to be played out. During the role play itself, the actors are expected to get inside the problem and "live" it spontaneously, responding realistically to one another. The role play may not flow smoothly; actors may experience uncertainty and be at a loss for words just as they would in real life. The first time a role is played, the problem may not be solved at all. The action may simply establish the problem, which in later enactments can be probed and resolved.

To increase the effect of role playing, the actors may exchange roles after playing a scene once and replay the same scene so that they grow to understand the other characters' points of view. Actors may be allowed to select consultants to discuss and improve the roles they are playing.

In the second phase, the observers discuss the actions and words of the initial role players. The teacher helps the observers review what they have seen and heard, discuss the main events, and predict the consequences of actions taken by the role players. Following the initial discussion, the teacher will probably decide to have new class members replay the roles to show alternative ways of handling the problem. The situation can be replayed a number of times if necessary. When a role-played situation generates a useful solution or suggests an effective way of handling a problem, the situation can be adapted and subsequent role plays can focus on communication skills that will enhance or improve the situation even further.

Role playing has many applications in both the cognitive and affective goals of the curriculum. Through role playing, students can experience history by researching the life of a public figure and taking the role in a historical interaction. Each student in the class, for example, can study the life of a U.S. president and be the president for a day. Frequently, teachers ask students to play the role of characters in books they have read as a means of reporting their own reading and stimulating others in the class to read the books. Students can enact the feelings of slaves and slave traders, the roles of scientists as they are "doing" science, or the interactions between an author and editor as they try to perfect a piece of writing.

Vocabulary role play is a simple yet effective tool for getting students involved in an active process of learning new words and applying their meanings. In this type of activity, appropriate vocabulary words are physicalized by having students act out the words to internalize their meanings. Primary children may participate with action words such as *jumping*, *squeezing*, and *shrugging*, words that require physical involvement and movement. Older students may use scenarios to demonstrate the meaning of more complex words and expressions such as *honesty*, *revolution*, *respect*, and *serenity*. The physicalization of these words and terms provides a different route of internalization and makes the vocabulary come alive for the students. This strategy has been found to be especially effective with English language learners (Herrell & Jordan, 2012).

Students can learn new behaviors and social skills that may help them win greater peer acceptance and enhance their own self-esteem. Interpersonal conflicts that arise in the classroom can be role-played as a means of helping students discover more productive and responsible ways of behaving. For example, when two students argue about taking turns with a toy in the kindergarten class, the teacher can ask the students to role-play the situation in an effort to learn new ways of speaking to one another, asserting their own desires, and creating a plan for sharing the scarce resource. In a classroom, the teacher may notice that one student is isolated and treated like a scapegoat by others in the class; the dilemma can be role-played, with the role of the isolated student assigned to be played by some of the students who have been most critical and aggressive toward the student. Through this active, vicarious experience, students may learn to be more tolerant and accepting of one another.

Storytelling

Adrienne Herrell recently taught a graduate class in *storytelling* as well as story writing. In this course, the 25 students were all teachers in the public schools, from pre-K all the way through high school. Using Hamilton and Weiss's (2005) wonderful book *Children Tell Stories*, the graduate students viewed the DVD that comes with the book and then developed storytelling units tailored to the ages and needs of their students. The graduate students learned to tell stories themselves to stir enthusiasm for their students and to experience the nervousness of telling stories to their peers.

This course was taught during the spring semester when all Florida students in grades 4, 8, and 10 are administered the Florida Writes examination. The graduate students who taught at these grade levels arrived at class the week after the writing scores came out, and they were raving about how well their students had done on the exam. The test is an actual writing sample that is scored by a team of teachers using a writing rubric. One fourth-grade teacher shared that her principal approached her, wanting to know how she had managed to prepare her students so well for the exam. The teacher's reply was, "We've been telling stories as prewriting." The graduate students were all amazed at the number of standards that were addressed in a storytelling unit: speaking and listening skills, writing stages, and editing skills, just to mention a few. The tenth-grade students did especially well on the persuasive writing section because they had been writing and telling stories to attempt to convince their peers to change their minds about specially chosen topics as part of their storytelling unit.

Simulations

Student drivers drive simulated vehicles before they learn to drive a real car on the highway, and airplane simulators provide a realistic but safe way for student pilots to practice flying. Mistakes made in these simulations lead to realistic consequences without threatening lives. *Simulations* usually involve some type of role playing but also include other game-like features such as a set of rules; time limits; tokens or other objects that are gained or lost through the action of the simulation; and a way of recording the results of the players' decisions and actions. Simulations almost always focus on dilemmas in which the players must make choices, take action, and then experience feedback in the form of consequences from their choices. The purpose of simulations is primarily to allow young people to experience tough real-life problems and learn from the consequences in the safe, controlled environment of the classroom.

Many valuable academic and social simulations can be used to enrich the classroom experience and cause students to understand the relationships among their choices, actions, and consequences. The teacher can purchase or create simulation games. A company named Interact publishes catalogs of simulations in all areas of the curriculum that can be purchased for a relatively small price; you can access their web page at www.interact-simulations.com. Their kits include teacher manuals describing the rules, time limits, and procedures to follow as well as a set of student materials that may include fact sheets, game pieces, and record-keeping devices. Titles of some of the simulations they publish include *Goldrush, Egypt,* and *Underground Railroad.* In their web-based simulation called *Internet Cruises,* students become members of six "advance teams" each sent by a cruise line to explore a different travel destination. They use the Internet to explore geographic locations (which can be tailored to your classroom needs); conduct focused Internet research on the history, geography, nature, food, and culture of the region; and report back to the class with travel brochures they have created.

The role of the teacher during a simulation is to explain the conditions, concepts to be covered, and expectations at the outset of the event. A practice session may be held to further familiarize participants with the rules and procedures that govern the simulation. After assigning roles or creating groups that will interact, the teacher moderates, keeps time, clarifies misconceptions, and provides feedback and consequences in response to the participants' actions. At the conclusion of the simulation, the teacher leads a discussion of what occurred and what was learned by asking students to summarize events and problems and to share their perceptions and insights with one another. At the end of the discussion, the teacher may compare the simulation to its real-life counterpart and ask students to think critically about what they would do in real life as a result of having taken part in the simulation.

An example of a simulation in economics involves the creation of a small company or store in which students decide on a product, create the product, set up the company or store, price and sell the product, and keep records on the transactions. The purpose, of course, is to learn about the principles of supply and demand as well as the practical skills of exchanging money and making change. Along with the primary goals of the simulation are secondary learning experiences. Students are also likely to increase their capacity for critical thinking and to learn about their own actions and decisions regarding competition, cooperation, commitment to a goal, and communication.

Students may simulate the writing of the U.S. Constitution by writing a classroom constitution. After studying various countries of the world, sixth-grade students may take part in a mock United Nations simulation in which students are delegates and face daily world problems presented to them by the teacher.

In language arts, students may establish a class newspaper to learn how news is gathered and printed in the real world; they may even establish a number of competitive newspapers to add another dimension of reality to the simulation. Students may simulate the writing, editing, and publishing processes as they write, print, and distribute their own original books.

Simulations may be used as the introduction to a unit or as the culminating activity of a unit. They may take a few minutes or the entire year, or they may be continued from week to week but played for only a specified amount of time during each session; some may take a full day or longer. Simulations are powerful learning experiences that may change the way students view themselves and the world.

Mastery Learning

Teaching strategies known as *mastery learning* derive from the philosophy that all students can learn if they have sufficient time to master the new skill or concept. Bloom (1984) proposed that students have different learning rates rather than different ability levels. He created a practical system for instruction using mastery learning based on the assumption that learners can achieve the educational objectives established for them, but because they learn at different rates, they need different amounts of time to complete the required work. Bloom points to cases in which students are tutored to prove his point. In a controlled experiment, he demonstrated that "the average tutored student outperformed 98% of the students in the control class" (p. 5). He attributes this finding to the fact that a tutor is able to determine what each student knows in a given subject and is then able to plan an educational program that begins instruction at the student's level and proceeds at the student's own pace.

The basic structure of the mastery learning model, including adaptations known as *individually prescribed instruction (IPI)* and *continuous progress,* lend themselves best to the learning of basic skills in sequentially structured subjects. Specific behavioral objectives are written for each unit of study. Pretests are used to assess students' prior knowledge, which then determines their placement or starting level. As students work individually to master each objective in the sequence of learning, they are able to proceed to the next one. Periodically, unit tests covering several objectives are given to check on the students' mastery and retention of a whole range of knowledge and skills.

The teacher's role in this process is quite different from teaching skills with a whole-class approach. The teacher rarely instructs the entire class at one time; instead, as students work independently, the teacher monitors their progress by walking around the classroom and responding to requests for assistance. This frees the teacher to work with small groups of students rather than devoting all of his or her time responding to individual needs.

The value of mastery learning is that it allows students to actively learn new material and skills on a continuous basis. Motivation to achieve also presumably increases because students are working at their own pace and have the prerequisite skills necessary for success. Also, because testing is done individually and students have opportunities to repeat what they did not learn, they suffer less embarrassment when they make mistakes. The effective goal of mastery learning programs is to help students become independent, self-directed learners.

Learning Contracts

Because mastery learning is appropriate for use only in sequential subjects that require a great deal of independent practice, many teachers are searching for methods of promoting independence and self-directed learning in other subjects as well. An alternative to direct whole-class instruction is the use of what is called *learning contracts*, for both individuals and groups. A learning contract such as the one in Figure 7.2 is usually created by the teacher at the beginning of a unit of study. The learning contract specifies a list of required activities, such as reading a chapter in the textbook, finding a library resource and writing a summary of the topic, completing a fact sheet, and meeting other necessary prerequisites for developing a knowledge base on the subject.

Figure 7.2   Independent learning contract.

Westward Expansion of the United States

Required Learning Activities

Date   Approval

_____   _____   Read Chapter 6 in the social studies textbook.

_____   _____   Write answers to the questions at the end of the unit.

_____   _____   Locate and read a book on the American West or Indians.

_____   _____   Write a 2- to 4-page summary of the book.

_____   _____   Play the computer game Oregon Trail until you successfully reach the state of Oregon alive.

Alternative Learning Activities

_____   _____   Imagine that you are a member of a wagon train heading west. Write a series of letters back home describing your journey.

_____   _____   Write a play about a meeting between Indians and settlers. Find a cast for your play, and present it to the class assembly.

_____   _____   Draw or paint a large picture of a scene that you imagine took place during the westward expansion.

_____   _____   Create a song or ballad about life in the west. Be prepared to play and sing it for the assembly.

_____   _____   Create a diorama or a model of a Plains Indian village.

_____   _____   Research the lives of the Plains Indians today. Be prepared to give a speech about the conditions in which they live now and how this is related to the westward expansion.

_____   _____   Create an alternative plan for a learning experience on this topic.

I, _____ , agree to complete the required learning activities by the date _____ . In addition, I select two to five alternative activities to pursue on my own. I will present my creative work to my classmates at our assembly on _____.

_____   I have reviewed this contract and understand the work my
Student Signature   child has agreed to do. I agree to support this effort.

_____   _____
Teacher Signature   Parent Signature

A second list of activities is offered that provides choices or alternatives for students to pursue. This list includes opportunities to do additional independent research or to create plays, stories, songs, and artwork on the topic. When learning contracts are offered to develop independence, individuals usually select the activities they want to accomplish. A variation on this strategy would be to combine the concepts of cooperative groups and learning contracts and allow each group to sign a joint contract specifying the tasks and products they will complete.

Science investigations, social studies research projects, and creative language arts activities can be described in learning contracts. The primary advantage of this strategy is that it allows individuals at various ability levels to work on an appropriate amount and type of work during the unit of study. Students who work quickly and accurately can select the maximum number of tasks and products, while other students select fewer tasks; theoretically, both types of students can actively learn and experience success during the same amount of time.

Learning Centers

Learning centers are stations or areas of the classroom where students can go to do independent or group work on a given subject or topic. Learning centers vary enormously in appearance, usage, and length of time for which they are set up. Teachers who use learning centers use them for a variety of purposes and with a variety of expectations.

Some centers may be informal and unstructured in their use. For example, a classroom may have a permanent science center containing a variety of science equipment and materials, and the students may go to the center to do science experiments in their free time. The same classroom may have a permanent reading center furnished with a rug, comfortable chairs, and shelves or racks of books where students can go to read quietly.

Other centers are set up for a limited amount of time and have highly structured expectations. For example, to accompany the unit on settling the western United States described in the learning contract, the teacher may have set up an area of the classroom as a research center. It would contain a computer with the Minnesota Educational Computer Consortium (MECC) computer program called Oregon Trail turned on and ready for students to use. It would also contain posters and maps of the western United States and a variety of reading materials on the topic. When the unit is finished, the center will be redesigned; new learning materials will replace the ones from the finished unit, and the center will become the focus of a new unit of study.

In primary classrooms, learning centers are often an important adjunct to reading and language arts. Many teachers set up four or five learning centers with different activities each week, and students in small groups travel from one station to another according to a prespecified schedule. For example, Jenny Bishop uses a weekly theme as the basis for her first-grade language arts program. Each week, she sets up activities related to that theme in her five stations: reading, writing, art, listening, and math. To accompany her fall theme, students find books on pumpkins to read at the reading station, paper and directions for a writing project at the writing center, paint and brushes to create a picture at the art station, a prerecorded tape to listen to at the listening station, and a math game involving pumpkin seeds and acorns at the math center.

Jenny uses five centers—one for each day—and that means each group can visit each center once a week. In Jenny's classroom, students can go to their stations only after completing their daily work assignments. In her system, the stations extend the students' learning experiences on the weekly theme but are also used as an incentive system for students to complete their required work. Figure 7.3 shows a sample of Jenny's posted schedule for groups and centers.

Figure 7.3   Learning station schedule.

Groups	Monday	Tuesday	Wednesday	Thursday	Friday
Acorns	Art	Music	Reading	Cooking	Math
Pumpkins	Music	Reading	Cooking	Math	Art
Gourds	Reading	Cooking	Math	Art	Music
Leaves	Cooking	Math	Art	Music	Reading
Apples	Math	Art	Music	Reading	Cooking

Source: Jenny Bishop.

Teachers who work with students who have limited English proficiency are finding that rotations from one learning center to another give the students many rich opportunities to use the English language with their peers as well as with adults. In a first-grade classroom at Viking Elementary School in Fresno, California, Susan McCloskey welcomes students who often speak limited or no English. In her classroom, she has created a learning environment that enables her English language learners to take risks with English so that they develop oral fluency in their new language. In the following case study, you can read about how she changed her classroom to implement free-flowing learning stations to provide her students with a variety of opportunities to practice their evolving English language skills.

Reflective Action Case Study

ESTABLISHING LEARNING CENTERS

Susan McCloskey

First-Grade Teacher, Viking Elementary School, Fresno, California

Teacher Begins to Plan

At the beginning of the school year, I do most of my instruction with the whole group sitting on the carpet at the front of the room. We begin reading books and having the students talk about the story. I take their dictation to show them how their words can be written down and reread.

Teacher Considers What Students Already Know

Because almost all of my students are learning English as a second language, I want to give them many opportunities to practice their developing English proficiency. Most of my students have experienced a year of state preschool where they participated in daily play stations where language interaction was encouraged.

Teacher Has Expectations

I began to think about ways that I could engage students in academic-related activities that would encourage verbal interactions and practices that would support the skills they are learning.

Teacher Does Research and Invites Feedback

I talked to other kindergarten teachers to determine how they use learning stations, how they organize them, and what types of stations they use in the beginning of the kindergarten year. I also asked how those stations change as the year progresses. I read articles about using learning stations and talked to my professors at Fresno State, where I had recently completed my master's degree in early childhood education with an emphasis on teaching English learners. I wanted to institute free-flowing centers where students could stay and work as long as they needed to complete a task, but many of my colleagues advised me to start with a schedule and move into free-flowing centers as my students gained experience.

Teacher Reflects Again Using Feedback, Research, and Creativity

As I reflected on the information I gathered from my colleagues and my research, I realized that I would need some support from parents and volunteers to provide help at stations, especially for children who did not yet speak English fluently. I talked to parents and asked several to come to school to volunteer during learning station time. I also enlisted help from one of my professors, who sent some college students to observe and help in my classroom as part of their field experience. In order for the volunteers to be of help, I had to schedule learning stations at a set time each day, so I decided that having station time right after group time made sense.

Teacher Creates New Action Plan

I set up a volunteer schedule on the days that I would not have student teachers from the university. I created a number of learning stations that supported our current theme, and I introduced stations gradually. I wanted my students to explore centers in depth, so I did not want to set a time limit on their involvement in a single station; I also did not want to require all students to work in all stations each week. My main concern was giving my students opportunities to practice their English in relation to the new concepts to which they were being exposed. I began with three stations, which I introduced and demonstrated. I let some students choose one station the first day while I worked with the students who did not choose to work in stations. I planned an activity that would encourage verbal interactions. We read a simple book and then retold the story. I wrote their words down, and then we reread their summary. The first three stations I introduced were planned to give them practice in verbal interactions:

1. One group of three students read a story on the computer with a program that verbalized the words for them and then asked them questions about the story. One of the volunteers sat with them to keep them on task.

2. Another station involved listening to a story on a tape and then drawing a picture to illustrate it. Once the students finished, they told the volunteer about their pictures, and the volunteer took a language sample in anecdotal record form to document their telling about their pictures.

3. The third station was a sorting center, where the students named the pictures in their deck of cards and then sorted the cards into piles of birds, animals, and fish. They created sentences about each card as they found its category; the sentence could be as simple as "This picture is a fish." The volunteer was instructed to help them expand their verbalizations by asking questions such as "What color is your fish?"

Teacher Has Unforeseen Problems

My original plan was to allow the students to choose the station they wanted to go to, but it became evident that some children wanted to return to the same station each day and that some stations were much more popular than others. I realized that I had to keep careful records of the stations and who participated in each.

Teacher Uses Withitness to Respond to Problems

I instituted several procedures to address these problems:

1. I asked students to choose a station each day that they had not yet attended.

2. I made sure that students who stayed with me for the station time rotated daily.

3. I gradually added stations to the rotation until all students went to stations each day and there were extra stations for them to go to if they finished their task at their initial station.

4. I did have some students who tended to flit from station to station without really accomplishing what they were supposed to do. I assigned these students to a specific station each day and had them report back to me to show what they had accomplished before allowing them to go to a second station.

I am very pleased with the way the students are using the free-flowing centers, and I make sure to reinforce their good work at stations by having them show their work in a celebration circle at the end of station time. They know I value what they do at the stations, and it shows in their work.

Cooperative Learning Strategies

Cooperative groups are a welcome change of pace for many students because they enjoy the opportunity to interact with their peers for part of the school day. Teachers may be hesitant to try the strategy for fear that the students will play or talk about outside interests rather than work at the assigned task. Cooperative groups can degenerate into chaotic groups if they do not meet certain conditions.

Imagine that a teacher hears some general ideas about cooperative groups at a conference or reads the first few paragraphs of an article on the strategy. Thinking that it seems to be an intriguing idea, the teacher may hurry back to the classroom, divide the class into several small groups, and tell them to study the Civil War together for a test that will be held the following Friday. After a few moments of discussing what they have (or have not) read about the Civil War, the groups are likely to dissolve into chaos or, at best, evolve into groups who sit near one another and talk to one another as each person studies the text in isolation.

When the group has a poor understanding of the goals of the task, the results may be unproductive and frustrating. To prevent this, the teacher must clearly state the goals and expectations of each group task and provide a copy of them in writing so the group can refer to them from time to time. This includes assigning specific duties to each group member, which results in smoothly functioning interactions in the group.

Cooperative learning is designed to encourage students to help and support their peers in a group rather than compete against them. This purpose assumes that the perceived value of academic achievement increases when students are all working toward the same goal. Cooperative groups emphasize the notion of pride in one's "team" in much the same way that sports teams do. A teacher using cooperative learning must be constantly vigilant to ensure that one or two students are not dominating the group to the educational detriment of the other children in the group. Quite often, dominant students will disregard the contributions of other members of the group based on a perception of educational "worthiness." Students who are not strong readers, for example, are often left out of discussions their ideas are minimized or disregarded altogether. Students are also sometimes the objects of negative interactions simply because of their linguistic or ethnic backgrounds. It is the responsibility of the teacher to monitor the groups' progress and intervene when necessary to make sure that all children are given the opportunity to participate in the group process (Cohen, 1994).

Another major purpose of cooperative learning is to boost the achievement of students of all ability levels. The assumption is that when high-achieving students work with low-achieving students, they both benefit. Compared to tracking systems that separate the high achievers from the low achievers, cooperative groups are composed of students at all levels so that the low-achieving students can benefit from the modeling and interactions with their more capable peers. It is also believed that high-achieving students can learn to be more tolerant and understanding of individual differences through this type of experience than if they are separated from low achievers.

Still another point is that cooperative teams are believed to be more motivating for the majority of students because the students have a greater opportunity to experience the joy of winning and success. In a competitive environment, the same few high-achieving students are likely to win over and over again, but a classroom divided into cooperative teams, each with its own high- and low-achieving students, more evenly distributes the opportunity to succeed. To this end, the reward systems do not honor individuals but depend on a group effort. As on sports teams, good individual performances are encouraged because they benefit the whole team.

Teachers may believe that they are using cooperative learning when, in reality, they are simply making physical changes in the classroom desk arrangement or allowing students who work rapidly and well to tutor or mentor their slower classmates. Johnson and Johnson (1993) provide us with a valuable perspective by telling us what cooperative learning is *not*: It is *not* having students sit side by side at the same table to talk with one another as they do their individual assignments, it is *not* having students do a task with instructions that whoever finishes first is to help the slower students, and it is *not* assigning a report to a group of students wherein one student does all the work and the others put their names on the product, too.

Using Learning Teams to Enhance Achievement

Slavin (1995) emphasizes the team concept in cooperative learning. For example, the teacher presents information to the entire class in the form of lectures, discussion, and/or readings. As a follow-up, students are formed into four- or five-member heterogeneous teams to learn the new material or practice the new skills.

These learning teams are designed to provide a way to encourage both individual accountability and group efforts. A baseline score is computed for each team by combining the data from individual pretests. Students then work together and assist each other in learning new material. At the conclusion of the study period, individual posttests are given to determine how well each member of the group has learned the material. Students are not allowed to help one another on the tests, only during the practice sessions. The individual test scores are then combined to produce a team score, but the winning team is not necessarily the team with the highest combined score. The results that count are the *improvement scores,* computed by determining the difference between each individual's original baseline pretest score and the final posttest results and adding these individual improvement scores together to create a final group improvement score.

For example, students may be pretested on 20-word spelling lists. High-scoring students are grouped with lower-scoring students to study and practice together, with the goal of having all students in the group earn improvement points for their team. One group's scores and points might look like this example:

Name	Pretest Score	Posttest Score Difference = Improvement Points	
John	13	15	+ 2
Mary	17	14	−3
Jorge	12	19	+ 7
Carla	8	18	+ 10

The teacher may use the total score of 16 to calculate an average improvement score for this group; then 16 is divided by 4, for an average group improvement score of 4. This group's score can then be compared with other groups in the class, and a competition among the study groups may be used to stimulate interest and motivation in working together to improve everyone's scores. If all groups do well and achieve impressive group improvement scores, then all groups can earn awards or extra privileges. Teachers can design award certificates or plan a menu of extra privileges to encourage students to work hard individually and in cooperation with each other.

Utilizing Cooperative Learning to Master Basic Skills

Cooperative learning can also be used to assist students in the mastery of basic skills such as computing the basic addition, subtraction, and multiplication facts. In a traditional classroom, teachers may prepare students for this assessment by providing them with daily worksheets for practicing and memorizing the math facts. Students may win rewards or recognition for being the fastest or the most accurate on these work assignments.

Although this type of competitive environment may please and motivate the high achievers, it is not likely to encourage the remainder of the class. To modify the process of learning math facts from a competitive to a cooperative experience, teachers could adapt the student team achievement division model to fit the needs of their classrooms. Using a learning team approach, the teacher would begin by giving a pretest of 100 math facts to the entire class. By sorting the pretests into high, medium, and low scores, the teacher can divide the class into heterogeneous groups with equivalent ability in math facts. Each group would contain one of the top scorers, one of the lowest scorers, and two in the middle range.

How the teacher sets up the conditions and expectations for this cooperative learning experience is very important. The achievement goal and the behavioral expectations must be clearly explained at the outset. For example, the teacher may state that the groups are expected to practice math facts for a given time each day. Worksheets, flash cards, and other materials will be provided, and the teams are free to choose the means they use to practice. The goal, in this instance, is to raise all scores from pretest levels as much as possible. A posttest will be given on a certain day, and each individual will have an improvement score, which is the difference between the correct responses on the posttest and the correct responses on the pretest. The group improvement score will be computed by adding the individual improvement scores. This method of scoring encourages the group to give extra energy to raise the scores of the lowest scorers because they have the most to gain. Top scorers, in fact, may not gain many points at all, since their pretests may already be near the total. Added incentives for this group, such as a certain number of points for a perfect paper, may be devised.

The incentives that will be awarded for success depend a great deal on the class itself. The teacher may choose to offer one reward for the group whose scores improve the most or reward each group based on their gains. For example, a single reward for the most improved group may be tangible, such as a certificate of success or temporary possession of a traveling math trophy. Less tangible incentives, such as the opportunity to be first in line for a week, to go to the library together during a math class, or to eat lunch with the teacher, are also important to third graders. To spread the incentives among all groups, the points that each group earns may be translated into an award such as 1 minute of free time per point or the opportunity to "buy" special opportunities and materials.

Once students become accustomed to helping their classmates in one subject area, they are likely to take considerable interest in assisting and supporting their class members in doing well in other subjects. Similar groups could operate to improve spelling, vocabulary, mechanics of writing, or other basic skills. The membership of each group would be different because students are likely to score differently on pretests for various subjects.

Using Cooperative Learning to Teach Science

In many classrooms, the conventional approach to teaching science once centered on textbook reading, discussion, an occasional demonstration by the teacher, and written tests of understanding. More recently, science curricula have been revised to include many more hands-on experiments and investigations. The current philosophy is that students need to learn how to *do* science rather than simply learn about it.

Hands-on science is an area that is a natural fit for cooperative group strategies. By participating in cooperative science investigations, students learn how scientists themselves interact to share observations, hypotheses, and methods. Although many teachers value these current science goals, they may be reluctant to try them because they are unsure of how to manage the high level of activity in the classroom when science experiments are happening. Cooperative groups can provide the support and structure needed to manage successful science investigation in the classroom.

When a topic or unit approach is taken for teaching science, each unit offers opportunities for cooperative learning. For example, jigsaw groups may study the topic of astronomy, with each studying one planet, creating models and charts of information about that planet, and reporting their findings to other groups. Investigations into the properties of simple machines, magnets, electricity, and other topics in physics can be designed by establishing a challenge or a complex goal for groups to meet by a given date. Groups may be given a set of identical materials and told to create a product that has certain characteristics and can perform a specific function. For example, given a supply of toothpicks and glue, groups are challenged to construct a bridge that can hold a pound of weight without breaking. Given a raw egg and an assortment of materials, groups work together to create ways to protect their eggs when they are dropped from a high window onto the pavement below.

Science groups can be mixed and matched frequently during the year, offering students an opportunity to work cooperatively with most other members of their class. This strategy is likely to reinforce the principles of the social sciences as well. For example, during the astronomy unit, the emphasis could be on learning how to come together as a group quickly, quietly, and efficiently when getting started on the day's project. During the bridge-building unit, the groups could practice encouraging everyone to participate, taking time to ask for opinions and suggestions from every member of the group before making an important decision. After completing each unit, the groups should participate in evaluating how well they worked together and how well they demonstrated the interpersonal skills emphasized during that unit.

Creating Well-Balanced Cooperative Groups

Assigning students to cooperative groups can be the most difficult part of the process for teachers. The philosophy of heterogeneous grouping is excellent in theory but is difficult to achieve in a real-life classroom. A classroom is likely to have one or two superstars whose ability cannot be matched in some subject areas; similarly, one or two students may have very unusual learning difficulties or behavior problems. For most types of learning situations, the teacher must simply make his or her best judgment about the combinations that are approximately equivalent in ability.

It is advisable to put non-task-oriented students into groups with highly task-oriented teammates so that peer pressure will work to keep them on task. This theory, however, does not always work in the classroom. Angry or highly restless students may refuse to participate or otherwise prevent their team from succeeding, and when this happens, the group itself should be encouraged to deal with the problem as a means of learning how to cope with and resolve such occurrences in real life.

In arranging the room during cooperative group activities, each group should have a comfortable space, and members should be able to face one another and have eye contact with every other member of the group. Separating the groups from one another is also necessary so they can each work undisturbed by the conversations and activities taking place in other groups.

Materials intended for cooperative groups may differ from those used in conventional teaching and learning situations. It is suggested that only one set of materials explaining the task and the expectations be distributed. This causes students in the group to work together from the very beginning. In some cases, each member of the group may receive different information from other members; this promotes interdependence because each member has something important to share with the others. Interdependence can also be encouraged by the assignment of complementary and interconnected roles to group members. These roles will vary with the type of learning and task but might include discussion leader, recorder of ideas, runner for information, researcher, encourager, and observer.

Tasks that result in the creation of products rather than participation in a test or tournament are more likely to succeed if the group is limited to the production of one product. If more than one product is allowed, students may simply work independently on their own products. Members of the group should also be asked to sign a statement saying that they participated in the development of the group's product.

To ensure individual accountability, students must know that they will all be held responsible for learning and presenting what they learned. During the final presentations, the teacher may ask any member of the group to answer a question, describe an aspect of the group's final product, or present a rationale for a group decision.

Evaluating Effects of Cooperative Learning

In a school setting, students learn in classes made up of their age mates, for the most part. With conventional teaching methods, relationships among peers in a class are likely to become somewhat competitive because most students are aware of how well they are doing in relation to their classmates. Grading systems reinforce the competitive nature of school, as do standardized tests and entrance exams.

Individual competition can enhance the motivation for high-achieving students, who perceive that they have a possibility of winning or being the best. However, the public nature of competitive rewards and incentives leads to embarrassment and anxiety for students who fail to succeed. When the embarrassment and anxiety are intense, students who recognize that they are unlikely to win no matter how hard they work eventually drop out of the competition in one way or another.

Despite these negative effects of competition, it is difficult to imagine a classroom without some type of competitive spirit or reward system, and despite its obvious flaws, competition does create an energetic response from many students. Slavin's (1995) models of cooperative group structures are designed to maintain the positive value of competition by adapting it in the form of team competition so that each student is equally capable of winning.

Reflective teachers who undertake some form of cooperative learning will need to be aware of all possible effects and observe for both positive and negative interactions among teammates. When using competitive teams, teachers should take steps to ensure that every team has an equal chance to win and that attention is focused more on the learning task than on which teams win and lose. When anger or conflicts arise within groups, teachers must be ready to mediate and assist students as they learn the interpersonal and communication skills necessary to learn from their team losses.

Slavin (1995) and Sharan (1999) also report that cooperative groups may actually improve race relations within a classroom. When students participate in multiracial teams, studies show that they choose one another for friends more often than do students in control groups. Researchers attribute this effect to the fact that working together in a group as part of a team causes students to promote more differentiated, dynamic, and realistic views (and therefore less stereotyped and static views) of other students (including peers who are handicapped and students who are from different ethnic groups) than do competitive and individualistic learning experiences (Johnson & Johnson, 2005).

Promoting dynamic interactions among your students is the likely effect if you choose to learn and master the use of cooperative learning strategies for your future classroom. All of the teaching strategies presented in this chapter have the potential of creating a stimulating, motivating, and highly interactive learning environment and enhance the relational aspects of teaching. Discovery learning and inquiry learning foster independence and intrinsic motivation. Role playing encourages self-awareness and understanding of others' points of view, and simulations encourage interactions; learning centers and cooperative groups promote interdependence. By using many of these strategies in your classroom, you will be inviting your students to learn for the sake of learning while at the same time providing them with opportunities for becoming reflective and relational human beings.

Additional Formats for Cooperative Groups

Literature Circles

Reading instruction may be conducted in a variety of formats. Primary teachers may teach small groups of students reading individual storybooks in flexible literature circles that change almost weekly. These groups of students are often engaged in active learning experiences after each small book is completed. In some classrooms, more conventional methods of teaching reading, three homogeneous reading groups based on ability, may still be used at many grade levels: Each group reads stories, essays, poems, and plays collected in a basal reader geared for their reading ability, and the teacher leads discussions of reading materials and assigns seat work to be done while he or she works with other groups.

Many upper elementary teachers, however, prefer to use literary materials in their own format rather than as collections in basal readers or anthologies. They believe that students' motivation to read will improve if they are encouraged to choose and read whole books, novels, poetry collections, and plays. A variety of paperback books in sets of six to eight books apiece are needed to carry out this type of reading program.

At Our Lady of Mercy School in Chicago, sixth-grade teacher Roxanne Farwick-Owens has developed a system that allows choice, maximizes cooperative efforts, and holds individuals accountable. To maximize student motivation and enjoyment of reading, Roxanne believes students must be allowed to choose their reading materials. Each month she provides three or four reading selections, in the form of paperback books, to the class; students are allowed to choose the book they want to read, and groups are formed according to interest rather than ability level. Roxanne may advise students about their selections and try to steer them toward appropriate selections, but in the end, she believes that they have the right to choose for themselves what they will read, especially because she has provided only books that have inherent value for sixth graders.

During initial group meetings, students decide for themselves how much to read at a time and assign themselves due dates for each chapter. Periodically, each group meets with Roxanne to discuss what they are reading, but most discussions are held without her leadership. Usually, she holds the groups responsible for generating their own discussions on the book. To prepare for these discussions, all members are expected to prepare questions as they read. For example, each person in the group may be expected to contribute three "why" questions and two detail questions per session. Roxanne reviews the questions each day as a means of holding each individual accountable for reading the material and contributing to the group.

Another task is to plan a presentation about the books—using art, music, drama, and other media—to share with the rest of the class at the end of the month. This allows groups to introduce the books they have read to the other members of the class, who are then likely to choose them at a later date. One group made wooden puppets and a puppet stage to portray an event from Mark Twain's *Tom Sawyer*. After reading Judy Blume's *Superfudge*, a group created a radio commercial, complete with sound effects and background music, for the book. Familiar television interview shows are sometimes used as a format, as are music videos.

About once per quarter, two teams are formed to compete in a game show–type tournament. Questions about the books are separated into categories such as character, plot, setting, author, and miscellaneous. Each person is responsible for writing five questions and answers on index cards to prepare for the tournament. One student acts as emcee while another keeps track of the points; the team with the most points wins the tournament.

Roxanne finds that this cooperative group structure increases her students' social skills, especially their ability to work with others and to find effective ways to handle disagreements. The primary reasons for the program are to help her students see that reading can be enjoyable and that reading can have a social aspect instead of being just a solitary pursuit. Roxanne believes many of her students may become lifelong readers from this yearlong experience.

Peacemaking Groups

Some cooperative peacemaking groups are formed for the social purpose of teaching students how to resolve conflicts, handle anger, and avoid violence in their lives. Many schools are taking an active role in training their students to incorporate conflict management skills in their daily lives. Johnson and Johnson (2005) have created a series of learning experiences teachers can use for this purpose. Students are taught to recognize that conflict is inevitable and that they can choose between entering into destructive or constructive conflicts. They learn how to recognize a constructive conflict through cooperative group experiences and simulations.

For example, a group of students may be told that they have just won an all-expense-paid field trip to the destination of their choice. Now comes the hard part: Where will the group choose to go? Students pair up to list their choices and create a rationale for them. Through negotiation, the group must resolve the dilemma and make a plan by consensus. In other peacemaking groups, students learn to identify how they personally react to conflicts and learn how to be assertive rather than to be aggressive or to withdraw from arguments and difficult situations. For example, one session may be devoted to assisting students in dealing with insulting remarks and put-downs; in another, they may deal with a simulated situation in which one student refuses to do her part in a cooperative group assignment. Even when anxiety over competition is less intense and is held under control by students with average or high-average achievement, they may become preoccupied with grades to the extent that they withdraw, avoiding complex or challenging tasks that will put their academic standing and grades at risk.

Peacemaking group activities such as these are designed to encourage students to seek peaceful solutions in their school environment. Teachers who use these cooperative methods are also likely to believe they may be useful to their students as adults and may lead to future generations seeking more peaceful solutions in business, politics, and other issues in their families and communities.

Involving the Larger Educational Community

The use of active learning during the teaching of curriculum units provides a great opportunity for parent involvement during culmination exercises. Inviting parents back to school for displays of student projects, reader's theater, oral presentations, and the like provides a clear connection between learning and stated outcomes. Allow the parents and significant others to share this learning with the children and to become co-participants in the educational processes that you have chosen to use in your classroom.

Some teachers like to invite parents to a back-to-school night to explain the active learning approach they have chosen to use, and they sometimes structure the room with learning centers that the parents can participate in to acquaint them with the active learning concepts. Often, teachers will use displays from the previous year to demonstrate some of the learning processes and to spur the parents on to getting involved with their children's learning.

Group Focus Activity

Planning a Cooperative Learning Activity

1. Your professor will divide the class into small groups and give each group a cooperative learning activity to plan.

2. Work with your group to answer the following questions:

    a. Why would this be a good activity for cooperative learning?

    b. What training will the students need in order for them to work cooperatively?

    c. What roles could be assigned to support the students in working together?

    d. How would you structure the activity?

    e. How would you have the students report their results?

3. Report your group's plan to the whole class.

Suggestions for Cooperative Learning Activities

- Prepare a report on one of the systems of the human body (skeletal, digestive, muscular, etc.)
- Prepare a report on one state in the U.S.A.
- Plan a party for a holiday celebrated in one of the countries studied (Central and South America).
- Identify and plan a project for your class that will contribute to the surrounding neighborhood.
- Plan a research project to identify the eating habits of the students in your classroom and some activities to help them learn to eat more healthy food.

Preparing for Your Licensure Exam

In this chapter you read about ways to build your repertoire of teaching strategies. Reread "A View into the Classroom" at the beginning of the chapter, and think about it as a case study you might encounter on your licensure exam. Answer the following questions to demonstrate your understanding of the process of building a repertoire of teaching strategies:

1. How can you include simulations or role plays in your teaching of math and science at your grade level?

2. How can you include the use of Internet resources in your teaching?

3. How did Celeste use simulations and role plays to build background knowledge in her students?

Portfolio of Professional Practices Activity

Visit and review three of the simulation sites listed in Figure 7.4 appropriate for the grade level that you would like to teach. Choose one of the simulations you reviewed and explain how you could integrate it into a unit of study at your chosen grade level. Write a reflection on how the simulation would build the students' background knowledge, how the simulation would help address grade-level standards, and what learning outcomes you would expect with the use of the simulation.

Figure 7.4   Simulations available online.

www.techtrekers.com/sim.htm (This site provides simulations in language arts, math, science, and social studies.)

www.edutopia.org/side-sims (Useful, usable simulations are available for practically any subject at any level; most are free or inexpensive.)

www.simplek12.com/virtualfieldtripfreepackage (This site supplies a guide for your teachers on creating their own virtual field trips as well as tips and uses in the classroom.)

www.3rdworldfarmer.com (This site lets players manage a small virtual farm in a developing country and thus experience the hardships and dilemmas faced by the poor.)

www.timetoteach.co.uk/simulations.html (A variety of simulations are available to use in your own classroom; select from a collection of topics and subjects.)

www.shambles.net/pages/students/simulation (This site supports school communities worldwide with over 30,000 links to moderated teaching and learning resources.)

References

Bloom, B. (1984). The search for methods of group instruction as effective as one-to-one tutoring. *Educational Leadership, 41*(8), 4–17.

Cohen, E. (1994). *Designing groupwork* (2nd ed.). New York, NY: Teachers College Press.

Hamilton, M., & Weiss, M. (2005). *Children tell stories.* Katonah, NY: Owen Publishing.

Herrell, A., & Jordan, M. (2012). *50 strategies for teaching English language learners* (4th ed.). Upper Saddle River, NJ: Merrill/Prentice Hall.

Johnson, D., & Johnson, R. (1993). *Circles of learning.* Alexandria, VA: Association of Supervision and Curriculum Development.

Johnson, D., & Johnson, R. (2005). *Teaching students to be peacemakers* (2nd ed.). Edina, MN: Interaction Book.

Joyce, B., Weil, M., & Showers, B. (2008). *Models of teaching* (8th ed.). Boston, MA: Allyn & Bacon.

Mann, H. (1989). *On the art of teaching* (Little Books of Wisdom). Bedford, MA: Applewood Books.

Sharan, S. (1999). *Handbook of cooperative learning methods.* Westport, CT: Greenwood Press.

Slavin, R. (1995). *Cooperative learning* (2nd ed.). Boston, MA: Allyn & Bacon.

chapter eight

Engaging Students in Classroom Discussions

iStockPhoto

"The teacher who is indeed wise does not bid you to enter the house of his wisdom but rather leads you to the threshold of your mind."

Kahlil Gibran, Lebanese-American author, poet, noted essayist, and author of *The Prophet*

When students become actively and enthusiastically interested in thinking about and discussing an idea, they are experiencing *cognitive engagement*, a powerful concept for teachers to aim for when they select teaching strategies for their classrooms. Cognitive engagement results in the opposite of the sterile, passive classroom environment in which students attend listlessly to the lessons and carry out their seat work and homework with little real effort or interest. When students are fully engaged in reading, listening, discussing, or doing creative activities, the classroom climate is more likely to be lively and stimulating. When teachers structure classroom discussions to engage their students fully in substantive, meaningful, and highly interactive exchanges of information and ideas, authentic learning is more likely to occur.

Can you recall a classroom learning experience so powerful that you have almost total recall of it many years later? When you recall the event, do you feel as if you are reliving it because the memory is still so vividly etched in your mind? Do you think of this event as life changing? Perhaps it altered the way you think about an issue or caused you to change your career goal or provoked you into making a lifestyle change. Bloom (1981) calls these relatively rare classroom events *peak experiences*. For many students, peak learning experiences occur during especially stimulating classroom discussions in which all members of the classroom community are expressing ideas, opinions, and points of view. Students experience these discussions as authentic, substantive, and valuable; teachers have a sense of exhilaration and pride when they are able to create the environment and structure needed for such powerful exchanges. In this chapter, we will examine some of the strategies you can use to stimulate and guide substantive and satisfying classroom discussions.

Questions for Reflection as You Read the Chapter

1. How can the teacher lead students into higher-level thinking as part of a classroom discussion?
2. What strategies must a teacher use to stimulate participation in classroom discussions?
3. What can a teacher do to keep classroom discussions on track?

A View into the Classroom

Dawn Schiffer teaches fourth grade in Modesto, California. One of the California History/ Social Sciences Standards requires that students compare life in the twenty-first century to life in the past. To support her students in understanding the ways in which life changes as new inventions and technologies are discovered, Dawn asks her students to interview their parents and grandparents about ways in which their lives were different when they were children. As a class, the students generate questions that they might ask in order to learn more about how their parents and grandparents lived as children. As the students develop questions, Dawn encourages them to ask more leading questions to get their parents and grandparents to speak freely and give even more information. Following are some questions they generated:

How was your life as a child different from the lives of children today?

What inventions have been discovered that make children's lives different today?

What do you think is the most important invention that has been discovered in your lifetime?

What was a day like when you were a child?

How was school different when you were a child?

What types of after-school activities did you participate in?

After the students had time to conduct their home interviews, Dawn engaged her students in a class discussion to explore what they learned. She opened the discussion with an open-ended question: "What was the most interesting thing you discovered in your interviews?"

Robert was the first to respond. "My parents never had television when they were children. They said televisions sets were very expensive and the reception in the hills wasn't too good, so their parents never bought a set."

Dawn asked, "How did they feel about that?"

"They were okay with it," said Robert. "They both liked to read, and they had lots of chores to do so they didn't have much time to watch TV anyway."

"My parents had TVs, but they weren't allowed to watch any shows on school nights," Celine added. "They said their parents never watched TV on weeknights either. Everybody in the house went to bed early."

"Why do you suppose their attitudes toward TV were so different in those days?" asked Dawn.

"Maybe the shows weren't as good in those days," suggested Juan.

"I think they got up earlier, and so they went to bed right after dinner," Pat added.

"My grandfather still goes to bed right after dinner," Susan said. "He gets up very early in the morning, too."

"My dad said he had lots of chores to do before school, so he got up very early and went to bed early, too," added Jorge. "He lived on a farm. He only watched TV on weekends, and he wasn't allowed to watch more than one or two shows a day."

"My parents didn't talk about TV much, but they thought air-conditioning was the most important invention," stated Ginger. "I was surprised that they didn't think computers were the most important."

"Why do you suppose they made that choice? asked Dawn.

"Well, it gets really hot in Modesto in the summer," Ginger offered tentatively.

"I think kids our age wouldn't think to name air-conditioning," added Peter. "We've always had it. We think of computers because they are newer and we're just learning to use them a lot."

"That's a very good point, Peter," responded Dawn. "What other things do your parents or grandparents think are important inventions?"

"My mom said the microwave oven was the most important invention," stated Jeremy. "I don't remember not having a microwave, so I wouldn't have thought to name it as an invention."

"I like the way you're analyzing the answers," said Dawn with a smile. "Parents and grandparents have a lot of inventions to think about in their lifetimes."

"Could we research inventions?" asked Danny. "I don't know when things were invented."

"Great idea, Danny! We can make a time line and then look to see what was invented during your grandparents' lifetimes, what was invented during your parents' lifetimes, and what was invented during your lifetimes."

"Then we can really see how life was different for our grandparents and parents," added Jeremy.

"Wonderful idea!" responded Dawn.

REFLECTING ON THE CLASSROOM EXPERIENCE

Conducting meaningful classroom discussions is more complicated than it appears on the surface. Teachers must listen to the students, adapt their questions to the interaction levels of their students, model good listening techniques, and continue to find ways to engage everyone in the activity.

Some teachers find that they have to do some direct teaching of listening and responding to another's comments. In today's busy world, many students have limited experience with conversation. The level of questions that you ask to engage your students is vital, as well. You want to state your questions in a way that encourages expanded answers rather than "yes" and "no" responses.

Two of the most challenging aspects of classroom discussion are keeping the students on topic and finding ways to encourage participation. Some teachers have devised hand signals that they use to indicate that the group has ventured off topic or that one student is monopolizing the conversation. This type of signal requires discussing the problems and introducing the signals in a nonthreatening way.

Dawn introduced hand signals by saying, "I want to make sure that everyone has a chance to express themselves in our discussion. Let's try a hand signal that indicates that I want to wind up your contribution so that someone else can have a turn. When this happens, I will pull on my ear, like this." She demonstrates.

Often Dawn finds that she doesn't have to give the signal—one of the students does it for her. Because she has introduced the signal in a nonthreatening way, it is usually accepted graciously.

Asking Questions to Stimulate Higher-Level Thinking

Imagine you are observing a classroom discussion after the students have read a biography of Dr. Martin Luther King Jr. The teacher asks the following questions:

When and where was Dr. King born?

Who were the other members of his family?

How did Dr. King's father and mother earn a living?

What career did Dr. King choose?

What does the word *ghetto* mean?

What does the word *prejudice* mean?

What did Dr. King accomplish that earned him the Nobel Peace Prize?

As you watch and listen to this discussion, you might reflect on the way you would lead it and the questions you would like to ask the students. Perhaps you believe that there are other, very different types of questions that the teacher could use to stimulate higher-level thinking and engage the students in a discussion that connects what they have read to their own lives.

Many reflective teachers use Bloom's revised taxonomy (Anderson & Krathwohl, 2001) to generate discussion questions that promote the use of higher-level thinking processes. Discussion questions can be readily planned at every level of the taxonomy, just as other learning experiences are planned. The term *higher level* refers to the top four levels of the hierarchy.

Higher-Level Thinking Processes	*Lower-Level Thinking Processes*
Creating	Understanding
Evaluating	Remembering
Analyzing	
Applying	

In the previous example, the teacher asked only lower-level (remembering and understanding) questions. But you can plan your discussions to highlight the thinking processes of applying, analyzing, evaluating, and creating. Although this system can be used at any grade level and with any topic, the following examples are taken from the discussion of Dr. King's biography.

Remembering Level

At this level, the learners are asked to recall specific bits of information, such as terminology, facts, and details:

> When and where was Dr. King born?
>
> Who were the other members of his family?
>
> What were the jobs Dr. King's father did to earn a living?
>
> What jobs did his mother do?
>
> What career did Dr. King choose?

Understanding Level

At this level, the learners are asked to summarize and describe the main ideas of the subject matter in their own words:

> What does the term *ghetto* mean?
>
> What does *prejudice* mean?
>
> How did the church affect Dr. King's life?
>
> What did Dr. King accomplish that earned him the Nobel Peace Prize?

While the teacher in the previous example stopped here, a reflective teacher is likely to use those questions only as a beginning to establish the basic facts and ideas so that the class can then begin to engage in a spirited discussion of how Dr. King's life and accomplishments have affected their own lives.

Applying Level

At this level, the learners are asked to apply what they have learned to their own lives or to other situations:

> Are there ghettos in this community? What are they, and who is affected by them?
>
> Can you give an example of prejudice that has affected you?
>
> If Dr. King were alive today, what do you think he would be most concerned about? What do you think he would do about it?

Analyzing Level

At this level, the learners are asked to describe patterns and cause-and-effect relationships:

> How did Rosa Parks's decision to sit in the front of the bus change Dr. King's life? How did her decision change history?
>
> In what ways was Dr. King a minister, a politician, and a teacher?
>
> If Dr. King had never been born, how would your life be different today?

Evaluating Level

At this level, the learners are asked to express their own opinions or make judgments about some aspect of the topic:

> What do you believe was Dr. King's greatest contribution?
>
> Which promotes greater social change: nonviolence or violence? Give a rationale or example to defend your answer.
>
> Why do you think Dr. King's work endangered his life?

Creating Level

At this level, the learners are asked to contribute a new and original idea on the topic:

> How would you complete this sentence: I have a dream that one day . . .
>
> If there were suddenly a strong new prejudice against people who look just like you, what would you do about it?
>
> How can we as a class put some of Dr. King's dreams into action?

Some teachers find that Bloom's taxonomy is a useful and comprehensive guide for planning classroom discussion questions as well as other classroom activities. Others find that the taxonomy is more complex than they desire and that it is difficult to discriminate among some of the levels, such as understanding and analysis or applying and evaluating. Other systems of classifying thinking processes are also available. Doyle (1986) proposes that teachers plan classroom tasks in four categories that are readily applicable to classroom discussions: (1) memory tasks, (2) procedural or routine tasks, (3) comprehension tasks, and (4) opinion tasks. Classroom questions and discussion starters can then be created to fit these four task levels.

MEMORY TASKS.   Learners are asked to reproduce information they have read or heard before:

> When and where was Dr. King born?
>
> Who were the other members of his family?

PROCEDURAL OR ROUTINE TASKS.   Learners are asked to supply simple answers with only one correct response:

> What jobs did Dr. King's father and mother do to earn a living?
>
> What career did Dr. King choose?

COMPREHENSION TASKS.   Learners are asked to consider known data and apply them to a new and unfamiliar context:

> What does the term *ghetto* mean?
>
> What does *prejudice* mean?
>
> How did the church affect Dr. King's life?
>
> What did Dr. King accomplish that earned him the Nobel Peace Prize?
>
> How did Rosa Parks's decision to sit in the front of the bus change Dr. King's life? How did her decision change history?
>
> In what ways was Dr. King a minister, a politician, a teacher?

OPINION TASKS. Learners are asked to express their own points of view on an issue, with no correct answer expected:

Are there ghettos in this community? What are they, and who is affected by them?

Can you give an example of prejudice that has affected you?

If Dr. King were alive today, what do you think he would be most concerned about? What do you think he would do about it?

How would you complete this sentence: I have a dream that one day . . .

If there were suddenly a strong new prejudice against people who look just like you, what would you do about it?

What do you believe was Dr. King's greatest contribution?

What can we as a class do to carry out some of Dr. King's dream?

Which promotes more social change: nonviolence or violence? Give a rationale or example to defend your answer.

What social problem do you most want to change in your life?

You will notice that the questions in Doyle's four categories are the same as the ones listed in the six levels of Bloom's taxonomy's. Questions at the understanding and analyzing levels are both contained in Doyle's comprehension category, and questions at the applying and evaluating levels are contained in the opinion category. Both of these systems offer teachers a comprehensive framework for planning a range of thought-provoking questions. You may choose to write out the questions you ask ahead of time, or you may just remind yourself as you participate in a discussion that you need to include questions from the higher-level thinking categories.

Strategies for Interactive Discussions

In some classrooms, what pass for discussions are really dull and repetitive question-and-answer periods. Some teachers may simply read aloud a list of questions from the teacher's manual of the textbook and call on students to recite the answers. As you probably recall from your own school experiences, when this type of "discussion" occurs, many students disengage entirely. They read ahead, doodle, or do homework surreptitiously. They seldom listen to their classmates' responses, and when it is their turn to recite, they frequently cannot find their place in the list of questions.

Reflective teachers value the process of considering alternatives and debating opinions and ideas. That is how reflective teachers approach the world themselves, and they are likely to want to stimulate the same types of behaviors among their students. Authentic learning experiences depend heavily on the promotion of high-quality and actively engaged thinking. Teachers who are committed to creating authentic learning for their students do so by planning discussions that stimulate higher-level thinking processes, problem-solving skills, critical thinking, and creative thinking and by acknowledging the multiple intelligences of their students.

These terms and concepts can be confusing and overwhelming for the beginning teacher, who may think it is necessary to establish separate programs for each of them. That is not the case; it is possible to discover common attributes among them and plan classroom discussions and other experiences that promote high-level thinking, problem-solving skills, and critical and creative thinking in all seven of the multiple intelligences at the same time. One question may pose a problem, another may call for a creative response, a third may be analytical, and a fourth may ask students to evaluate a situation and make a critical judgment. The best (which is to say, the most highly engaging) classroom discussions do all of these in a spontaneous, nonregimented way.

The following sections describe various thinking processes along with alternatives for planning classroom discussions to promote these processes. As you read these sections, reflect on the similarities and differences, look for patterns and sequences, and consider how you would use, modify, and adapt these systems in your classroom.

Although these processes can be applied to both academic and nonacademic areas of the curriculum, we will illustrate how classroom discussions are created and managed using the topic of racial discrimination as a common theme. In this example, the operational goals are to promote understanding of how racial discrimination affects the lives of human beings and to generate a sense of respect for individuals who are different from oneself.

Problem-Solving Discussions

Much has been written about the need for developing students' problem-solving and decision-making abilities. This can be done by presenting students with a complex problem and providing adequate scaffolding support for them to learn how to solve problems. Although some solutions require paper and pencil or a hands-on experimental approach, classroom discussion can solve other problems.

To create productive problem-solving discussions, the teacher must understand the processes involved in problem solving and then structure the questions to guide students through that process. A problem is said to exist when "one has a goal and has not yet identified a means for reaching that goal. The problem may be wanting to answer a question, to prove a theorem, to be accepted or to get a job" (Gagne, 1985, p. 138).

According to cognitive psychologists, the framework for solving a problem consists of identifying a goal, a starting place, and all possible solution paths from the starting place to the goal. Some individuals are efficient and productive problem solvers; others are not. An excellent classroom goal for the beginning teacher is to help students become more efficient and more productive problem solvers.

Nonproductive problem solvers are likely to have difficulty identifying or defining the problem. They may feel that a puzzling situation exists but may not be aware of the real nature of the problem. Students who are poor problem solvers need experience in facing puzzling situations and defining problems; they also need experience in identifying and selecting worthwhile goals.

When a problem has been defined and a goal established, it is still possible to be either efficient or inefficient in reaching the goal. Efficiency in problem solving can be increased when students learn how to identify the alternative strategies to reach a chosen goal and recognize which ones are likely to provide the best and quickest routes to success. This can be done by helping students visualize the probable effects of each alternative and applying criteria to help them choose the most valuable means of solving the problem they have defined.

As in the teaching of higher-level thinking processes, several useful systems are available to teachers who want to teach students to become better problem solvers. Many teachers enjoy using the technique known as *brainstorming*, which includes four basic steps:

1. Defining the problem
2. Generating, without criticism or evaluation, as many solutions as possible
3. Deciding on criteria for judging the solutions generated
4. Using these criteria to select the best possible solution

Brainstorming is an excellent way to generate classroom discussion about a puzzling issue. Rather than formulating a series of questions, the teacher supplies a dilemma or a puzzle, teaches the students the steps involved in brainstorming, and then leads them through the process itself.

In discussing the life of Martin Luther King Jr. and helping students to understand the effects of racial discrimination, the teacher might use a portion of the classroom discussion to brainstorm answers to one of the more perplexing questions. For example, the teacher might choose to use brainstorming to expand discussion of the following question:

If Dr. King were alive today, what do you think he would be most concerned about? What do you think he would do about it?

The techniques of brainstorming call for the teacher to pose the question or problem in such a way that it engages students' interest and motivates them to take it seriously. Because students may not be proficient at discussion of this sort, it is frequently necessary for the teacher to give additional cues and suggestions as a scaffold. In this instance, the teacher might need to pose the original question and then follow it up with some prompts:

What do you think he'd be concerned about in our community?

What has been in the news lately that might alarm him?

Who are the people in the world who are presently in need?

What are some threats to our environment?

Open-ended questions such as these will generate many more responses than if they were not used. After recording all the student responses on the chalkboard, the teacher leads the students through a process of selecting the most important items for further consideration, which may be done by a vote or general consensus. When the list has been narrowed to several important issues, the teacher must then help the students to establish criteria for judging the items.

Because the question is related to Dr. King's values, one possible criterion is to judge whether Dr. King showed concern for the issue in his lifetime; another criterion might be the number of people who are threatened or hurt by the problem. After judging the items by these criteria, the class makes a judgment about which items would most concern Dr. King. Then the process of brainstorming begins again, but this time the problem the class is considering is what Dr. King would be likely to do to help solve the problem. Generating responses to the first question—"If Dr. King were alive today, what would he be most concerned about?"—will help students understand the many aspects of racial discrimination that exist today. By selecting one of these as the main concern and generating responses to the question "What do you think he would do about it?" the students will reflect on their own responsibility to treat other human beings respectfully and on ways to increase tolerance and build a sense of community in their neighborhoods.

To moderate a brainstorming discussion, the teacher faithfully records every response generated by the students, no matter how trivial or impossible it sounds. The teacher then leads students through the process of eliminating the least important items and finally works through a process of establishing criteria to use in evaluating the best possible solutions.

Brainstorming alone does not solve problems; it merely trains students to think productively about problems and consider alternative solutions. In some classrooms, teachers may wish to extend the hypothetical discussion of possible solutions to an actual attempt to solve a problem or at least contribute to a solution.

Group Investigations

Occasionally, a crisis or an unusual event will excite students' interest and concern. When the topic is appropriate—and especially if it relates to the curriculum for that grade level—teachers may allow students to participate in an investigation of the puzzling event to learn as much as they can about the subject and, in the process, learn research and communication skills. Often teachers create puzzling situations or present unusual stimuli as a means of causing students to become curious and learn how to inquire and investigate to gather information that leads to accurate assessments and judgments.

Perhaps there is a change in local government or a national election that students want to know more about. Perhaps a change occurs in the way their own school is managed, or a community event that affects their lives unfolds around them. The first hint of student interest may occur in a classroom discussion. To the extent that reflective teachers are sensitive to their students' concerns, they may wish to allow students time to talk about the event.

The first discussion may simply be a time to let students air their opinions and express their feelings about the event. If the teacher decides that the event is a worthwhile issue, the class may be encouraged to read about it, ask questions, or interview other members of the community and bring back their findings for more expanded discussions. These, in turn, may lead students to form small investigative groups that attempt to discover as much as they can about the event and even suggest solutions to the problems or issues under discussion.

The teacher's role in this type of investigative discussion is to encourage students to find out more about the subject and to allow them opportunities to express their opinions and share their findings. The discussion may continue for a few days or a few weeks, depending on the seriousness of the event and its impact on the students' lives. Under the guidance of a caring, reflective teacher, this type of discussion is authentic learning at its very best.

When teachers want to stimulate curiosity and discussion, they may present a social dilemma or demonstrate a strange event. For example, the teacher may drop a number of different fruits and vegetables into a large, clear bowl of water and ask students to predict which will sink and which will float. Students are encouraged to ask the teacher questions and to formulate hypotheses about floating and sinking objects. As the discussion progresses, the large group discussion may be adjourned to allow small groups to make investigations of their own, reaching their own conclusions. After small-group investigations are completed, class members reconvene to share their hypotheses, demonstrate their investigations, and present their conclusions.

Discussions to Promote Critical Thinking

The term *critical thinking* is not a separate and distinct concept that is different from higher-level thinking processes and problem solving—it overlaps both of them. It is presented here in a separate section because during the past few years, it has become a field of study with its own research base and suggested classroom processes. This field of study known as critical thinking grew out of the philosophical study of logic, which was designed to train people to think about a single hypothesis deductively and arrive at a rational conclusion. Logical thinkers are prepared to deal with a single issue in depth, but sometimes they are not prepared to deal with unexpected evidence or ideas and may be stumped when they are asked to think "outside the box" or to deal with complex ideas that defy one right answer.

Critical thinking, then, is partially defined as a complex set of thinking skills and processes that are believed to lead to fair and useful judgments. Lipman (1988) points out the strong association between the words *criteria* and *critical thinking*. Through the use of problem-solving discussions, students learn the technique of brainstorming and applying criteria to select the best solution. But critical thinking is a more multifaceted concept than problem solving. Critical thinking involves more than simply training students to use a set of strategies or procedures; it also involves establishing some affective goals for students to support them in becoming more independent and open minded. Paul (1988), director of the Center for Critical Thinking at Sonoma State University in Rohnert Park, California, proposes that some of the affective attributes of critical thinking include independence, avoidance of egocentricity and stereotyping, and suspension of judgment until appropriate evidence has been gathered.

Paul recommends that school curricula be designed to teach students cognitive strategies such as observing, focusing on a question, distinguishing facts from opinions, distinguishing relevant from irrelevant information, judging credibility of sources, recognizing contradictions, making inferences, and drawing conclusions. Because almost every specialist in critical thinking proposes a slightly different set of thinking processes and skills that compose critical thinking, reflective teachers need to judge for themselves which of the strategies to stress in their own classrooms.

A more recent addition to the knowledge base on critical thinking is the topic of critical literacy. Vasquez (2003) describes critical literacy as an approach to reading that empowers the reader to ask questions about the origin of the reading material. Readers are encouraged to ask questions about the author's point of view and the purpose of the text; they should also determine who benefits from the knowledge that is being shared. The reader is also taught to ask questions such as "Is there another voice that should be heard in this discussion?"

Discussions to Improve Observation Skills

When possible in your curriculum, bring in photos or objects related to the subject you are studying. Invite students to read their stories, essays, or poems aloud for other students to listen and respond to, or possibly stage an event to elicit student observation skills. For example, as you study the concept of community, ask some students to role-play a disagreement; then ask them to describe what they observed, using as many details as they can. Call on as many students as possible, and encourage each of them to make a personal response to the situation. If they seem to be making impetuous or repetitive observations, guide their thinking with questions that ask them to explain or support their observations.

Show your students that they can observe with all five senses, not just sight. As you study nutrition, for example, allow students to taste a variety of foods and describe their taste observations. During a study of sound waves, provide a variety of different sounds, and ask students to identify what they have heard. The more students use their five senses and discuss what they observe, the more likely they are to develop accurate, detailed schemata for the subject matter they are studying.

Discussions to Enhance Comparing Skills

In classroom discussions, compare two or more objects, stories, characters, or events by asking students first to articulate ways that the two subjects are the same, taking as many responses as possible. Then ask students to tell how the two are different. This type of discussion can occur in any subject area: You may ask them to compare fractions with percentages in math, George Washington and Abraham Lincoln in history, Somalia and the United States in geography, electric- and gasoline-powered engines in science, or the wording and effects of two different classroom rules in a classroom meeting.

Discussions to Guide Classification Skills

Introduce a collection of words; for young children, use a set of manipulative materials, such as a collection of buttons, small toys, macaroni shapes, or shells, appropriate to their grade level. When possible, conduct this type of discussion using cooperative groups. Ask each group to examine the collection, look for distinguishing attributes, and create a system for classifying the objects into groups. During follow-up discussions, a spokesperson for each group can describe the attributes the group observed and present a rationale for the classification system used.

Older children can classify words on their spelling lists, favorite books or stories, foods, games, clothing, famous people, or television programs. The best results occur when the teacher has no preestablished criteria or notions of right or wrong regarding classification systems. As children discuss the characteristics of the shells or television programs they are classifying, they may discover some of the same attributes that adults have already described, or they may discover a completely original rationale on which to base their categories. The object of the students' discussion is not to get the most "right" answers but to participate in the open-ended process of sharing observations and making critical judgments they can defend with evidence.

Discussions to Identify Assumptions

Use advertisements for products your students want to buy as a means of stimulating a discussion to identify assumptions people make. Show a newspaper ad for a product, and ask students to describe what they believe the product will be like based on the advertisement alone. Then discuss the actual product, and compare the students' prior assumptions with the real item.

Talk about assumptions human beings make about each other. Ask students to examine the meaning of clothing fads in their lives. When a subject arises that illustrates the effects of making decisions based on assumptions, take the time to discuss these events with your class; for example, ask students to discuss what assumptions are being made when they hear someone say, "He's wrong," or "She's the smartest girl in the class."

Socratic Dialogues

One form of discussion that reveals individual assumptions to the speaker and the listeners at the same time is the technique known as *Socratic dialogue*, in which the teacher probes to stimulate more in-depth thinking among students. Teachers who use this method believe that individuals have many legitimate differences in opinions and values and want to encourage their students to listen to each other to learn different points of view.

To conduct a Socratic dialogue, the teacher presents an interesting issue to the class and asks an individual to state an opinion on the case. With each participant, the teacher probes by asking the student to identify the assumptions and values that led to his or her opinion. Further questions may be posed to the same student to encourage clarification of the consequences of the student's opinion or the relative importance it has in the student's priorities.

This type of exchange between the teacher and one student may take several minutes and include 3 to 10 questions. While the teacher conducts the discussion with one student, the others are expected to listen carefully, comparing what they believe to what is being said by their classmate. Another student with a different opinion is likely to be the next subject of the Socratic dialogue. When the teacher believes that the most important issues have been raised by the dialogues, then a general class discussion can be used to express how opinions may have been changed by listening or participating in the Socratic dialogues.

Discussions to Enhance Creative Thinking

Can individuals learn to be creative? Perhaps the more important question is: Do individuals learn to be uncreative? More than a century ago, William James (1890) stated his belief that education trains students to become "old fogies" in the early grades by training them to adopt habits of convergent, conformist thinking.

Divergent thinking is the opposite of convergent thinking in that it deviates from common understandings and accepted patterns. Guilford (1967) contributed a definition of divergent thinking that is still well accepted and has become the basis for E. Paul Torrance's (1984) well-known tests for creativity. Guilford describes (and Torrance's test measures) four attributes of divergent thinking: *fluency, flexibility, originality,* and *elaboration*. In other words, a divergent thinker is one who generates many ideas (fluency), is able to break with conformist or set ideas (flexibility), suggests ideas that are new in the present context (originality), and contributes details that extend or support the idea beyond a single thought (elaboration).

Classroom discussions can be designed to help students develop these four attributes of creativity. In a technique similar to brainstorming, the teacher can ask students to generate many responses to a single question as a means of helping them to become more fluent in their thinking. For example, given our topic of King's "I Have a Dream" speech, the teacher may begin the process with the unfinished sentence, "I have a dream that someday . . ."

Students may be asked to write their own responses for several minutes before the actual discussion begins. This allows each student to work for fluency individually. Then the ideas on paper are shared, and other new ideas are created as a result of the discussion. To promote flexibility, the teacher may ask students to imagine making their dreams come true and to suggest ways that they could do this, using flexible and original strategies rather than rigid and ordinary methods. Finally, to extend the students' originality and elaboration, the teacher may select one dream and ask the entire class to focus on it and create a more detailed vision and a more in-depth plan to accomplish it.

Einstein and Infeld (1938) add a further dimension to our understanding of creative thinking:

> The formulation of a problem is often more essential than its solution, which may be merely a matter of mathematical or experimental skill. To raise new questions, new possibilities, to regard old problems from a new angle, requires creative imagination and marks real advance in science. (p. 92)

Problem solving, then, is related to creative thinking. It is readily apparent that the methods described for improving problem solving involve critical thinking and that both involve the use of higher-level thinking processes. Whatever we call it, the goal of aiding students in developing better thinking skills is an integral part of any classroom discussion.

Just as we respect Einstein's ability to pose new problems, so should we respect and develop our own and our students' capacity to ask questions and suggest new ways of solving age-old problems. Certainly, the teaching profession needs people with the capability of regarding old educational problems from a new angle—often it is the newest and youngest members of a faculty who see things from a helpful new perspective and suggest different ways of dealing with difficult school issues.

Another dimension of creativity involves the production of something useful, interesting, or otherwise valued by at least a small segment of society. In synthesis, a creative thinker is one who poses new problems, raises new questions, and then suggests solutions that are characterized by fluency, flexibility, originality, and elaboration. The solutions result in a product unique for that individual in those circumstances.

Discussions to Encourage Imagination and Inventiveness

In the process of discussing almost any type of subject, teachers always have opportunities to ask students to consider "What if . . . ?" Imagine living on an island with no electricity. What would your life be like? How would it be different than it is now? What could we do to make our school a better place? What would you do if you were the main character in the story? How would your actions change the ending of the book? For many reflective teachers, these questions are as important as those that test student recall of information or understanding of the main idea. While it is seldom necessary to plan a discussion with the sole intent of stimulating children's imaginations, it is a worthy goal to include these types of questions in any classroom discussion.

Another technique is to assign a group of students a certain task that requires them to discuss strategies and invent a method to carry them out: Give students a single dollar bill, and ask them to discover how high a stack of 1 million dollar bills would be; give them a few pieces of cloth and some string, and ask them to make an effective parachute; or have each group work together to design one map of the school property. These real-life and simulated tasks provide incentives for authentic discussions on substantive and meaningful topics.

Prewriting Discussions

Another method teachers may use is to focus on images, analogies, and metaphors in creative discussions. These are very effective discussions before students begin writing, encouraging students to use these word pictures in their writing as well. Gordon and Poze (1975) suggest that analogies allow us to make the strange familiar and the familiar strange. In discussions, teachers can present an unfamiliar idea or object and assist students in describing it using sensory images or comparing it with another, more familiar concept. For example, when presented with a rusty lawn mower engine, students may be led to describe it according to size, shape, imaginary sounds, or uses, or they can compare it to other, more familiar objects. The teacher may ask students what the machine reminds them of. This may generate responses such as "The machine is like my old shoes." Then the teacher probes by asking the child to tell why the machine and the old shoes are alike, and the student responds, "Because they are both old and muddy." Another child may see the machine in a whole different context: "The machine is like a kangaroo because it has a lot of secret compartments." Discussions like these can begin to have a life of their own and can lead to fresh new ways to express ideas in writing.

Do schools enhance or undermine the conditions and processes that encourage creativity? Do textbooks, curriculum guides, rules, regulations, and expectations support the development of creative thinking and the processes needed to create a unique product? Caring and reflective teachers do. They work very hard to create stimulating classroom discussions that assist students in learning to become creative thinkers. Teachers may need to plan some creative activities to stimulate this type of thinking; see Figure 8.1 for an example of this type of activity.

Figure 8.1   Creative thinking exercise.

1. Display a picture of a statue from your community or use a picture of the Statue of Liberty

2. Ask the students to brainstorm parts of the statue that could be renovated (crown, book, robe, face, hair, etc.)

3. Working in small groups, ask the students to suggest companies that could sponsor the renovation of one part of the statue. Encourage them to use local companies if they exist. (Avon for the face, Barnes and Noble for the book, Omar the tentmaker for the robe, etc.)

4. Bring the groups back together and have each group share their favorite suggestion. Allow the students to add to their lists by using ideas from the other groups.

5. Have the students brainstorm the benefits a company might receive for participating in this community renovation project.

6. Have each group choose one company and have them create a presentation they could make to that company to convince them to sponsor the renovation of a part of the statue. Encourage them to create visuals for their presentations.

7. Allow the groups to share their presentations.

Discussions to Address Multiple Intelligences

You have created a thematic unit plan that has an interesting topic and many opportunities for students to read, research, and report on their findings. One day near the end of the unit, you want to have a lively interactive discussion to allow your students to report on what they have learned and discovered on their own about the topic. For example, Judy Eby once planned and taught a unit titled "Aviation and Mapmaking." This unit began with students making maps of their school and neighborhoods. Then the class examined maps made by the early explorers who traveled the globe by ship and created maps of the new worlds they discovered. The students had compared the early maps with modern maps and laughed at how inaccurate the early maps appeared. As a culmination of this unit plan, Judy hired a pilot and a 10-seat airplane to take the students on short flights over their school and neighborhoods; they took photos of the ground and then created new aerial maps based on their photos.

Let's imagine a discussion taking place a few days after their flights. The general topic of discussion is "How has aviation changed mapmaking?" To promote verbal-linguistic intelligence, questions involving vocabulary might be asked: "What is a map legend? What is the difference between latitude and longitude?" Logical-mathematical intelligence can be stimulated by asking questions about the map scales: "How accurate are the first maps you made? Does the entire map have the same scale, or does it vary? How accurate are the scales of the aerial maps you are making? Why are they likely to be more consistent?"

This whole project was an excellent example of a school program that develops visual-spatial intelligence. There can be many discussion questions in which students refer to their maps or show something on their photos. "Can you show us an example of how your map is more accurate now than it was before the aerial photo experience?"

Musical intelligence does not come easily for this unit. If it is not appropriate, there is no need to include it just for the sake of including it; other units may have many musical applications. It would be a stretch, but you could ask students to create short songs about their experience in the air or sing a song or two from early American history that refers to maps or travels or distances.

Bodily-kinesthetic intelligence was involved in creating the first maps. Students can be asked to describe the processes they used to walk around their school or their neighborhoods finding ways to see the big picture of what they were drawing. "Did you have to climb on something high and look down at the area in order to draw it accurately? Did you pace off the distances and then convert them to inches or centimeters?"

To promote interpersonal intelligence, the discussion could turn to how well people worked together to create their maps. If a cooperative learning model was used, the maps may have been the work of a small committee rather than an individual. "How well did your group work together on the first map you made? Did you work more or less effectively on the second map?"

Naturalist intelligence can be promoted by referring to the land and its uses. "In your view, is the land near our school used well, or are there things that you would like to see changed? By looking at your photos and maps, what do you appreciate about the world that you didn't seem to notice before?"

During the evaluation phase of this unit, the teacher can tap into students' intrapersonal intelligence by conducting an interactive assessment of what each student accomplished. "What are you most proud of accomplishing during this unit? What new interests have you developed during this experience? What do you want to improve?"

Role of the Teacher in Leading Discussions

Discussions that promote the use of multiple intelligences and critical or creative thinking can be exciting classroom events for both students and teachers, but beginning teachers may find it difficult to elicit responses from students who are not used to taking part in such activities. What if you ask a wonderful question and the students do not respond? There is nothing quite so demoralizing for a teacher as a lack of response from students. "Now boys and girls, how do you think the sound got onto this tape?" There is no response, just interminable silence. Finally, the teacher leaps in to break the tension and gives the answer. Everybody, including the teacher, visibly relaxes. Whew! Let's not try that again.

This example of a nondiscussion is more common than is desirable. Students in your classroom may not have had opportunities to think creatively and express their own ideas. If not, they may be reluctant to do so at first, believing that you expect one right answer, just as most of their teachers have in the past. Because they do not know the one right answer, they may prefer to remain quiet rather than embarrass themselves by giving a wrong answer. Your response to their silence will tell them a great deal. If you jump in with your own response, they will learn that their responses were not really wanted after all.

There are many ways a teacher can encourage participation in class discussions:

• *Practice scaffolding responses.* Scaffolding is a necessary component of teaching critical thinking and discussion strategies to students. Be explicit about what you do expect from them in a discussion, and tell them that there are no wrong answers and that all opinions are valued. If they still hesitate, provide cues and prompts without providing answers. Simplify or rephrase the question so that they are able to answer it. For example, if the question "How do you think the sound got onto this tape?" gets no response, rephrase it: "What sounds do you hear on this tape? Can you imagine how those sounds were captured on a piece of plastic like this? Do you think machinery was used? What kinds of machines are able to copy sounds?" These supporting questions provide scaffolds for thinking and talking about unknown and unfamiliar ideas.

• *Value silence.* Another consideration in leading discussions is to *value* silence rather than fear it. Silence can indicate that students are truly engaged in reflection. By allowing a few moments of silence, a teacher may find that the resulting discussions are much more creative and productive. Students need time to process the question, to bring forward the necessary schemata in their working memories, and to consider the question in light of what they already know about the topic. Some students need more time than others to see connections between new ideas and already stored information and to generate responses of their own.

• *Always allow wait time.* Some teachers consciously use *wait time,* a short period of silence after each significant question is asked. Students are taught to listen quietly and then think quietly for several seconds, not raising their hands to respond until the wait time has passed. Rowe (1974) found that when teachers use a wait time of 3 to 5 seconds, more students are able to generate a response to the question. Without a planned wait time, the same group of fast-thinking students is likely to dominate all discussions; with the wait time, even students who are slow thinkers will have an opportunity to consider what it is they do believe before hearing the opinions of others.

• *Employ some practice exercises.* Lyman (1989) recommends that teachers employ a system called *listen, think, pair, share* to improve both the quantity and the quality of discussion responses. This technique employs a structured wait time at two different points in the discussion. When a question is asked, wait time goes into effect while students jot down ideas and think about their responses. Students are then expected to discuss their ideas in pairs for a minute, after which a general discussion takes place. After each student makes a contribution, other members of the class are expected to employ a second wait time of 3 to 5 seconds to process what their classmate has said before they raise their hands to respond.

• *Introduce the discussion questions before the study.* The quantity and quality of students' responses may be improved by introducing the questions early in the class period, followed by a reading, a lecture, or another type of presentation before the actual discussion of the questions themselves. This strategy follows the principle of using the questions as an advance organizer. Giving students the questions before the presentation of new material alerts them to what to listen or read for and allows sufficient time for them to process the information they receive in terms of the questions. When teachers use this technique, they rarely experience a lack of responses.

• *Arrange the seating so students can see one another.* Another strategy that promotes highly interactive discussions involves the physical setup in the classroom. To facilitate critical and creative thinking, students must be able to hear and see one another during the discussion. Arranging the chairs in a circle, rectangle, U shape, or semicircle will ensure that each student feels like a contributing member of a group.

• *Set up an accepting environment.* Meyers (1986) notes that a hospitable classroom environment is the most important factor in engaging students' attention and interest and promoting their creative responses during discussion:

> Much of the success in teaching critical thinking rests with the tone that teachers set in their classrooms. Students must be led gently into the active roles of discussing, dialoguing, and problem-solving. They will watch very carefully to see how respectfully teachers field comments and will quickly pick up nonverbal cues that show how open teachers really are to student questions and contributions. (p. 67)

• *Model critical and creative thinking.* Reflective teachers are critical and creative thinkers themselves, so they welcome opportunities to model their own thinking strategies for their students and plan experiences that encourage the development of their students' higher-level thinking processes. They are likely to make even the simplest discussion an exercise in problem solving, reasoning, logic, and creative and independent thinking. They examine the subjects taught in the curriculum in search of ways to allow their students to learn to think and communicate their ideas. They plan discussions involving the creation and testing of hypotheses in science; they promote thinking that avoids stereotypes and egocentricity in social studies. They teach their students to suspend judgment when they lack sufficient evidence in discussions of math problems, and they promote flexible, original thinking in discussions of literature. Discussions in every part of the curriculum can be crafted in ways that teach individuals to think reflectively, critically, and creatively.

Involving the Larger Educational Community

Supporting students so that they feel comfortable and confident enough to actively participate in class discussions can be greatly enhanced if parents understand the goal and participate in the solution. A combination of communication strategies is often needed to convey the importance of home–school cooperation, so introduce the topic at a parent meeting early in the year. Help parents to understand the importance of their children participating in class discussions; the engagement, higher-level thinking, and problem-solving skills that their children gain from these types of discussions; and the need for parental involvement at home. Many parents think of their role in discussions as providing the answer; help them to understand that students quickly learn to turn off thinking and just wait for the answer when they are conditioned to that role.

Help parents learn to provide scaffolding questions by engaging them in an activity where they have to generate such questions. In other words, just as you are training your students to engage in discussions, teach your parents to participate as those who scaffold. Tell parents that you will be working on learning discussions all year and that one of their responsibilities should be to ask, "Did you have any good discussions in school today?" By having the students recall and recount the class discussions, students will have a second opportunity to explore the ways in which the ideas were generated and the solutions (if any) that were brainstormed.

Ask the parents to involve their children in these same types of discussions at home. Discussions around the dinner table can give all the children in the family confidence in engaging in higher-level discussions and problem solving. Everyday problems or challenges, community problems, or current events can serve as topics for these types of discussions.

Periodically during the year, send home a class newsletter that includes some news about the ways in which you are using class discussions to address problems, current events, or creative challenges. These articles will serve as reminders to the parents to ask about class discussions and to engage their family members in these types of discussions, and the newsletter items can serve as a starting point of family discussions.

Group Focus Activity

Your professor will provide the class with an experience in generating discussion questions.

1. The class will work in small groups. Each group will be given a discussion topic that has a variety of objectives. Each group will use some transparency film and transparency markers to record questions they generate.

2. Each group will generate scaffolding questions they could use to stimulate thinking and discussion, write their topic and scaffolding questions on the transparency, and prepare to give a short presentation on their results.

3. The groups will be given time to work, discuss, and create their transparencies.

4. The groups will be brought back together to share their results.

Preparing for Your Licensure Exam

In this chapter you read about strategies to use in conducting classroom discussions. Reread "A View into the Classroom" at the beginning of the chapter, and think about it as a case study you might encounter on your licensure exam. Explore each of the following sggestions to demonstrate your understanding of the process of asking higher-level questions and conducting an academic discussion:

1. Analyze each of Dawn's questions, and identify their levels on Bloom's revised taxonomy.

2. Reword each of Dawn's questions to change their level.

3. Suggest ways that Dawn could have directed the discussion in different directions.

Portfolio of Professional Practices Activity

Your task is to write a short paragraph on how you would plan a class discussion following a lesson on a topic of your choice.

Points to Consider

1. Capture students' attention.

   - Ask questions.
   - Use a film clip.
   - Relate a story or case description.

2. Ask questions.

   - Ask open-ended questions directed to the whole group.
   - What will you do if no one answers?

3. What happens if an answer is wrong?

   - How can the student find the correct answer?
   - What happens if the answer is partly right?

4. Keep students' talk focused on the topic.

   - Ask them to summarize what they've done.
   - Have them summarize what they need to do.
   - How will you record this summary—whiteboard, butcher paper, overhead projector?

5. What happens when an audience member's comment is off the topic?

   - "Thanks for giving us that information, Emma. Let's think about it in relation to . . ."

6. Use the whiteboard or overhead transparency to summarize the discussion.

   - What are the advantages of this?
   - What are the disadvantages of this?

7. What will you do if the discussion gets out of control or off the topic?

8. What will you do if some people don't contribute to the discussion?

9. What will you do if one person becomes the "class clown" and dominates the discussion with his or her negative contributions?

10. What will you do if students don't do the reading and feel it's okay to talk "off the top of their heads"?

References

Anderson, L., & Krathwohl, D. (Eds.). (2001). *A taxonomy for learning, teaching, and assessing: A revision of Bloom's taxonomy of educational objectives*. Boston, MA: Allyn & Bacon.

Bloom, B. (1981). *All our children learning*. New York, NY: McGraw-Hill.

Doyle, W. (1986). Classroom organization and management. In M. Wittrock (Ed.), *Handbook of research on teaching* (3rd ed.) (pp. 392–420). Upper Saddle River, NJ: Merrill/Prentice Hall.

Einstein, A., & Infeld, L. (1938). *The evolution of physics*. New York, NY: Simon & Schuster.

Gagne, E. (1985). *The cognitive psychology of school learning*. Boston, MA: Little, Brown.

Gordon, W., & Poze, T. (1975). *Strange and familiar*. Cambridge, MA: Porpoise.

Guilford, J. (1967). *The nature of human intelligence*. New York, NY: McGraw-Hill.

James, W. (1890). *Principles of psychology*. New York, NY: Holt.

Lipman, M. (1988). Critical thinking—What can it be? *Educational Leadership, 46*(1), 38–43.

Lyman, F. (1989). Rechoreographing the middle-level minuet. *Early Adolescence Magazine, 4*(1), 22–24.

Meyers, C. (1986). *Teaching students to think critically*. San Francisco, CA: Jossey-Bass.

Paul, R. (1988). *31 principles of critical thinking*. Rohnert Park, CA: Center for Critical Thinking and Moral Critique.

Rowe, M. (1974). Wait time and reward as instructional variables, their influence on language, logic and fate control. Part 1: Wait time. *Journal of Research on Science Teaching, 11*, 81–94.

Torrance, E. (1984). *Torrance tests of creative thinking*. Bensenville, IL: Scholastic Testing Service.

Vasquez, V. (2003). *Getting beyond "I like the book": Creating space for critical literacy in K–6 classrooms*. Newark, DE: International Reading Association.

chapter nine

Balancing Standards and Creative Activities

Shutterstock

"Like a ten-speed bike, most of us have gears we do not use."

Charles Schulz, creator of the Peanuts comic strip

As standards-based education has become the norm in American education, reflective teachers are facing the challenge of finding time to include creative activities in their curriculum. They recognize the need for a balance between a carefully sequenced standards-based lesson with clearly defined objectives and the need for students to experience creative outlets that stretch the imagination and provide authentic opportunities for problem solving and innovation (Burke-Adams, 2007). Elliot Eisner (2002), a professor in education and art at Stanford University, maintains that lessons in the arts accomplish a number of outcomes for students:

- They teach children to make judgments about qualitative relationships. Unlike other areas of the curriculum in which rules and correct answers are valued, students learn to make judgments, choices, and decisions in the arts.
- The arts teach students that problems can have more than one solution and that questions can have more than one right answer.
- The arts teach that there are many ways to see and interpret the world.
- Learning in the arts requires students to surrender to anticipated possibilities and to engage in complex problem solving.
- In the arts, students find that words cannot always capture the essence of what we know.
- The arts teach the promise of subtlety. Students learn that small differences can have large effects.
- The arts teach students to think thoroughly and find ways to make images become real.
- The arts support students in expressing their emotions and finding their own poetry.
- The place of arts in the curriculum symbolizes to students what adults believe is important.

Questions for Reflection as You Read the Chapter

1. How can you include creative activities in a standards-based classroom?
2. How can you set up your classroom to include areas for creative activities?
3. What benefits do students derive from engaging in creative activities?

A View into the Classroom

Delores Burke teaches second grade in an urban school in New York City. She tries to involve her students in hands-on activities that address the curriculum standards and also give them experiences in creativity. To engage her students in creative approaches using math and science concepts, Delores asks her students to design a house for a family of gummy bears using thick spaghetti and miniature marshmallows as building materials. Before she begins the activity, she gives her students an opportunity to play with the spaghetti and marshmallows to see how they can combine them to create structures. She also demonstrates some ways of combining the materials to make the structures stand up.

To begin the more academic part of the activity, she divides her class into groups of three students and gives each group a family of gummy bears. Some groups have a couple, some have a family of three, some have four, and some have even bigger families. She asks each group to form a construction company and think of a name for their company. She stops after each direction is given to allow the groups to complete the task before moving on to the next one. Each company must then identify a construction manager, a materials manager, and a budget manager. The students discuss the positions and are given name tags to indicate their roles in the companies.

Delores explains the building materials to her students: "You will use pieces of spaghetti connected with miniature marshmallows. You have to buy your building materials using a budget of $25. Each strand of spaghetti will cost you $1, and each marshmallow will cost your company 25 cents. Work with your group to decide on your company name, and then draw a diagram of the house you want to build. Figure out how much spaghetti and how many marshmallows you want to buy; then send your materials manager to me to buy your materials." Delores then gives each group $25 in play money and displays a poster she has made that says:

Spaghetti $1

Marshmallows 25 Cents

As each materials manager comes to her to buy materials, Delores helps them to pay for the materials and to keep a list of materials they have purchased. She uses sales slips she created on the computer so that the companies have records of their purchases. The budget managers are responsible for keeping a running record of expenses.

The first question comes from Joseph, the materials manager from the Good Builders Company. "Mrs. Burke," he asks, "can we break the spaghetti and use smaller pieces?"

"Good question, Joseph," replies Delores. "You may break the spaghetti, and you may even break the marshmallows into smaller pieces if you want. You may also use any other materials you find in your desk or anywhere in the room." She further explains, "We call those materials 'found materials.'"

The groups work busily creating their houses. Some groups also create swimming pools and trees using construction paper or cardboard found in the classroom. When the houses are complete, Delores asks the groups to write an advertisement for their houses, telling all about the unique features they have created. They also are asked to create a television commercial for their house, and Delores videos each commercial. One group writes a jingle to sing as part of their commercial; another group imitates a well-known local car salesman as they present their commercial.

At the end of the project, Delores shows the commercials to the class as they eat popcorn. After the showing of the commercials, Delores reviews what they learned in this project. "We practiced our math facts as we added up our bills for materials. We learned about structures that are strong and those that need support as we built the houses. We also learned about using creative ideas to make our houses different, and we learned ways to work together, to listen to each other, and to make compromises to get the job done."

"And we learned how to write television commercials!" piped up Karen.

REFLECTING ON THE CLASSROOM EXPERIENCE

Planning creative lessons is an art. The good news is that there are many websites available that provide suggestions for teachers. Your fellow teachers are also a rich source of ideas; learning to collaborate with other teachers, sharing ideas, and adapting lessons to the needs of your students are all skills that take time to develop. Reflective teachers observe their students carefully and find ways to motivate them by using a variety of approaches.

Using technology to support learning is something that is often motivating for students. It is always important, however, to evaluate the effect of the technology on students' learning. If the technology does not improve learning or motivate students, there may be a different approach that would be more creative. Hands-on learning is one of the most motivating teaching approaches—students enjoy creating and having the opportunity to explore new and different materials.

Importance of Imaginative Childhood Experiences

Creative adults often talk about their imaginative childhood experiences. Giving a child the chance to play without the invading eyes of adults is one way adults can be supportive of a child's creativity. *Play* is children's *work* during the early years, and it is during play that they learn to imagine, pretend, and even create original dialogue. Children who have created dialogue for favorite toys find writing dialogue for characters in their original plays and stories much easier. When children have engaged in creative play, they move much more naturally into artistic and learning endeavors such as art, music, and writing. Children who play with blocks, Legos, and Lincoln logs know much more about how things work and their spatial relationships, so they often delve into scientific experimentation without fear. Creativity is often nurtured in an environment that provides a time and place for solitude and private thoughts and experimentation.

You may think, "But I also need to ensure the child's safety." This is a natural concern, especially in today's society. For teachers and parents, the answer to this concern lies in finding a secluded place that is within earshot but that gives the child a sense of privacy for his or her creative play. In a busy classroom, this can be a table set apart by using a screen or portable bulletin board or a tent set up indoors just outside the classroom but within sight. An empty refrigerator box filled with throw pillows is a great privacy place; allowing the children to paint the outside of the box with their own designs gives them ownership.

One teacher had a dad who did construction work build a loft in the classroom. He put up a see-through fence around the edge of the loft to make it safe and carpeted it (with a remnant purchased for $10) to make it quiet. The students called it the writing loft and put some small tables up there, along with writing materials, and they did a lot of writing that year. The area under the loft was called the Hidey Hole and contained tables and art materials. The second graders tended to write their stories in the loft and then come down to the Hidey Hole and illustrate them, using a wide range of art materials.

Since time to think and experiment will always be scarce in classrooms, it is important that parents understand the child's need for privacy and time to explore new concepts. Teachers can help by discussing this need at parent meetings and giving parents suggestions for finding private space for their children's creative endeavors. At home, especially in large families, it is often difficult to find secluded places for creative activities. Families will need support to understand the importance of this need for a small private space that belongs to each child. When children are creating, they sometimes leave their projects unfinished during "incubation time" for additional creative thoughts, and they need to know their projects will be safe when left for a while.

Some of the same suggestions for secluded areas in classrooms also work in the home setting:

Adrienne Herrell recalls that one of her sons did a lot of writing under the dining room table, an area that was rarely used except on holidays. In a family with five sons, this was his creative solution for private space.

Another son had a set of bunk beds in his room; he slept on the top bunk and removed the bottom bed to create a private space for his creative projects. He curtained off the bottom area using old drapes he found in a storage closet, and he moved a card table and folding chair into his private space but usually worked stretched out on the rug.

A third son set up a work space in the garage since his projects always seemed to involve power tools. He found two old two-drawer filing cabinets and an old door and set up a workbench. The filing cabinets gave him storage space, and he was close to power outlets and a water supply for clean-up.

Making all of these creative spaces requires patience, understanding, and valuing of creative projects on the part of the rest of the family—they are often not the neatest areas in the house.

Providing Materials for Creative Projects

Materials from Homes

Providing materials for the creative child sometimes requires some creativity on the part of teachers and parents. Art and writing materials, dancing lessons, and music lessons all cost money. In schools, there are some materials provided, but many of the materials end up being paid for by the teachers. Enlist parents in saving things that would normally be thrown away for use in creative projects. Include a "Classroom Needs" section in your classroom newsletter, and ask parents to donate useful items for the classroom. Things that are commonly saved for classroom use include the following:

- Empty paper towel and toilet tissue rolls (for making paper sculptures and finger puppets)
- Empty egg cartons (for making 3-D animals, for mixing paint colors, for storing small beads and other decorative items)
- Leftover gift wrap and wall paper (for making collages, for creating book covers for publishing books)
- Scrap paper of all kinds (for writing drafts, for making paper sculptures)
- Newspapers (for creating papier-mâché projects, for protecting desks and carpets)
- Small plastic containers from yogurt and camera films (for storing small items such as buttons and beads, for mixing paints)

Materials from Merchants

Learn to ask for items from merchants who will be discarding them. Leave an empty cardboard box at a local print shop with your phone number on the box, and ask the manager to put any paper scraps in the box for use in your classroom. Make it a practice to go by the print shop every week to claim the paper scraps so that the manager is never inconvenienced. One teacher reports that she put paper scraps in one of the art centers and suggested that the students might want to make fancy bookmarks. The first girl who went to that center made "book bracelets." She drew illustrations from her favorite books on each scrap and then taped them together to make bracelets; before the end of the day, all the students—even the boys—were wearing book bracelets.

Your local print shop may keep a big bag of "holes" from their hole-punching machine. Because they are punching holes in many colors of paper, the holes are multicolored. The children can use them to create texture in their artwork.

Other Sources of Materials

Some schools have projects where they ask for donations of musical instruments for the music program and are often amazed at the number of instruments that are stored away and not used; at least one school even found a retired musician who was willing to give music lessons as a volunteer. It is important to keep your community in mind. Service clubs are often looking for projects, and all they ask is that you come and speak to the service club and explain your project. They also like to see the results of their donations, so make a habit of taking a lot of pictures.

Remind parents that art and writing materials make wonderful birthday gifts, and before major gift-giving holidays, you might include gift suggestions in your class newsletter. Busy parents often get caught up in the shopping mode influenced by television commercials instead of sound child development theory. A gentle reminder that art and writing materials such as clay, paint, paper, markers, and writing tablets serve to inspire creative activities is often appreciated. Legos, blocks, Lincoln logs, and magnetic rods all serve to encourage scientific experimentation. Durkin's (1975) research found that all the children who entered kindergarten reading had toy chalkboards at home with which to experiment.

Setting a Creative Tone

The atmosphere in the school as well as the home can support creativity. When you walk through the halls of a school that values and supports creativity, it is obvious: Products of creative work are displayed everywhere; children's art, sculpture, writing, and science experiments, both completed and in progress, are in evidence.

In order for children to expand their creative potential, it has to be nurtured. Adults who work with children can set a creative tone by modeling creative behaviors, encouraging creative thoughts, and exposing children to the creative works of others.

It has been said that what we love, we pass along to our children. Mister Rogers of television fame is a good example of this adage. At a national conference of the National Association of Education of Young Children (NAEYC) in Anaheim, California, the topic of his speech was passing along our passions, and he talked about exposing children to art forms they might never experience without our influence. He showed film clips from his TV program, *Mister Rogers' Neighborhood*, where he had guests who played the cello or performed modern dance. We may never know how many children were led into creative pursuits by watching his enormously popular program.

A large elementary school in Titusville, Florida, was built around a lovely indoor courtyard. Due to budget cutbacks, the school had no art teacher, and some of the teachers were not comfortable teaching art. The primary specialist tried to support them as best she could, but her time was spread too thin. As a way of providing the school with a creative atmosphere, the primary specialist invited local artists, starting with some of the parents, to set up and work in the courtyard about once a week. They would set up and paint or sculpt in the courtyard, and the teachers would bring their classes through to watch and to ask questions; the children were fascinated with the processes they observed. The teachers planned follow-up art activities in their classrooms. One of the dads built some wonderful picture frames that had slots in the sides so the pictures could be changed regularly. Each classroom was responsible for choosing an art product to be displayed in the courtyard monthly, using these lovely frames. The first of each month, the artist of the month was called to the courtyard to have his or her picture taken with the framed artwork. This exposure to creative activities caused the teachers to incorporate more creative expressions into their curricula.

Importance of Creative Atmosphere

Developing a creative atmosphere at your school is vital to the students with creative potential, but it also opens avenues of expression for other students. Many of today's students have not been exposed to different forms of creative expression, so the school can provide this exposure. Explore possibilities by contacting local orchestras, ballet companies or schools, theater groups, and artists to see if they have any children's programs because local groups and artists are often available to come to the schools and provide programming that is appropriate for children.

Technology is another way that creative activities can be made available to students while still addressing state standards. When one school acquired one computer per classroom, a lot of the teachers were uncomfortable using computers in the classroom, so the principal planned after-school workshops to teach them how to use a free word processing program. The local Parent-Teacher Association (PTA) purchased rolling carts for each of the computers and storage disks for each student. The computers were housed in each classroom until 1:30 each day. When the kindergartners went home at 1:30, a "computer mover" student from each class moved the computers to a large multipurpose room that also housed the two kindergarten classes. The kindergarten teachers then taught a computer lab for the school from 2:00 to 3:30

each day. This lab was used for publishing student work. The students could work on the computer in their classroom during the morning if they had time, but they could also bring their storage disks to the computer lab during their scheduled class time or during after-school computer time. They got to publish their writing in the computer lab, and parent volunteers were available to help students make covers for their books (using donated materials such as contact paper or wallpaper as covers).

At the end of the school year, an English teacher from the nearby high school was invited to bring one of her creative writing classes to the school for a writers' conference. The elementary students shared their books in small groups, and the high school students shared some of their writings. The high school students answered questions and gave encouragement to the younger budding writers. The elementary students were so excited about the experience that many of them participated in a summer writers' workshop that year. The high school students told their teacher how impressed they were with the writing done by the younger students, and several of them volunteered during the summer workshop.

Ways to Encourage Creativity in Children

There are a number of things teachers can do to foster creativity in their students and provide a balance between the structure needed to achieve curriculum standards and the open-ended teaching and thought processes needed for creative thinking.

BE A ROLE MODEL.   Teachers and parents can set a wonderful example by involving themselves in creative activities and sharing their passions with their children. As a teacher, when you are teaching writing, share your writing with your students. Use your own writing as an example when teaching revision and editing. It is empowering for students to see that their teacher's writing can be improved and that a teacher wants their feedback before making decisions about what to revise.

EXPOSE CHILDREN TO THE CREATIVE WORKS OF OTHERS.   Teachers can support parents by helping them become aware of creative projects that are part of the community. Use your class newsletter to let parents know about art fairs, music festivals, theater productions, and other artistic endeavors in your local area; many of these activities are free or very low cost. If your community theater doesn't have a student ticket price, approach them with that need.

In larger cities, there are art galleries and museums available for field trips. The teachers are usually the ones who choose the field trips to be taken, but we are beginning to see a trend of eliminating field trips because of cost and liability issues. As teachers and parents, we need to serve as advocates for our children in these areas. Children who have never seen great art or heard professional symphonies or experienced live opera, ballet, or theater are much less likely to participate in these activities as adults. They won't know how to enjoy these beautiful artistic expressions without having some early experiences and instruction.

IMPLEMENT INTERDISCIPLINARY WORK AND AUTHENTIC PROBLEM-SOLVING CHALLENGES.   Units of study that integrate different disciplines and allow students to approach a topic from many different perspectives provide more opportunities for creative thinking and activities (Erez, 2004). Open-ended projects and assignments that give students choices will allow them to express themselves using their strongest intelligences and passions (Ritchhart, 2004).

Projects where students are encouraged to design new products for everyday common items such as a paper clip allow students to use creative thinking in problem solving. A helpful website for creative problem solving can be found at www.LGReal.org.

OFFER EXTENSION AND/OR ENRICHMENT PROJECTS.   In today's fast-paced classrooms where meeting basic standards is vital, finding time to delve into creative projects in depth is difficult. Teachers who value creative activities are innovative in finding the time. Some teachers plan extended-day activities a day or two each week; with parental permission, the students stay after school to participate in activities that allow them to explore some of their academic topics in more depth and integrate them with art, music, science, and technology. In some schools, teams of teachers work together to provide these experiences, each leading students in activities according to the teacher's area of expertise. Do not overlook community resources for these types of activities; for example, local colleges often have professors or students who can be enlisted to lead creative projects. As volunteerism and community involvement become more popular, many businesses are giving their employees time to volunteer as club leaders after school.

UTILIZE TECHNOLOGY.   There are many computer programs that foster creative activities. Support students in using word processing programs for writing. Concept maps, graphic software, and computer-aided design (CAD)/computer-aided manufacturing (CAM) applications all support creative production. Students can use multimedia such as PowerPoint to support their oral presentations. Using digital cameras and video productions to produce videos and graphic displays encourages students to write scripts for their productions and design costumes and props appropriate for different times in history (Herrell & Fowler, 1997).

MAKE A CONSCIOUS EFFORT TO DIFFERENTIATE INSTRUCTION.   Use both sequential and creative modes of instruction to meet the individual needs of your students. This balance is a critical piece to providing equitable opportunities for all students to demonstrate their strengths (Burke-Adams, 2007).

VALUE UNIQUENESS OF STUDENTS.   Some of our most creative scientists, musicians, and artists were not successful in school because of the limited definition of what it meant to be a "good student" in the past. In today's schools, with Gardner's (2006) research on multiple intelligences and our understanding of the importance of authentic problem solving, teachers can celebrate innovative thinking and unique solutions with the idea that they may quite possibly be supporting the next Albert Einstein.

Self-Fulfilling Prophecy

Children are extremely perceptive. They understand and react to subtle differences in adult expectations. This effect has come to be known as the *self-fulfilling prophecy*. The process appears to work like this: (1) The teacher makes decisions about the behavior and achievement to be expected from his or her students; (2) the teacher treats students differently depending on his or her expectations for each one; (3) this treatment communicates to the students what the teacher expects and affects the students' self-concept, achievement motivation, and aspirations either positively or negatively; (4) if the teacher's treatment is consistent over time, it may permanently shape the children's behavior and achievement. High-expectation students tend to achieve at higher and higher levels, whereas the achievement of low-expectation students tends to decline.

What is it that teachers do to communicate their high or low expectations for various students? This is the question that interested Good and Brophy, who found that some teachers treat low achievers in certain ways (2002, p. 55):

1. Seat them far away from the teacher.
2. Call on them less often.
3. Wait less time for them to answer questions.
4. Criticize them more frequently.
5. Praise them less frequently.
6. Provide them with less detailed feedback.
7. Demand less work and effort from them.

Negative Impacts on Creativity

The Marlboro man and the Barbie doll are not the most appropriate creative models. On a continuum from extremely masculine to extremely feminine, creative children and adults tend to fall in the middle (Piirto, 2004). Rigid sex roles can have a negative impact by limiting creative behavior and discouraging sensitivity. In a world where boys don't cry and girls don't climb, children's opportunities for creativity are limited. In order to be successful in maintaining the discipline and hard work necessary to succeed in the arts, children must become very self-sufficient and yet maintain their sensitivity. This requires being able to work like a man and feel like a woman. As teachers and parents who value creativity in our children, we need to guard against stereotyping of any type; we know that gender stereotyping, in particular, often stifles creativity.

Adults have a very powerful influence on the atmosphere both in the classroom and at home. To encourage creative children, they have several important responsibilities. In addition to modeling and valuing creative behavior and exposing children to high-level creative expression through art galleries, ballet, music, and theater productions, they can also do the following:

- Talk to children about their ideas and the dedication and hard work that are involved in producing creative products.
- Avoid reinforcing sex-role stereotypes.
- Encourage conversation and support children in learning to express themselves.
- Never accept "pat answers."
- Advocate for creative programs for children in the community.
- Join the library and take children there often.

Become aware of the creative programs available near you, and involve your children in them regularly. As a parent or a teacher, you have the power to encourage or kill the creative potential in your students and children—a very frightening thought.

Adrienne, herself a teacher and parent, tells the following story regarding the negative impact that words can have. "My mother, both a parent and a teacher, supported me through dance lessons, art lessons, piano lessons, and many art projects. She took me to the theater, the ballet, and concerts, and we went to the public library every Monday night. I thank her for all that support and appreciate her contributions to my love of the arts. But she did one thing that discouraged me. She told me that I couldn't carry a tune. All my life I have been afraid to join in on sing-alongs. I sing *very* quietly in church. When my church choir director asked me why I didn't join the choir, I said, 'Oh, you wouldn't want me to spoil your beautiful music.' Yet I love to sing. I sing along with the radio in the privacy of my car but would never consider singing if anyone else were listening. Can I sing? I don't think I can. After all, my mother, whom I cherished, told me I couldn't. That is the power that parents and teachers have over the children and students they love and teach."

As adults who are responsible for the tender sensibilities of children, we must be very aware of the impact of our words and actions. When working with children, remember the difference between words of praise and words of encouragement. Choose words that focus on a child's feelings and efforts. If a child shows a picture that can't be deciphered, say, "Tell me about your picture," hoping that the child will give you a clue about what is represented. This is hard to do because we have stored scripts in our minds and tend to revert to those scripts when responding to children. In order to use words of encouragement, we have to reprogram. Instead of saying, "I really like your picture" (praise), say, "You must be very proud of that picture because you worked very hard on it" (encouragement). Turning the discussion to the child's feelings and sense of self-worth supports his or her incentive and motivation and gives him or her the recognition for a job well done.

Ways to Demonstrate Valuing Creativity

Besides words of recognition and encouragement there are several other ways that adults can demonstrate that they value children's creative efforts:

- Find ways to display art in the home and classroom.
- Find time to read students' writings.
- Respond when students write in a dialogue journal.
- Help students publish their writing, and then include the books they've written in the class library.
- Keep a portfolio of their work at home, and display some on the refrigerator.
- Frame some of their work and hang it on the wall.

These actions show children that we value their creativity, which serves to encourage their efforts.

There is another thing that serves to demonstrate the value we place on children's creative efforts: providing our time and attention. Spending time with children while actually participating in their creative work sends a very powerful message to them. When adults sit down and create along with children, it encourages children in a very real way. Children are aware of how busy teachers and parents are, and they want more of our time and attention. Working together on creative projects is a wonderful way to spend that elusive "quality time" and also establish creative classroom and family traditions.

Core Attitudes in Creative Thought

In studying creative people and the creative process over the past 50 years, researchers have identified a number of attitudes that creative people have in common (Piirto, 2004). Creative people have an attitude of *naiveté*, a word that literally means "openness." It is the ability to see uniqueness in very common things. Vincent Van Gogh, for example, is said to have been able to see drawings and pictures in everything he viewed, even shabby huts or dusty rooms. Naiveté is the ability to see interesting textures, lines, color values, designs, or combinations in common objects that the ordinary person would look at but not really see.

The gift of observation has often been linked to this creative attitude of naiveté, and observation is surely a part of it, but it seems to be much more. The creative person observes but also seems to see unusual potential or to simply delight in things or ideas that are odd or strange. There are elements of acceptance and curiosity inherent in naiveté as well. Igor Stravinsky (as quoted in Piirto, 2004) said that "the true creator may be recognized by his ability always to find about him, in the commonest and humblest thing, items worthy of note" (p. 192).

To teach this attitude to students, teachers must *model* an openness and acceptance of the unusual. Ironically, many teachers reveal that they find the creative student's unusual approaches to tasks and discussions in the classroom disruptive (Torrance, 1983). To foster openness, creative approaches, and unique problem solving in a classroom setting requires teachers who are open and accepting of unique thought processes and who validate these unusual points of view and observations.

Creative people—at least the ones who are productive and successful in bringing their creative ideas to fruition—also possess self-discipline, often working long and arduous hours, days, months, and even years in the pursuit of creating something unique and special. They are risk takers, willing to brave public opinion and even public censure for their unique ideas. When they work in a collaborative way with other creative people, they practice a mutual trust and respect for one another's ideas. Creative people must sometimes get beyond the opinions of others in order to bring their creative projects to fruition.

People can have self-discipline in many areas. Some have self-discipline in controlling their diets; others are very disciplined in maintaining a healthy exercise program. Creative people in the arts and sciences are very disciplined in their creative work. The successful inventor usually has many, many versions of his invention before he discovers the one that really works well, and a writer may write thousands of words, but she ends up publishing a very small percentage of them.

Albert Einstein is quoted as saying, "I know quite certainly that I myself have no special talent. Curiosity, obsession, and dogged endurance combined with self-criticism have brought me my ideas" (Piirto, 2004, p. 47). Author Sydney Harris (as quoted in Piirto, 2004) agrees that self-discipline contributes to success and is quoted as saying, "Self-discipline without talent can often achieve astonishing results, whereas talent without self-discipline dooms itself to failure" (p. 48). Great creators are known for their great productivity. Choreographer Agnes de Mille noted that "all artists—indeed all great careerists—submit themselves, as well as their friends, to lifelong, relentless discipline, largely self-imposed and never for any reason relinquished" (de Mille, 1991, p. 158).

Parents and teachers have long struggled with the challenge of fostering self-discipline in their children and students. Many adults still struggle with a lack of self-discipline in themselves. In a fast-paced world of instant gratification, what type of activities lead students to develop self-discipline? There have been a number of books and articles published on self-discipline and ways to develop it. Most of them begin with a similar strategy: *start small*. Begin with a small task that you dread, and spend a few minutes getting started. Then try to develop a habit of doing small things regularly for the practice of self-discipline. But this type of self-discipline is not quite the same thing as the self-discipline that Einstein mentioned. Einstein was talking about obsession—being so involved and interested in something that you do it again and again until you feel that you have it right, have mastered it, or have found a solution to a difficult problem.

Parents and teachers can support children in the development of self-discipline in two important ways:

1. They can model it. They can demonstrate the self-discipline of staying with projects until their completion and then share the exhilaration of completing a task that took time and commitment.

2. They can include their children and students in their own creative activities; they can also find new pursuits that will fascinate and engage their children and students.

Another important contribution parents and teachers can make is genuine interest in and celebration of a child's efforts. Notice when a child has spent a lot of time and effort on a project (remembering the difference between praise and encouragement). If you are trying to inspire self-discipline, then the object of your encouragement should be the time and effort the child put into the project (not the quality of the result); with practice, effort, and self-discipline, the child's project will improve. Your encouragement fosters the child's self-confidence, and a very powerful cycle is begun.

We know that our children often see life in 7-minute segments—the time between television commercials. To develop self-discipline, children have to become actively involved and engaged in life; they have to be exposed to a number of interesting topics and then be given time to explore them in depth. In today's busy homes and classrooms, children rarely have the opportunity to engage in an activity that requires time and perseverance.

Creative people are, almost by definition, risk takers. Creative risk taking is not the same as physical risk taking. Taking creative risks involves exposing your innermost thoughts, feelings, and passions to a world that may not accept them or even understand them. To quote the noted social psychologist Dean Keith Simonton, "Great creators are great risk-takers besides" (1995, p. 255). The risk the creative person takes is public censure and rejection. Because artists and writers, poets, and inventors put so much of themselves, their heartfelt feelings as well as their efforts, into their work, the risk they take is very real, but it is also a necessity for them to create. Creative people are often quoted on the topic of risk taking, possibly because this attitude is so vital to their ability to express themselves in their chosen field, whether it is painting, poetry, essays, dance, or invention.

One second-grade teacher encourages her students to share the books they have read by creating projects based on the books when they finish reading them. Most of her students draw pictures, create time lines, make posters, or build dioramas. One year, she had a student who was taking modern dance lessons and wanted to choreograph a dance showing the events in the story she had read. The teacher encouraged her, knowing that the student would be taking the risk of being laughed at by her peers (especially the boys). The little girl dressed up in costume as the heroine of the story and danced to music she had selected to help create the context of the story, which was set in the old west. The class was enthralled! The creative child was given very positive feedback from her teacher and her peers. She had been given a chance to take a creative risk, and it paid off.

An important aspect of valuing children's creativity is focusing on the core attitudes shared by creative people. Children should be introduced to the concept of hard work and practice in enhancing creative potential. Become aware of the children's favorite authors, illustrators, and musicians; then look for information about these creative people and share your knowledge about their training, the number of creative works they have produced, and their work ethic. For example, a number of children's authors have published autobiographies. Read these to the students, and discuss how these authors all continue to work to perfect their art.

In order to encourage students to complete projects, there are several approaches that can be incorporated into the school setting:

- Schedule blocks of time for reading and writing that allow students to get beyond the superficial. Encourage students to keep drafts of their writing in a writing folder and to work on more than one project at a time. Often they will need to leave one project and work on another to allow time for the incubation of ideas.

- Avoid changing activities like learning stations on a set schedule. Allow the students to move to a new station when they have completed their work in the first one (and cleaned up, of course).

- Encourage students to complete projects. Have conferences with them to check on their progress. Teach them strategies to use when they get stuck.

Using Creativity in the Classroom

Creative Activities in Language Arts

When we think of creative activities in language arts, we almost automatically think of writing, but there are now six recognized areas in language arts: reading, speaking, listening, viewing, visually representing, and writing. All six of these can be used for creative activities. Reading should involve reading with expression, using different voices for different characters, maybe even using accents or unique speech patterns to define characters. Speaking activities can include some extemporaneous speaking to encourage fluency and flexibility in oral expression as well as assignments where speakers must convince the listeners of a point of view or lead them to change their opinions. Listening skills are developed as students listen to their classmates read and speak. Viewing and visually representing give learners the opportunity to create visuals to accompany their oral presentations or to explain by speech or other means the feelings that a visual image evokes.

We continue to develop new ways to engage in creative writing with our children. If children are going to become writers, they need to have time to develop writing skills. Writers' workshop classrooms support the students as they become better writers. If you structure the workshop to address standards in language arts and another academic subject like social studies, you can meet a number of standards in the process. Having students read books related to social studies and then write reader's theater scripts, plays, or simulation journals incorporates creative writing into the study of history and geography.

Children can work together to write and publish their books. They can write the "About the Author" page and place a copy of their school pictures in their books. The teacher could demonstrate appreciation of their efforts by letting them read their books to the class and questioning them about where they got their ideas. Allowing the students enough time to complete in-depth projects like this is another way of fostering creativity in the classroom.

E-MAIL STORIES.   E-mail stories is another way to use students' natural interest in using the computer to support creativity and the language arts standards. The teacher starts a story and e-mails it to a student. The student adds to the story and sends it to another student or back to the teacher; the story is exchanged several times before it is complete. When it is finished, the teacher publishes it by printing it out and making it into a book. Pictures of the authors can be included in the back along with a brief "About the Author" section. The children keep the books in their personal libraries but also share them with their teacher and classmates.

For additional suggestions for creative activities in language arts, see Figure 9.1.

Figure 9.1   Suggested activities in language arts.

Language Arts	Activity	Adaptations
Speaking	Painting a verbal picture	Students create a visual (picture, clay sculpture, diagram). The visuals are displayed without names attached, and each student must create a verbal picture by describing his/her product so that others can identify it. This can also be done using art prints.
Listening	Re-creating something that is heard	The teacher or a student describes a picture that the others cannot see. The students re-create the picture strictly by listening to the description.
Reading	Making a character come alive	Using published or class-written reader's theater scripts, each student assumes a character and creates a way of depicting that character with gestures, voice, and movements so that the other students can identify the character readily. The teacher can provide additional motivation by offering "Oscars of the Day."
Writing	Writing reader's theater scripts for favorite books	This can be done as a class project to introduce the format. Then students can write their own scripts as they read books and can involve their peers in producing the scripts.
Viewing	Viewing an art print and creating a story to explain what the artist was thinking or feeling	This can be done in writing or verbally. After students become more comfortable with expressing new ideas verbally, this provides a wonderful way to encourage extemporaneous storytelling.
Visually representing	Listening to music and creating a verbal picture	The teacher plays a musical piece, and students respond in writing, creating a story behind the music and telling what the composer was thinking or feeling. This presents another opportunity for extemporaneous speaking when it is done verbally.
Making a literary response	Reading and creating a response using a variety of media	After reading a book, students create a product to convey the essence of the book. Some suggestions: • Create a diorama of the setting. • Create a script for a favorite scene. • Write a new ending. • Create a mural of the plot. • Create a time line of the plot. • Compose a song that tells the story. • Create a comic strip of the main events. • Create a simulated journal of the events from one character's perspective. • Design a response format of your own.

Creative Activities in Mathematics

We think of mathematics as the one discipline where there is always a correct answer. While this is usually true, students can be challenged to think of situations in which an answer might change. Students have great imaginations and can usually find some ways in which the "right" answer might be different. Another way to introduce creative thought into the use of mathematics is to combine math with another discipline such as writing.

One fifth-grade teacher introduced the concept of math riddles by reading the book *One Riddle, One Answer* (Thompson, 2000), in which the emperor found a husband for the princess by posing a mathematical riddle. The teacher then gave a short lesson on how to write math riddles and allowed the students to write their own. The students were so fascinated by the topic that they continued writing riddles through their lunch period. After lunch, the students presented their riddles, and the class enjoyed another period of creative mathematical thought as they attempted to solve them. They were so excited by this application of mathematics that the teacher kept a learning center in the classroom for several weeks. At the center, they wrote math riddles and left them for others to solve. As a result of reading this one book aloud and giving the students opportunities to extend their knowledge in math, the students published a book of math riddles which they shared with the other fifth-grade classes.

There are a number of mathematically based stories that can be used with students to challenge their understanding of math principles and include math in their creative projects. See Figure 9.2 for a list of some of these books.

Creative Activities in Social Sciences

The social sciences give many opportunities for creative projects as well as integration with other areas of the curriculum. For example, a unit of study on the three branches of government led one fifth-grade teacher to challenge her students to each design their own island country. They had to make a topographical map of their island showing all the landforms and creating a legend so that other students could read their map. They then designed an economic plan for their country, including ways to supply the people with food, water, other supplies, and jobs. The students had to decide what form of government their island would have, how the laws would be made and enforced, and how they would balance the power in the government. In the process of this study, students addressed social studies standards in mapping,

Figure 9.2 Children's books to encourage creative applications in mathematics.

Demi. (1997). *One grain of rice: A mathematical folktale.* New York, NY: Scholastic.

Friedman, Aileen. (1994). *The king's commissioners.* New York, NY: Scholastic.

Murphy, Stuart J. (1996). *Too many kangaroo things to do!* New York, NY: HarperCollins (a book about multiplying).

Murphy, Stuart J. (1998). *A fair bear share.* New York, NY: HarperCollins (a book about regrouping).

Neuschwander, Cindy. (1997). *Sir Cumference and the first round table: A math adventure.* Watertown, MA: Charlesbridge.

Neuschwander, Cindy. (1999). *Sir Cumference and the dragon of Pi: A math adventure.* Watertown, MA: Charlesbridge.

Neuschwander, Cindy (2001). *Sir Cumference and the great knight of Angleland: A math adventure.* Watertown, MA: Charlesbridge.

Piligard, Virginia. (2000). *The warlord's puzzle.* Gretna, LA: Pelican Publishing.

Thompson, Lauren. (2001). *One riddle, one answer.* New York, NY: Scholastic.

Figure 9.3   Suggested activities in social sciences.

Activity	Standards Addressed	Websites/Adaptations
Online simulations	History, geography, economics	www.simulations.com www.jimcrowhistory.org
Virtual field trips	History, geography	www.uen.org
Debates	History, economics, current events	Slave owners vs. abolitionists, prohibitionists vs. bar owners, hawks vs. doves
Illustrated concepts	History, economics, current events	Defining a concept in writing and then illustrating it; making a class book (e.g., Bill of Rights)
Time lines	History	Clothesline time lines, picture time lines, artifact time lines
Creative note taking	All areas of curriculum	Flap books, foldables, graphic organizers
Edible maps	Geography	Creating a map using edible materials (e.g., graham crackers and icing)
Exploring the Internet	All areas of curriculum	www.brainpop.com www.nationalgeographic.com www.history.com (for great speeches)

Source: Adapted from Dr. Angela Fiske, Florida State University, personal communication.

government, and economics and also included additional standards in music and art as they designed a national anthem and a state flag.

For additional suggestions for creative activities in social studies, see Figure 9.3.

Creative Activities in Science

Science is an extremely creative discipline. Great inventions are important in history and are almost all scientifically based. Students can be encouraged to become creative in science by involving them in explorations and elaboration. Introduce a simple object, and invite the students to change it slightly to make it serve a different function.

One science teacher added a new twist to the science fair project by having the students make a videotape documenting what their project was, where the idea came from, and how it was planned; all the steps along the way (including the mistakes) were also documented. The students were extremely creative in making their videotapes because the teacher added one caveat: Make it interesting!

For additional books to inspire creative activities in science, see Figure 9.4.

Creative Activities in Visual and Performing Arts

Visual and performing arts are usually the first things that come to mind when you think about creativity. Under the stress of meeting academic standards and trimming school bud-

Figure 9.4   Books to inspire creativity in science.

Casey, S. (2005). *Kids inventing! Handbook for young inventors*. Hoboken, NJ: Jossey-Bass.

Erlbach, A. (1989). *The kids' invention book*. Minneapolis, MN: Lerner.

Harper, C. M. (2001). *Imaginative inventions: The who, what, where, when, and why of roller skates, potato chips, marbles, and pie (and more!)*. New York, NY: Little, Brown Young Readers.

Hauser, J. F. (1999). *Gizmos and gadgets: Creating science contraptions that work (and knowing why)*. Charlotte, VT: Williamson.

Jones, C. (1994). *Mistakes that worked*. New York, NY: Doubleday.

Panati, C. (1989). *Extraordinary origins of everyday things*. New York, NY: Harper & Row.

Thimmesh, C. (2002). *Girls think of everything: Stories of ingenious inventions by women*. New York, NY: Houghton Mifflin.

Tucker, T. (1998). *Brainstorm! The stories of twenty American kid inventors*. New York, NY: Farrar, Straus, & Giroux.

Wulffson, D. (1999). *The kid who invented the popsicle: And other surprising stories about inventions*. New York, NY: Puffin.

gets, these arts-based programs are often the first to be cut back or eliminated altogether, but there is a movement to find innovative ways to keep or reintroduce the arts in education in many areas of the country. In an article published in the *San Diego Union-Tribune*, several California school districts were finding ways to raise funds to support the arts in their schools. The money raised was used for teacher training, art docents, resident art and music teachers, and arts education curricula.

Another approach is being used in Hawaii, where the local arts council and the school district have found ways to integrate the visual and performing arts into almost every aspect of the academic curriculum. The arts council/school district collaboration has made an arts toolkit available with lessons for all grade levels and all academic disciplines (this toolkit can be downloaded at http://arts.k12.hi.us). The results have been extremely positive: This integration is helping to raise test scores along with student motivation.

Humor and Creativity

What does humor in the classroom have to do with creativity? Humor is a very abstract form of language that often requires using language in unique ways. Understanding humor requires a facility with manipulation of ideas and concepts that develops over time. Some children cannot understand certain types of jokes until they attain a certain sophistication in their language development. Intelligent children sometimes have highly developed abilities to design and understand humor. This "off the wall" humor may be a sign of intelligence but can often be misunderstood by the majority of the children in the class—and sometimes by the teacher. When you have children in your classroom who enjoy "playing with language" to create jokes, consider ways to channel that talent. They can have time to share their jokes just as you would give students time to share any other form of writing. Always stress the importance of not using jokes to demean or hurt others.

Children love humor, and creative children enjoy it more than most. When teachers think of humor in the classroom, they tend to be a little cautious. Humor in the classroom that is sarcastic is hurtful. Humor in the classroom should be a case of joint enjoyment and laughter, not humor at anyone's expense. There are questions that you, as a teacher, should ask yourself: Are you naturally a humorous person? Do you enjoy your students? Have you found that you can tease them without hurting their feelings? Bryant and Zillman (1989) studied humor in the classroom and found that elementary teachers used more humor than middle school and high school teachers and that humor used with older students tended to be more sarcastic and hurtful.

STYLES OF HUMOR-ORIENTED TEACHING.   Diane Loomans and Karen Kolberg (2002) have written a book called *The Laughing Classroom*, which is filled with motivating strategies for teachers to use in all areas of the curriculum. They identify four different styles of humor-oriented teaching:

1. *Joy master.* This is a teacher who inspires students to become warmhearted and humane toward one another. She might use a strategy such as creative debate in which students are assigned a role and debate an issue; Abe Lincoln may be debating on one side and Charlie Chaplin on the other.

2. *Fun-meister.* This type of teacher uses slapstick and clowning as motivational techniques. When teaching a mathematical operation, he may pretend to make mistakes so that students catch them, thereby giving the students a reason to monitor his demonstration more carefully; peals of laughter may fill the room as the students point out the teacher's error. This style of teaching, however, can have its dark side, as fun-meisters sometimes mock others, including their students, causing students to laugh at one another's mistakes.

3. *Life mocker.* This teacher is almost entirely negative based on the students' viewpoints. Teachers who are cynical and sarcastic may cause a few laughs, but the students may experience this style as coldhearted and dehumanizing.

4. *Joke maker.* This type of teacher has a way with telling stories and jokes that are always entertaining for her students. These stories can be very instructive and provide insight as examples of an abstract concept. Occasionally, teachers can use jokes or stories that are experienced as insults or stereotypes, and those can have a negative impact on students.

The Laughing Classroom is an excellent resource for teachers at all grade levels and can assist you in planning humorous activities that are supportive, positive, and healing.

Creativity Training

Classes in creativity training are being offered for teachers and students of all ages. Some school districts have invested in this training for teachers, especially teachers who are teaching gifted programs. There are a number of different programs available:

• Creative Problem Solving (CPS) is the oldest of the training courses and is the foundation of such programs as Future Problem Solving and Odyssey of the Mind. In this program, groups of students work together to solve problems using divergent and convergent processes such as "problem finding" and "solution finding."

• Gordon's Synectics program is based on putting unlike things together to form a new object. It is a popular teaching approach in textbooks about models of classroom instruction.

• Meeker's Divergent Production Exercises are found in *Sourcebooks*, which are workbooks at both basic and advanced levels. The workbooks contain exercises in all of Guilford's Divergent Production Factors.

- Torrance's programs are available from the Torrance Center for Creativity at the University of Georgia. Many of the materials were developed by Torrance's graduate students.

- Taylor's Talents Unlimited is a program based on Taylor's nine talent totem poles: academic, productive thinking, communicating, forecasting, decision making, planning (designing), implementing, human relations, and discerning opportunities.

- *Schools of Curious Delight* is a book written by Starko, a professor of elementary education; the book gives suggestions to teachers of ways to infuse creativity training into the curriculum (Starko, 2005).

There is concern about the approaches used in some of the creativity training courses — people find it odd that workbook exercises would be used to teach creativity. Some researchers at the Buffalo Creativity Studies program are now looking at creativity training in relation to personality types.

Torrance (1983) studied the creativity training programs being offered and found that most of them focused on six approaches:

1. Teaching specific creative problem-solving skills
2. Teaching problem solving and pattern recognition
3. Using guided fantasy and imagery
4. Using thematic fantasy
5. Using creative writing
6. Using Quality Circles for quality control

Some of these training exercises are based on popular approaches to creativity training. The fantasy exercises encourage students to imagine sights, sounds, and tastes as they hear a fantasy story read aloud. The Quality Circles approach is one that originated in Japan to involve employees working in small volunteer groups to brainstorm ways to improve production and solve problems.

In some school districts, creativity training is being used as a way of differentiating instruction for gifted students. Many of the publishers of reading textbooks are now including some creativity training exercises in their teaching materials. It is a concept that is growing in popularity, but the jury is still out on the results of such training.

Torrance (1983) lists six results of creativity training in elementary and secondary schools:

1. Increased satisfaction
2. Evidence that academic achievement is not affected by creative performance
3. More creative writing in different genres
4. Growth in personality and healthy self-concept
5. Improvement in attitudes toward mathematics
6. Openness to pursuing creative choices

Attitudinal and conceptual changes are difficult to measure. Because creativity involves emotional risk taking, there are certain factors that must be included in any creativity training. Affective issues must be valued as well as the importance of building trust among the group members experiencing the training and the leader. Piirto (2004) suggests that maybe "training" is not the correct word and suggests creativity "experiencing" or creativity "simulation" as possible alternatives.

Involving the Larger Educational Community

When you talk with parents, make it clear to them that they are constantly creating what is called a "family mythology." Explain to them that this is a very powerful aspect of family dynamics that can help students to understand the core values in their family. For parents, their family mythology is important (Piirto, 2004). When they begin a sentence with "In our family, . . ." they are creating a mythology related to their family beliefs and values. For example, "In our family, we go to college."

Many of you knew from kindergarten that you would attend college—there was never a question about it. Think about the message that children get from the choices parents make: "In my family, we went to art museums, the ballet, and the symphony." This part of a family mythology is passed along to each generation. If parents are interested in something and share that interest with their children, the children are much more likely to show an interest in the same or a similar thing. If parents are raising boys, they can point out that athletes use ballet training to help their sons appreciate ballet and other forms of dance. As a teacher, you can use your class newsletter to support parents in finding inexpensive ways to expose and involve their children in a variety of activities in your community. If parents are aware of the power of their influence, it helps them to make these types of choices.

If you are teaching in the upper grades and have students in your class who have not been exposed to the arts or have had teachers who have not valued unique approaches to learning, you may have to do some work to adjust students' attitudes toward the arts. For example, one local ballet company gave a performance at an elementary school. The company comprised six female dancers and two male dancers, all teenagers. After the performance, the dancers fielded questions from the audience, and one sixth-grade boy directed his question to one of the male dancers: "Don't you think that ballet dancing is a sissy thing for men to do?"

The dancer's response was classic: "I started studying ballet because I wanted to learn to move quickly and exactly to improve my broken-field running in football. But I stayed with it because I enjoy the weight lifting I do; lifting beautiful girls is better than the weight lifting I do with barbells."

Students who have had no exposure to classical music will benefit from instruction in the different aspects of this type of music and the ways in which classical themes have been incorporated into popular music over the years.

Students with little exposure to the aspects of art will also need to be taught that line, form, color, and movement all have a part in creating visually pleasing products.

Changing attitudes toward risk taking is more difficult. If your students always ask questions like "How long does the paper have to be?" or "Is this the right answer?" you have some catching up to do. They need to feel comfortable with making decisions about how long a paper has to be to convey the important aspects of a topic and with having a problem with more than one correct answer. Even more importantly, they need to understand that you, the teacher, value unique responses and don't want everyone's answer to be the same unless there happens to be only one correct answer.

Group Focus Activity

For this activity, your professor will follow these steps.

1. Divide the class into several groups.

2. Draw samples of geometric shapes on the board, and discuss them with the class. Present the students with the definition of each shape and one example of each in use.

3. Ask each group of students to brainstorm as many applications of each shape as possible and then present their findings to the class.

Preparing for Your Licensure Exam

In this chapter you read about strategies to engage students in creative activities while still meeting curriculum standards. Reread "A View into the Classroom" at the beginning of the chapter, and think about it as a case study you might encounter on your licensure exam. Answer the following questions to demonstrate your understanding of the role of creativity in educational settings:

1. What purposes do creativity activities serve in elementary learners?

2. How can a teacher encourage creativity in students?

3. How do hands-on activities support students in learning to cooperate with others?

Portfolio of Professional Practices Activity

A parade is a public march or procession honoring a certain occasion. There are countless themes for parades, many of which have become celebrated traditions. Paintings on cave walls depicted the earliest parades believed to be celebrations of hunters arriving home. The first recorded use of a float was in Athens during a sixth-century parade in honor of the god Dionysus. Floats have changed—especially how they are powered. But what if animals or modern inventions could not be used? We would have to use our own power to move floats in parades.

Design a lesson and write a lesson plan in which the class chooses a theme. Then divide the students into groups, and have each group design a float to be entered into a "parade." As a culmination activity, the students might also build a model of their float and share it with the rest of the class.

References

Bryant, J., & Zillman, D. (1989). Using humor to promote learning in the classroom. In P. McGee (Ed.), *Humor and children's development* (pp. 49–78). Binghamton, NY: Haworth Press.

Burke-Adams, A. (2007). The benefits of equalizing standards and creativity: Discovering a balance in instruction. *Gifted Child Today, 30,* 58–63.

DeMille, A. (1991). *Martha: The life and work of Martha Graham.* New York: Random House.

Durkin, D. (1975). A six year study of children who learned to read in school at the age of four. *Reading Research Quarterly, 10,* 9–61.

Eisner, E. (2002). The arts and the creation of the mind. In *What the arts teach and how it shows* (National Art Education Association Publication, pp. 70–92). New York: Yale University Press.

Erez, R. (2004). Freedom and creativity: An approach to science education for excellent students and its realization in the Israel arts and science academy's curriculum. *Journal of Secondary Gifted Education, 15,* 133–140.

Encouraging your child to write creatively. (2007, May 7). Scribble Pad. Retrieved from www. scribblepad.co.uk/EncouragingYourChildToWriteCreatively.html.

Gardner, H. (2006). *Multiple intelligences: New horizons in theory and practice*. New York: Basic Books.

Good, T., & Brophy, J. (2002). *Looking in classrooms* (9th ed.). Boston, MA: Allyn & Bacon.

Herrell, A., & Fowler, J. (1997). Camcorder in the classroom. New York: Prentice Hall.

Loomans, D., & Kolberg, K. (2002). *The laughing classroom*. Tiburon, CA: H. J. Kramer.

Piirto, J. (2004). *Understanding creativity*. Scottsdale, AZ: Great Potential Press.

Ritchhart, R. (2004). Creative teaching in the shadows of the standards. *Independent School*, 63(2), 32–41.

Simonton, D. H. (1984). Genius, creativity, and leadership. Cambridge, MA: Harvard University Press.

Starko, A. (2005). *Creativity in the classroom: Schools of curious delight*. Mahwah, NJ: Erlbaum.

Stravinsky, I. (1990). Poetics of music. In F. Barron, A. Montuori, & A. Barron (Eds.). *Creators on creating: Awakening and cultivating the imaginative mind* (pp. 189–194). Los Angeles, CA: Jeremy Tarcher/Putnam.

Thompson, L. (2000). *One riddle, one answer*. New York, NY: Scholastic.

Torrance, E. P. (1983). The creative personality and the ideal pupil. *Teachers College Record*, 65, 220–226.

Assessing and Reporting Student Accomplishments

Shutterstock

"The most important single factor influencing learning is what the learner knows. Ascertain this and teach accordingly."

David Ausubel, educational psychologist and developer of theory of advance organizers

What is good work? As a teacher, you may find evaluating students' accomplishments among the most difficult judgments you have to make. You have worked hard to create authentic learning experiences. Now how can you create an assessment system that allows students to demonstrate what they learned? How can you create an assessment system that allows students a range of possibilities to demonstrate their own particular strengths and talents? How can you create an assessment system that is fair and that your students can understand? Educators committed to providing authentic learning for their students are also searching for meaningful and useful assessment systems that provide the kinds of information that allow students to move ahead and develop their skills and knowledge base.

Teachers use assessment devices in their classrooms for two very different purposes. On the one hand, teachers give students tests that will be used to assess the progress of the class as a whole. Teachers want information on how their students are doing on average as a guide to making judgments about what to teach and how to teach it most effectively, and they use the test data for the purpose of planning for the group as a whole.

The second purpose of assessment is to inform teachers of individual student progress. Professional teachers are astute observers of students—tracking their movements, their words, and their minds. Teachers use a variety of assessment devices to collect information on individual student progress and recognize that each assessment tool has its own strengths and weaknesses. These assessments may be formative in nature, given during a sequence of instructions to help determine what learning is taking place and whether more instruction might be needed to assist the students in mastering needed material before further progress can be made in the study. Summative assessments are typically given at the end of a unit of study or sequence of lessons to determine how well individual students have mastered the material presented.

Professional teachers create their own assessment tools, including but not limited to portfolios, videotapes, demonstrations, and exhibitions; in addition, they use more traditional methods of assessment such as quizzes and exams. Teachers use questions and group discussions to determine how well students are responding to the lesson, and they talk with individuals in conferences to learn more about each student's needs and accomplishments.

Questions for Reflection as You Read the Chapter

1. How do teachers align assessment strategies with lesson objectives?
2. What purposes do assessments serve?
3. How can teachers consider individual learning styles as they assess students?

A View into the Classroom

Edina Winters's sixth graders are becoming excited about writing books. They have studied several different genres in literature; historical fiction, realistic fiction, and tall tales. After reading a variety of good examples from a particular genre, they write a story in that genre. Edna now wants to begin to move them toward evaluating their own work and supporting each other in improving their stories. Since they have written tall tales most recently, she decides to involve them in creating a scoring rubric for their tall tales. She wants them to be able to use the scoring rubrics to identify areas needing improvement so that they will be able to do some self-evaluation.

Edna introduces the scoring rubric idea by asking her students to name the elements of a good story. They list such things as creating interesting characters, using description to set the stage, using rich vocabulary, creating a plot that engages the reader, and using exaggeration to create explanations for events in a tall tale.

She then leads the students through the steps to create a 5-point scale under each of the headings they have identified. In creating a 5-point rubric, students begin with the best example, followed by the most minimal example; then they work through the three middle descriptions. They began with the idea of creating characters; after much discussion, they identified the high and low descriptors, using 5 for the highest rating and 1 for the lowest:

5—Creates characters you want to know more about, characters who are clearly defined and believable, have positive traits, but have some flaws

1—Creates poorly defined characters who don't have much depth, are not believable, are too good or bad to be true

They then described an "almost perfect" character rubric:

4—Creates characters who are interesting but not too rich, who you don't feel you know very well

After describing the "almost perfect" character, they worked on the next-to-lowest score. This took a lot of discussion, but they finally compromised:

2—Creates characters who make you want to ask questions like "Could you describe this person?" or "How does the character feel about what's happening?"

Finally, the group discussed the middle score, identifying it as an okay character needing improvement. Edna asked them to be more specific, so they agreed on this description:

3—Creates some characters who are well defined while others feel like strangers when you read about them; uneven characterization

After the rubric for characterization is complete, Edna engages the students in a discussion of how to use the rubric to help them identify ways to improve their characterizations. She puts the students into groups of three to read their tall tales and score their characterizations using the newly created rubric. After they score each piece independently, the trio must help each other identify ways to improve their characters. The students use their feedback to go back to write and improve their characterizations.

Edna walks the students through this procedure until they have built a complete scoring rubric for their tall tales. They use the rubrics to improve their stories and then write a new tall tale using the scoring rubrics to improve their products.

REFLECTING ON THE CLASSROOM EXPERIENCE

Aligning assessment with the purpose of the lesson is an important aspect of lesson planning and an opportunity to use assessment as an actual teaching tool. If students are involved in creating the standards for a project, they understand the important aspects that must be included in an excellent product. It is very important that the standards of excellence be shared with students. Students should be able to begin to evaluate their own work in order to know how to improve it, so the criteria to be met should never be a surprise. Writing scoring rubrics with rich descriptions that define the levels takes practice. Students can contribute to creating these rich descriptions; in doing so, they clarify their own definition of good work.

How Teachers Select and Use Assessment Procedures

One piece of the authentic learning puzzle is to link your grading and reporting criteria with the criteria used in the learning process. When students know what the criteria for success are and see how they are linked to the learning experiences in the classroom, the learning environment seems fair to them (Guskey & Bailey, 2000). Varying evaluation procedures is also seen as beneficial; no one evaluation strategy works well for all subjects, grade levels, or student learning styles. For that reason, students should have a variety of ways to earn their grades.

Imagine you are a teacher planning a unit on astronomy for your classroom. You have gathered some interesting learning materials, including DVDs on the solar system, National Aeronautics and Space Administration (NASA) material (www.nasa.gov/offices/education/programs/national/core/home/index.html) on the space shuttles and telescopes, and many exciting books with vivid illustrations. You have planned a field trip to an observatory and have invited an astronomer to visit the classroom; you have also worked out a time line for several weeks' worth of individual and group investigations and projects.

Now it is time for you to think about evaluation and to clarify your values regarding complex evaluation issues. How will you know what students have learned at the end of this unit? What do you expect them to learn? What techniques will you use to find out whether they have learned what you expect? What about the possibility that they may learn something different than what you expect or even that some students who become very actively engaged in the study may learn more than you expect? How will you know what they learned? How will you assign students science grades at the end of this unit? How will you communicate to the students' parents what was gained from it?

The following sections describe several assessment devices, each having a variety of uses and applications and each providing answers to different questions teachers have about evaluation. Reflective teachers will consider each alternative and decide whether and how to use such measures in their own classrooms. Recognizing that this introductory text can only provide minimal information about each assessment method, the reflective teacher will want to search actively for more information about certain methods in order to fully understand their value and use before incorporating them into a program that affects children's lives (http://fcit.usf.edu/assessment).

Informal Observations

Teachers use informal observations intuitively from the first moment the students enter the classroom at the beginning of the term. They watch groups to see how students relate to one another; they watch individuals to spot patterns of behavior that are either unusually disruptive or extremely productive. To manage a classroom effectively, withit teachers are alert to the overt and covert actions of their students at all times.

Informal observations also have academic implications. Teachers who observe their students while teaching a lesson are able to evaluate their understanding. Spotting a blank look, a nervous pencil tapping, or a grimace of discomfort on a student's face, the teacher can stop the lesson, check for understanding, and reteach the material to meet the needs of any student who did not understand.

As students read aloud, primary teachers observe and listen for patterns of errors in decoding words. They may also listen to the expression in a student's voice to determine whether the student comprehends the material or is simply saying words aloud. They listen for signs that indicate whether students are interested in or bored with the material. An additional tool in informal observations is asking the students pertinent questions to check for understanding and to determine the students' thought processes. This one-to-one interaction provides data and information not measured in any paper-and-pencil test.

By observing a student read, asking a few questions, and comparing the results with other students of the same grade or age, the teacher is able to assess many things: (1) the extent to which the student is able to use phonics and context clues to decode reading material, (2) the student's approximate reading level in terms of sight vocabulary, and (3) the student's comprehension level. In addition, the reflective teacher uses informal observations to gather information about the student's affective qualities (including confidence level), his or her interest in the subject or in reading itself, the amount of effort the student is willing to give to the task, and his or her expectations about success or failure in the subject.

By observing as students write or by reading what they have written, teachers can gather similar data about children's writing abilities, interests, and expectations. As students work out unfamiliar math problems, teachers are careful to observe who works quickly and who is struggling. Then they can gather the struggling students together for an extra tutoring session.

In the astronomy unit, the teacher may observe as students take part in discussions to determine the extent to which various students understand the concepts. When students are visiting the observatory, the teacher will watch them to learn about their interests in various aspects of the topic. When an astronomer visits the classroom, the teacher will listen to the students' questions to assess the depth of understanding they have achieved.

Informal observations are one of the most powerful assessment devices the teacher can use to gather new information about children's learning patterns and needs. Teachers may gather data about students from academic and psychological tests, but in the end, it is the informal observations that most teachers rely on to understand the test data and make a final evaluation about an appropriate placement or a grade value for students' work.

Performance Tasks to Show Mastery of Objectives

In contrast to informal observations that provide useful subjective information, behavioral objectives are relatively formal and provide useful objective data about what students have learned. Do not assume that teachers choose one or the other of these two devices—reflective teachers know that it is valuable to gather both subjective and objective data. They may choose behavioral objectives as a means of gathering hard data about what students have achieved during classroom learning experiences and compare those data with the subjective information they have gathered during their informal observations.

To plan an assessment system based on students showing mastery of certain specified outcomes or objectives, the teacher must begin before teaching the lesson. By preplanning a unit with specific outcomes or a lesson with very concrete behavioral objectives, the teacher specifies the skills that students should be able to demonstrate at the conclusion of the lesson and the criteria for success. The teacher then plans learning experiences that are linked with the outcomes. After each objective has been taught and students have had an opportunity to practice the new skill, a quiz, worksheet, or other assessment product asks students to demonstrate that they have mastered the new skill and can perform it with few errors.

When each lesson is introduced, the teacher describes the prespecified criteria for success to the students. Criteria for success may be specified as a percentage or as a minimum number of correct responses. For example, the following behavioral objective specifies 80 percent (or 16 of the 20 possible items) as the acceptable demonstration of mastery of this objective:

Spelling objective: When the teacher reads the list of 20 spelling words aloud, students will write the words, demonstrating correct spelling and legible handwriting on at least 80 percent of the words.

A criterion-referenced test, such as the weekly spelling test common in many classrooms, demonstrates whether the students have mastered the new skill. To record student achievement, teachers may write the percentage of correct responses that each student attained in a grade book.

For more complex objectives, teachers design performance tasks that require students to demonstrate what they have learned. Marzano (2000) describes a system that allows teachers to design performance tasks that measure growth in communication skills, information processing, and other complex acts. For example, students may present oral reports on a NASA satellite launch, and the teacher evaluates their knowledge and communication skills by using a scoring rubric. A scoring rubric consists of a fixed scale and a list of characteristics for describing performance for each of the scoring points on the scale. Since rubrics describe levels of performance, they provide important information to teachers, parents, and others interested in what students know and are able to do. Perhaps most importantly, rubrics provide a clear statement to students, teachers, and parents about what is considered important and worth learning, even before the learning has occurred. A teacher may choose to use the following rubric for communication skills and oral presentations:

1. Clearly and effectively communicates the main idea or theme, and provides support that contains rich, vivid, and powerful details
2. Clearly communicates the main idea or theme, and provides suitable support and details
3. Communicates important information but without a clear theme or overall structure
4. Communicates information in isolated pieces in a random fashion

CRITERION-REFERENCED QUIZZES AND TESTS.   Quizzes such as matching quizzes are frequently used with behavioral objectives to determine whether students are successfully gaining each new skill or bit of knowledge in a unit of study. Quizzes are generally short, consisting of only a few questions or items, and are thought of as formative assessments, providing teachers with a way to know whether the students are learning the material day by day.

Tests, however, may consist of many items and are generally thought of as summative assessments. Tests are often given at the end of a unit and contain a variety of items that measure students' achievement of content and skills that have been taught during a longer period of time.

In both cases, the term *criterion referenced* refers directly to the criteria established for each behavioral objective. Each item on a criterion-referenced test should match a preestablished criterion. Criterion referencing provides objective data about material that all students in the class have had an equal opportunity to learn.

Objective tests may take a variety of forms. The most common are matching, true-false, multiple-choice, and short-answer or completion tests. Matching items are those that provide both the question and response. Students have only to recognize the correct response for each item and draw a line to connect the two. Items appear in a column on one side of the paper and the responses in a different order on the other side. In terms of Bloom's taxonomy, matching items are an excellent way of measuring knowledge-level objectives that require students to recognize correct responses. An example of a matching quiz related to the astronomy unit might look like this:

Jupiter	Planet that has rings and many moons
Earth	Planet that is closest to the sun
Mercury	Planet that is 3/5 water
Saturn	Planet that is largest

To construct fair matching items, each right-column response must be clearly identified with only one item on the left. In our astronomy test, for example, descriptions of the planets need to contain unambiguous elements so that only one matches each planet. If several responses are vaguely correct, the reliability and therefore the objectivity of the test decline.

True-false items are also knowledge-level items and consist of statements that students must recognize as either true or false. These items are difficult to write, as they must be factual and objective if they are to provide useful data. If items contain unsupported opinions or generalizations, the students must guess what the teacher intended.

For our astronomy unit, we might construct a true-false quiz with these statements:

True	False	The sun orbits the Earth.
True	False	Venus is smaller than Jupiter.
True	False	Mars is closer to the sun than Neptune.

These items are reliable in that the correct responses are not likely to change in our lifetime. They are also valid because every item is an element directly related to our objective of teaching students about the physical characteristics of the solar system. As examples of less reliable and less valid items, consider these:

True   False   Venus is a more interesting planet than Uranus.

True   False   The sun will never stop shining on the Earth.

Multiple-choice items also measure knowledge-level objectives because they call for the student to recognize a fact or idea. A multiple-choice item contains a question, problem, or unfinished statement followed by several responses; the directions tell the student to mark the one correct answer. While college admission tests may contain several near-right responses and students are expected to use reasoning to determine which one is best, classroom tests should probably be constructed with only one correct response. As in other objective measures, reliability and validity of each item must be considered.

In a multiple-choice quiz on the astronomy unit, these would be two valid and reliable items:

1. Which planet is known as the red planet?
   A. Venus
   B. Orion
   C. Mars
   D. Jupiter

2. It would take longest to travel from the Earth to:
   A. Neptune
   B. Mercury
   C. Venus
   D. Saturn

Short-answer or completion items supply a question or an unfinished statement, and students are expected to supply a word, phrase, number, or symbol. These items are used primarily to test students' knowledge of specific facts and terminology. A short-answer quiz on the astronomy unit might contain these two examples:

1. The planet Saturn has _____ rings around it.

2. Which planet has the most moons? _____

An advantage of the four types of objective items that comprise most criterion-referenced tests is that they objectively measure students' knowledge of the basic content of a subject. They can be written to directly match the criteria of the teacher's objectives for the lessons. They are also relatively easy to correct, and the scores are easily recorded and can be averaged together to provide the basis for report card grades.

A disadvantage of such items is that they only measure students' understanding of basic knowledge-level content and skills. They do not provide information about what students comprehend, how they would apply the knowledge they have gained, what they would create, or how they would analyze and evaluate the ideas they have learned.

MASTERY LEARNING ASSESSMENT.   Some teachers prefer to use a teaching strategy termed mastery learning to motivate students to learn a sequence of skills. In mastery learning, individual students work through a series of learning experiences at their own pace and demonstrate mastery as they complete each objective. The teacher uses the information from the tests to provide helpful feedback for reteaching rather than to create a record of achievement. Summative evaluations occur only at the end of a unit of study, when students are expected to demonstrate mastery of a whole sequence or unit of learning; grades of these unit tests are recorded and become the basis for determining students' grades.

For the astronomy unit, the teacher may have written a number of outcome statements:

Outcome 1: After viewing the film strip on the solar system, the students will be able to match pictures of each planet with its name, with no more than one error.

Outcome 2: Students will be able to draw and label an illustration of the solar system with the sun and nine planets in their respective orbits, with 100 percent accuracy.

Together, these two outcomes will inform the teacher whether students have learned the names, distinctive visual elements, and locations of the planets in the solar system.

To measure whether students have mastered this content, the teacher simply carries out the tasks described in the objectives after students have had sufficient opportunity to learn the material. The teacher prepares a matching quiz with a column of nine names and another column of nine pictures of the planets. For those who do not achieve the criterion of eight correct answers, the teacher can provide a reteaching experience or require students to do additional reading on their own. They can be retested until they achieve the criterion.

On another occasion, the teacher distributes blank paper and asks students to draw and label the solar system. From these two objectives and others like them, the teacher can begin to answer the question, "How will I know what they have learned?" Also, the data gathered from this assessment system are more readily translated into letter grades than are the data from informal observations.

ESSAYS EVALUATED WITH RUBRIC GUIDELINES.   Essays have the exact opposite advantages and disadvantages of criterion-referenced tests. They are subjective rather than objective; unless they are given specific criteria on which to base their ratings, two or more teachers rarely evaluate an essay the same way. Essays are also time-consuming to read and mark.

However, essays provide teachers with an excellent means of knowing what students comprehend, how they would apply their new learning, and how they would analyze and evaluate the ideas and concepts. Essays also provide students with opportunities to be creative by asking them to synthesize a number of previously unrelated notions into an original expression of their own. Essays can answer the question, "How much more have they learned than what I taught in this unit?"

To improve the way that teachers rate essays, many school systems employ a rubric guide specifying what an essay must contain and how it must appear on the page to earn a specific mark or grade. Teachers who use a rubric to guide their assessment of essays usually limit the topic of the essay with specific parameters and may even specify what must be included in the response. For example, for the astronomy unit, the teacher may want to assess whether students can describe the concept of outer space in their own words, which will provide information about how much students truly comprehend about the subject rather than what they simply remember. For example, a teacher may present students with the following guidelines for writing their essay on the solar system:

Write a two-paragraph essay in your own words comparing the Earth's atmosphere with space. Tell why humans cannot live in outer space without life support. Use examples and provide evidence to support your ideas.

These guidelines are fairly explicit in terms of both length and content, so this form of essay is relatively objective. To make it even more likely that two or more teachers would look for similar elements when correcting the papers, school systems may provide teachers with rubric evaluation samples of student work, along with specific descriptions for measuring success on a particular essay topic.

Grade   Characteristics of Essay

A   Paragraphs are well organized and contain at least six sentences. Facts are accurate, and evidence is clearly given to support the student's viewpoints.

B   Paragraphs contain at least four sentences. Most facts are accurate. Examples are given to support ideas.

C   Paragraphs contain at least three sentences. Some facts are accurate, although one or more errors are present. One example is given.

D   Paper contains only one paragraph. Some facts are accurate, though no evidence or examples are given to support them.

F   Unconnected sentences contain few accurate facts. Many errors are stated. No examples are given.

This format for essay evaluation is especially useful for assessing students' levels of comprehension on a topic. It also provides an opportunity for students to demonstrate their ability to analyze the topic, but it limits the use of synthesis and evaluation. If students are provided with the rubric system before they begin writing, they are more likely to know what the teacher expects of them and thus be able to deliver it.

For other purposes, the extended-response essay gives students more freedom to express ideas and opinions and to use synthesis-level thinking skills to transform knowledge into creative new ideas. In the astronomy unit, the teacher may hope that students gain a sense of responsibility for the Earth after studying its place in the universe. This affective goal for the unit may also be expressed as a series of problem-solving or expressive objectives:

> At the end of the unit, students will write an essay titled "The Big Blue Marble," in which they express their own hopes and fears for the future of the Earth. The essays will be edited, rewritten, illustrated, and displayed for parents to view on parents' night.

This extended-response essay calls on students to integrate all they have learned in this unit and combine it with previous learning from geography and social studies units; their individual experiences and outside readings are likely to affect their responses as well. Objectivity in marking this essay is very low, so it is quite likely that teachers will view the each student's responses differently. Nevertheless, within a single classroom, a teacher can say or state a set of criteria or expectations that can lead students to write a successful essay. In this instance, as stated in the objective, students will have an opportunity to receive critical feedback and make corrections on their essays before the final products are displayed.

Despite the lack of objectivity of extended-response essays, there are good reasons to include them in an educational program. They provide invaluable information about the creativity, values, philosophy, and maturity of students. Moreover, they encourage students to become more creative and give them practice in making difficult judgments. One of the most effective ways to provide students with the information they need to succeed is to provide them with the rubric descriptions prior to the time they write their essays. When students can see the criteria on which their work will be evaluated, they are able to meet the expectations with much greater degrees of success than when they try to guess what the teacher expects or wants from them.

ORAL REPORTS AND EXAMINATIONS.   Like essays, oral reports can be restricted or unrestricted, depending on the type of assessment the teacher wants to generate. To increase objectivity and communicate expectations to students, teachers can create rubric systems describing the length and format of the oral report as well as what must be included. Examples of restricted oral reports include book reports in which students are expected to describe the main characters, the setting, the plot, and their favorite part of the story. In a restricted oral examination, teachers may ask questions that students must answer within specified parameters. For the astronomy unit, an oral examination may be scheduled for a certain day. Students are told to prepare for it by reading material supplied by NASA on the U.S. space program. In the examination, teachers ask questions taken from the reading material:

Tell how the astronauts prepared for weightlessness.

Describe the food astronauts eat in space.

As teachers listen to the students' responses, it is possible for them to make judgments about whether the students' answers are right or wrong and to assess whether the students have a poor, average, or unusually good understanding of the ideas they speak about. A teacher's evaluation of the students' responses can be recorded in some form and shared with the students later.

Unrestricted oral reports allow students more opportunities to speak about matters of great interest and importance to them. These oral reports encourage students to use their imagination to generate synthesis-level responses or to be persuasive about a matter of opinion or judgment. Following are some possible topics:

Describe the space journey you'd like to take.

Tell what you think should be NASA's next big undertaking.

Debate is a form of oral examination that provides students with an opportunity to prepare and then speak about a subject after learning a great deal about content and evidence and opinions prior to the event. During the debate, teachers can assess the students' energy and effort used in gathering information as well as their understanding of the topic.

In evaluating oral presentations, teachers may write comments as they listen, or they may videotape the presentations so they can evaluate them more comprehensively later. Students may be involved in self-evaluation of their efforts as well; they can view the videotape and discuss with the teacher what they did well and what they need to improve.

Designing Authentic Assessment Tasks

It is possible to construct assessment tasks that measure student performance in terms of using higher-level thinking skills of analysis and evaluation, as well as critical thinking skills of observation and inference and problem-solving strategies such as the creation and testing of hypotheses. These tests can be constructed as paper-and-pencil exams, presenting a situation or dilemma and asking students to respond to it in various ways. Such a test may consist of a passage to be read that describes a problem or dilemma; maps, charts, graphs, or other forms of data might also be available on the test. The test items then consist of questions that allow the student to observe, infer, formulate a hypothesis, design methods of testing the hypothesis, and speculate about the possible outcome.

Another common method of assessing students' authentic learning is to encourage them to do independent research on one aspect of a unit theme and to create a product that shows what they have learned. This method allows students to demonstrate their knowledge, comprehension, and all four higher-level thinking skills on a topic. This assessment technique is appropriate for every area of the curriculum: Students can do independent research or make an independent investigation in math, science, social studies, literature, music, or art. This method lends itself especially well to interdisciplinary units.

The teacher introduces a unit or theme and provides some teacher-centered instruction on it at the outset. Readings may be assigned, and quizzes and worksheets may be used to assess the extent to which students are developing a knowledge base about the topic. Essays or oral presentations may be assigned to assess whether students comprehend the main ideas and concepts of the topic. Finally, each student selects one aspect of the main topic on the basis of individual preference or interest and begins to research that subtopic independently. Each student decides on a final product that will demonstrate what has been learned and achieved during the independent study.

The kinds of products that students might create as a result of this type of investigation are limitless. Many teachers prefer to plan their evaluations of student accomplishment to correspond with Bloom's taxonomy. Specific student products are appropriate for learning objectives at all six levels, and a sample of them can be found in Figure 10.1.

Teachers may evaluate these student products using a rubric checklist or rating scale. Specific rubric systems may be prespecified so that students know exactly what their products must demonstrate to earn a high mark or positive evaluation from the teacher. Reflective teachers who wish to encourage critical thinking and reflection among their students are also likely to involve the students in self-evaluation of their own products. When students evaluate their work critically, they are learning how to become more independent and responsible for revising and improving their work without an outside evaluator.

Figure 10.1 Student products related to Bloom's revised taxonomy.

	Characteristics of Each Level	Products Associated with Each Level
Remembering Level	Recognizing and recalling specific terms, facts, and symbols	Doing worksheets, labeling diagrams, memorizing poems or lists, responding to flashcards
Understanding Level	Constructing meaning from oral, written, and graphic messages	Paraphrasing information, giving examples, sorting or classifying by a given criteria, summarizing orally or in writing
Applying Level	Using knowledge or procedures Diagramming or illustrating	Completing a math calculation, writing and solving story problems, using writing skills to create a paragraph
Analyzing Level	Breaking material apart and showing how the parts relate to one another	Showing cause and effect as well as similarities and differences, determining the author's point of view, finding relevant numbers in a word problem, comparing and contrasting
Evaluating Level	Making judgments based on criteria and/or standards	Ranking or prioritizing, choosing the best solution from two or more possibilities, writing critiques
Creating Level	Putting elements together to create a functional whole Creating new material	Planning, researching, and writing a report, creating a new example, generating and supporting hypotheses

Source: Adapted from Anderson, L. W., & Krathwohl, D. R. (Eds.). (2001). *A taxonomy for learning, teaching, and assessing: A revision of Bloom's taxonomy of educational objectives.* Boston, MA: Allyn & Bacon.

Checklists, Rating Scales, and Rubrics

When teachers wish to assess students' products or presentations, they can tell the students their reactions in a conference or write comments on a piece of paper and give these comments to the students. These methods suffice for informing the students in a general way whether they have met the teacher's expectations in the product, and they may be adequate for evaluating an unrestricted product or presentation (see Figure 10.1 for products and how they relate to the revised Bloom's revised taxonomy).

When the teacher has prespecified the criteria for a product or presentation and several important elements must be included, the teacher may choose to create a checklist to use for notation when evaluating each student. This is frequently done when the objective is for students to use effective speaking skills in a presentation. In preparing the students for the speech, the teacher will likely specify several important elements that the students should incorporate, such as maintaining eye contact with the audience, using appropriate volume to be heard by everyone in the room, and speaking rather than reading during the presentation. By preparing a simple checklist with these items on it, the teacher can quickly and accurately record whether each student uses these skills in their presentations. To make the whole system even more valuable, when the teacher shares the rubrics with the students ahead of time, students are able to make much better judgments about what to study, what to include, or how to present the information they have learned.

Checklists can record mastery of many basic skills in the primary grades. Each item on the checklist can correspond directly to a behavioral objective; together, the items on a checklist provide an overview of a sequence of objectives. Kindergarten teachers frequently employ checklists to record the letter recognition of each pupil, letter by letter. Primary teachers use checklists to record mastery of basic math operations. Intermediate and middle school teachers may use checklists to record whether students have demonstrated fundamental research skills. In our astronomy unit example, the teacher may combine a goal of developing research and study skills with the goal of achieving content mastery; to record the accomplishment of these skills, the teacher may use a checklist such as the one in Figure 10.2.

Checklists provide useful and efficient means of recording information about the accomplishments of individual students. They are also valuable during a student–teacher

Figure 10.2 Astronomy unit checklist of research and study skills.

Name _____ **Grade** _____

This is a record of research and study skills demonstrated by this student. The teacher's initials and date indicate when the skill was successfully demonstrated.

Date	Initials	Skill Area
_____	_____	A. Located a book on astronomy in the card catalog
_____	_____	B. Located a book on astronomy on the library shelves
_____	_____	C. Used the table of contents to find a topic
_____	_____	D. Used the index to find a subtopic
_____	_____	E. Interpreted orally a graph or chart
_____	_____	F. Took notes on a chapter in a book on astronomy
_____	_____	G. Summarized the chapter from notes
_____	_____	H. Wrote a bibliographic entry for the book

conference. Both student and teacher can quickly see what has been achieved and what still lies ahead. Checklists are also valuable when teachers confer with parents about a student's progress along a set of learning objectives.

Rating scales are used in circumstances similar to those of checklists. They provide additional information, however, in the form of a rating of how well the student achieved each element or skill on the list. Rating scales are useful in providing students with feedback that rates their performance on an objective. In the astronomy unit, for example, students' products may be turned in and evaluated by the teacher, using a rating scale of important elements. In many classrooms, teachers involve the students in their own evaluations of their products and the efforts expended in creating them. In Figure 10.3, a rating scale is structured so that both the student and the teacher rate the finished product.

A rubric is similar to a checklist but also employs detailed descriptions of the specific levels of mastery the teacher hopes students will attain. Student products are then compared to the levels of mastery described in the rubric. Figure 10.4 shows a rubric that allows the teacher to compare student products related to the astronomy research project against a set of specific criteria. As has been suggested before, if students are given this rubric prior to beginning the unit, they are empowered to make better choices about how to use their time, what to study, and how to present the material they have learned.

Many times you will see rubrics with four levels of quality (as shown in Figure 10.4). What do the levels 4 through 1 mean? Are they the same as the grades A, B, C, and D? Andrade (2000) observes that "satisfactory labels are hard to come by, although it is obvious at a glance that a 4 is what everyone should try to achieve and a 1 is something to avoid. Some teachers indicate a cutoff point on the rubric, for instance, by drawing a box around the level that is considered acceptable."

How do you, as a classroom teacher, learn how to create fair and useful rubrics for your classroom assignments? Andrade (2000) suggests that you look at other models of rubrics but then involve your own students in the process. She envisions the teacher and students discussing the criteria together, listing the most important criteria, and then writing descriptions of the various levels of quality.

Figure 10.3   Astronomy unit rating scale of the solar system model.

Name _____ **Grade** _____

To the student: Please evaluate your own product, using the following scale:

   O = OUTSTANDING; it is one of my best efforts

   S = SATISFACTORY; I accomplished what I set out to do

   N = NEEDS IMPROVEMENT; I need to revise and improve this element

Student's Rating	Skill Area	Teacher's Rating
_____	Adequate research and information gathered	_____
_____	Elements of the model are accurate in shape	_____
_____	Elements of the model are accurate in scale (except for orbits of planets)	_____
_____	Labeling is accurate and legible	_____
_____	Legend is accurate and legible	_____
_____	Model is visually interesting and pleasing	_____

***Figure* 10.4** Rubric grading evaluation system for astronomy research project.

To the student: Read these criteria before you begin your research so that you will know how to earn the level you want to attain.

Turn in a 5- to 10-page booklet on the solar system. The booklet may contain a combination of words, pictures, graphs, and any other types of illustrations that show an understanding of the physical elements of the planets, moons, and sun that make up our solar system. The booklets will be evaluated according to the following criteria.

Level 4: The student clearly and completely identifies the important planets and moons of the solar system and shows how they are related to the sun and each other in size and space. There is a combination of verbal descriptions and visual illustrations that make the distinguishing features of each planet very evident. The writing is well organized, and references are given for sources of information. At least four references are provided.

Level 3: The student clearly identifies the planets and some of the most important moons of the solar system. Relationships of size and space are given, though they may be distorted in some cases. Verbal information is fairly well organized, and illustrations are useful in distinguishing among the planets. At least two references are given as sources of information.

Level 2: The student correctly names the nine planets and shows that they travel around the sun. Relationships among planets are not accurate. The booklet uses more pictures than words. Only one source of information is provided.

Level 1: The student incorrectly labels planets and shows little understanding of their relationship to the sun and to each other. Verbal information is given as captions for illustrations only. No source of information is given.

One method Andrade suggests for creating rubrics uses these four sentence stems: "yes"; "yes, but"; "no, but"; and "no." For example, if the criterion is "Briefly summarize the plot of the story," the four levels might be the following (Andrade, 2000, p. 14):

Level 4—"Yes, I briefly summarized the plot."

Level 3—"Yes, I summarized the plot, but I also included some unnecessary details or left out key information."

Level 2—"No, I didn't summarize the plot, but I did include some details from the story."

Level 1—"No, I didn't summarize the plot."

Learning Contracts

A learning contract is a device that can be thought of as both a teaching strategy and a means of assessment. The learning contract described in Chapter Seven lists several required activities and a number of options for the unit on settling the western United States. Teachers using this strategy meet with individual students to agree on a suitable number and type of optional activities; the activities on the contract then provide the structure for daily learning experiences. When the unit is complete, the contract is used as the basis for assessing what each student has accomplished. Just as in adult life, students are held accountable for meeting the terms of their contracts. If they succeed, they can expect a positive evaluation, but if they have not met the terms of their contract, they can expect to have to explain why and describe what they will do to honor their contract.

Learning contracts can take several forms and can even be structured so that the student makes a contract to receive a certain grade for a specified amount of work. A point system can be employed to allow students to select from among options and earn the grade they desire. For example, in the astronomy unit, a learning contract with a built-in point system for earning a grade is shown in Figure 10.5.

Learning contracts also serve as the basis for recording accomplishments. In the sample learning contract for the astronomy unit, the parent is also required to sign the contract, agreeing to support the student's efforts. This strategy is an efficient way to communicate with parents about the goals and expectations for the class. Later, during parent–teacher conferences, the parent can see the work that was accomplished, and if a student did not complete the contract, the parent can see what was left undone.

Figure 10.5 Sample learning contract.

Astronomy Unit Learning Contract

I, _____, a student in the fifth grade at Otis School, do hereby contract to complete the following tasks during my investigation of the solar system.

Furthermore, I agree to complete these tasks by _____.

I understand that I am agreeing to earn _____ points, which will earn a grade of _____ if my work is evaluated to be acceptable. I understand that the point values listed below are the maximum number that can be earned for each task and that fewer points may be awarded.

Points Needed to Earn Specific Grades

>90 = A; >80 = B >70 = C; >60 = D; <60 = F

_____	10 pts	Read Chapter 7 in the science text. Do exercises, pp. 145–146.
_____	10 pts	Matching quiz
_____	10 pts	True-false quiz
_____	10 pts	Multiple-choice quiz
_____	10 pts	Short-answer quiz
_____	15 pts	Drawing of the solar system, labeled correctly
_____	20 pts	Model of the solar system, labeled and scaled to size
_____	10 pts	Essay on Earth's atmosphere and outer space
_____	10 pts	Essay on "The Big Blue Marble"
_____	5 pts	Per each answer on NASA oral exam
_____	10 pts	Oral report on "A Space Journey I'd Like to Take"
_____	10 pts	Finished Checklist on Research Skills

Signed this day _____ at _____ School.

_____   _____
      student signature   teacher signature

_____   _____
      parent signature   witness signature

Portfolios of Student Products

Portfolios are collections of work samples designed to illustrate a person's accomplishments in a talent area. Photographers collect portfolios of their best photos, artists collect their artwork, composers collect their compositions. Assessment portfolios are used to document what a student has achieved in school. To use this technique, teachers collect samples of each student's work and put them in a file folder with that student's name on it. Some teachers collect many types of work in a single portfolio; others have writing portfolios that contain only writing samples, math portfolios filled with worksheets and tests, and other portfolios for other subject areas.

It is important to understand that a collection of student work in a folder is not a portfolio assessment. As an assessment tool, a portfolio contains a selection of work samples, anecdotal records, tests, and other materials that document the student's progress, and the student's progress must then be analyzed and summarized by the teacher and the student. There should be a statement of goals written jointly by the student and teacher. Students can select samples of work to be included in the portfolio and write brief explanations of the reason each item was selected and the progress it shows. Often there are summary sheets that serve to document the student's growth. A portfolio assessment allows students to demonstrate their content knowledge without being dependent on English fluency or reading ability. Portfolios also allow the teacher and student to approach the anxiety-laden process of evaluation more comfortably because it celebrates progress rather than weaknesses.

Portfolios may be kept for a short or a longer time. Many teachers collect writing samples in the first week of school and then periodically throughout the school year. In some cases, the teacher may assign a writing topic during the first week and then assign the very same topic during the last week of school. When the two samples on the same topic are compared, the growth and development of the students' writing abilities are plain for everyone to see.

A short-term portfolio may be collected for the duration of a learning unit. For example, in the astronomy unit, all of the student's work, including quizzes, essays, pictures, and photos of the model solar system, can be collected in a portfolio to document that student's accomplishment during the unit. If a contract was used during the unit, the contract will be included in the portfolio along with the work samples. In the following reflective action story, Diane Leonard, a first-grade teacher, shares her experience with developing portfolios.

Reflective Action Case Study

TEACHER'S REFLECTION ON PORTFOLIO ASSESSMENT

Diane Leonard
First-Grade Teacher, Balderas Elementary School, Fresno, California

Teacher Begins to Plan

I teach in an inner-city school, where the vast majority of the students are from lower socioeconomic settings and are second-language English learners. I notice that my students respond best when I can give them concrete examples and model what I want them to do.

Teacher Considers What Students Already Know

Because my students are all second-language learners, I feel it's important to document and celebrate their growth. For first graders, their work changes rapidly, and I've found collecting samples of their work showing the growth they've made to be a good way to communicate with their parents, many of whom speak very little English. It also helps me to focus on exactly what they need to be taught based on where they are in relation to the achievement of standards.

Teacher Has Expectations

I needed a system to accomplish several things at once. I need to be able to relate the students' progress to their achievement of the standards. I need to be able to clearly summarize the growth they make on their report cards. I need to be able to show their parents the progress they are making, and I need to be able to give 6-year-olds concrete examples of things they can be working on to improve their own learning. I had heard about portfolios, but no one at my school was actually using them. I wanted to find out more about them, so I went on a search for resources.

Teacher Does Research and Invites Feedback

Because I was in a master's program at my university, I decided that researching and implementing portfolios in my classroom might be a good project. I did a literature review on portfolio assessment and decided that I could implement this approach and create my master's project at the same time. Because my undergraduate major had been video production, I decided to document each step of my implementation on video. I hoped that the implementation would be successful, and then I could share the process and the product with my colleagues.

Teacher Uses Reflective Withitness

I started with a small piece of portfolio assessment by setting up storage boxes in my classroom. Each child had an individual portfolio labeled with his or her name. I collected baseline examples of their writing, drawing, cutting, and reading (a running record). I made video clips of each step of the process and shared the video with three of my colleagues. Their input into the ongoing process helped me to clarify the elements in the video, make adjustments, include explanations of the process.

Teacher Reflects on Event

As I continued my refinement of the portfolios and my sharing with colleagues, it became obvious that this was more than just a classroom problem; it was a schoolwide challenge. Because I had included my colleagues in the process, several of them asked if they could implement portfolio assessment in their classrooms, based on my model. By the end of the school year, all of the first-grade teachers were using portfolio assessments. This gave us the opportunity to sit together and help each other evaluate the products in the portfolios in relation to the first-grade content standards. It also gave us an opportunity to share ideas for lessons that would help our students move toward meeting the standards.

Teacher Creates New Action Plan

The first-grade teachers who had implemented portfolio assessments and collaborative scoring asked the principal if we could share this approach with the entire faculty. The principal set up a series of faculty meetings so we could share the implementation video and talk about the success of the collaborative approach in implementing the process.

Portfolios may be used at all grade levels and for any subject or course a student takes. When portfolios are meant to be used to document student accomplishment, they must be organized so that they reveal the development of a skill or the growing understanding of a set of ideas. To demonstrate growth and change, Wolf (1989) suggests collecting "biographies of works, a range of works and reflections" (p. 37).

The biography of a work consists of several drafts of a work showing the student's initial conception of the project, the first attempts, and the final product. By collecting these items, the teacher can document the growth and development of the student. Wolf (1989) further recommends that after completing this collection, the teacher ask the student to reexamine all the stages of the work and reflect on the process and the products from beginning to end. The student's reflection may be done in writing or captured on audiotape (and later transcribed onto paper) and should then be included in the portfolio itself. This self-evaluation process is valuable in helping the student develop metacognitive abilities that then can be applied to future self-assessments in academic or real-life settings.

Wolf (1989) also suggests that teachers deliberately collect a range of works, meaning a diverse collection consisting of journals, essays, poems, drawings, charts, graphs, letters, tests, and samples of daily work. When using the portfolios as a basis for a parent–teacher conference, this range allows the teacher to discuss and document many different aspects of a student's school accomplishments.

Primary teachers must take responsibility for setting up a system for assisting the children in collecting and filing items in their portfolios. Colored portfolios in storage boxes or bins can be used so that younger students do not have to search the whole box to locate their own portfolios. The teacher should put similar names in different-colored folders to assist the children in locating their personal work. Each item entered into the portfolio should be stamped with a date, and even young children can be taught to put their work in chronological order by date in the folder. This adds another dimension to the portfolio by using authentic learning tasks (alphabetizing and filing in chronological order) during the process of maintaining the portfolios. The portfolios should contain periodic representative examples of the child's sequential improvement and advancement through the learning process. At the upper grades, however, students may be asked to assume more responsibility for choosing representative examples that document their growth and learning. The teacher may suggest items to be included, and the students may decide on others. At the end of a people and nature unit, for example, each student may have a portfolio containing the tests, lab reports, essays, creative writing, and charts created for the unit.

Portfolios are especially powerful in documenting the growth of English learners through representative samples of classwork when the teacher encourages students to document their understandings in less traditional ways. Diagrams, illustrations, recordings, multimedia presentations, and the like can be included to document content knowledge growth without being bound by students' English writing ability. Their growth in English language development, both oral and written, is also documented in the portfolio.

Portfolios of student work are an excellent way to communicate with parents about a student's accomplishments. When the parent and teacher look at the representative writing samples together, they can both reflect on the student's growth and better understand what the student's strengths and weaknesses are at a glance. When a parent sees the signed contract and the completed work, both parent and teacher see the same evidence to support the resulting grades.

Some teachers, and even entire schools, schedule portfolio days at the end of the school year. Each student selects his or her best work for the year and prepares a short presentation to talk about the work and what it represents in effort and accomplishment. Parents and community members are invited to the school to hear the students talk about their work and to ask questions of the students. In schools where portfolio days are a regular part of the school schedule, teachers help the students to plan by scheduling these presentation days in advance so that students have an opportunity to carefully select the work they will present and to write and practice their presentations. Teachers may also choose to assess the students' oral presentation skills as part of the portfolio day.

Video Records

When the purpose of evaluation is to record the accomplishment of a student and allow later analysis and more comprehensive evaluation, a video is an excellent way to capture and store a variety of learning events. Speeches can be videoed easily, as can dramas, skits, presentations, and displays of students' products.

Videos are also excellent ways to communicate to parents the accomplishments of individual students or the entire class. They allow all interested parties to view the final products or performances of a unit of study. Teachers can store a whole year's worth of accomplishments on video.

Video recordings also provide teachers with data they need to evaluate their own plans. By reviewing a video of a classroom learning event, reflective teachers are able to gain new understandings about what students need from their learning environment to be successful.

Grading of Cooperative Group Projects and Products

Many of the assessment methods described in this chapter can be adapted for cooperative groups. Evaluation of cooperative group efforts should include an assessment of both a task that requires a group effort to complete and an assessment of individual efforts to ensure that each member of the group takes responsibility for doing personal reading and preparation.

As an illustration of how to adapt ordinary lessons and units to function as cooperative lessons and units, consider the example of the astronomy unit. To adapt this unit for use by cooperative groups, each group can function as a study team with directions to assist one another in reading and preparing for the quizzes. Group scores can be computed and recorded for each quiz at the same time that individual scores are recorded.

The contract system works well with cooperative groups. When used in this way, there is one contract per group instead of per individual, and each group negotiates what the group members will accomplish together. Evaluations can include peer assessments, with members of the group providing critical feedback for one another.

Assessment of student accomplishment is a complex and multifaceted undertaking. There is no one best way to assess what students have learned or accomplished in school. Some methods work better than others at various grade levels; some work better than others with different individuals. This chapter has provided you with a number of assessment methods so you can develop a repertoire of assessment devices to use as the basis for making judgments about the accomplishments of your students.

Reporting Student Accomplishments

Report cards—these two words are likely to elicit memories filled with anxiety and a variety of other conflicting emotions for most people. In your many years of schooling, you have probably received more than 50 report cards. You may have viewed many with relief and happiness and proudly showed them to your parents; others may have you caused torment and disbelief. On occasion, you may have wondered about the teacher's fairness or integrity; you may have questioned whether the teacher really got to know you or understood the effort you put into your work. Perhaps you have even approached a teacher and challenged the grade you received, showing evidence of why the assigned grade was unjustified.

After 8 or 9 weeks into your first school year, you will face the task of deciding on and recording report card grades for your students. Many first-year teachers consider that responsibility one of their most difficult challenges; experienced teachers often say that the task does not seem to get easier as the years pass. In fact, many reflective teachers find that the more they know about grades and children, the more difficult it is to sum up the work and efforts of students in a single letter grade.

Reflective teachers struggle with many conflicting ideas, thoughts, and concerns when they confront existing evaluation systems. Systems using letter grades are likely to be based on the assumption that students vary in ability and acquire learning by passively receiving knowledge from the teacher. From this assumption, it is logical to conclude that students should be evaluated by determining what they have learned and how this compares to other students of the same age. Categorizing or rank-ordering students is the next step and is done by assigning letter grades to label their respective categories of ability. Teachers with this perspective can be overheard saying, "John is an A student, and Sally is a C student."

Reflective, caring teachers are often very uncomfortable with such statements. They recognize the complex mix of environmental, nutritional, genetic, and experiential factors that contributes to each student's success or lack of success in school. Moreover, according to their view of teaching and learning, it is the teacher's responsibility to diagnose their students' needs and then plan a series of learning experiences as well as scaffolding that each student needs to experience success. The competitive nature of letter grades contrasts sharply with this philosophy.

Due to the time-consuming nature of the task of correcting students' work and the complexities of the evaluation processes described previously, it is easy to see why school personnel have resorted to a form of shorthand to record and report student progress. Most teachers have too many students and too little time to hold discussions with each student's parents or to write extensive narratives of each student's learning on a regular basis. Schools use standardized shorthand methods known as grades and test scores to communicate with parents, future teachers, college admissions personnel, and future employers (Oakes & Lipton, 1990).

The practice of awarding letter grades as measures of individual achievement has been part of the U.S. educational scene for many decades. In the 1960s and 1970s, personnel in some school districts attempted to replace conventional report cards with detailed anecdotal records, describing what each student had accomplished in each subject area during the course or term. But these attempts to change the prevailing evaluation system met with opposition from parents, who insisted on a return to the letter grading system with which they had grown up. Parents were not satisfied with a description of their own child's achievements they wanted to know how their child compared with other students and expressed concern that these records would not be accepted at prestigious colleges.

In response to these debates, school boards and administrators in most school districts arrived at a compromise. While they reestablished the letter grades and report cards for the intermediate and upper elementary grades, they retained the use of anecdotal report cards for the primary grades. As more and more states have adopted standards-based education, reporting systems are being developed to reflect each student's progress toward meeting the standards in each content area. If you are planning to teach in the primary grades (kindergarten through second or third grade), you may be expected to write anecdotal report cards describing and documenting the progress each student in your classroom has made toward meeting the content standards for that grade. If you are planning to teach in the intermediate grades (second or third grade through sixth grade), you may still be expected to compute letter grades for the students' report cards; however, the letter grade may include references to the student's progress toward achievement of standards in a standards-based system.

Computation of Grades

At the end of the astronomy unit described earlier, the grades for all of the reports, tests, and projects may be recorded in the teacher's grade book (as shown in Figure 10.6). Computation of the final grades for this curriculum unit involves a straightforward computation of an average grade by awarding numerical equivalents to each letter grade, adding the seven items, and dividing the total score by 7; the average scores can then be assigned a letter grade. After they are computed, the grades are recorded in the students' cumulative folders and on the report cards that are sent home to parents. Intermediate report cards are likely to use letter grades to sum up

Figure 10.6 Teacher's grade book.

	Graded Objectives						Average Score	Report Card Grade
Name of Student	1	2	3	4	5			
Lisa	A	B	B	A	C			
	4 +	3 +	3 +	4 +	2	=	16/5 = 3.1	B
Peter	B	C	A	C	D			
	3 +	2 +	4 +	2 +	1	=	12/5 = 2.4	C+
Alejandro	B	A	A	B	A			
	3 +	4 +	4 +	3 +	4	=	18/5 = 3.6	A–

A = 4 points
B = 3 points
C = 2 points
D = 1 point
F = 0

each student's achievement in each academic subject. Some report cards may also provide checklists of subskills beneath the letter grade as a means of explaining to parents how the letter grade was determined.

Report Cards and Anecdotal Records

In most school districts, teachers are responsible for writing three or four report cards per year. These contain descriptions of each student's current level of accomplishment in each of the major areas of the curriculum, plus a summary of the student's work habits and social adjustment to school and peers. At the primary grades, report cards usually consist of either anecdotal records or checklists of skills rather than letter grades, and some school districts may use both. The advantage to this double format is that it allows teachers to describe and report their direct observations of a student's actual behaviors and accomplishments with sufficient detail so that parents understand the student's strengths and deficiencies. This is especially useful for such skill areas as listening, speaking, and writing as well as study habits, social skills, and interests (Linn & Gronlund, 2000).

When a concern about a student arises, the teacher's daily observations of the student's work habits and social interactions can be important sources of data to help parents or other school personnel understand the student's particular needs and strengths. These observations may be augmented by the use of written anecdotal records of what the teacher observes. For example, if a student comes to school late, appears tired, and has difficulty sitting still at her desk, the teacher may want to document these observations by keeping a short anecdotal record for a week, recording how late the student is every morning and describing episodes of falling asleep or being inattentive. When this written record is shown to the parents, it is more likely to enlist their cooperation with the teacher in seeking answers to the problem than if the teacher simply reports orally that the student is "always late and too tired to work."

To be used to their best advantage, anecdotal records should be limited to observations of specific skills, social problems, or behavioral concerns. If a teacher sets out to record every behavior and event in a student's school day, the process will become too tiring and difficult to be feasible. Instead, when a student is exhibiting a particular behavior or deficiency in a skill area, the teacher can focus on daily descriptions of that one area and be successful in producing a useful document.

The major limitation or disadvantage of the anecdotal record is teachers' tendency to project their own value judgments onto the description of a student's behavior or accomplishment. This is due, in part, to the tendency to observe what fits the teacher's preconceived notions. For example, nonreflective teachers may tend to notice more desirable qualities in those pupils they like better and more undesirable qualities in those they like less. The recommended way to avoid this tendency is to keep descriptions of observed incidents separate from your interpretations. First, state exactly what happened in nonjudgmental words; then, if you wish to add your interpretation of the event, do so in a separate paragraph and label it as such (Linn & Gronlund, 2000).

In general, a single observation is seldom as meaningful as a series of events in understanding a student's behavior. Therefore, anecdotal records should contain brief descriptions of related incidents over time to provide a reliable picture of a student's behavior.

Involving Students in Evaluation Procedures

For reflective teachers, the natural extension of the teaching process is the interactive evaluation process that encourages students to become active evaluators of their own efforts and products. The current writing programs organized around periodic student–teacher conferences and the grouping of students who edit one another's work are excellent examples of this type of evaluation. In classrooms that feature such writing programs, the teacher's role in evaluation is to confer with the students about their current writing projects and to ask questions that engage them in analyzing what they have written.

Teachers may use open-ended questions designed to gather information on what the student has intended to do in a piece of writing. When the teacher has a sufficient understanding of the student's goal, the teacher and student may begin to zero in on ways to improve the quality of the writing so that it more nearly matches the student's purpose. This may mean correcting the mechanics of the writing so that it can be understood by others or guiding the student to rethink the way a passage is written and to consider new ways of stating the ideas.

The editing groups used in such writing programs encourage students to learn how to listen to and respect the work their peers are creating. Typically, each student in a group reads aloud from a current piece of writing and then answers questions about the content from the other students in the group. Through this type of interactive evaluation, students may be learning how to work cooperatively, accept critical feedback, and write better at the same time.

This interactive evaluation system can be used in other parts of the curriculum as well. "What did you learn?" should form the core of the classroom evaluation. The more often this question is asked, the easier it is for students to identify and receive the help they need. It is a question children can learn to ask themselves (Oakes & Lipton, 1990).

Providing students with self-evaluation checklists or rating scales assists them in learning more specific types of questions about their own progress and achievement. Checklists and rating scales that ask students to evaluate specific outcomes may be developed for any learning activity, especially a unit of study that takes place over several weeks. Teacher evaluations may be entered on the same form to allow each students and his or her parents to compare the student's self-evaluation with the teacher's assessment of the student's accomplishments. For example, students are allowed to assess themselves after completing a research unit on leadership in Figure 10.7.

Interactive evaluation procedures are designed to breed success and enhance students' metacognitive capacities, which are as much a part of the learning process as they are a part of the assessment process. In fact, the long-term goals of most caring, reflective teachers are likely to emphasize the development of independence, self-responsibility, self-discipline, and self-evaluation as important affective goals of education. These goals are achieved through the development of metacognitive processes as children learn to understand how to succeed in any learning environment.

Figure 10.7 Interactive student–teacher evaluation for leadership unit.

Name of student _____ **Grade** _____ **Date** _____

Leader selected for research _____

The student completes the left side of this evaluation, and then the teacher will complete the right side.

Afterward, student and teacher discuss the accomplishments made by the student, decide on areas that need to be improved, and plan goals for future learning experiences.

O = Outstanding;   S = Satisfactory;   N = Needs Improvement

Student Evaluation: **Teacher Evaluation:**

____ I completed the readings and assignments for this unit on time.   ____

____ I showed responsibility by bringing appropriate materials to class.   ____

____ I showed growth in my planning, decision making, and organizational skills.   ____

____ I have gained skills in doing research and taking notes to gather information.   ____

____ I used a variety of relevant and challenging resources to learn about my subject. ____

____ I improved my ability to speak in public.   ____

____ I gained confidence in my ability to speak in public.   ____

____ I gained independence in working on my own to achieve a goal.   ____

____ I am able to evaluate my own accomplishments and identify what   ____
      I need to improve with accuracy and honesty.

The most important thing I learned in this unit was:

Regarding my work in this unit, I am most proud of:

Involving the Larger Educational Community

Parents are important members of the teaching and learning team. You need to inform parents about the types of assessments that you will be using in your classroom. Make sure they understand that although letter grades are a great way to provide a snapshot of a child's work, they do not necessarily paint a complete picture of a student's progress. Use parent–teacher conferences to inform them of the variety and types of assessments you are using with their child. Show them examples and explain the importance of looking at their child's work through a multitude of lenses and avoiding judgments based on a single assessment. Talk with them about their role in creating a positive level of expectations, avoiding inappropriate and severe criticism, and providing positive reinforcement for successes in and out of school. Encourage them to join you and form a team focused on finding the best way to teach and assess their child.

Group Focus Activity

Your professor may choose to engage the class in a hands-on exploration of assessment in the following manner.

1. The professor divides the class into groups.

2. Each group is to design a 4-point rubric for assessing a student portfolio on a social studies unit. The group may decide on the grade level but must remember to align the assessment with the grade-level standards for the chosen grade.

3. Members from each group will present their rubric to the class, followed by a short discussion of each rubric.

Preparing for Your Licensure Exam

In this chapter you read about a wide variety of approaches to assessing and reporting student achievement. Reread "A View into the Classroom" at the beginning of the chapter, and think about it as a case study you might encounter on your licensure exam. Explore each of the following questions to demonstrate your understanding of the process of involving students in creating rubrics and evaluating their own work:

1. In what other areas of study could students appropriately be involved in creating the scoring or grading standards?

2. How did Edna involve her students in the discussion of scoring standards?

3. How can scoring rubrics be used to support students in improving their writing projects?

Portfolio of Professional Practices Activity

Write a 10-question criterion-referenced test for a unit on the solar system. You may choose your grade level. Be sure to base the questions on the science standards for your chosen grade level.

References

Anderson, L. W., & Krathwohl, D. R. (Eds.). (2001). *A taxonomy for learning, teaching, and assessing: A revision of Bloom's taxonomy of educational objectives.* Boston, MA: Allyn & Bacon.

Andrade, H. (2000). What do we mean by results? Using rubrics to promote thinking and learning. *Educational Leadership, 57*(5), 11–14.

Guskey, T., & Bailey, J. (2000). *Developing grading and reporting systems for student learning.* Berkeley, CA: Corwin Press.

Linn, R., & Gronlund, N. (2000). *Measurement and assessment in teaching* (8th ed.). Upper Saddle River, NJ: Prentice Hall.

Marzano, R. (2000). *Transforming classroom grading.* Alexandria, VA: Association for Supervision and Curriculum Development.

Oakes, J., & Lipton, M. (1990). *Making the best of schools.* New Haven, CT: Yale University Press.

Wolf, D. (1989). Portfolio assessment: Sampling student work. *Educational Leadership, 46*(7), 35–39.

chapter eleven

Involving the Larger Community: Collaboration to Support Continuous Improvement

"It takes a whole village to raise a child."
African proverb

The classroom teacher is but one person in an important learning team whose members work together to ensure continuous improvement for students. There are a number of key individuals and groups who can provide support for the teacher and students. As a new teacher, you will be developing a support team for your students and for yourself. The most successful school improvement projects in recent years have reached out to parents and the community to gain a rich infusion of ideas, energy, and momentum for school improvement.

Questions for Reflection as You Read the Chapter

1. Who are the key players in academic collaboration?
2. How do successful school improvement projects manage to get all the key players involved?
3. How do teachers gain support from the larger community?

A View into the Classroom

Barbara Mason teaches a multiage group of students in a homeless shelter in an urban setting in California. She was deeply touched one Sunday night after watching a movie titled Beyond the Blackboard, *a true story of a teacher working in a homeless shelter in Salt Lake City, Utah. It documented the impact of a teacher who tapped the talents and interests of homeless parents living in a shelter with their children. Barbara's goal was to improve their children's educational setting and increase the parents' level of learning as well.*

Tapping the resources of her parents was a new concept for Barbara. "I never actually thought of my parents as having resources. I saw them more as simply struggling to survive," Barbara says.

"After I saw Beyond the Blackboard, *I realized that the parents needed to be involved in order to appreciate the importance of education and to begin to take personal pride in the progress their children were making."*

Barbara organized a parent club and got to know her parents. She found that one mother was a talented artist, another played the piano, several spoke Spanish fluently, one mother was an aerobics teacher, and one dad practiced tai chi. The list went on and on. Barbara asked the parents to volunteer their time for enrichment activities and organized cleaning and painting parties on Saturday. She scheduled afternoon enrichment activities using her parents as group leaders. While the parents conducted the enrichment activities, Barbara worked with individual and small groups of students, ensuring they were meeting grade-level standards.

The students were thrilled with the additions to their curriculum and the beautiful new classroom environment. The parents became more aware of what was being taught and the importance of having their children in school every day. Daily attendance improved as parents engaged in the activities and learned assignments along with their children. An after-school homework club was organized, and parents took turns supervising and helping; some parents even taught reading and math to other parents who needed additional educational skills.

Barbara managed to get a wide variety of donations, including an old piano, several computers, a printer, and art supplies, from local businesses. She made the local merchants aware of the needs of the shelter and often received contributions of snacks and clothes from nearby grocery stores, clothing retailers, and churches.

Barbara's students often moved out of the shelter after a short period of time. She always sent each student to his or her new school with a message for the new teacher highlighting each student's special talents and sharing the ways the student's parents had been active in her school.

"I'm always afraid the new teachers will have lower expectations for my students once they see that the students have been in the shelter school. We maintain high standards here and support our students in meeting standards. If it means providing extra instruction or Saturday lessons to get the students up to grade level, we provide it. We're very proud of the progress our students make. Most of our parents now value education and see the difference it can make in their own lives as well as their children's lives," says Barbara. "I'm so grateful that I saw Beyond the Blackboard. It opened my eyes to the importance of making the whole community a part of the educational team."

REFLECTING ON THE CLASSROOM EXPERIENCE

As Barbara's story shows, teachers can underestimate the support they can gain from parents and community sources. New teachers often feel reluctant to ask for support, often feeling they have to do everything themselves. It is true that parents and community members often gain great satisfaction and knowledge by collaborating with schools. Some of the most successful school improvement projects have documented the importance of community collaboration (Davenport & Anderson, 2002).

Key Players in Educational Collaboration

Administrators

One of the most popular themes in educational leadership research in the past two decades has been in the field of instructional leadership, with principals and assistant principals as leaders and coaches in instructional planning and implementation. Wilma Smith and Richard Andrews (1989) identify four dimensions or roles of instructional leadership:

1. *Resource provider.* This means ensuring that teachers have the materials, facilities, and budget they need to perform their duties, including making changes for needed reforms.
2. *Instructional resource.* This involves actively supporting day-to-day instructional priorities and programs by modeling desired behaviors, participating in in-service training, and consistently giving priority to instructional concerns.
3. *Communicator.* This necessitates having clear goals for the school and articulating these goals to faculty and staff.
4. *Visible presence.* This involves engaging in frequent classroom observations and being highly accessible to faculty and staff.

Throughout the research on instructional leadership, there are recurring themes of personal attributes that demonstrate a principal's effective instructional leadership (Baskett & Mikkos, 1992; Rutherford, 1987). Following are five desired attributes:

1. *Have a vision.* Work toward a shared understanding of the goals, and progress toward their achievement.
2. *Translate the vision into action.* Work as a team, emphasizing schoolwide goals and expectations.
3. *Create a supportive environment.* Promote an academically oriented, orderly, and purposeful school climate.

4. *Know what's going on in the school.* Find out what teachers and students are doing and how well they're doing it.

5. *Act on knowledge.* Intervene as necessary in accommodating different teacher personalities, styles, and teaching approaches.

In addition to these five qualities, Fullan (1991) found in his research that "schools operated by principals who were perceived by their teachers as being strong instructional leaders exhibited significantly greater gain scores in achievement in reading and mathematics than did schools operated by principals who were perceived as average and weak instructional leaders" (p 156). You may not have much input into the approaches of your administrators, but that doesn't mean that you are helpless as a teacher. There are many documented school improvement projects that have been initiated by classroom teachers. You just have to learn to present your ideas well, explain how the approach will benefit the students, and identify the roles of your administrators in supporting and becoming involved in the project. It is important that you keep your administrators informed and that you let them know what support is needed in order to continue moving forward.

Parents as Team Members

A Southwest Educational Development Laboratory synthesis of research on parent involvement over the past decade (Henderson & Mapp, 2007) reported that students with parents who are involved in their education benefit in a number of ways:

- They earn higher grades, post higher test scores, and enroll in higher-level programming.
- They pass classes, are promoted, and earn credits at a higher rate than their peers.
- They attend school more regularly.
- They have better social skills, improved behavior, and adapt well to school.
- They graduate and go on to postsecondary education.

Research in this area also indicates that the schools themselves play an important role in determining the level of parent involvement. Finding ways to include parents as collaborative educational team members is important as students continue with their schooling, especially in communities with limited resources (Rutherford, 1997). Three major factors have been found to influence the level of parent involvement in school:

1. The parents' beliefs about what is important, necessary, and permissible for them to do with and on behalf of their children

2. The extent to which parents believe that they can have a positive influence on their children's education

3. The parents' perceptions that their children and their children's school want them to be involved

The strongest and most consistent predictors of parent involvement at school and at home are the existence of specific school programs and teacher practices that both encourage parental involvement at school and guide parents in how to help their children at home (Williams & Chavkin, 1989).

Parents need specific information on what to do in order to help their children. Schools that initiate and monitor programs that help parents learn how to help with homework, how to provide quiet study places and times, and how to show interest in reviewing the students' work at home have been found to have the strongest influence on students' school performance (Epstein et al., 2009).

Some parent involvement activities that encourage a student's academic improvement are fairly easy to encourage and implement:

- Listen to the student read daily.
- Read to the student.
- Have books available for the student to read.
- Take trips to the library as well as local museums, factories, and businesses, and engage in conversations about how these places work and what the people who work there do.
- Guide television watching and engage the student in discussions of what he or she is watching.
- Provide stimulating experiences that spark questions and discussions.

Joyce Epstein, professor of sociology of education at Johns Hopkins University, has developed a framework for defining and encouraging the development of school and family partnerships. She cites the most important reason for developing these relationships as "to help all youngsters succeed in school and in later life." Epstein's framework defines six types of parent involvement and lists sample practices in each type as well as expected results of implementing them for students, parents, and teachers (Epstein et al., 2009):

1. *Parenting.* Help families establish home environments to support children as students.

   - Parent education and other courses or training for parents (GED, college credit, family literacy)
   - Family support programs to assist families with health, nutrition, and other services
   - Home visits at transition points to preschool, elementary, middle, and high school

2. *Communicating.* Design effective forms of school-to-home and home-to-school communication about school programs and children's progress.

   - Conferences with every parent several times a year
   - Language translators to assist families as needed
   - Regular schedule of useful notices, memos, phone calls, newsletters, web posts, and other communications

3. *Volunteering.* Recruit and organize parent help and support.

   - School and classroom volunteer programs to help teachers, administrators, students, and other parents
   - Parent room or family center for volunteer work, for meetings, and for resources for families
   - Annual postcard survey to identify all available talents, times, and locations of volunteers

4. *Learning at home.* Provide information and ideas to families about how to help students at home with homework and other curriculum-related activities, decisions, and planning.

   - Information for families on skills required for students in all subjects at each grade level
   - Information on homework policies and how to monitor and discuss schoolwork at home
   - Family participation in setting student goals each year and in planning for college or work

5. *Making decisions.* Include parents in school decisions, developing parent leaders and representatives.

- Active PTA/PTO or other parent organizations, advisory councils, or committees for parent leadership and participation
- Independent advocacy groups to lobby and work for school reform and improvements
- Networks to link all families with parents' representatives (class websites, online newsletters, etc.)

6. *Collaborating with the community.* Identify and integrate resources and services from the community to strengthen school programs, family practices, and student learning and development.

- Information for students and families on community health, cultural, recreational, social support, and other programs and services.
- Information on community activities that link to learning skills and talents, including summer programs for students

One outstanding example of parent involvement was published in the September 2010 issue of *Family Circle* magazine. Barbara Blalock, a parent in Tempe, Arizona, became concerned about the amount of personal money individual teachers were spending to provide basic learning supplies such as pencils and paper to their students. She began to collect materials from volunteers in the community and then approached local businesses for donations. She obtained so many supplies that she had to find a place to keep them all. She searched for and found a vacant warehouse and even persuaded the owner to donate the use of it for her project. She named the warehouse "Treasures 4 Teachers," and it is now open several days a week for local teachers to "shop" for large bags of school supplies, art materials, colorful buttons, and books. The teachers pay only $2 for as much as they can fit into a large shopping bag. Although the materials are helping students learn, Barbara is most excited about the pride her own children show in her project and how she is helping all the teachers in the area.

WAYS TO ENCOURAGE PARENT INVOLVEMENT.   It is very important for parents to feel that their involvement is wanted and needed. In today's society, many parents may work outside the home or be involved in a variety of time-consuming activities. This makes it necessary for teachers to find ways for parents to become actively involved even if they might not be available during the school day:

1. Begin each year with a meeting in the evening to get to know the parents, and let them know that they are important members of the learning team.

2. Survey the parents to find out about their interests and expertise.

3. Hold "how to" sessions to help parents become familiar with the roles you would like them to play in their children's learning, such as how to help with homework, how to ask questions about their children's reading assignment, how to make learning math facts fun, and how to make learning games to support their children's developing skills.

4. Provide ideas for parents who would like to volunteer without having to come to school during the day. Mention such things as making learning materials from provided patterns and instructions and collecting materials such as milk cartons, bottle caps, and egg cartons for art and learning projects.

5. Communicate class needs weekly, providing a list of items necessary for projects for the coming week. This might be just one item in a weekly newsletter or in a computer blog from the classroom.

6. Organize a make-and-take session, with coffee and cookies as well as someone to watch their little ones, for parents staying at home with small children; during this time, the parents make learning materials and get to know each other.

7. Make a big deal out of anything parents contribute, and make sure the child is recognized for what the parent contributes. ("Look at these beautiful chair covers that Suzie's mother made for our classroom! Let's write Suzie's mom a nice thank-you note!") Include a section in the class newsletter or blog where you also recognize contributions from parents.

8. Encourage parents to volunteer in the classroom by always having meaningful tasks ready for them when they drop in. You can keep a file of suggestions for volunteers, or have a parent sit and listen to a child read. You can also keep a shelf with materials that need to be prepared for an upcoming lesson. Parents can learn to run the copy machine, the dye-cut machine, and the laminating machine, as well.

9. Provide a list of times and activities when you could use an extra pair of hands in the class newsletter if you are not comfortable with volunteers just dropping in. If you have a set time for learning centers, maybe you can encourage parents to volunteer during those times; also, some parents may be good at arts and crafts and can provide help during those periods. Just keep the lines of communication open to help parents to feel involved, and they will provide help in many surprising ways.

Local Museums, Community People, and Libraries

Every community has a wealth of resources available to its citizens. A reflective teacher must search for these valuable resources and find ways to use them to enhance the curriculum in the classroom. Museums have long been a source of support for learning about the past. History, art, and science are often displayed in ways to help young learners picture the concepts that are being taught in the classroom. Students can get an opportunity to study past cultures, extinct animals, and the general evolution of our planet. Museums provide a unique prospective into all of these different aspects, and many include an extremely interactive atmosphere in which tactile, aural, and visual experiences provide new windows of understanding to the important events and creatures from the past. Even if your community doesn't have a museum, there are a number of virtual museum tours available online. See Figure 11.1 for a list of these virtual museum tours.

Bill Coate, a teacher in Madera, California, engaged his students in creating a local museum, encouraging his students to make displays documenting the history of their

Figure 11.1 Virtual museum tours.

There are over 300 museums worldwide. Go to www.virtualfreesites.com/museums.html. For some specific museums, consult the following list:

Egyptian museums.

www.museum-tours.com/museum.

The Louvre.

www.louvre.fr/llv/musee/visite_virtuelle.jsp?bmLocale=en.

National Gallery of Art.

www.nga.gov/exhibitions/vgwel.htm.

Oriental Institute Museum.

http://oi.uchicago.edu/museum/virtual/tours.html.

Smithsonian Museum of Natural History.

www.mnh.si.edu/panoramas.

community. They gained knowledge of Madera history through visiting graveyards, exploring local birth records and personal journals, and interviewing the elders of their community who had lived the history. The principal of the school was so impressed with the work of these fifth graders that he dedicated a room for their Madera Museum of Local History. The parents helped build a replica of the historical jail, and the students and parents worked together to build a Conestoga wagon to show how the residents of the area arrived there. The students even took short historical treks in the Conestoga wagon to experience the hardships of traveling experienced by the early settlers. When visitors came to visit the museum during open hours, students would dress in period costumes and tell the stories of early residents, sharing their research and enthusiasm for the project. This project continued for several years in the late 1990s. As a result of the impact of this project and Bill's method of teaching, the approach to studying history through local records and student involvement and replication is now known as the Madera method.

To read an interview with this dedicated teacher and another history project his class conducted, go to http://chong.zxq.net/ancestry/prt3/InterviewBillCoate.htm. As a result of Bill's class project, a film was made of their experiences. This film is a great way to introduce the study of local history to elementary students. Read about the film at www.cetel.org/madera.html.

As Bill's approach demonstrates, another local resource is the people of the local community. As a teacher, you need to locate important local resources for your students. Who are the community elders and leaders? How can their knowledge impact the learning of your students? Interviewing significant local personalities can be an exciting project for your students while at the same time addressing a number of English/language arts standards related to speaking and listening. Using interviews as a basis for creating reports and/or projects involves reading and writing as well as creating visual representations and planning.

Local or community libraries are valuable resources to teachers and students. Many libraries house special collections of books related to local history or other areas of interest to students. It is important to introduce libraries as community resources since many families are unaware of the wealth of information, activities, and learning opportunities offered through libraries.

Susan McCloskey, an urban first-grade teacher in California, takes her parents and students on a walking field trip to their nearby community library. On this field trip, each family applies for and receives a library card, a tour of the facilities, a sample activity time designed for the children, and a schedule of coming events. Susan says, "I am constantly amazed that my students and their parents are totally unfamiliar with this community resource. I often hear remarks such as, 'We can take the books home?' Because my families are not wealthy, they really value this experience and the learning activities offered at the library. The parents also learn to use the computers and use them regularly after our initial visit."

WAYS TO USE MUSEUMS AND LIBRARIES IN PLANNING CURRICULUM.
There are several options for using museums and libraries when planning your curriculum:

1. Do your homework by making a list of all the resources, opportunities, and activities available in your community.
2. Share information with your parents, advertise activities through your class newsletter, and plan a field trip with your students and their parents to help them learn how to access and use the facilities.
3. Explore the collections and activities thoroughly to determine if there are things that can be incorporated into your daily curriculum.
4. Teach your students how to access the resources as they work on projects and reports.
5. Introduce virtual tours of national museums and libraries to expand your students' horizons beyond the local community.

6. Read more about the Madera method and how Bill involved his students in conducting their own interviews and research.

WAYS TO EXPAND THE COLLABORATION: LOCAL BUSINESSES AND IN-
DIVIDUALS.   Various local businesses and individuals provide support to schools through volunteers released during work hours, donations of materials and expertise, and even monetary support. Many schools now solicit businesses and civic organizations as sponsors.

In Titusville, Florida, the Indian River Methodist Church has adopted a local elementary school, Coquina Elementary, and provides free after-school tutoring for students using church members (retired teachers) as tutors. Sunday School classes at the church collect children's clothing and donate it to the school's clothing closet; members of the church also provide support in setting up and providing child care during activities such as grade-level meetings for parents. The youth group at the church became actively involved in the Coquina project and holds Sunday afternoon picnics and games at the neighborhood park. Several groups at the church work together to provide grounds care and plantings to beautify the school.

For other suggestions of community groups to solicit for support for school projects, see Figure 11.2.

Figure 11.2 Enrichment activities using community volunteers.

Disciplines	Activities
Mathematics	Doing in-depth or enrichment studies to explore use of math in various career choices
	Using guest speakers and challenge activities (Can you do architectural math?)
	Involving volunteers: retired math teachers, engineers, architects
History and writing	Exploring primary sources in local area to create regional history publication
	Exploring areas of geography and history that are not given much attention in regular curriculum
	Writing from perspective of people of other times (Roman gladiator, explorer on the Oregon Trail)
	Involving volunteers from local historical societies
Writing	Doing in-depth exploration of writing genre such as poetry, science fiction, documentary writing, script writing
	Involving volunteers: local poets, writers, dramatists
Fine arts	Viewing art history in connection with history studies
	Doing in-depth exploration of different media with support from local artists
	Taking field trips to museums and viewing works of art representing famous artists' styles
	Involving volunteers: local artists
Drama and writing	Writing and performing plays or using reader's theater
	Involving volunteers: local community theater actors, writers, directors
Integrated thematic study	Doing thematic study of heroism spanning mythology, multicultural definitions and examples, present-day heroes, personal heroes, heroes of famous scientists, musicians, artists
	Involving volunteers: retired teachers, historians, policemen, firefighters
Problem-based service projects	Identifying local or school concern, brainstorming and researching solutions, gathering support, funding and implementing plan
	Checking Internet sources: www.newhorizons.org/strategies/service_learning/front_service.htm

WAYS TO TAP COMMUNITY RESOURCES FOR SUPPORT FOR SCHOOLS.
There are several steps in identifying community resources that can provide help for your school:

1. Work with your faculty to identify schoolwide needs such as child care during parent meetings, after-school tutoring, school beautification, and support in academic areas such as math, science, art, and music.

2. Identify nearby businesses, civic groups, and churches that might provide support.

3. Identify any faculty or staff who might already have contacts with the groups you identified.

4. Set up meetings with the groups identified to explain the school's needs and solicit their support. Use examples provided in this chapter to explain ways that the groups might be of assistance.

5. Make sure their support is recognized when a group begins to help. Write thank-you notes, and have the students write thank-you notes. Let your local newspaper know what the group is doing, and ask them to write an article about the support your school is receiving.

6. Assign a faculty or staff member as liaison to the support group so that the lines of communication remain open. As new needs arise, let the support groups know.

The Continuous Improvement Model (CIM)

Key Tenets of CIM

The Continuous Improvement Model (CIM) is based on the idea that student, teacher, and schoolwide success must be a continuous effort. This involves collecting and utilizing data, developing time lines, providing quality instruction, and doing frequent assessment of students to determine their understandings and needs. CIM is derived from the eight-step instructional process developed by Mary Lehman Barksdale (2003) while teaching third grade in Texas:

1. Disaggregate test data.
2. Develop an instructional time line.
3. Deliver the instructional focus.
4. Administer frequent assessments.
5. Use tutorials to reteach nonmastered target areas.
6. Provide enrichment opportunities for mastery students.
7. Reinforce learning through maintenance.
8. Monitor progress.

Based on the Barksdale model, teachers and administrators must do the following:

- Raise expectations for all students.
- Create a vision to guide reform.
- Develop measurable objectives with time frames for accomplishing them. (Barksdale & Davenport, 2003)

The Barksdale model, the Effective Schools Research area in education, and the Total Quality Management (TQM) method from the world of business constitute the main research bases of the Florida Continuous Improvement Model (FCIM). Effective Schools Research is an area that has gained in importance over the past 50 years in the United States. In the 1960s, researchers from Michigan State University identified five characteristics that were common to all effective schools (Barksdale & Davenport, 2003):

1. Strong instructional leadership
2. High expectations of student achievement
3. Pervasive and broadly understood instructional focus
4. Safe and orderly school climate conducive to teaching and learning
5. Measures of pupil achievement as indicator of program success

The Plan, Do, Check, Act (PDCA) Cycle

CIM is based on the eight-step instructional process developed by Barksdale (2003) and is reflected in a series of activities called the Plan, Do, Check, Act (PDCA) cycle that are repeated continuously. The acronym PDCA is used to assist educators in remembering the order in which the actions take place. Following are the cycle and the activities contained in it:

P (Plan). It involves data disaggregation and calendar development (steps 1 and 2 of the Barksdale model).

D (Do). It involves a direct instructional focus (step 3 of the Barksdale model).

C (Check). It involves assessment, maintenance, and monitoring (step 4 of the Barksdale model).

A (Act). It involves tutorials, enrichment, maintenance, and monitoring (steps 5, 6, 7, and 8 of the Barksdale model).

Once the cycle is completed, then it immediately begins anew. You might note that a number of these activities are familiar, but a number of them are *not* routinely involved in school as usual—that is the strength of this program. TQM in education means we base our decisions on data, focus on the students, and are more process oriented. The goal is continuous improvement, not just for the students but for all the others involved—parents, administrators, and the community.

In her book (with coauthor Davenport) titled *8 Steps to Student Success* (2003), Barksdale lists many benefits of the eight-step instructional process:

- It is applicable to any curriculum subject area, grade level, or student group.
- It promotes a culture of excellence where teachers can teach and students will learn.
- It removes subjectivity and specifically identifies the needs of the campus group, classroom group, and individual students according to data.
- It ensures that all state standards are taught before the test.
- It neutralizes the "blame game." It requires ongoing collaboration between the student and teacher, teacher and teacher, instructional coordinator and teacher, instructional coordinator and principal, principal and student, and superintendent and principal, from grade level to grade level.
- It promotes ongoing analysis of student performance.
- It eliminates excuses. High standards and expectations are set for all.
- It promotes consistency in instruction from classroom to classroom, grade level to grade level, and campus to campus.
- It promotes quality instruction, active learning, and higher-level thinking skills.
- It maintains a strong instructional focus and provides direction.

No Excuses

In their book *Closing the Achievement Gap: No Excuses*, Davenport and Anderson (2002) chronicle the story of using CIM in Brazosport, Texas. The authors lay out the steps they used to guarantee success and continuous improvement for the students, teachers, parents, and administrators in their school district.

CIM bases decision making on the students' test scores in a way that is unusual in most school districts. Students' scores are examined carefully to see which concepts they are using successfully at grade level, which appear to need a different teaching approach, and which are thoroughly mastered and can be built upon and extended.

A yearlong plan is formulated to address the needs of the students and the continuing education of the teachers, parents, and administrators. All aspects of the curriculum are monitored carefully, and teachers are supported in acquiring new teaching strategies in order to improve instruction and learning.

The overarching theme of CIM is "**no excuses.**" If certain concepts are not being learned, additional support is given to the students who need it and also to the teachers so that their approaches to teaching the concepts are improved.

Community resources are used to free teachers to teach tutorial groups each afternoon to ensure that all students are mastering all standards. Students who master concepts are given enrichment activities to build on and utilize the skills they are mastering. Very often, community volunteers are used to conduct the enrichment activities. The tutorials ensure that students receive as much instruction as they need in order to be successful—no excuses.

Planning for Success: Tutorials and Enrichment

Today we realize that students have many reasons for not making academic progress. CIM schools take the responsibility for adherence to quality principles and student learning, and they intend that all students master the essential skills. The PDCA instructional cycle ensures that all students can learn through an aggressive program of frequent assessments, maintenance, and tutorials.

Brazosport Independent School District's first attempt at tutorials didn't work when they held the tutorials after school and on Saturdays. The faculty initially said, "Well, we offered the help, but they didn't show up." Then they began to explore the reasons why the students didn't choose to participate:

- They lacked transportation.
- They had babysitting duties with younger siblings.
- They had paper routes and after-school jobs.
- They had parents who had other plans for them and wouldn't allow them to come.

The "customers" (students) were not being served by the schedule or by the "packaging" (students thought the tutorials were punishment for not "getting it" in class). However, Brazosport educators learned from their first venture and found these solutions:

- *Create "quality team" periods—a minimum of once a week—for teachers to assess progress and to determine any barriers to learning.* Elementary and middle school faculty meet by grade level; high school faculty meet by subject area. They discuss progress in general, review the assessment results, and determine which students needed "refocusing" through tutorials and which students would benefit from enrichment.

- *Build team time—one for tutorials and one for enrichment—into the school day.* Let individual schools determine the appropriate time for them. Most schools choose to schedule them the last hour of the school day.

- *Assign team time for each student based on frequent assessment results.* For example, if the grade level has 100 students divided among 4 teachers and 40 of them fail the standard assessment and 60 pass, then 40 are assigned team time for tutorial and 60 go to enrichment activities during the time set aside. It may mean the teachers teaching enrichment have larger groups than the tutorial teachers, *but* the needs of the students are met. Tutorials should be small direct-instruction groups, while enrichment activities may be more self-directed and require less individual instructional attention. After the next assessment, the group size balance may go the other way. For this reason, the teachers rotate among tutorials and enrichment activities.

- *"Repackage" tutorials as a positive way to achieve mastery.* Talk to your students in an encouraging way about the opportunities to participate in team time tutorials. Approach it simply by suggesting, "You have some standards you haven't mastered yet, and this is a chance for extra time and practice so you can pass them. We're going to provide team time so you can be successful."

- *Don't sacrifice excellence for equity.* Don't make the mistake of focusing on tutorials to the detriment of enrichment. Enrichment needs to be a priority, too. Kids should be scrambling for opportunities to go to *both* types of team time.

- *Use new material for enrichment.* Don't use the same materials for enrichment that you use in the regular class. Budget funds for different and more challenging materials, and look on the Internet for challenging activities. Mastery students respond to higher-level thinking activities just as gifted student do. Encourage your colleagues to suggest new and exciting material and approaches.

- *Encourage mastery students to go beyond.* Students who go to enrichment need new challenges. Give them an opportunity to attend an additional elective or advanced placement course; allow them to attend a local college to earn college credits. At Brazosport, many students are using their enrichment time for earning their diplomas from the local high school and working toward their associate's degree at the local community college at the same time.

- *Utilize staff members and paraprofessionals for enrichment and tutorials.* Most school systems think only math, English, or reading teachers can teach those courses. Because small classes are critical at Brazosport, everyone teaches—the coaches, physical education instructors, librarians, the principal, the assistant teachers (aides), parents, and even older students. Students enjoy the change of teachers and approaches, so have the music teacher teach math and the gifted teacher teach tutorials. It can vary from school to school, but remember it works best when traditional roles are broken down. The idea is for the students to go home and say, "Our math class was neat today. The music teacher taught us how to do the math problems and showed us how you have to know math to read and write music." The students need to recognize that everyone needs and uses the skills they are learning.

- *Involve parents whenever possible.* Parents are ideal choices for serving as additional tutors or for leading enrichment programs. Invite them to serve as teachers or assistants; get to know their strengths and interests and use those because they can provide some interesting enrichment and tutorial classes.

While some nonmastery students will begin by spending most of the year in tutorials, they will spend more and more in enrichment as they complete mastery assignments. When Brazosport started CIM, they had 80 percent of their students in tutorials; 9 years later, 80 percent of their students are in enrichment activities.

TUTORIALS.   The decisions that need to be made to make sure that tutorials are effective are numerous. You first need to decide if the tutorials are going to be uniform throughout the school or if each grade level will make decisions about their own tutorials. As we said earlier, Brazosport decided to allot the last hour of the school day to tutorials and enrichment activities, but they can be scheduled in the middle of the day or in an extended-day setting.

It is important both to approach instruction in slightly different ways so that tutorials aren't just more of the same and to use time wisely (not just in tutorials but all day long). Successful teachers use every teaching opportunity. They do not allow the end of class period to become downtime but use those last few minutes for a quick review, often in the form of a quick game like Jeopardy.

One school uses lunchtime as a review game time. The teachers and paraprofessionals create learning games that can be used while supervising lunch, asking review questions and giving points to the tables answering correctly. At the end of the week, the table with the most points gets free ice cream snacks. The lunchroom supervisors report that the students enjoy the games *and* the cafeteria is much quieter with the more structured environment. The game playing also serves to build students' confidence as they review skills.

Another school schedules tutorials during lunch and calls them "working lunches." Obviously, this limits the types of activities that can be used, *but* it does create a positive attitude for tutorials since the teachers provide dessert when the students are working diligently. Some other approaches that are being used include:

- Assigning double math and English periods for at-risk students
- Creating a remedial class that at-risk students attend instead of an elective
- Creating a study room where students can go for extra help at any time during the day
- Using block scheduling (90- to 95-minute periods) for a subject at the high school and intermediate levels, which allows time for instructional focus *and* tutorials within the period, and scheduling longer periods for reading and math to allow for tutorial and enrichment time within the period at the elementary level

In addition to team time for tutorials during the day, Brazosport uses an extended-day intervention program. For 3 weeks before the state assessment test, teachers work with at-risk students after school. Each teacher has 10 students, grouped by standard nonmastery level, and they meet from 3:30 p.m. to 5:30 p.m., Monday through Thursday. As an incentive, snacks and transportation home on the bus are provided. This is funded with summer school money, which makes more sense if you are trying to prepare students to pass the test since summer school takes place *after* the state assessment test. The students take their snack break immediately after school; then each teacher takes the 10 students assigned to him or her and reviews the standards that were not mastered. Just as with team time, the teachers are rotated so students are assigned to someone other than their own homeroom teacher. Some of the mastery-level students even volunteer to serve as teacher aides.

As a result, 92 percent of the students considered to be "on the bubble" passed the state assessment test after this 3-week review. After the first few years, Brazosport no longer offered summer school for students who had passed the grade but had not mastered all standards because they found this extended-day program to be more effective for helping students meet standards.

One school implementing CIM invested in interactive whiteboards for each teacher. The teachers found ways to use the boards for tutorials since the information that was taught in the regular class could be reviewed on computers by downloading materials from the whiteboards. They had several innovative ideas for using whiteboards for tutorials:

- Videotape the lesson and download it onto the computer using Blackboard or another online management system; then use it as a review lesson for each standard that is taught. This allows the students to review any lessons they miss due to absences or to review a concept they haven't mastered.
- Use the textbook publisher's suggestions for interactive whiteboard activities for individual center time for students who have not yet mastered a particular standard.
- Download your teaching notes from the interactive whiteboard, and print them out for students to use in reviewing and studying for tests.

ENRICHMENT.   Although the dictionary definition of the word *enrichment* mentions making something fuller or more meaningful, another definition, used by farmers, is apropos here: adding nutrients. In order to meet the needs of mastery learners, there are several considerations:

- The need for time to explore topics in depth
- The focus on real-world applications, including the use of specialized interactions, tools, and techniques
- The opportunity to do interdisciplinary work and interact with experts

Because of the power of interdisciplinary work with experts, enrichment activities are a good match for work with parent and community volunteers. One school has sent out a survey to parents and the community to find people with expertise in the arts and sciences who are willing to volunteer to work with students. The results of this survey were exciting: The school located painters, weavers, sculptors, musicians, actors, and scientists. The school then set up a schedule for the volunteers to share their expertise with students as part of the enrichment period at the end of each school day. The students built rockets, designed solar cars, wove baskets and placemats using mathematical patterns, sculpted with several different materials, learned to draw human figures, and painted with watercolors and other media. They used math to design a gazebo for the school; they also figured out the best design for a community garden, applied geometry and other principles to lay out the garden, and used math to figure out the money needed to purchase the materials and seeds for the garden. According to Bloom's revised taxonomy, these activities require two types of higher-level thinking: creating and evaluating.

Tap community resources by approaching local businesses and universities for experts. Many businesses have programs in place where they release employees for school–community collaborations. These people serve as valuable resources for gifted learners and present a real-world connection to knowledge that is not commonly addressed in school settings. Some examples of these collaborations are listed in Figure 11.3.

To plan an enrichment program for your students, ask some questions:

1. What are the specific interests, strengths, and needs of your students? Gather this information through surveys, interest inventories, class discussions.

2. What are the time constraints? Will you be able to expand your in-school program to allow more time for in-depth exploration? Can your students stay after school? If the program needs to be limited to time available during the school day, can you break projects into small steps that can be done within the time constraints?

3. Have you approached your administrator for approval, resources, and a commitment to follow through?

4. What is your expertise? What areas of interest and expertise do the rest of the team members possess?

Figure 11.3 Community collaboration resources.

Topic of Study	Experts	Who to Contact for Support
Playing the stock market	Investment bankers, financial planners, business professors	Banks, universities, investment companies
Building a house	Contractors, architects, electricians, decorators	Local businesses, Habitat for Humanity
Saving the environment	Environmental scientists, water systems engineers, recycling engineers, utility consultants	Electric companies, water companies, science professors, recycling plants
Using creative science and math	High school science and math teachers, science and math professors, engineers	High schools, colleges, engineering firms

5. What resources are available in your school and community? Do you need to write a grant for funding? Are there local businesses that you can contact for support? Are there other teachers on your faculty with expertise in the area you will be addressing? Are there parents who can provide expertise?

Once these questions are answered, you are ready to sit down with your team members and plan the activities.

Because one school had a number of computers available and the mastery students were interested in learning more about computers and the Internet, the enrichment activities centered on Internet usage. The instructors focused on ethical Internet usage and had the students work in small groups to research in-depth studies and to plan a PowerPoint presentation for their classrooms. After the students' introduction to the Internet, the teachers involved them in an electronic scavenger hunt to give them practice searching for specific resources online.

Another school used the instructional focus currently being addressed and had the enrichment students research more in-depth information about the topic and create "Want to Know More?" booklets for their classrooms. They researched and wrote the text and used visuals downloaded from the Internet to create the illustrations. Because the enrichment groups are not all from the same classroom, these booklets were shared in all the grade-level classrooms. The students were extremely innovative in making real-world connections. For example, one group wrote booklets with examples of how the use of incorrect grammar in real-life situations can cause miscommunication, loss of opportunities, and social mishaps, interviewing their parents and community members for real-world examples.

It is very important that the enrichment activities *not* be neglected in order to focus more attention on the tutorials. Both are equally important. The enrichment program, if rich enough, can be a powerful incentive for students to pass the basic standards.

A Summary and Review of CIM

CIM is based on several types of research. For CIM to be successful, Effective Schools Research demonstrates these needs:

- Schoolwide instructional focus understood by all
- Strong instructional leadership
- High expectations of student achievement
- Safe and orderly school climate
- Measures of student achievement as indicator of program success

TQM, a business model, provides these principles when using CIM:

- Identify the main customer (the student) and the main product (student achievement).
- Involve all major stakeholders (parents, students, teachers, principals, superintendent, school board, and the community) in planning and implementing the program.
- Set continuous improvement as the goal for *all* stakeholders. Everyone improves!
- Use the PDCA cycle to provide the structure to ensure continuous progress.

To review, the PDCA cycle contains four steps:

1. *Planning.* This step includes data disaggregation and development of an instructional focus time line (instructional calendar).
2. *Doing.* This step involves the actual teaching of the instructional focus
3. *Checking.* Next come frequent student assessments to adjust the time line and plan new instructional approaches. Monitoring by the instructional leader determines the

needs of students, teachers, and other stakeholders. Also included here are maintenance activities to make sure that students are retaining previously mastered skills and
standards.

4. *Acting.* The last step provides tutorials and enrichment activities to meet individual needs
of *all* students and to make sure *no one* falls through the cracks. All students are given every opportunity to succeed.

CIM is *not* a new program. It has been successfully implemented for more than 10 years
and is being used in more and more states every year. Stories of successful collaborative efforts
often begin with one person or a small group of committed people. In the case of Brazosport
and CIM, one teacher had already implemented a collaborative project in her classroom that
was expanded and adapted to the needs of the whole district. This collaboration also grew
from the frustrations of parents, who asked the superintendent to examine the reasons their
children were not achieving as well as the students across town. The results of this request led
the district superintendent and curriculum coordinator to identify teachers whose students
were being successful. A powerful collaboration involving parents, administrators, students,
and local businesses resulted.

MEASURES OF PUPIL ACHIEVEMENT AS INDICATORS OF PROGRAM

SUCCESS.   We know that effective schools use assessment data to measure both the
individual growth of each student and the effectiveness of the program itself. The effective school is self-reflective. The teachers and administration look at assessment data
to judge how their teaching strategies are working and make adjustments as needed to
increase both student and teacher success. The students are given support in amelio-
rating their weak areas, but so are the teachers *and* the program as a whole. This is a
very different approach than simply looking at student test scores and providing adapted
instruction. The attitude in an effective school is one of learning for all—teachers and
administrators included. Everyone is working together to improve outcomes in both
teaching and learning.

COMMUNITY INVOLVEMENT PROJECTS BASED ON NEEDS OF COM-

MUNITY.   Community involvement projects in schools should be based on the needs
of the community being served. In low-income neighborhoods, projects could include
community gardens, computer literacy classes for students and adults, and other enrichment activities that open up unknown possibilities for the students and maybe their
parents. In communities where the students have many economic advantages, they
can become involved in projects to support students in less affluent neighborhoods or
countries.

City Heights is an area of San Diego, California, where most of the students and their
parents speak languages other than English. San Diego State University has formed a collaborative arrangement with the three schools in the area: Rosa Parks Elementary School,
Monroe Clark Middle School, and Hoover High School. The university places student teachers in all three schools, sponsors literacy coaches for the schools, and offers graduate classes at
the schools to support the teachers in continuing their education. Education professors often
team-teach classes to support the use of innovative approaches for English language learners.

Professors in local business schools provide help in grant writing to encourage families in applying for federal and state grants to start businesses in the area. Using a combination of grants and incentives for urban redevelopment, high-rise condos are offered
to teachers at reduced interest rates to encourage teachers to live and stay in the area. As
a result of this collaborative project over the past 10 years, local family businesses have
increased in number, teachers have moved into the area and made it their home, and
the quality of teaching and learning in the schools has greatly improved. The identified
needs of the community were met through collaboration with the local university and
colleges, the school district, local businesses, and federal agencies offering grant money.

Involving the Larger Educational Community

There are some steps to follow if you want to get different groups in your community involved in helping your school improve:

- Identify areas in your school in need of improvement.
- Identify possible key players to approach regarding possible collaborative plans to remedy school concerns.
- Identify connections in the community. Who are the people who can become involved in the collaboration? Think outside the box.
- Plan an approach that involves all the key players. What will the teachers need to do? What resources are needed? How can administrators, parents, and local businesses be involved?
- Use some of the available examples of successful collaborations to help you brainstorm ways to achieve your goals.
- Think big!

Group Focus Activity

Your professor will divide the class into small groups and have each group select a project from Figure 11.4. Each group will do an initial plan to explore solutions to their assigned project and carry out the following steps.

1. Identify the key players.
2. Identify roles for each of the key players.

Figure 11.4 Possible collaborative projects.

Following are six possible scenarios for collaborative projects:

1. Your school is experiencing an influx of students from Russia who do not speak English. How can a collaborative project support both their inclusion in the school community and their academic and social success?

2. Your school district is experiencing budget cuts, and all art and music teachers are being cut. How can a collaborative project ensure that students continue to have rich art and music experiences without teachers?

3. Your school is experiencing problems with bullying on the playground and in the hallways. How can a collaborative project help solve this problem?

4. Your school building is old and deteriorating; the school district has very limited funds for school building improvements. How can a collaborative project be used to remediate this problem?

5. Your school district recently spent money to supply each classroom with several computers, but the faculty needs training. Funds for teacher in-service training have all been used for the year. How can a collaborative project help solve this problem?

6. You are planning a teaching unit and want to include community resources and expertise. How would you go about involving and collaborating with community players in this project?

3. Identify community resources that can be used to solve the problem.

4. Identify ways in which the effectiveness of the project can be evaluated.

5. Report your plan to the entire class.

6. Discuss with the whole class some additional ways to include key players to enrich each plan.

Preparing for Your Licensure Exam

In this chapter you read about ways to build collaborative projects. Reread "A View into the Classroom" at the beginning of the chapter, and think about it as a case study you might encounter on your licensure exam. Answer the following questions to demonstrate your understanding of the process of using collaboration to enrich your students' learning:

1. In what ways can the teacher's assumptions influence the use of collaboration in the classroom?

2. How can collaboration benefit students?

3. What possible barriers to collaboration must be overcome in order to get all key players involved?

Portfolio of Professional Practices Activity

Brainstorm a list of possible collaboration projects. Choose one project that will enrich your students' understanding of the practical applications of curricula that are being studied, and create a tentative approach to using collaboration to help your students see the practical applications of their learning. Include the following:

- Examples of practical applications for the curricula

- Possible community resources for helping students see practical applications for their learning

- Several ways to involve people and businesses in the community to give students a deeper understanding of the practical applications

- Detailed plan for presenting your idea to administrators and parents

- Possible methods for evaluating the effectiveness of your plan

References

Barksdale, M., & Davenport, P. (2003). *8 steps to student success: An educator's guide to implementing continuous improvement K–12*. Austin, TX: Equity in Education.

Barksdale model. (n.d.). Retrieved June 4, 2009, from http://focus.florida-archives.com

Baskett, S., & Mikkos, E. (1992). *Perspectives of effective principals*. Canadian Administrator, 32(1), 1–10.

Blalock, B. (2010, September). Supporting our teachers. *Family Circle*, 23–24.

Davenport, P., and Anderson, G. (2002). *Closing the achievement gap: No excuses*. Houston, TX: American Productivity and Quality Center.

Electronic scavenger hunts. (n.d.)Retrieved July 22, 2009, from http://edtech.boisestate.edu/teki/scavengerhunts.htm

Epstein, J., Sanders, M., Sheldon, S., & Simon, B. (2009). *School, family, and community partnerships: Your handbook for action* (3rd ed.). Thousand Oaks, CA: Corwin Press.

Fullan, M. (1991). *The new meaning of educational change.* New York, NY: Teachers College Press.

Henderson, A., & Mapp, K. (2007). *Schools, families, and student achievement.* District Administration, 43, 64.

Interactive whiteboards.(n.d.) Retrieved from www.fsdb.k12.fl.us/rmc/tutorials/whiteboards .html

Rutherford, D. (1987) *The effective principal.* New York, NY: Teachers College Press.

Rutherford, B. (1997). *Parent and community involvement in education.* Ann Arbor: University of Michigan Press.

Schoolwide enrichment. (n.d.). Retrieved July 22, 2009, from www.gifted.uconn.edu/sem/ semeffct.html

Smith, W., & Andrews, R. (1989). *Instructional leadership: How principals make a difference.* Alexandria, VA: ASCD.

Williams, D., & Chavkin, N. (1989). Essential elements of strong parent involvement programs. *Educational Leadership, 47,* 18–20.

chapter twelve

Improving the Effectiveness of Your Teaching

iStockPhoto

"Develop a passion for learning. If you do, you will never cease to grow."
**Anthony J. D'Angelo, contributing author and editor
of *Chicken Soup for the College Soul***

An important focus of a reflective action model of teaching is self-improvement. Reflective teachers are always reviewing the effectiveness of their teaching and working to improve student learning. When you earn your teaching credential, you are given the opportunity to begin a lifelong process of working with students while constantly reviewing and updating your effectiveness as a teacher. You have chosen to embark on an ongoing adventure in learning fostered by a professional responsibility for providing your students with the best possible opportunities in learning and understanding. Reflective teachers use a variety of resources to help them identify ways to improve their effectiveness.

In this chapter, we will explore challenges you may face in many areas of the curriculum and in day-to-day activities of the classroom, and we will offer a variety of suggestions for improving your approaches to teaching and classroom management. We will include a continuum of effectiveness, starting at the beginning level, moving through gaining confidence and expertise as well as building effectiveness, and reaching professional levels of teaching interactions in order to guide your choices for improvement and self-improvement. Teaching can truly be a whirlwind journey of learning for the professional teacher as well as for the students. Welcome to what may be the wildest roller-coaster ride on the planet. There's only one question left to answer: "Are you having fun yet?" That's an easy question to answer for those who commit to ongoing continuing education and self-renewal.

As you read through each of the sections in this chapter, you will be able to reflect on your own teaching and look at the teaching effectiveness continuum for each particular area to determine what you will need to improve in order to make continuous progress and move along on the continuum. Following is an example of an effectiveness continuum for classroom transitions:

Beginning	Developing	Accomplished	Exemplary
Students are asked to move from activity to activity without advance instructions.	Teacher gives instructions before students are asked to move to a new activity.	Teacher gives advance instructions and has a set plan for distributing materials that involves students taking responsibility.	Teacher gives advance instructions and makes the plan for distribution of materials clear to students. Teacher checks for understanding and makes all expectations clear before moving students in an organized fashion.

Questions for Reflection as You Read the Chapter

1. What are some of the symptoms revealing that an approach is not effective?
2. What resources are available to teachers for improving their effectiveness?
3. How is reflective action used to ensure continuous improvement in teaching?

A View into the Classroom

Mark Wathrop is a first-year teacher in Madera, California. He has completed his basic teaching credential and is teaching in a school district that uses a Beginning Teacher Induction Program to provide support and mentoring for new teachers for their first 3 years of teaching. Mark is assigned to a third-grade classroom. His students speak three different languages at home—English, Spanish, and Hmong—and Mark's credential qualifies him to teach English language learners at the elementary school level.

The Beginning Teacher Induction Program in Mark's district requires him to compile a yearly improvement plan that includes an area of teaching in which he wants to improve as well as classes, reading materials, and workshops to help him improve his effectiveness in the identified area. Mark is assigned a mentor teacher at his school and a supervisor from a nearby university to provide him with support and periodic evaluations.

Because Mark's district has recently purchased interactive whiteboards for each classroom, Mark identifies one goal as learning effective teaching strategies for using the new whiteboard. He plans to attend district training sessions, read professional journal articles about interactive whiteboard usage, and research online for ideas for effective use of whiteboards.

Mark's mentor teacher invited him to come into her classroom to observe the teaching of a lesson using the interactive whiteboard. Mark observed the lesson; then his mentor, Susan Williams, asked him an interesting question: "What could I have done differently to make my lesson more effective?"

Mark thought about it. "Well, I noticed that only one student at a time was interacting at the whiteboard. Some of the others were losing focus."

"Exactly!" said Susan. "I noticed the same thing. What can we do to make sure they're all involved?"

"We've got to have them doing something at their seats . . . maybe using individual whiteboards?" suggested Mark.

"That's a great idea," Susan responded. "I have a set of individual whiteboards. I'll use them next time and see how it works."

After observing Susan's class, Mark reflected on the observation. He began to search online for activities for interactive whiteboards. He also added another goal to his professional development plan: find ways to actively involve all the students.

As Mark attended workshops related to the use of interactive whiteboards, he was able to collect a nice repertoire of effective strategies for their use as well as ideas for student involvement. He was especially excited about the way the use of everyone responds (ER) activities cut down on the need to refocus students because they were involved and more focused. See Figure 12.1 for a list of the websites Mark found related to interactive whiteboards and Figure 12.2 for materials for ER activities.

REFLECTING ON THE CLASSROOM EXPERIENCE

As the visit to the above classroom demonstrates, teachers must constantly reflect on the effectiveness of their lessons and be working toward improving their effectiveness. Mark is a good example of a reflective teacher: He uses interactions with more seasoned teachers; he researches possible solutions to his questions, tries them out, and makes adjustments based on self-reflection. He is

Figure 12.1   Websites with ideas for using interactive whiteboards.

www.amphi.com/departments/technology/whiteboard/lessonplans.html

www.scholastic.com/interactivewhiteboards

www.learningtoday.com/corporate/interactive-whiteboard-lessons.asp

www.interactivewhiteboardlessons.org

www.globalclassroom.org/ecell100/javamath.html

http://rmtc.fsdb.k12.us/tutorials/whiteboards.html

http://teacher.scholastic.com/whiteboards/languagearts.htm

Figure 12.2   ER (Everyone Responds) activities.

Materials	How to Use Them	How to Create Them
Individual whiteboards	All students write a response to every question. Answers are reviewed and corrected if needed.	Go to your local home improvement store, and have white shower board cut into 8" × 11" pieces. You'll have to lightly sand the edges, but this method dramatically cuts down on the cost of providing individual whiteboards for your students. They will need whiteboard markers for this activity.
"Show me" cards	Students make cards for multiple-choice responses and display them to respond to each question when the teacher says, "Show me."	Determine all possible answers for the activity you will be doing. Then give students pieces of sentence strips or 3 × 5 cards and markers, and walk them through the creation of their cards. Have them write on the cards the numerals or the words "Yes" and "No" or the terms "Verb," "Noun," "Adjective," "Adverb"—whatever answers are appropriate for your activity. Have students keep their "Show me" cards in envelopes for future use.
Individual magnetic boards	Each student needs a small cookie sheet or range burner cover and makes cards backed with magnetic tape to attach to the magnetic board. Students respond by attaching their answers to their magnetic boards.	Follow directions for "Show me" cards, but put magnetic tape on the back of the cards.
Magic slates	Students write their responses on the magic slates using the stylus that comes with each slate. When the teacher says their names, they know their answer is correct and lift the film to erase it.	Magic slates can often be found in Dollar Stores. You may have to collect a few at a time. They come in a variety of sizes, and small ones work well.
Thumbs (each student comes equipped with two)	Students respond to each question by showing a "thumbs up" for a "Yes" or "I agree." "Thumbs down" signifies a "No" or "I disagree" response.	Students should be instructed to wait for a signal before they reply.

lucky enough to have support in his first years of teaching, but the strategies he uses are available to all teachers. The reflective action model encourages self-reflection, research, and action. Reflection without action will not produce improvement.

Resources for Professional Growth

Professional Organizations, Journals, and Conferences

Most of the areas of curriculum or disciplines taught in the elementary school have professional organizations dedicated to setting standards, publishing research and exemplary practices, and conducting state, regional, and national conferences each year. In addition to the organizations related to individual curricular areas, there are several organizations dedicated to more global teaching quality issues. You may already be familiar with some of these organizations because they have student groups on college campuses. See Figure 12.3 for a list of professional organizations, their foci, and their websites.

As a future educator, you can join the student affiliates of these organizations, receive their professional journals at a discount price, and attend their conferences at a reduced rate. This is an important opportunity to help you starting building your professional development plan. Most teachers join the organizations according to their interests and the needs of their students.

Figure **12.3**   Professional organizations in education.

Organization	Purpose	Website/Journal
National Association for the Education of Young Children (NAEYC)	It is dedicated to improving the well-being of all young children, with particular focus on the quality of educational and developmental services for all children from birth through age 8.	www.naeyc.org Young Children
American Federation of Teachers (AFT)	The mission of the American Federation of Teachers, AFL-CIO, is to improve the lives of members and their families; to give voice to their legitimate professional, economic, and social aspirations; to strengthen the institutions in which they work; to improve the quality of the services we provide; to bring together all members to assist and support one another; and to promote democracy, human rights, and freedom in our union, in our nation, and throughout the world.	www.aft.org American Teacher
National Council of Teachers of English (NCTE)	It is devoted to improving the teaching and learning of English and the language arts at all levels of education.	www.ncte.org Language Arts
National Education Association (NEA)	Its mission is to advocate for education professionals and to unite our members and the nation to fulfill the promise of public education to prepare every student to succeed in a diverse and interdependent world.	www.nea.org NEA Today
National Council of Teachers of Mathematics (NCTM)	It is a public voice supporting teachers to ensure equitable mathematics learning of the highest quality for all students through vision, leadership, professional development, and research.	www.nctm.org Teaching Children Mathematics
National Council for the Social Studies (NCSS)	Its mission is to provide leadership, service, and support for all social studies educators.	www.socialstudies.org Social Studies & the Young Learner
National Science Teachers Association (NSTA)	It is committed to promoting excellence and innovation in science teaching and learning for all.	www.nsta.org Science & Young Children
American Alliance for Health, Physical Education, Recreation, and Dance (AAHPERD)	Its mission is to promote and support leadership, research, education, and best practices in the professions that support creative, healthy, and active lifestyles.	www.aahperd.org American Journal of Health Education

Keep an open mind about professional organizations. For example, you might find that you are more interested in the teaching of reading but seem to be struggling with ideas to enliven your social studies curriculum. This is a perfect opportunity to subscribe to a professional journal in social studies education and maybe even attend a social studies education conference. Classroom teachers and education professors often make presentations at these conferences, sharing ideas and successful strategies that will greatly expand your teaching repertoire. You will find information about the journals and conferences on the websites listed in Figure 12.3.

UNIVERSITY COURSEWORK. Once you are employed as a teacher, you will be required to continue your professional development through workshops given in your school district, attendance at professional conferences, and enrollment in university classes. You will also be asked to identify areas in which you want to improve and to create a professional development plan for meeting your teaching effectiveness goals.

Many states are now requiring new teachers to complete a master's degree within a few years of being hired. Since you will be required to submit a professional development plan showing how you will be working toward improving your teaching effectiveness, it makes sense to include university classes that will move you toward your professional development goal as well as get you started on completion of master's degree requirements. In order for these courses to help you move upward on the salary schedule, they usually have to be related to your teaching assignment. For example, taking courses to prepare you to qualify as an administrator often may not help you advance on the salary scale as a teacher, whereas courses toward a master's in reading or math might.

Personal Research

Personal research is a very powerful approach to improving your knowledge and skills. There are a number of ways to do personal research that are vital components of becoming a reflective teacher:

- *Online research.* Look online for articles and websites related to teaching.
- *Professional journals.* Look in professional journals for research related to teaching and examples of effective teaching practices.
- *Observations.* Observe in other teachers' classrooms for effective teaching strategies.
- *Professional book clubs.* Form a book club with a group of teachers; read and discuss books about teaching and learning.

SELF-REFLECTION RUBRIC. Examine the following continuum of professional development, and reflect on your current status and what you need to do to improve:

Beginning	Developing	Accomplished	Exemplary
Read articles in professional journals or go to teaching websites for ideas.	Join at least one professional organization, and read their journal regularly, trying out ideas obtained from the journal and online.	Join more than one professional organization, and participate actively in at least one professional conference a year.	Continually explore new professional journals and websites, attend and actively participate in more than one professional conference each year, and use ideas from journals and conferences to improve teaching effectiveness.

Self-Reflection and Improvement Plans

Voice, Body Language, and Enthusiasm

In today's world of advanced technology and communication, teachers often find themselves competing for their students' interest and attention. All manner of visual, auditory, and tactile experiences are available, literally at the touch of a button, and students have become increasingly adept in accessing and utilizing these new and exciting sources of information. Given this challenge, it becomes increasingly important for teachers to look for and embrace a broad variety of classroom techniques and methodologies to capture and hold the students' attention. Performance skills involving voice, body language, and enthusiasm are becoming a more and more important tool in a teacher's repertoire for enriching classroom presentations and student learning.

SYMPTOMS.   You may have visited classrooms where children seem inattentive and off task during lesson presentations. Students' symptoms of this situation can vary from not participating in the lesson to whispering to neighbors to causing disruptions that interfere with the instructional process. Teachers often respond by using traditional methods of presenting material without offering a more challenging and stimulating classroom atmosphere for their students. By incorporating a few changes in their classrooms, teachers can create a "positive and welcoming classroom environment that encourages student achievement" (Hart, 2007, p. 38).

SOLUTIONS.   For the reflective teacher, various areas can be targeted to find solutions to the problem of student inattentiveness:

- *Vocal expression.* Using different vocal modulations—varying pitch, speech rate, volume, and intensity—provides a great deal of variation and creates interesting and engaging presentations in the classroom. Many teachers are able to communicate a high level of passion and interest in every subject they teach, even the ones that may not necessarily be their favorites. By varying your vocal inflections and control, you are able to engage students and model the excitement you feel about learning. *Teachers are between 3 and 5 times more likely to experience voice problems than the general population and are a staggeringly 32 times more likely to report voice problems than the general population. Since your voice is your primary means of communicating with students, it is paramount that you handle and care for it properly. One website provides some excellent tips for teachers related to taking care of their voices:* www .dukehealth.org/services/voice_care_center/care_guides/voice_hygiene/tips_for_teachers.

- *Body language.* Effective teachers are always excited about sharing their enthusiasm for learning with students and display this in their demeanor, delivery, movement, and energy level. Effective body language is a quality reported time and again as associated with student success across all grade levels and disciplines (Strong, 2010). Liberal use of positive facial expressions, gestures, posture, and movement as nonverbal forms of expression can enhance emphasis and importance. Students need to see positive acceptance and reinforcement in their teacher's face and gestures. Listening with a smile, giving a reassuring touch, accepting student input—these are all evidence that the teacher values his or her students.

- *Point of concentration.* It is vitally important that each lesson have a point or an objective. Authors and playwrights often refer to this as the climax of the novel or play. It always helps to structure your lessons so that they build to their climax or objective (Tauber & Mester, 2007). Every lesson should have this so-called point of concentration that helps to plan and focus the outcomes for the students. The students may have difficulty remembering everything presented in a lesson, so it is the task of the teacher to determine the points of the lessons to clarify and concentrate on, ensuring student understanding and learning.

- *Enthusiasm.* Teacher enthusiasm can be displayed in many ways in the classroom. It doesn't have to mean running around the classroom, using a loud voice, and making larger-than-life gestures. A discussion about what things are important to you, why you decided to be a teacher, or how you take pride in your students' accomplishments will serve to alert them to the commitment you have to their education and future. These enthusiastic teachers never let their students know they are not excited about learning, always conveying a sense of commitment and interest and encouraging them to follow their lead and to love learning. You will never regret giving that extra effort to involve your students in your enthusiasm for exploring.

- *Subject-matter knowledge.* Teachers must know their subject matter before they can expect to teach it effectively. One of the hallmarks of outstanding teachers is an in-depth knowledge of their subject matter. The ability to explore material in depth begins with over-preparation and mastery of the appropriate subject matter. When a teacher feels weak in an area of the curriculum, it is important that he or she do whatever is necessary to bolster his or her command of subject-matter material in that area. This might include workshops, additional or remedial coursework, or online research. Lack of adequate preparation on the part of the teacher often results in less than constructive student achievement in that particular subject matter.

- *Creative use of classroom space.* Teachers should use the entire classroom to present information, moving about, making contact with students, and checking for understanding. Much like an actor who would not deliver an entire play from the center of the stage, don't confine yourself to the front-and-center position of the classroom.

Though these may be used less often, the following areas have also been found to complement those mentioned above:

- *Humor.* Teachers should always use constructive and nonhostile humor directly related to the educational objective. The use of sarcasm in the classroom is not appropriate and certainly should never be used at a student's expense.

- *Role playing.* A teacher assuming the role of a famous person or character can be a very strong tool for motivating students and capturing their interest—it can make material come alive. This technique can be used to motivate students, to hold their attention, to clarify or intensify material, or to stimulate discussion. It might involve using costumes and props or be as simple as donning a hat or employing particular gestures or facial expressions. It should be well researched and should focus on the character and information rather than the "performance."

- *Props.* Props for teachers can vary from real-life artifacts and manipulatives to common objects found in the classroom such as chalkboards, flip charts, and overhead projectors. They are most effective when used to focus on and advance specific learning goals. B. E. Bradley reminds teachers to use visual aids to enhance a presentation rather than expect the aids to be the sole source of information (Bradley, 1991). Rehearsing with the prop beforehand is essential to the success of its use.

- *Eye contact.* Eye contact provides teachers with an avenue to gain and maintain students' attention. You can communicate an interest in what students are doing or saying and provide tacit encouragement through a simple look. Students respond well to the initiation of eye contact, recognizing that they are important and have something to contribute. By looking directly at a student whose interest appears to be wavering, you can refocus him or her. Reasonably consistent eye contact between teacher and students results in greater attention and retention on the students' part (Cooper & Simonds, 2007).

SELF-REFLECTION RUBRIC.   Following is a sample voice, body language, and enthusiasm continuum for teachers:

Beginning	Developing	Accomplished	Exemplary
Voice and body language sometimes are negative; enthusiasm sometimes is lacking.	Voice is used in different ways to direct attention. Body language is neutral. Enthusiasm is sometimes evident.	Voice is used effectively to direct attention and make major points. Body language is positive; enthusiasm is evident.	Voice is used effectively to demonstrate, direct attention, and emphasize important points. Body language is positive and responsive, and enthusiasm is evident and clearly authentic.

Clarity and Pacing in Presentations

SYMPTOMS. If your students often ask questions that you think you've already explained, ask you to slow down, or appear inattentive during explanations or discussions, you may want to work on improving your clarity and/or pacing. Clarity is an important part of every lesson a teacher prepares; pacing involves several aspects, including rate of delivery, wait time, timely feedback, and checks for understanding before introducing new material.

SOLUTIONS. As we discussed in Chapter Five, different students learn best through visual, auditory, tactile, or kinesthetic modes. Reflective teachers make a point to include a variety of approaches in every lesson so that each student is receiving instruction in his or her preferred mode (Dunn & Dunn, 1992). In addition to exploring different modes of instruction, clarity and pacing also involve careful observation of your students to look for signs of confusion, frustration, or noninvolvement.

There are several ways to improve clarity and pacing in your teaching:

1. As you plan lessons, identify the modes of delivery you are using. If all the instruction is verbal, add visuals, gestures, and active student involvement.
2. Once you plan a lesson that includes a variety of learning modes, video the lesson as you deliver it. Make sure that you record the students as well as yourself while you are presenting the lesson. This may require obtaining help from another teacher or an administrator.
3. Watch the video of your lesson while doing the following:

   - Note the expressions on students' faces. Are they attending to the lesson, or are they distracted? Do they look confused or noninvolved?
   - Keep track of how many questions students ask. Do your responses to the questions require clarifying something you presented?
   - Actually count the seconds of wait time that you give before you provide support or rephrase the question. Also note whether you provide support to the student answering the question or move on to another student.
   - Tally the number of times you call on boys as compared to girls. Also note students to whom you address multiple questions. Are there any students who are not involved at all?
   - Listen carefully to your rate of delivery. Are you speaking clearly and distinctly at a rate that is easily understood?

4. Once you have reviewed the recorded lesson, list the areas you want to improve.

See Figure 12.4 for suggestions of approaches for improving clarity and pacing.

Figure 12.4 Suggestions for improving clarity and pacing in teaching.

Symptoms	Suggestions
Teacher has short wait time (less than 5 seconds).	• Count silently from the time you ask the question, giving student at least 5 seconds before scaffolding. • Support original student in responding before moving on to another student to add more information or give another opinion.
Teacher has rapid verbal delivery.	• Build in strategies to slow down your speech. • Pause and write key points on overhead transparency or whiteboard. • Pause at key points to check for understanding if you use prepared transparencies. • Be aware of importance of maintaining an instructional rate of speech that may differ from your conversational rate. • Don't let the clock determine your rate of delivery. If you are running out of time, note areas you need to address in the next lesson, but don't try to finish lesson now at the expense of clarity.
Students often have to ask questions to clarify points made in lesson or directions.	• Plan your lesson carefully by making list of key points you intend to make. • Make sure you are using a variety of learning modes in each lesson. • Make a habit of writing key points on whiteboard or overhead projector as they are made. • Always provide numbered visual reminder of steps you want students to follow. (This can be in the form of pictures for kindergartners.)
Students seem confused or uninvolved.	• Build in periodic checks for understanding. • Always review background knowledge and connect known concepts to new ones. • Always provide assessment to determine students' background knowledge in an area before beginning instruction. Provide needed background knowledge in the form of photos, visuals, video, reading materials. This can also be done with a brief discussion or building of a KWL chart. • Identify students who need further instruction, and provide small-group guided practice while the rest of the class moves into independent practice. • Provide enrichment activities for students who have already mastered skills or concepts being presented.

SELF-REFLECTION RUBRIC. Once you have viewed your video lesson, identify the behaviors you observed on the following teaching effectiveness continuum:

Beginning	Developing	Accomplished	Exemplary
One delivery mode dominates the lesson. Students often ask questions for clarification. Wait time may be less than 3–5 seconds.	One delivery mode is still dominant, but multiple modes are included periodically. Visuals are included in the lesson for key points and directions.	Multiple modes of delivery and visuals for key points and directions are consistently used. Pacing is adjusted to the needs of the students.	Different approaches and modes of delivery are continually explored. There is consistent use of student observation to adjust pacing, enlist active involvement of students, and direct verbal interactions.

Classroom Management

Classroom management is the area most often cited by beginning teachers as an area of concern. The concept of effective classroom management reaches far beyond discipline and involves planning interesting and interactive curriculum, clearly stating expectations, and consistently monitoring student behaviors (Kohn, 1999). Conducting smooth transitions between activities requires planning and consistency as well.

SYMPTOMS.   When you observe a classroom in which the teacher employs effective classroom management strategies, the methods may be invisible. The students follow directions and move between activities easily. As a result, beginning teachers often remark that they didn't observe any classroom management strategies being used.

If you notice any of the following behaviors in a classroom, you will note that some classroom management strategies may need to be changed or instituted:

- Students call out answers to questions without raising their hands or waiting to be recognized.
- Students move around the classroom with no apparent purpose.
- Student behaviors or verbalizations interrupt the teaching.
- Students make verbal comments that are not respectful to teachers or other students.

Some of the symptoms that related to clarity and pacing can also be causes of classroom management difficulties. Students who cannot follow instructions, understand directions, or actively participate in classroom activities may find other ways to occupy their time and may disrupt the learning of others in the classroom.

SOLUTIONS.   Two of the most important aspects of classroom management are consistency and expectations. You, the teacher, must be consistent in setting and expecting students to follow classroom rules and routines; the students must clearly understand what is expected of them. Reflective teachers involve their students in setting the classroom rules, and these teachers spend time at the beginning of the school year both having students practice following the rules and routines and making their expectations clear.

It is important to observe the activities and situations in the classroom in which the management concern arises. The first step is to note when you need to correct behavior and what the causes of the misbehavior seem to be. Students learn best when they are actively involved. ER activities are a good way to keep all students involved since they all respond to every question; these activities also provide the teacher with opportunities to observe responses and note students who need additional practice or instruction. See Figure 12.2 for suggestions of ways to use ER activities.

Transition times in the classroom must be carefully planned. Moving students from one activity to another or one place to another works best if done in an orderly and organized fashion. Primary teachers may use a phonics review to move the students by asking all the students whose names start like "ball" to go to their desks, followed by students whose names start like "jump, etc. Math teachers of older students can use other academic benchmarks such as "students whose birth month is the square root of 16." One common way to move students is simply row by row, but using transition times to review academic concepts makes it more interesting and keeps students listening.

Organization and advance planning eliminate a number of classroom management concerns. Part of your advance planning should involve careful consideration of all the materials you will need to conduct the lesson. These materials should be accessible, and students may be involved in their distribution. A plan for distributing the materials is important. One student per table, row, or group can be the "materials manager." Many teachers rotate tasks each week so that every student has an opportunity to participate. Setting up expectations for these roles in advance is very important. Choosing classroom helpers can be done in several different ways: Some teachers simply choose names from a container with popsicle sticks labeled with all the students' names; other teachers choose exemplary students each week and verbalize their reasons for choosing certain students. For example, a teacher might say, "I noticed that Jason was very helpful last week. He helped Betty when she fell down on the playground, and he shared his lunch with Daniel when Daniel forgot his. Jason will be our line leader this week because he is behaving like a leader."

Teachers in classrooms with students who are English language learners must always remember to demonstrate directions as they verbalize them. If you want students to get their math books out, you should be holding and showing the math book as the directions are given (Herrell & Jordan, 2012). This addition to verbal directions—showing what you're saying—helps English language learners and visual learners.

Consistency is a vitally important part of classroom management. Only the teacher can control the consistency of his or her actions and reactions. If you and your students agree that raising your hand to be recognized before speaking is the rule, it is important to be consistent in calling on only students who raise their hands. If you recognize students who blurt out answers or allow certain students to dominate classroom conversations, the students will soon ignore the rule. Some teachers find it effective to use hand signals to let a student know that a rule was broken and then call on a student who is following the rule. For example, a student who blurts out an answer gets a reminder to raise her hand; the teacher might put her finger to her lips to signal "quiet" and then immediately call on a student whose hand is raised.

Hand signals are a very effective way to remind students to follow the rules so the teacher can go on with instruction without stopping to discuss the infractions. Some students may need a private conversation to set up a hand signal in advance. For example, if you have a student who dominates classroom conversations, you might want to call him aside and say, "Joseph, I know that you know a lot of the answers and get excited because you want to share the information. I want to encourage other students to talk, so we're going to have a signal. When I touch my nose and look at you, I'm telling you that I *know* you know the answer but that I want to allow others to talk." Of course, this signal only works if you remember to be consistent in using it.

There are several other signals teachers can use to help students remember the rules:

- A hand raised in a "stop" position might signal a student to wait.
- A hand raised and a finger to the lips might signal students to remember to raise their hands.
- A tap on a book in front of a student might remind the student to attend to the book if he is distracted.
- A nod to a student whose hand is raised while calling on another student might let that student know that you will come back to her.
- A hand on the shoulder of a student who is talking while you are teaching might signal him to stop talking while you continue to teach or give directions.
- Moving into close proximity to students who are off task might signal to them that you are aware of their being off task. This is called *proximity control* and allows you to make a correction without stopping the momentum of the lesson.
- A bell or set of chimes can be used as a signal to the class that the noise level has gotten too high.

Voice control is a very powerful classroom management tool. Many teachers recognize that raising the volume of their voices is *not* a good classroom management tool, that it's best *not* to try to talk over the students' voices. Use a signal such as ringing a bell or chime, wait for quiet, and then talk. Many teachers have found that talking very softly requires the students to listen more carefully. Primary teachers discovered long ago that their students will stop and listen if they simply start singing. Many kindergarten and primary teachers have made up songs such as "Jason's ready, so is Batty," which get the students' attention quickly.

"Use your teacher's voice" is a suggestion that has been made to many beginning teachers. The "teacher's voice" has more to do with authority in the tone than with volume of the voice. The tone must project to the student that this direction is *not* a request but comes with an expectation of compliance.

Reflective teachers consistently monitor their classroom management. If concerns arise, they immediately think about the circumstances and what actions they could have used to avoid the situation and what they will change in the routines of the classroom to avoid the situation in the future. Monitoring your own progress in classroom management requires reflection and planning.

SELF-REFLECTION RUBRIC.   As you reflect on your classroom management, identify your placement on this classroom management effectiveness continuum:

Beginning	Developing	Accomplished	Exemplary
Classroom rules are inconsistently enforced.	Classroom rules are enforced and new strategies attempted when problem areas are encountered.	Classroom rules are consistently enforced, and the teacher uses voice control and signals to create a supportive learning environment.	Consistency and student involvement in making rules, distributing materials, and adjusting rules are evident. Classroom signals are in place and used regularly.

Group Focus Activity

Your professor will have you work in small groups. Each group will be given a scenario to read and discuss, a transparency sheet, and a transparency marker and will follow these steps when doing the activity.

1. Identify the area of concern.

2. Brainstorm a list of possible solutions to the problem. List the problem and the possible solutions on the transparency.

3. Discuss and evaluate each possible solution, and rank the solutions from best to least likely to be successful. The best solution should be marked 1 and the others labeled by their rankings.

4. Present your work to the class, summarizing the reasons why your group ranked the first solution as the best.

Scenarios

- Martha has a very loud voice and teaches at top volume all day. Her class is very noisy because she simply overpowers the students' voices when they are talking.

- Carl's students are often confused by his directions. He is constantly saying, "I've already told you what to do. Get to work."

- Greg gives very detailed, complete directions and lectures. He expects his students to take meticulous notes and gives tests from his lectures. His students are not doing well on the tests.

- Megan believes that students should be allowed to express themselves freely. She doesn't require that students raise their hands and be recognized before speaking. Two of her students dominate every class discussion, and other students tend to wander off task.

- Sandra often gives directions and information facing away from the students. Her students often misunderstand her directions and explanations.
- Eugene uses PowerPoint presentations for all his lectures. His students have difficulty following the lessons because he talks so quickly.

Figure 12.5   Teaching effectiveness continuum.

Beginning	Developing	Accomplished	Exemplary
Commitment to Professional Development			
Read articles in professional journals or go to teaching websites for ideas.	Join at least one professional organization and read its journal regularly, trying out ideas obtained from the journal and online.	Join more than one professional organization, and participate actively in at least one professional conference a year.	Continually explore new professional journals and websites. Attend and actively participate in more than one professional conference each year, and use ideas from journals and conferences to improve teaching effectiveness.
Voice, Body Language, and Enthusiasm Continuum			
Voice and body language are sometimes negative; enthusiasm is sometimes lacking.	Voice is used in different ways to direct attention. Body language is neutral. Enthusiasm is sometimes evident.	Voice is used effectively to direct attention and make major points. Body language is positive; enthusiasm is evident.	Voice is used effectively to demonstrate points, direct attention, and emphasize important points. Body language is positive and responsive, and enthusiasm is evident and clearly authentic.
Delivery of Instruction			
One delivery mode dominates lesson. Students often ask questions for clarification. Wait time may be less than 5 seconds.	One delivery mode is still dominant, but multiple modes are included periodically. Visuals are included in lesson for key points and directions.	Multiple modes of delivery and visuals for key points and directions are consistently used. Pacing is adjusted to needs of students.	Teacher continually explores and varies approaches and modes of delivery. Teacher consistently uses student observations to adjust pacing, solicit active involvement of students, and direct verbal interactions.
Effectiveness and Consistency of Classroom Management			
Classroom rules are inconsistently enforced.	Classroom rules are enforced and new strategies attempted when problem areas are encountered.	Classroom rules are consistently enforced, and teacher uses voice control and signals to create supportive learning environment.	Consistency and student involvement in making rules, distributing materials, and adjusting rules are evident. Classroom signals are in place and used regularly.
Classroom Transitions			
Students are asked to move from activity to activity without advance instructions.	Teacher gives instructions before students are asked to move to new activity.	Teacher gives advance instructions and has set plan for distributing materials that involves students taking responsibility.	Teacher gives advance instructions and makes plan for distribution of materials clear to students. Teacher checks for understanding and makes all expectations clear before moving students in organized fashion.

Preparing for Your Licensure Exam

In this chapter you read about ways to improve your teaching effectiveness. Reread "A View into the Classroom" at the beginning of the chapter, and think about it as a case study you might encounter on your licensure exam. Answer the following questions to demonstrate your understanding of the process of self-reflection and continuous improvement in teaching:

1. What evidence did you see that Mark is committed to continuous improvement?
2. What characteristics did his mentor show that convinces you that she too is committed to improving her teaching effectiveness?
3. What resources are available to teachers to support them in lifelong learning?

Portfolio of Professional Practices Activity

Complete all the teaching effectiveness continuums in this chapter, and document your growth throughout your student teaching. Include these continuums in your professional portfolio. See Figure 12.5.

References

Bradley, B. E. (1991). *Fundamentals of speech communication: The credibility of ideas* (3rd ed.). Dubuque, IA: William C. Brown.

Cooper, P., and Simonds, C. (2003). *Communication for the classroom teacher.* Boston, MA: Allyn & Bacon.

Dunn, R., & Dunn, K. (1992). *Teaching elementary students through their individual learning styles: Practical approaches for grades 3–8.* Boston, MA: Allyn & Bacon.

Hart, R. (2007, January 1). Act like a teacher: Teaching as a performing art. *Electronic Doctoral Dissertations for UMass Amherst.* AAI3275803. Retrieved from http://scholarworks.umass.edu/dissertations/AAI3275803.

Herrell, A., & Jordan, M. (2012). *Fifty strategies for teaching English language learners* (4th ed.). Boston, MA: Pearson.

Kohn, A. (1999). *The schools our children deserve: Moving beyond traditional classrooms and "tougher standards."* Boston, MA: Houghton Mifflin.

Strong, J. H. (2010). *Effective teachers = student achievement: What the research says.* Larchmont, NY: Eye on Education.

Tauber, R., & Mester, C. (2007). *Acting lessons for teachers.* Westport, CT: Praeger Publications.

Subject Index

Active learning, scheduling time for, 43
Advance organizers
    definition of, 143
    importance in lesson planning, 144
    related to schema theory, 143
Assessment
    anecdotal records, using, 131
    authentic, 134, 232
    at the beginning of the year, 26
    cheating, 40, 41
    checklists, creating and using, 234
    criterion-referenced, 228
    cooperative projects, grading of, 241
    devices to identify student needs, 130–131
    essays, rubrics for evaluation, 230
    essays, rubrics for grading, 231
    informal observations, 226
    for mastery learning, 229–230
    observation as, 131
    oral reports and examinations, 231–232
    percentile ranking, 130
    performance sampling as, 131, 227
    portfolios as, 131, 238, 240
    pretesting for diagnosis, 133
    rating scales, creating and using, 234, 235
    rubrics, creating and using, 224, 234, 236
    selecting and using procedures, 225
    tailored to lesson objectives, 63, 64
    using observations, 27
    using video recordings, 241
Authentic learning
    definition of, 141–142
    essential elements of, 153
    strategies for, 151

Bullying
    conflict resolution related to, 43
    defining, 41
    intervention programs, 42
    national campaign against, 43
    teaching communication skills, 42
    teasing, distinguishing from, 42
    using withitness to respond, 42

Caring, ethical, 17
Classroom climate
    building a community of learners, 130
    encouraging cooperation, 29, 30
Classroom discussions
    accepting environment, setting up, 198
    to address multiple intelligences, 196
    to begin the writing process, 195
    brainstorming in, 190–191

    critical and creative thinking, modeling, 198
    to encourage imagination and inventiveness, 195
    to enhance creative thinking, 194
    to enhance comparing skills, 193
    group investigations, definition of, 191
    group investigations, implementing of, 191–192
    to guide classification skills, 193
    to identify assumptions, 193
    to improve observation skills, 193
    interactive, strategies for, 189
    open-ended question in, 191
    practice exercises, employing, 198
    problem-solving, strategies for, 190
    to promote critical thinking, 192
    scaffolding in, 197
    seating for, 198
    silence in, 197
    Socratic dialogues, 194
    teacher's role in leading, 197
    wait time, allowing, 198
Classroom examples
    1st grade phonics, 2, 3
    1st grade teacher designs a self-improvement plan, 268–269
    2nd grade creative activities to meet standards, 203–204
    2nd grade standards-based classroom, 22–26
    2nd grade unit on family history, 86–88
    3rd grade differentiated classroom, 114–116
    4th grade family interview project, 184–165
    4th grade lesson sequencing based on standards, 52–54
    5th grade hands-on learning, 140–141
    6th grade social studies simulations, 162–163
    6th grader students create writing rubrics, 224–225
    multiage class and parent involvement, 248–249
Classroom interventions, 125
Classroom management
    classroom meetings, 39
    dealing with disruptions, 27, 28
    establishing rules and consequences, 36–38
    importance of withitness, 6
    leadership style, 35
    monitoring behavior, 35
    proximity control, 36
    ripple effect, 6
    self-reflection rubric, 279
    symptoms of poor, 277
    system of moral discipline, 40
    teacher body language, 35, 36
    troubleshooting guidelines, 67
    using hand signals in, 278
    using voice control in, 278–279

planning scaffolding for discussion topics, 199
practicing brainstorming, 221
practicing reflective action, 18, 19
recognizing English language development levels, 136–137
room arrangements related to educational philosophy, 47
solving classroom dilemmas, 278
sorting and completing objectives, 81, 82
using multiple intelligences in teaching, 159
Grouping, of students
by ability, pros and cons of, 146
based on standardized scores, 134
for cooperative learning, 173
using observation and pretesting, 134
Grouping formats
literature circles, 178–179
peacemaking groups, 179

Humor
in relation to creativity, 218
styles of, 218

Interactive whiteboards, 269
Inquiry training
definition of, 164
implementing, 165
model of, 165
Involving the larger educational community
community involvement, 264
interactive back-to-school night, 180
involving parents and community in unit study, 110
involving parents in scaffolding discussion, 199
involving parents in supporting creativity, 220
parents as members of the learning community, 81
planning authentic learning experiences, 158
planning for parent–teacher conferences, 246
sharing rules and expectations with, 47
sharing your philosophy of education, 17
using community resources for differentiation, 136

Knowledge, types of, 55

Labeling students
dangers of, 132
examples of, 132–133
Language acquisition
adapting instruction for, 120
affective filter, 121
basic interpersonal communication skills, 118
cognitive academic language proficiency, 118
leveling instruction for, 120
scaffolding in, 117–118
stages in, 119
theories related to, 117

Learning centers
leveling for student needs, 115
organizing and scheduling, 170–171
using with English language learners, 171
Learning contracts
definition of, 169
implementing, 169, 236
example of, 169, 237
Learning styles
definition of, 126–127
inventories of, 127
matching to teaching styles, 156
teaching to, 127
Lesson planning
for active learning, 61, 62
assessing lesson objectives, 63, 64
behaviorial objectives, 59
educational objectives, 58
formats for, 68–70
four-step procedure, 126
goals and outcomes in, 55, 56
for higher-level thinking, 60, 61
leaders in, 54, 55
organization of, 66
predicting outcomes, 64, 65
problem-solving objectives, 59, 60
types of outcomes, 56
writing objectives, 58
writing outcome statement in, 56, 57
Lesson plans, samples
problem-solving, 78, 80–81
science, 78, 79
writing, 75–77
Literature circles
definition of, 178
implementing of, 178–179

Mastery learning
definition of, 168
role of individual prescribed instruction in, 168
teacher's role in, 168
Meeting individual needs
catching up, 26
creating challenge activities, 123
curriculum compacting, 146
English language learners, 145
enrichment, 26, 145, 146, 255
exceptional education students, 122–123, 145
504 plans, 122
gifted students, 122
individual education plans (IEPs), 124, 145
Maslow's hierarchy, 28, 29
mastery learning, 146
students not working on grade level, 124